CAULDRON OF RESISTANCE

A volume in the series

The United States in the World

Edited by Mark Philip Bradley, David C. Engerman, and Paul A. Kramer

A list of titles in this series is available at www.cornellpress.cornell.edu.

CAULDRON OF RESISTANCE

Ngo Dinh Diem, the United States, and 1950s Southern Vietnam

Jessica M. Chapman

Cornell University Press
Ithaca and London

Copyright © 2013 by Cornell University

First published 2013 by Cornell University Press
First paperback printing 2018

Printed in the United States of America

Library of Congress Cataloging-in-Publication Data

Chapman, Jessica M. (Jessica Miranda), 1977–
    Cauldron of resistance : Ngo Dinh Diem, the United States, and
1950s southern Vietnam / Jessica M. Chapman.
        p. cm.
    Includes bibliographical references and index.
    ISBN 978-0-8014-5061-7 (cloth : alk. paper)
    ISBN 978-1-5017-2510-4 (pbk. : alk. paper)
    1. Vietnam (Republic)—Politics and government.   2. Ngo, DInh
Diem, 1901–1963.   3. Vietnam (Republic)—Foreign relations—
United States.   4. United States—Foreign relations—Vietnam
(Republic)   I. Title.
    DS556.9.C454 2013
    327.59707309'045—dc23   2012028850

Cornell University Press strives to use environmentally responsible
suppliers and materials to the fullest extent possible in the publishing
of its books. Such materials include vegetable-based, low-VOC inks
and acid-free papers that are recycled, totally chlorine-free, or partly
composed of nonwood fibers. For further information, visit our
website at cornellpress.cornell.edu.

For my parents,
Sharon and David Chapman

Contents

Preface

A few notes on language and sources are necessary at the outset. Readers familiar with the Vietnamese language will notice the absence of diacritics and tone markers on Vietnamese words in the pages of this book. These marks are, of course, critical for understanding and identifying Vietnamese words. I have chosen to exclude them from the text to render it more accessible to a wider range of readers. However, several important proper names, place names, and names of organizations appear with diacritics in an appendix.

This book is a product of many years of research in Vietnam, France, and the United States, in the languages of those three countries. My desire to understand the complex political sphere of 1950s southern Vietnam took me first to Ho Chi Minh City, where I poured over documents from the Republic of Vietnam in the Vietnamese National Archives #2, as well as stacks of southern Vietnamese newspapers from that same period in the General Sciences Library across town. While those sources did not always illuminate the inner workings of Ngo Dinh Diem's government, they spoke volumes of his administration's broad objectives, methods, and processes. Just as important, they presented a full picture of the southern Vietnamese civil society with which his government interacted.

French sources from the colonial archives in Aix-en-Provence and the army archives in Vincennes provided a surprisingly rich supplement to the materials I collected in Vietnam. The collections I explored contained detailed French intelligence reports and translations of pamphlets, petitions, letters, and radio broadcasts produced by a variety of southern Vietnam's most influential political groups. These sources revealed a great deal about the perspectives of those organizations and their leaders, as well as the views of the French officials who commented on them.

The insights I gleaned from Vietnamese and French sources led me to approach American archives with a very different set of questions than I might have otherwise. Rather than simply asking how Washington made the early decisions that would eventually lead the United States to wage war in Vietnam, I wondered how American officials perceived southern Vietnam's wide range of political actors, why they assessed them as they did, and what the consequences of their views might have been. Trips to the National Archives II in College Park, Maryland, the Library of Congress in Washington, DC, and the Eisenhower Presidential Library in Abilene, Kansas, provided ample material to help me answer those questions.

I could not have conducted all of this research without generous funding from a number of sources. I am deeply grateful for support from the following: the Foreign Language and Area Studies Program, the Fulbright Program, the Pacific Rim Research Program, the Institute for Global Conflict and Cooperation, the University of California at Santa Barbara (UCSB) Interdisciplinary Humanities Center, the UCSB Department of History, the Woodrow Wilson National Fellowship Foundation, the Society for Historians of American Foreign Relations, the American Council of Learned Societies, the National History Center, the Oakley Center for Humanities and Social Sciences, and the Hellman Foundation. Williams College provided funding to support the research and publication of this book.

Special thanks must be reserved for Fredrik Logevall, who was a wonderful graduate adviser and remains a remarkable colleague and friend. So many steps along the way to this book began with sage advice from Fred, from the suggestion that I learn Vietnamese to the proposal that there might be something interesting to discover about Vietnam in the 1950s. I am deeply appreciative of his enduring interest in this project. I am also extremely grateful for the stimulation, support, encouragement, and critical feedback that I received from professors and fellow graduate students at the University of California at Santa Barbara. Toshi Hasegawa, Mark Elliott, Jennifer See, and John Sbardellati especially helped me see how the subject of this book fit into the larger processes of decolonization and the Cold War in which we all share a great interest. Thanks also to Darcy Ritzau, a wonderful graduate assistant, for making sure I never fell through the administrative cracks.

I could not possibly name all of the scholars who have contributed in some way to my thinking about this book. I owe a great debt to those who patiently helped me learn the Vietnamese language and navigate my way through Vietnamese archives and libraries, especially Bac Tran, Mai Thi Thuyet Anh, Nguyen Van Kim, Nguyen Thi Huong Giang, and Nguyen Thi Hue. Bob Brigham, Mark Lawrence, Hue Tam Ho Tai, Edward Miller, Nu Anh Tran, and Peter Zinoman provided especially useful feedback as I wrote this book. I could never sufficiently thank Mark Bradley for his insightful and patient comments on several drafts. I am so thankful as well for Michael McGandy's amazing work ushering this book through the publication process, for the editorial support provided by Sarah Grossman, Karen Laun, and Jack Rummel, and for the detailed, thoughtful comments provided by two anonymous readers. For their companionship, insights, and countless laughs along the way I thank Scott Laderman, Julie Pham, Jessica Elkind, Chi Ha, Lien Hang Nguyen, and Paul Chamberlin. My colleagues at Williams College have provided invaluable feedback and support, for which I am grateful. My wonderful research assistant, Madeleine Jacobs, went above the call of duty and helped reinvigorate my excitement about this book. Of course, any mistakes remaining in the book are mine alone.

Last but certainly not least, I thank J. J. Kercher, Jolene Griffith, Dave Gore, Andrea Thabet Waldman, Maeve Devoy, April Rose Haynes, Elizabeth Pryor, and Amanda Peeples for their enduring friendship. Without them I could never have finished this project. I can only hope that my parents, Sharon and David Chapman, realize how grateful I am for their encouragement. Better parents do not exist. Whatever I say about Bill Colvin will be insufficient. He has brought light to all things in my life, including this book.

Abbreviations

ARVN	Army of the Republic of Vietnam
CCC	Candidates' Campaign Committee
CIA	Central Intelligence Agency
DRV	Democratic Republic of Vietnam
EDC	European Defense Community
ICC	International Control Commission
ICP	Indochinese Communist Party
NATO	North Atlantic Treaty Organization
NLF	National Front for the Liberation of South Vietnam
NRM	National Revolutionary Movement
PRC	People's Republic of China
RVN	Republic of Vietnam
SRV	Socialist Republic of Vietnam
SVN	State of Vietnam
VNQDD	Vietnamese Nationalist Party
VWP	Vietnam Workers Party

CAULDRON OF RESISTANCE

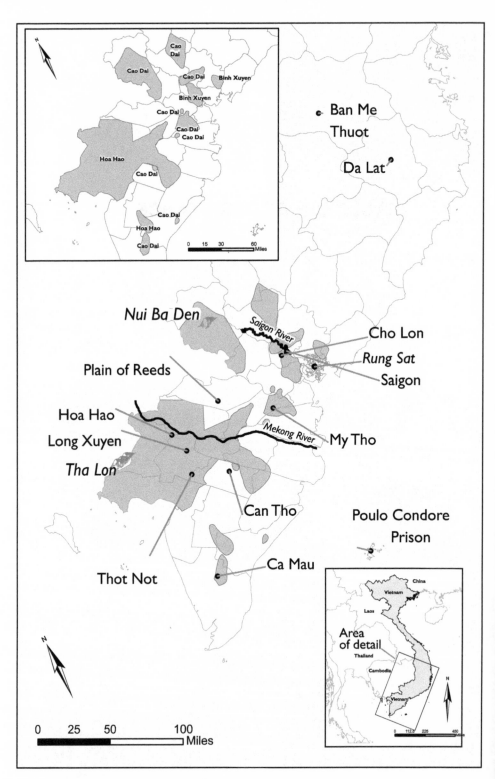

Map 1. Southern Vietnam circa 1954

Introduction

In February 1957, Hollywood director Joseph Mankiewicz arrived at the Cao Dai Holy See in Tay Ninh to film one of the organization's colorful festivals for the original cinematic version of Graham Greene's *The Quiet American*. The previous year, Cao Dai pope Pham Cong Tac—the group's religious leader and one of southern Vietnam's most notable nationalist politicians—had been forced to flee across the border to Cambodia to escape capture by South Vietnamese government forces. As Mankiewicz's crew arrived at the Holy See, a rumor spread that Hollywood magic had somehow arranged for the pope's return to Tay Ninh. The festival kicked off pleasantly enough, but quickly turned hostile when the vice pope Bao The announced, "Our dear Pope is not here, but his spirit is among us." At this, the crowd of Cao Dai followers began shaking their fists at the Americans and chanting in Vietnamese, "We want our Pope." Followers wielded photographs of their beloved Pham Cong Tac and unfurled banners with similar requests for his return printed in both Vietnamese and English.

This was simply the latest in a long string of Cao Dai efforts to gain American support in their struggle with Ngo Dinh Diem's increasingly oppressive government. The protest ended almost as quickly as it began, but not before one of the cameramen could comment, "This is not religious.

Figure 1.1. Cao Dai protest outside the Holy See in Tay Ninh, February 1957 (NARA II)

This looks political to me." The next day, the film crew returned to find that the vice pope and his staff had departed for parts unknown. The Cao Dai followers who remained refused to have anything further to do with filming the movie. Only then did a group of twenty thousand disillusioned Cao Dai followers sit down to elect a new pope, finally accepting that the old pope was gone for good.[1]

This incident was indicative of significant ongoing antigovernment activity within the once-powerful Cao Dai politico-religious organization that had seriously threatened Ngo Dinh Diem's rule during his first two years in power. To the Americans who observed the protest, however, it was barely a curiosity. The scene seemed to highlight the oddity of the Cao Dai more than any political problem of significance within South Vietnam. It caused little alarm and did nothing to overturn the prevailing view that Ngo Dinh Diem's recent consolidation of power in Vietnam at the expense of his rivals among the Cao Dai, Hoa Hao, and Binh Xuyen was nothing short of a miracle.[2] By the end of Ngo Dinh Diem's second year in power, Americans in the White House, the State Department, and the press corps alike eagerly relegated to the past the political infighting that just two years earlier had seemed destined to topple the South Vietnamese government.

The president of South Vietnam had, by then, annihilated his armed politico-religious opponents and established uncontested military control over the countryside. He had put on an election to depose the chief of state Bao Dai and authorize the formation of a new state—the Republic of Vietnam (RVN)—with himself as president. The RVN's Personalist Labor Revolutionary Party (Can Lao Nhan Vi Cach Mang Dang) led by Ngo Dinh Diem's brother Ngo Dinh Nhu and the Ministry of Information led by Tran Chanh Tranh had set in place a network of political, security, and propaganda programs designed to ensure total government control over all political activity throughout South Vietnam. Ngo Dinh Diem declared all-out war on communism south of the seventeenth parallel and refused to participate in the countrywide reunification elections mandated by the Geneva accords to take place in summer 1956, thereby solidifying Vietnam's division. With all this accomplished, RVN officials and their American advisors were poised to embark upon an ambitious nation-building program.

The Ngos' miracle quickly proved a mirage, however. In 1963, Ngo Dinh Diem and Ngo Dinh Nhu died at the hands of their own military, having failed to quell a growing insurgency against the RVN, funded and organized by the communist Vietnam Workers Party (VWP) in Hanoi but composed of disaffected South Vietnamese citizens of various ideological stripes. This study helps explain Ngo Dinh Diem's failure to establish political legitimacy by venturing beyond the traditional Cold War framework that shapes the majority of extant scholarship on the Vietnam Wars. Whereas that framework privileges the communist leader Ho Chi Minh and the noncommunist leader Ngo Dinh Diem as subjects of historical inquiry, this book examines the activities of Ngo Dinh Diem's most prominent southern Vietnamese political rivals and assesses his government's conduct and the U.S. policy of support for it in light of that domestic political context.

Of course, the Cold War was central to American involvement in Vietnam. But American intervention on Cold War grounds intersected with Vietnamese domestic political affairs that had more to do with a mix of often cross-cutting concerns such as nationalism, decolonization, regionalism, and religion only peripherally related to the struggle between communism and capitalist democracy. Decentering the Cold War and focusing on a wider range of Vietnamese political actors generates what one scholar has described as "an admittedly messier picture, though probably one truer to the period itself, and one that capture[s] the uncertainty, hesitations, and contestations among and between states and people as they sought to make sense of the powerful ruptures that the global turn toward decolonization after 1945 posed for Vietnam."[3]

I explore the chaotic competition for postcolonial political control that unfolded in southern Vietnam between the Second World War and the formation of the communist-backed National Front for the Liberation of South Vietnam (NLF) in 1960. In many respects, instability had been a hallmark of southern Vietnamese society for generations, even prior to its colonization by the French. Indeed, the region's long history of political, social, and cultural heterodoxy made it notoriously difficult to govern and contributed to the rise of three powerful politico-religious organizations that constitute the foci of this study: the Cao Dai, Hoa Hao, and Binh Xuyen. By the end of the Franco–Viet Minh War in 1954, these noncommunist nationalist groups controlled roughly one-third of the territory and population below the seventeenth parallel. The Binh Xuyen operated the Saigon-Cholon police and security agency, which its leader Bay Vien had purchased from chief-of-state Bao Dai the previous year. All three benefitted from support payments issued by the French in exchange for the defense of their strongholds against Viet Minh forces. They had their own administrative structures, which some have referred to as "states within a state," collected their own taxes, and fielded their own armed forces. As the French war drew to a close, they wielded great power on the ground in southern Vietnam, while newly appointed prime minister Ngo Dinh Diem controlled little beyond his palace gates.

In the prevailing understanding, these groups appear as little more than fleeting obstacles on Ngo Dinh Diem's path to establishing absolute power over South Vietnam. Their potential to undermine his frail government worried French and American officials from the time he took office until he defeated them in the "sect" crisis in the spring of 1955, at which point the Americans quickly forgot about them and lauded Ngo Dinh Diem for his ability to prevail over the chaos and anarchy that they appeared to generate. They were, however, much more than fleeting obstacles. They were key players in Vietnamese nationalist politics long before Ngo Dinh Diem took power, and they remained critical to South Vietnam's political trajectory even after their supposed annihilation.

Close examination of the Cao Dai, Hoa Hao, and Binh Xuyen and their interactions with Ngo Dinh Diem, France, the United States, and Vietnamese communists goes a long way toward explaining the failure of the joint RVN-American nation-building project in South Vietnam. Developments in South Vietnam between 1954 and 1956 paved the way for the organized opposition to Ngo Dinh Diem's government that would emerge by the decade's end. And those developments centered on the challenges politico-religious organizations posed to the government and the methods Ngo Dinh Diem, with American backing, employed to combat them.

Most fundamentally, I contend that the Hoa Hao, Cao Dai, and Binh Xuyen organizations that vied for power with Ngo Dinh Diem during his first two years in office had national political ambitions and substantial power and influence south of the seventeenth parallel. Although Ngo Dinh Diem and the Americans dismissed their leaders as immoral, feudalistic, politically immature warlords, the manner in which Ngo Dinh Diem's administration set out to annihilate them during his first two years in office held great consequences for the future of South Vietnam. The tendency among historians to adopt official U.S. government assessments of these groups has obscured how significant they were within South Vietnamese society. They were not passing oddities as many American observers assumed, but rather organic products of southern Vietnam's unique history. They dominated religious, social, and political life throughout much of the southern countryside for decades prior to Ngo Dinh Diem's inauguration and commanded popular allegiances that would not be wiped away simply by decimating their militaries.

One of the ways that I recover the agency of these organizations and the individuals who participated in them is through an adjustment in terminology. While French and American officials referred to the Cao Dai, Hoa Hao, and Binh Xuyen by the derisive and inaccurate term *sects*, only the first two were religious while the third more closely resembled a mafia group. This fact alone makes it misleading to discuss political activity involving all three as sectarian in nature. More important, French and American officials' use of the term *sect*, like their application of the term *feudal* to the same entities, reflected their judgment that these groups and their leaders were parochial, antimodern, and incapable as well as morally unworthy of participating in a nationalist government. While the French were more willing to imagine a coalition government that included Hoa Hao, Cao Dai, and Binh Xuyen representatives—even those who actively challenged Ngo Dinh Diem—it was not because they were less prejudicial toward these groups, but because they held Ngo Dinh Diem in equally low esteem.

This is not merely a semantic issue, as it gets to the heart of U.S. attitudes toward the South Vietnamese leader and his domestic political challengers. From the outset, American officials conferred legitimacy on Ngo Dinh Diem and discounted the claims of his adversaries based on moral distinctions that made sense within their own framework of thinking about the Cold War, religion, and modernization, but that reflected a fundamental misreading of the complicated political contest that swirled within southern Vietnam. By mid-1955, the United States committed itself to supporting Ngo Dinh Diem based on these perceptions and sanctioned the campaign to eradicate the politico-religious organizations that challenged him in the intimidating and often brutal manner that his government employed. This made Washington complicit in creating the Saigon government that inspired widespread opposition within a short matter of years on the grounds that it was an oppressive, authoritarian, nepotistic, hypocritical puppet of the United States.

My second key claim is that Ngo Dinh Diem constructed his government and developed its most unpopular institutions and practices largely in an effort to neutralize the politico-religious threat that plagued him during his first two years in office. Between the summers of 1954 and 1956, as he went after the politico-religious organizations and the remnants of French power in South Vietnam to which they were linked, he created in opposition to them the organizational structure of his government and the rhetorical justification for his leadership. Contrary to Saigon chargé d'affaires Robert McClintock's claim that Ngo Dinh Diem was "a messiah without a message," the South Vietnamese leader aimed to lead his people in a "national revolution" based in a political philosophy that represented an amalgam of French personalism and Confucian political thought.[4] In that quest, he persistently made reference to his politico-religious rivals in an attempt to establish a rubric for good citizenship and effective leadership within the revolutionary state he imagined.

Politico-religious rather than communist opposition posed the greatest immediate obstacle to Ngo Dinh Diem's success in the early years, but it also presented him with critical opportunities. At the outset of Ngo Dinh Diem's administration the Communist Party south of the seventeenth parallel was weak, fragmented, underground, and directed by Hanoi to pursue its objective of national reunification by political rather than military means.[5] Communists gave him no concrete reason to initiate a violent crackdown; despite their potential to reconstitute as a major challenge to his government down the line, their current threat was rhetorical. The prime minister skirted this inconvenient truth by referencing violent politico-religious opposition to his government as an extension of not only the French, but also the communist, cause. Hoa Hao, Cao Dai, and Binh Xuyen challenges to Ngo Dinh Diem's government provided the very justification he needed to target them, Bao Dai, and the French for annihilation, ouster, and forced withdrawal, respectively. What is more, the very real material threats politico-religious forces posed to the Saigon government enabled the Ngos to rationalize their violent, oppressive, and indiscriminate antiterror programs aimed ostensibly at identifying and neutralizing communists.

Ngo Dinh Diem's administration went out of its way to cast politico-religious rebels as traitors against not only his state, but the Vietnamese nation more generally. He named a triad of enemies of the people consisting of feudalists, imperialists, and communists. And he worked to establish connections between politico-religious figures, French agents, and communists in order to bolster the claim that any and all opposition to his government signified membership in that group of conspirators. Thus he explained all of the most important early South Vietnamese government initiatives in terms of necessity brought about by politico-religious subversion. These included the Denounce the Communists Campaign and the activities of Ngo Dinh Nhu's related clandestine security apparatus, the referendum to depose Bao Dai, the very formation of the Republic of Vietnam, the timetable for a complete French military withdrawal, and even the decision to evade the reunification elections. While historians agree overwhelmingly that Ngo Dinh Diem built up an oppressive authoritarian state in South Vietnam, they have overlooked the extent to which he relied on early politico-religious challenges to his government as a foil for doing so.

My third contention is that the United States too readily accepted Ngo Dinh Diem's argument that authoritarian rule was necessary to quell chaos in Vietnam, and that such a government would be capable of generating popular legitimacy. By no means was this surprising, as Washington by the 1950s had a long history of supporting authoritarian regimes around the world as a means of promoting stability and preventing the spread of anarchy and communism.[6] Ngo Dinh Diem, moreover, presented U.S. officials with a familiar leader for Vietnam whose Catholic ethical framework coincided with their own. When he defied lowly expectations to prevail over the politico-religious armies in the spring 1955 Battle of Saigon, Washington praised his victory as a miracle and concluded that it had no real choice but to continue supporting him. In the coming years, American officials dismissed concerns about his growing authoritarianism and ignored complaints from South Vietnam's disenfranchised noncommunist nationalists that he was alienating his constituency and driving his opponents into reluctant collaboration with the communists.

Yet to ignore these voices was a grave mistake. By restricting participation in his government to a small clique of family members and close
confidantes and attempting to subsume South Vietnam's disparate political
parties under a single government entity, Ngo Dinh Diem frustrated the
country's postcolonial political actors, most of whom conceived of democracy more as a government representing the interests of all major national
political parties and regional leaders than a system based on popular political participation. On a more grassroots level, the violent and oppressive
measures Ngo Dinh Diem and his brothers used to combat any and all
who opposed them, coupled paradoxically with promises of ethical, democratic government, generated broad resentment throughout the countryside. Using violent and intimidating security and propaganda apparatuses,
they forced this opposition underground almost before it could emerge. For
a time, this led to an illusion of legitimacy surrounding Ngo Dinh Diem's
government, but he never extinguished the ember of resistance that smol-
dered beneath the surface.

My fourth argument is that the authoritarian state system and indiscriminate terror tactics Ngo Dinh Diem established during his first two
years in power, in reaction to challenges from the politico-religious organizations, generated the widespread opposition to his government that
encouraged Hanoi to form the National Liberation Front. Incidents like
the 1957 Cao Dai demonstration for the return of Pope Pham Cong Tac
foreshadowed the organized opposition to the RVN that would emerge
by the decade's end and belied the impression that Ngo Dinh Diem's
consolidation of power was the miracle his American supporters gauged
it to be. His military campaigns against the politico-religious organizations did cripple their armies and divide their political organizations. Ngo
Dinh Nhu's Denounce the Communists Campaign, and the oppressive
security apparatus and disruptive land reform program that accompanied
it, intimidated Ngo Dinh Diem's opponents and discouraged overt antigovernment expression. Yet, on final analysis, the Ngo brothers' attempts
to generate uncontested loyalty to their state, by combining moral and
nationalistic appeals based in personalism and Confucian traditions with a
program of brutality and repression directed at those who dared to oppose
them, served to inspire ever greater resentment and hostility toward their
administration.

Some Cao Dai, Hoa Hao, and Binh Xuyen followers continued to oppose the RVN even during South Vietnam's apparent golden years from
1955 to 1959. Though suspicious and even disdainful of communists as

a result of prior betrayals, many politico-religious followers would find that they had little alternative but to cooperate with communist cadres to form an organized opposition to Ngo Dinh Diem in the countryside.[7] In 1960, many of them would participate in the foundation of the NLF. Many others with no politico-religious affiliation would come to oppose Ngo Dinh Diem and join the NLF due to his authoritarianism, his nepotism, his ill-advised changes to local political administration and disastrous land reform policies, his restrictions on religious freedom, and his hypocritical promises of democracy. The foundation for each of these critiques was laid during the first two years of his administration, when the politico-religious organizations served as the focal point of his policies and much of his propaganda. Indeed, disenfranchised politico-religious leaders were the first to condemn Ngo Dinh Diem's fledgling RVN as a "family government" (*gia dinh tri*) and a "religious (Catholic) government" (*ton giao tri*)—indictments that would come back to haunt him at the end of his rule.

These arguments stem from a rather different approach to the Vietnam War than that which currently prevails, one that privileges Vietnamese sources and delves beneath the top tier of Vietnamese leadership to explore the country's broader political context. The vast majority of extant literature on America's Vietnam War and on the failed partnership between Washington and Ngo Dinh Diem reflects its predominant reliance on American sources. Based on those sources, most historians have concluded that Ngo Dinh Diem's chances for success were iffy from the outset, as many of his countrymen regarded him as a puppet of the United States, an outsider to Vietnamese politics with no ability to compete with Ho Chi Minh for nationalist legitimacy, and a Catholic with no comprehension of the Buddhist country he aimed to govern. According to this view, things went from bad to worse as his administration progressed, and by the end a slew of factors conspired to cause the demise of his government.[8] Among these were his authoritarianism, his lack of nationalist vision and stagnant mandarin ways, his blatant favoritism toward Catholic refugees, his ill-advised restructuring of village politics and catastrophic land reform programs, his total dependence on American aid, and his refusal to distance himself from seemingly toxic family members like Ngo Dinh Nhu and his wife Madame Nhu (Tran Le Xuan). While there is a great deal of truth to these claims, Ngo Dinh Diem too often stands alone or alongside his American advisors in these scholarly analyses, while the varied and complex Vietnamese experiences of the country's postcolonial moment remain understudied and largely unknown.[9]

It has become axiomatic for most historians of the Vietnam War and former policymakers alike that the United States lost its war in Vietnam— or made the mistake of fighting it in the first place—because it did not understand the country's domestic political, cultural, and social context suf- ficiently. Perhaps most strikingly, former secretary of defense Robert Mc- Namara has claimed in retrospect, "Our judgments of friend and foe alike reflected our profound ignorance of the history, culture, and politics of the people in the area and the personalities and habits of their leaders."[10] One historian has described the Vietnam War as "a war foretold" by the events of 1945–54, which included the "American cultural ignorance and con- descension" displayed toward the Vietnamese during the First Indochina War.[11] Even those who defend the American war as a "triumph forsaken" blame U.S. misunderstandings of Vietnamese politics and traditions for the mistakes that lost the war.[12] Despite this general consensus, we still know far too little about the domestic Vietnamese milieu in which American advi- sors, diplomats, and soldiers intervened.

This dearth of knowledge is the result of several factors. For a genera- tion after the war's end, American scholars and citizens alike attempted to reckon with their own national tragedy, and sought to understand how U.S. policies led to a humiliating and divisive defeat in Vietnam. Historians of Vietnam tended to focus on the period before the war, and students of the war engaged little with their area studies counterparts. In part this was a function of the inaccessibility of Vietnamese archives, which only began to open to Western scholars after the Socialist Republic of Vietnam initiated the *Doi Moi* reform program in 1986.[13] Even then, the Vietnamese government was slow to make post-1945 records available for consultation and, of course, those sources that were available were largely in Vietnamese, requiring that researchers possess the necessary language skills.

Following on the heels of Vietnam's initial archival openings, a handful of historians armed with Vietnamese language training delved into Viet- namese sources to produce an invaluable first cut of scholarship that began to bridge the gap between Vietnam studies and Vietnam War studies.[14] Since then, a growing number of historians have followed their lead, attempting to rectify the unbalanced focus on Washington that pervades the majority of American writing about the Vietnam Wars. Some, most notably Philip Catton and Edward Miller, have trained their interest on Vietnamese ac- tors in the south to deepen our understanding of Washington's relationship with Ngo Dinh Diem. In the process they have recovered a good deal of agency for the South Vietnamese leader and his government.[15] Indeed, most historians contributing to this new body of literature conclude that Ngo Dinh Diem was neither an American puppet nor a backward-looking traditionalist, but an autonomous leader with his own vision for modernizing Vietnam and leading it to independence on his own terms.[16] For the most part, they agree that Ngo Dinh Diem, having been largely responsible for South Vietnamese nation-building projects, owns an equal share of the blame for their failure. However, even in these Vietnam-centric studies too much of the weight rests on Ngo Dinh Diem's shoulders.

The pages that follow place the South Vietnamese leader into the domestic context that would ultimately determine his fate. The United States, wedded to a geostrategic vision that privileged Cold War considerations over local nuances, grossly misperceived that domestic political context. Its resulting support for Ngo Dinh Diem and its ultimate military intervention thus transformed a multifaceted postcolonial civil struggle into a large-scale proxy war, fueled by external funding, troops, and technology.

I begin this book with a discussion of the origins of the Hoa Hao, Cao Dai, and Binh Xuyen organizations and how they grew out of southern Vietnam's unique political context in the 1920s and 1930s, and conclude with an analysis of their participation in the formation of the National Liberation Front in 1960. The bulk of my analysis centers on the events from 1953 to 1956, the critical years of transition in which the French ended their war in Indochina and the United States threw its support behind Ngo Dinh Diem's newly formed Republic of Vietnam. The politico-religious organizations were front and center for all of the key events that unfolded during those years.

Well before the Battle of Dien Bien Phu opened in March 1954, Hoa Hao, Cao Dai, and Binh Xuyen leaders anticipated the end of the Franco–Viet Minh War and initiated political maneuvers to assert their claims to power in a postwar southern Vietnamese government. Amid the Geneva Conference that summer they stepped up their activities within Vietnam and made concerted efforts to appeal to American officials, only to see Ngo Dinh Diem appointed prime minister. They quickly realized that he aimed to exclude them from power and annihilate their influence, a fact that provoked them to confront his government, first during the Hinh crisis of fall 1954 and again in the "sect" crisis of spring 1955. I discuss the ways in which these organizations continued to exercise powerful opposition to Ngo Dinh Diem's government, even after he supposedly annihilated them and destroyed their remaining connections to power via military campaigns against their armies and a political campaign to depose their ally, chief of state Bao Dai. While it seemed to American observers as though Ngo Dinh Diem had successfully consolidated power once he defeated the politico-religious armies and established the RVN in October 1955, attention to his opponents' activities over the remainder of the decade tells a very different tale.

Chapter 1

Anticolonialism in Vietnam's Wild South

A group of rebel forces drawn from the millenarian Buddhist organization, Buu Son Ky Huong, was among the last holdouts against France's colonizing army in the Mekong Delta. The organization appeared in the delta
in the 1840s and quickly grew in popularity as its charismatic leader Doan
Minh Huyen offered healing amulets amidst the latest in a series of devastating cholera epidemics that swept through the swampy terrain over the
course of the nineteenth century. Buu Son Ky Huong doctrine represented
an amalgamation of Vietnamese and Khmer practices, magical incantations,
and folk readings of Buddhist scriptures. It attracted adherents from southern Vietnam's diverse communities and promised to inoculate them against
foreign conquest and natural calamities alike. In the early 1860s, Buu Son
Ky Huong followers joined a hodgepodge of other local resistance forces to
wage guerrilla war against colonizing forces. As the French tightened their
stranglehold on Saigon, Buu Son Ky Huong rebels retreated into the dark,
dense, boggy jungles surrounding the Mekong River where they managed
to evade French authorities for another six years.[1]

The prominent role Buu Son Ky Huong rebels played in resisting
French colonization, and the challenge France faced as it sought to subdue
them, stemmed from southern Vietnam's frontier character, wild in both

human and geographic terms. The Mekong Delta had for centuries been marked by geographic, economic, social, ethnic, and cultural heterodoxies so rich that one scholar has deemed it "the least coherent territory in the world."[2] Between the 1500s and the mid-1800s, when France imposed colonial rule, the region experienced a layered settlement pattern that brought together a range of diverse peoples, including Khmer, Chinese, Vietnamese, and a number of ethnic minorities. Successive waves of human migration contributed to the fluid and overlapping nature of identities that came to define southern Vietnam.[3] Throughout the precolonial era, the lack of any powerful centralized government, a plethora of opportunities for trade and commerce with the outside world, and the relatively weak influence of rigidly hierarchical Confucian philosophy encouraged an individualistic pioneer spirit amongst southern Vietnam's diverse population.

The heterogeneous, entrepreneurial character of southern society was only reinforced by the territory's unique geography. Its stark transitions from coastal plains to mountain highlands and the mazelike waterways of the Mekong Delta facilitated the emergence of distinct local communities with their own hierarchies and traditions, sometimes dominated by figures unaffiliated with the state. Despite the presence of a strong, often oppressive colonial administration from 1867 to 1945, such local power bases remained a hallmark of southern society throughout the colonial era. By the end of the Second World War the wild south responded to the dislocations caused by French colonial rule and Japanese occupation by balkanizing into competing armed administrative units.[4]

Building on southern Vietnam's existing tradition of syncretic Buddhism and on the region's Chinese-influenced practices of organizing politically via secret societies, several millenarian Buddhist organizations like the Buu Son Ky Huong that sought to alleviate the social, spiritual, and economic dislocations wrought by French colonialism gained strength in the early colonial era. Between the 1920s and 1940s, while nationalists in northern and central Vietnam developed Western-influenced anticolonial organizations such as Ho Chi Minh's Indochinese Communist Party (ICP) and the Vietnamese Nationalist Party (Viet Nam Quoc Dan Dang, or VN-QDD), millenarian groups took root as the south's most powerful agents of anticolonialism. Thus, in the complex and often violent anticolonial politics of Vietnam's wild south, where so much of the French and American wars would play out, the Cao Dai, Hoa Hao, and Binh Xuyen politico-religious organizations were among the most important actors. Their growing popular support and control of as much as a third of the territory of the south posed profound challenges to the efforts of the French, the Japanese, Ho Chi Minh's Democratic Republic of Vietnam, and eventually the American-backed government of Ngo Dinh Diem to bring southern Vietnam under centralized control. Whether for the French colonial state or its postcolonial successors, the wild south was not an easy place to govern. Indeed civil war—with the Cao Dai, Hoa Hao, and Binh Xuyen at its center—was just as apt a descriptor as colonial war or Cold War for the condition of southern Vietnam in the 1940s and 1950s.[5]

The Emergence of Southern Vietnam's Politico-Religious Organizations

The Cao Dai was the first of southern Vietnam's three most influential politico-religious organizations to emerge in the colonial era. Officially founded by colonial civil servant Ngo Van Chieu in 1926, it would grow to be the largest of the region's politically oriented religious entities, and in many ways the most powerful. The Cao Dai, known in the West primarily for its eclecticism, and for the novelty of claiming as saints in its pantheon such figures as Joan of Arc, William Shakespeare, Victor Hugo, Sun Yatsen, Vladimir Lenin, Phan Boi Chau, and Li Po, derived from a synthesis of the world's major religions: Confucianism, Geniism, Christianity, Islam, Buddhism, and Taoism.[6] According to Cao Dai doctrine, the Supreme Being (*cao dai tien ong*) revealed himself during a ritual séance on January 13, 1927, to exhort, "Nowadays all parts of the world are explored: humanity, knowing itself better, aspires to world peace. But because of the very multiplicity of . . . religions, men do not always live in harmony. That's why I decided to unite all in one to bring them back to primitive unity."[7] The central tenet of Cao Dai doctrine, then, was that a single God had revealed himself throughout time and across the globe in different forms, and had finally chosen Vietnam as the place to establish a universal religion aimed at harmonizing the world's beliefs and philosophies.[8]

More than a decade later, on May 18, 1939, Prophet Huynh Phu So introduced another politico-religious organization into southern Vietnam's anticolonial milieu by founding the Hoa Hao. Huynh Phu So, born in 1919 to the village of Hoa Hao in Chau Doc Province, near the Cambodian border, grew up a sickly and somewhat apathetic young man. When he fell seriously ill in 1939, his father sent him on a pilgrimage to the mountains of That Son and Tha Lon to seek help from a reputed healer. During his pilgrimage, Huynh Phu So studied magic, acupuncture, and Buddhist teachings. He returned home uncured, but soon after claimed to experience miraculous healing while praying in the middle of an intense storm outside his family home.[9] He explained the story of his recovery to astonished family members and neighbors, and it spread rapidly throughout the countryside and drew more and more followers to his side. He graduated quickly to performing miracle cures, preaching, and carrying out acts of extreme charity for the poor, and by the end of 1939 he had already attracted tens of thousands of adherents to the new Hoa Hao organization.

Huynh Phu So's teachings were an egalitarian reinterpretation of the Buddhist faith, which appealed immensely to Vietnamese peasants who often suffered nearly permanent states of indebtedness under the French colonial system. French administrators had severely disrupted the precolonial economic system by seizing rural lands and introducing a capitalist economy that replaced the barter system with cash for trade. This forced many small landholders into tenancy and thrust landless peasants into staggering debt. Such widespread indebtedness made it nearly impossible for people to worship gods and ancestors, marry daughters, and bury parents in a manner sufficiently ostentatious to prove their filial piety.[10] By placing great emphasis on the value of internal faith and the need to be charitable to the living while downplaying the tradition of lavishing grandiose gifts on the dead, Huynh Phu So posed a much-needed palliative for peasants' material and religious woes.[11]

The third politico-religious organization in southern Vietnam's anticolonial trifecta was in fact not religious at all. The roots of the Binh Xuyen organization can be traced back to the early 1920s, when a loose coalition of pirate bands sprung up in the marshes and canals to the south of Saigon-Cholon. Initially about two hundred to three hundred strong, some of these pirates were escapees from forced labor on colonial rubber plantations and many were ruffians straight off the streets of Cholon. They earned their livings extorting protection money from junks and sampans traveling the canals to deliver goods to the docks in Cholon. When pursued, they evaded the police and colonial militia by retreating into the mangrove swamps in the Rung Sat area at the mouth of the Saigon River. Local inhabitants regarded them not as criminals, but as heroes who stole from the exploitative colonial regime and redistributed wealth to the Vietnamese masses. In exchange, the residents of Rung Sat eagerly offered them shelter and protection. "If the Binh Xuyen pirates were the Robin Hoods of Vietnam," writes one historian, "then the Rung Sat ("Forest of the Assassins") was their Sherwood Forest."[12] While its key players were active in the Mekong Delta during the 1920s to 1940s, the Binh Xuyen would not emerge as a truly organized political force until the end of the Second World War.

All three of these organizations were products of southern Vietnam's heterogeneous frontier character. In the seventeenth century, as the Nguyen lords struggled simultaneously to legitimize their rule among the diverse peoples of the south and to fend off conquest from rival Trinh lords to the north, they embraced Buddhism as a potential vehicle for winning over their non-Vietnamese subjects while distinguishing their southern polity from the Confucian north. In an effort to naturalize Vietnamese settlers to their new communities, they encouraged the integration of a variety of in-digenous spirits and beliefs into a uniquely Vietnamese Mahayana Buddhist framework. Mahayana Buddhism's syncretic nature facilitated the easy in-corporation of local deities, to some extent drawing on Cham polytheism, which made southern Buddhism particularly inclusive of ethnic, regional, and even class variations. This shift away from Confucianism and toward Buddhism was made easier by the fact that new southern villages were settled not by traditional elites, but by lower-status people who were by no means wedded to existing patterns of social organization and behavioral expectations. Their willingness to change and innovate as circumstances demanded would become a hallmark of southern society.[13] The strength of Buddhism and the acceptance of religious variation from village to village in the precolonial south set the stage for a range of millenarian organiza-tions to emerge in southern Vietnam under French colonial rule.

The Cao Dai, Hoa Hao, and Binh Xuyen grew also out of a related tradition among the lower classes in the Mekong Delta of working through secret societies to address problems such as debt, poverty, seasonal migration, and heavy taxation. This practice was rooted in ancient Chinese traditions developed in the period immediately following the Manchu overthrow of the Ming dynasty, when Ming loyalists founded secret societies that were both political and religious, based on the belief that a native king would be born to lead them out of their current period of oppression. A network of Ming loyalist merchants brought this tradition to southern Vietnam in the eighteenth and nineteenth centuries.[14] Two organizations that exerted great influence on the social and political organization of the Mekong Delta— the Thien Dia Hoi (Heaven and Earth Society) and Buu Son Ky Huong (Strange Fragrance from the Precious Mountain)—had their origins in Chinese influence under the Qing dynasty (1644–1912).

During the reign of Minh Mang (1820–41), a religious leader named Tran Nguyen (Buddha Master, *phat thay tay an*) warned of the imminent demise of the Vietnamese Empire at the hands of "men come from the West," and spread to Vietnam the Ming prophecy of an Asian leader destined to fend off Western invaders.[15] He preached a form of Buddhism that eschewed the emphasis on exterior, material manifestations of the religion and advocated a more pure, interior practice of faith, ideas that would later factor heavily into Hoa Hao doctrine. Tran Nguyen's branch of Buddhism was called Buu Son Ky Huong because his followers wore protective talismans inscribed with that phrase, which was understood to represent the Buddha who would soon appear to end the suffering endured during French occupation.[16] Resistance to the French was a main tenet of Buu Son Ky Huong faith even prior to the formal colonization of southern Vietnam, as the organization mobilized in an ultimately doomed effort to expel French conquerors, thereby joining the region's millenarian tradition with the cause of anticolonialism.[17]

In the early 1900s, when no secular political ideology had yet emerged in Vietnam to express the people's widespread discontent with colonial oppression, religious groups like the Buu Son Ky Huong and its offshoots employed traditionalist, apocalyptic language to challenge the French administration. During the early colonial period, southerners turned to the Thien Dia Hoi and Buu Son Ky Huong as vehicles for underground struggle. In 1913 and again in 1916 these two organizations cooperated to stage armed rebellions in the Mekong Delta. They attracted broad support not only from the peasantry, but also from Vietnamese elites who sought to align themselves with popular grassroots political organizations.[18] The Cao Dai and Hoa Hao—new iterations of the existing secret society model— emerged in a context in which Vietnamese elites had come to recognize the failure of both legal dissent and armed rebellion against colonial rule, and sought new forms of organization through which they could unite southern Vietnam's social classes behind a novel form of challenge to French control. The formidable history of resistance to colonial rule through secret societies in the Mekong Delta enabled the Hoa Hao, Cao Dai, and even the Binh Xuyen to claim that they took part in the anticolonial struggle in the name of a longstanding tradition of Vietnamese national sovereignty.[19]

While the politico-religious organizations looked back to these earlier models for political organization and resistance, they also drew on ideas and technologies recently introduced to southern Vietnamese society under French colonialism. The Cao Dai, which enjoyed a longer period of development prior to the outbreak of World War II than either the Hoa Hao or the Binh Xuyen, stands out in this regard. Its emphasis on uniting the world's disparate religions stemmed from the intimate contact between East and West brought on by colonialism, and more generally from modern innovations in transportation and communication that made possible interactions between the full range of peoples and religions of the world.[20] Its organizational structure followed closely along the lines of the French Catholic Church. And perhaps most significantly, the Cao Dai evolved in tandem with Vietnam's more secular, Western-influenced anticolonial movements, including the reformers in the 1920s and the ICP and the VN-QDD in the 1930s and 1940s. The ideas and approaches politico-religious leaders borrowed from those movements were unmistakably Western and modern.

Indeed, despite the idiosyncrasies associated with its eclectic nature, the Cao Dai was an important political and social movement generated by the colonial context of 1920s Vietnam. It was no coincidence that the organization was founded just months after a rash of anticolonial student strikes in 1926, and that it appealed directly to the anti-French sentiments of radical Vietnamese youth.[21] At a time of increasing Vietnamese rebellion against colonial rule and growing animosity between patriotic Vietnamese youth and French-educated colonial collaborators among their parents' generation, the Cao Dai religion promised to do away with ethnic, racial, and national conflict.[22] It filled a political void in the south, where the individualistic nature of political culture and the dominance of moderate bourgeois reform movements impeded the emergence of a single, dominant radical revolutionary movement. Just as Marxism began to emerge as a vehicle for populist anticolonial organization in northern and central Vietnam, the Cao Dai served similar demands in the south.[23] Cao Dai leaders called for nothing less than a new moral, social, and political order, rooting their appeals in the organization's millenarian doctrine, claiming that the anticipated period of reconciliation between East and West would be the third and final epoch of spiritual development in Vietnam's history.[24]

The Cao Dai first spread to urban religious networks around Saigon-Cholon, and by 1928 businessmen and landowners had recruited enough of a cult following amongst the peasant population to persuade leaders to establish a Holy See in Tay Ninh Province.[25] The majority of the Tay Ninh population apparently converted to Cao Dai after the formation of the Holy See. The estimated number of early Cao Dai adepts ranges anywhere from 200,000 to 1 million in the first three years of the organization's formal existence.[26] Regardless of the exact figure, this overwhelming conversion of the local peasantry underscored the political allure that accompanied the sect's theological attraction. Cao Dai appeal extended well beyond the limits of religion, and indeed much of its popularity can be attributed to its overt embrace of anticolonial politics. The organization proved overwhelmingly successful at attracting peasant followers as a result of its clever use of nationalist appeals, often couched in more traditional language.[27] One example of this can be found in the case of a 1928 mass-conversion in a poor village in the Plain of Reeds, where Cao Dai leaders convinced peasants to swallow live toads in order to immunize themselves against French bullets in the impending revolution.[28] This simultaneous appeal to traditional animistic beliefs and anticolonial aspirations exemplified Cao Dai recruitment practices.

Initially, the Cao Dai was not necessarily poised to compete with Vietnam's western-influenced, countrywide anticolonial movements like the VNQDD and the ICP, but its fortunes shifted as the French colonial administration cracked down on those organizations following a series of uprisings in 1930–31. Early Cao Dai solutions to peasants' social and economic problems alleviated some of the worst manifestations of distress but did little to solve systemic problems.[29] The onset of the Great Depression in 1930 brought an abrupt end to prosperity and prompted peasants throughout Vietnam to take matters into their own hands and revolt against the colonial administration. The ICP and the VNQDD claimed leadership of those uprisings, provoking French officials to respond by imprisoning the revolutionaries, crushing their organizations, and developing strict measures of repression designed to prevent a repeat occurrence.[30]

After a nadir in the 1930s, the ICP would recover during the popular front era to eclipse the badly damaged VNQDD as the primary adversary of the French colonial regime in northern and central Vietnam. Yet the communists would never regain such strength in southern Vietnam, where the vacuum created by French repression of the VNQDD and the ICP cleared the way for locally based groups like the Cao Dai, Hoa Hao, and Binh Xuyen to emerge and thrive. The blow that French administrators dealt to the anticolonial movement in 1930 and 1931, which was further compounded by severe ongoing worldwide economic depression, prompted southern revolutionaries to seek refuge among the ranks of politico-religious organizations.[31] During the late colonial period and especially during the Second World War, these organizations would grow in power and influence as the Vietnamese communists struggled to regain a foothold in the south.

The absence of a strong anticolonial movement in the south facilitated the emergence of an ever more politicized leadership for the Cao Dai. The organization developed a unique program that appealed to a constituency distinct from that which the ICP tended to target. Traditionalist Cao Dai peasants in the 1930s tended to be poor and lived in marginal areas relatively sheltered from the impact of the colonial state, as opposed to peasants in areas exposed to the full brunt of colonialism, who were much more likely to support communist political parties and organizations.[32] Yet the trajectory of the Cao Dai platform was by no means predetermined, and its early years were marked by internal battles over the organization's political future. By the 1930s, when hatred toward the French and proroyalist patriotism was widespread, Pham Cong Tac emerged from a bitter power struggle within the Cao Dai ranks and ascended to the position of pope at Tay Ninh. He was a nationalist at heart and quickly moved the Cao Dai in a steadily more anticolonial direction. Pham Cong Tac possessed a remarkable skill for issuing abstruse anti-French statements that appealed to Vietnamese nationalists without alarming colonial administrators.[33] His leadership encouraged urban reformist politicians to view the Cao Dai as a vehicle for spreading their political influence and economic interests among the peasant masses.[34]

The Cao Dai had been developing its political position and building a base of followers for over a decade when the Hoa Hao burst onto the scene in 1939. Cao Dai was the best organized and the most successful of southern Vietnam's major mass movements during the colonial period, as it competed with the ICP and more briefly the Hoa Hao, ultimately attracting significantly more adherents than either of those organizations.[35] Cao Dai ambitions reflected the organization's dominant position. According to one of the organization's early military leaders, Tran Quang Vinh, Cao Dai officials aimed not only to expel French colonialists but to establish themselves as the primary ideological and administrative force within Vietnam. He claimed that the organizational structure of the Cao Dai "is that of a modern state. It does not lack ambitions which, however, remain within the realm of possibility: to make Cao-Daism into a religion of the State, into the national religion of Vietnam."[36] Despite these grand ambitions, Cao Dai dominance would not go unchecked.

If the Cao Dai was the most powerful of southern Vietnam's politico-religious organizations in the 1930s, and the most heavily influenced by the larger context of Vietnam's anticolonial politics of the 1920s and 1930s, that broader context also shaped the Binh Xuyen and the Hoa Hao. Both of those organizations sought to challenge the primacy of the Cao Dai in the southern struggle to oust the French and recover Vietnamese sovereignty. Indeed, Binh Xuyen political development was heavily colored not only by experiences of French colonialism, but also by intimate contact between the organization's future leaders and others who actively opposed the colonial regime.

Le Van Vien (Bay Vien), who would head the Binh Xuyen during its heyday throughout the First Indochina War, was born in 1904 in the outskirts of Cholon. At the age of seventeen, after losing his inheritance in a dispute, he began work as a chauffeur for a small-time gangster who introduced him to the leaders of the Cholon underworld. Like many of his fellow Binh Xuyen, Bay Vien's illegal activities earned him time in Poulo Condore prison. While there he participated in anticolonial political discussions among inmates, which were most often dominated by communists. To be sure, Bay Vien and the Binh Xuyen were motivated largely by the less-than-lofty ambition of protecting and enhancing their own wealth and power. Bay Vien and his Binh Xuyen colleagues were also determined to keep southern affairs out of northern hands and sought at all costs to preserve Binh Xuyen autonomy within the territory under its control.[37] Yet Binh Xuyen leaders were motivated as well by larger, national political concerns and worked during World War II to establish their organization as a significant player in Vietnam's anticolonial field. When Bay Vien returned to Saigon upon his escape from prison in 1945, he was politicized and embittered toward French colonialism, but certainly not converted to communist ideology.[38] He remained adamant that the Binh Xuyen did not represent a particular religion nor did it endorse a particular political philosophy. Instead, he claimed on several occasions that the organization placed patriotism above any creed.[39]

On the dawn of the Second World War, Hoa Hao leaders were much better poised than the Binh Xuyen to assert their claim to the mantle of Vietnamese nationalist leadership in the south. At its inception in 1939, Hoa Hao doctrine had a more overtly millenarian and anticolonial bent than that of even the Cao Dai.[40] Indeed, the organization emerged just as shifts in the international system that would eventually lead to the Second World War brought an end to the popular front era. With the end of that era, French colonial forces stepped up repression of revolutionary groups, increased taxes, and conscripted large numbers of soldiers from their colonies, placing ever greater strains on the Vietnamese peasantry. In this context, Huynh Phu So drew directly on the Buu Son Ky Huong tradition of resistance to French domination and sought to reform Buddhist practices in ways that were inherently critical of French colonial economic and social policies. Moreover, in his quest to address peasant concerns, the prophet proved willing to associate with secular nationalists. He would soon link the Hoa Hao organization with southern Trotskyites, who had lost their peasant base following a 1937 split with Stalinists who dominated the ICP. The association between the Hoa Hao and the Trotskyites, whose determination to emphasize social revolution over class struggle conformed nicely to Huynh Phu So's objectives, would continue to grow during the Second World War.[41] This contributed to the development of a Hoa Hao brand of anticolonial politics that would render future cooperation with the ICP's successor organization, the Viet Minh, difficult if not impossible.

The Second World War and the August Revolution

Almost as soon as the Hoa Hao organization was born, Japanese forces landed in Indochina, bringing the Second World War to Vietnamese soil. In a desperate attempt to retain authority in the face of threats from both Japanese troops and Vietnamese challengers, French officials tightened their grip on opposition movements, including the politico-religious organizations. This only inspired the Hoa Hao and the Cao Dai to embrace anticolonial politics more overtly. During the war, with Japanese support, both groups would become more nationalistic and initiate the process of militarizing their organizations. By pitting the Hoa Hao and the Cao Dai more squarely against not only the French but also the Viet Minh, and endowing them with the organizational and military resources they would need to compete with both, the Japanese contributed to the outbreak of civil war in southern Vietnam almost immediately after the war's end.

In September 1940, just months after France capitulated to Germany, Japanese troops took advantage of French weakness to station troops in northern Vietnam. To many Vietnamese nationalists, this seemed to signal the impending demise of French colonial rule. Communist cadres, many of whom feared the arrival of Japanese fascism at least as much as they loathed the prospect of continued French rule, attempted to avert both by staging an insurrection focused exclusively on southern Vietnam. The French response, reminiscent of that which followed the uprisings in 1930 and 1931, devastated the ICP and the rural base it had managed to rebuild in the south. Most party cadres were shot, imprisoned, or sent into exile, and the southern communist movement would not begin to recover until French authority collapsed in 1945.[42]

The ICP's failed southern insurrection in 1940 left many distraught peasants devoid of anticolonial leadership, which encouraged the radical-ization of the politico-religious organizations and facilitated the rapid ex-pansion of their power. With the party's secular alternative to millenarian politics once again crippled, the Hoa Hao, Cao Dai, and emergent Binh Xuyen organizations were poised to capitalize on the increased demands for mass action against the French that the Japanese occupation inspired among Vietnam's southern citizens.[43] Wartime security controls and Allied bombing raids isolated southern intellectuals from political developments in northern and central Vietnam, further contributing to the largely inde-pendent development of anticolonial political organization in the south.

As Hoa Hao and Cao Dai leaders adopted ever more bold anticolo-nial positions, they found that they were by no means immune to French repression. In an increasingly radicalized anticolonial milieu Huynh Phu So's millenarian prophecies became more political and anti-French.[44] His prediction that the Franco-Japanese War signaled the end of the world prompted thousands of adepts to abandon their material possessions and take to the hills. The French colonial administration of Indochina re-sponded to Huynh Phu So's inflammatory behavior first by exiling him from his home and then by committing him to an insane asylum in August 1940. He was later moved to the psychiatric ward of a hospital near Saigon where he converted his psychiatrist to the Hoa Hao faith, and was finally declared sane by a board of French psychiatrists in May 1941. Huynh Phu So's imprisonment may have done more to fuel Hoa Hao growth than impede it, as the organization's membership spread rapidly to well over 100,000 while he was behind lock and key.

In an effort to retain their predominant position in southern politics, Cao Dai leaders also migrated during World War II toward more explicitly anti-French modes of nationalism, and allied with the Japanese and other proindependence movements against the colonial regime.[45] Following the lead of other Vietnamese nationalists, Cao Dai leaders looked to Japan to help them free Vietnam from French colonial rule and bring Prince Cuong De, then living in exile in Japan, to the Vietnamese throne.[46] The organization used spirit messages to propagandize about its independence movement and spread rumors that the Japanese were poised to overthrow the French and install an independent Vietnamese government including Cao Dai members.[47] From 1940 on, this bold new approach brought the

Cao Dai into ever greater conflict not only with French administrators, but with competing nationalist organizations including the ICP and the Hoa Hao.

When Japanese troops finally rolled into southern Vietnam in May 1941, the Cao Dai leadership was disappointed by their decision to allow French authorities to retain civil control over their colonies while ordering Vietnamese resistance forces, including those associated with the Cao Dai, to stand down. This perceived betrayal caused many to decry the Japanese as traitors and called into question Japan's pledge to take the lead in securing "Asia for the Asians." But the Cao Dai leadership maintained a pro-Japan position in hopes that the Japanese would eventually make good on their promise of liberating Vietnam and installing Cuong De in power.[48]

Meanwhile, the French continued to suppress nationalist and religious groups, particularly the Cao Dai and Hoa Hao, which drove both organizations to seek Japanese protection and ultimately to take advantage of Japanese assistance to militarize their own organizations. French officials ransacked Cao Dai temples, drove leaders underground, and forced followers to disband. In July 1941, the French governor general Admiral Jean Decoux initiated draconian steps to circumscribe Cao Dai activities. He sent French troops to occupy the Holy See in Tay Ninh and forced followers to evacuate within twenty-four hours. On July 27, they arrested Pope Pham Cong Tac and five other Cao Dai dignitaries, incarcerating them briefly at Poulo Condor (Con Son), a French colonial prison off the coast of southern Vietnam, before shipping them off to Madagascar. Following Pham Cong Tac's exile, his surrogate Tran Quang Vinh placed the organization under Japanese protection and volunteered young adepts for service in the Japanese military and security agency.[49] The Cao Dai took advantage of this opportunity to improve its own military organization following a Japanese model and to recruit soldiers for its own army, thereby greatly strengthening the group's overall position in Cochin China.[50] Cao Dai leaders' ongoing ambivalence about the Japanese did not prevent them from capitalizing on available assistance to expand their political, religious, and military activities. In turn, this growth inspired many previously unaffiliated people to flock to the sanctuary of Cao Dai bases.[51]

After 1941 the Hoa Hao also began to militarize under Japanese protection. During the Second World War, the organization developed armed self-defense units charged with protecting Hoa Hao followers in villages under its control. As Hoa Hao activities became more brazenly anticolonial, and Huynh Phu So issued prognostications about the impending flight of French colonial administrators, Hoa Hao adherents flocked to join the self-defense units. The organization's military leadership strove to transform them from local security forces into paramilitary resistance units. During the war, this objective was hindered by a lack of access to modern weapons and professional training. Indeed, it was not until late-1944, when the prospect of an Allied invasion of Indochina began to appear more likely, that the Cao Dai and Hoa Hao found Japanese occupation forces more willing to train their military branches in tactics, marching, self-defense, and assault. Even then, the Japanese provided little by way of arms and equipment. Nonetheless, Hoa Hao armed forces made use of what they had to earn a reputation for murder and banditry within the western part of southern Vietnam.[52] Contributing to this trend was the emergence of two military leaders, the notoriously tempestuous Tran Van Soai, whose violent temper earned him the nickname Nam Lua ("Five Fires"), and Le Quang Vinh, who garnered the nickname Ba Cut ("Third Finger Cut") by chopping off his own middle finger to prove his fighting mettle.[53]

The processes of Cao Dai and Hoa Hao militarization experienced another boost in early March 1945, when Japan finally staged a coup to oust French colonial administrators and install Japanese troops in their stead. Cao Dai forces became unwitting collaborators in the coup itself, as the Japanese rounded them up and sent them off to gather intelligence and, on the day of the event, to arrest and detain Frenchmen. Members of the Cao Dai organization took pride in the role they played in eliminating French rule, although they were disappointed by Japan's decision to retain the emperor Bao Dai rather than returning Cuong De to lead Vietnam as promised.[54] But like other Vietnamese nationalists, including the Viet Minh—the new, ostensibly more broad-based iteration of the ICP headquartered in the north—they saw the Japanese coup as an opportunity to be exploited.[55] Cao Dai temples were reopened and the organization's leaders coordinated a nationalist forum "to celebrate the end of French rule and express gratitude to the Japanese" that attracted as many as fifty thousand participants.[56]

The Japanese coup fueled Hoa Hao military development and political ambition as well. Almost immediately after seizing power, the Japanese announced a mass political amnesty and released thousands of political prisoners from French jails, including Hoa Hao military leaders Nguyen Giac Ngo and Lam Thanh Nguyen. These two joined with Tran Van Soai and Ba Cut to mount campaigns of intimidation designed to drive French police and village administrators out of the countryside under Hoa Hao control.

They were able to acquire some modern weapons from the fleeing Frenchmen, and to purchase some additional arms from the Japanese military.

Almost as soon as the Japanese coup occurred, Vietnamese nationalist leaders throughout the country began to anticipate an Allied victory and worked to position themselves to take advantage of the impending Japanese capitulation. In early summer 1945, Hoa Hao leaders opened talks with the heads of other southern nationalists groups, including the Trotskyites, the Cao Dai, and the VNQDD in view of uniting nationalist forces in the south to fight for and defend an independent Vietnam when the war drew to a close. In the north, anticolonial politics was dominated by the Viet Minh, the organization that Ho Chi Minh and his fellow communists had created to replace the ICP in an effort to broaden the movement's appeal. Upon learning of an imminent Japanese surrender in early August, Viet Minh leaders began preparations to stage a general insurrection, in hopes that they might strengthen their claims to governance over an independent Vietnam before Allied forces could sweep into the country to oversee the process of Japan's surrender.

The Viet Minh launched their insurrection with a mass demonstration at the Hanoi Opera House on August 19, after which armed units moved to take over preselected installations. Prior negotiations between the Viet Minh and the Japanese ensured that these initial seizures would be bloodless. The demonstrations and occupations of government buildings in Hanoi were accompanied by uprisings in other cities and throughout the countryside in the coming days. Most, but not all of the Viet Minh takeovers in the north, followed shortly by seizures in central Vietnam, occurred without confrontation. Japanese forces often proved willing to step aside and transfer abandoned French weapons to Viet Minh leaders. Royalists and most of their supporters among the Dai Viet and VNQDD parties reluctantly accepted Viet Minh leadership, and under pressure Emperor Bao Dai abdicated his throne and recognized Viet Minh authority on August 30. Fighting persisted in select locales, but in northern and central Vietnam, protracted violence was the exception rather than the rule.

Ho Chi Minh declared independence for the newly established Democratic Republic of Vietnam, headquartered in Hanoi, on September 2, 1945. Still hoping to secure Washington's support for the new government, he quoted liberally from the U.S. Declaration of Independence. The new regime would mobilize images of its smooth seizure of power and of widespread, spontaneous support for Viet Minh leadership in the struggle for independence to legitimize DRV rule.[57] However, those images masked the disjointed, decentralized manner in which the Viet Minh captured, or attempted to capture, control of much of the country. The new government, struggling to deal with a war-torn economy and the aftermath of a devastating famine in the north as it tried to establish a postcolonial state, exerted the most tenuous authority over many urban and rural locales. In many cases, those who did fight for independence under the Viet Minh banner only loosely grasped the principles for which the organization stood. And local leaders frequently bristled at efforts by the Hanoi leadership to bring them under DRV authority. Nowhere was this more of a problem for the Viet Minh than in the southern part of the country.[58]

Given the weak status of the communist movement in southern Vietnam and the "legions of local competitors" there, consolidating power peacefully in former Cochin China posed a significant, perhaps insurmountable, challenge.[59] Viet Minh leadership in southern Vietnam was itself internally divided and uncertain of how aggressively it should follow Hanoi's revolutionary lead. In addition to fears of reprisals at the hands of Japanese troops that could cripple the organization as badly as the French retaliation that followed the uprisings in 1940, southern communist revolutionaries faced potential resistance from a newly formed nationalist coalition.

On August 17, a group of non–Viet Minh parties and organizations in the south, including the Trotskyites, the politico-religious organizations, Catholics, and other secular nationalists announced their merger into a United National Front (Mat Tran Quoc Gia Thong Nhat).[60] Many members of this coalition had aligned with Japanese forces during the war. They were shaken by Tokyo's surrender and worried that the Allies might accuse them of collaborating with the enemy. At the same time, they wanted to assert themselves as major players in the movement for independence and publicize their opposition to French imperialism.[61] Behind the scenes, leaders of the front's constituent organizations found it impossible to work together and feuded over whether or not to support the Viet Minh. They agreed to march in an August 25 demonstration to mark the establishment of nominal Viet Minh power in Saigon, but that symbolic gesture represented only the thinnest veneer of unity to mask the ongoing struggle for power and political representation between Viet Minh leaders and the powerful politico-religious groups of the south.

Ostensibly, the Viet Minh was designed to include all patriotic, antiimperialist Vietnamese forces, but its southern leadership quickly proved unwilling to entertain any type of power sharing arrangement with the politico-religious organizations that had come to dominate much of the south. Viet Minh leaders lacked a coordinated approach to southern Vietnam's nationalist groups, in large part because of the ICP's inability to plan or communicate effectively with southern cadres in the years leading up to the August Revolution. On one hand, some Viet Minh cadres made deliberate efforts to include Cao Dai, Hoa Hao, and VNQDD representatives on the People's Committees of individual towns. However, Tran Van Giau, leader of the Viet Minh's Southern Administrative Committee, quickly stepped in with a heavy-handed approach to bring southern nationalist forces in line with the new Viet Minh government. He made no effort to include Hoa Hao, Cao Dai, or Catholic representatives in the new Southern Provincial Revolutionary Committee, filling its ranks instead with established ICP members and individuals who had already made clear their willingness to follow Viet Minh orders.[62]

On top of this, just days after Ho Chi Minh declared independence, communists pummeled Cao Dai leaders with accusations of "a number of misdeeds, including aiding the enemy, supporting a decaying monarchy, and working against the interests of the masses."[63] One Cao Dai follower in a Viet Minh stronghold remembers a "movement to exterminate religious groups" (*phong trao diet dao*) aimed at Cao Dai and Hoa Hao places of worship.[64] Cao Dai leaders in Tay Ninh grew fearful that all hopes of playing a role in an independent Vietnamese government were slipping away. They divided over whether or not to support the Viet Minh, creating a schism in the organization that would become an increasingly important factor in southern politics over the coming years.

The gravest altercations between Vietnamese groups in the period immediately following the August Revolution broke out between Viet Minh and Hoa Hao adherents in the Mekong Delta.[65] The organization's spiritual leader Huynh Phu So, angry that the Viet Minh had excluded Hoa Hao figures from the Southern Provincial Administrative Committee, ordered ICP members off newly formed provincial and district committees in territories under Hoa Hao control. On August 29, more than thirty thousand Hoa Hao adherents staged a march to demand that the administrative committee be reorganized, only to be pushed back by better armed and organized Viet Minh forces. The next day, Viet Minh units rounded up and arrested several local Hoa Hao leaders. Rather than suppressing Hoa Hao dissent, this simply caused the conflict to shift to the Mekong River port town of Can Tho a few days later. Hoa Hao followers there were incensed by Viet Minh moves to take control over their town just four days after general Tran Van Soai marched through Saigon in a show of solidarity with the Viet Minh. On September 8, Hoa Hao adherents in Can Tho staged a demonstration of twenty thousand people to protest what they viewed as the "dictatorial" policies of Tran Van Giau and the Viet Minh. The gathering, organized by Huynh Phu So to garner support for the Hoa Hao resistance movement, was ostensibly aimed at opposing French colonialism, but ended up conveying an even greater sense of contempt to the Viet Minh.[66] This provoked violent Viet Minh reprisals against Hoa Hao followers in and around Can Tho, which in turn inspired a rash of revenge killings against the Viet Minh.[67] Meanwhile, back in Saigon, Huynh Phu So's attempts to strike a power sharing agreement with Tran Van Giau fell flat.

If Viet Minh leaders in southern Vietnam struggled to subdue the Cao Dai and Hoa Hao in the days and weeks following the August Revolution, they had better luck with the Binh Xuyen. The organization, at one time no more than a loose band of pirates, first emerged as a formidable political and military organization in South Vietnam toward the end of World War II, especially after Japan rapidly seized power from French agents.[68] With all French soldiers, police, and civil servants suddenly behind bars, the organization, then under the command of Duong Van Duong (Ba Duong), was able to organize openly for the first time, and with encouragement from the Japanese. The new Japanese occupation government turned to the Binh Xuyen for logistical support, granting amnesty to some and hiring others, including Bay Vien, to work as police agents. By the time Japan surrendered, the Binh Xuyen had evolved into the primary force to be reckoned with in Saigon-Cholon and the surrounding jungles. This inspired rival Vietnamese political factions to court the Binh Xuyen in hopes of gaining access to the money, intelligence, and manpower that the group could provide. In August, Tran Van Giau convinced the Binh Xuyen to align with the Viet Minh. For a time, then, the Binh Xuyen would serve as a key ally of the Viet Minh as the organization sought to consolidate power and fend off French reconquest in the south.

The First Indochina War and Civil War in the South

Just as the Viet Minh had begun to extend DRV control to all of Vietnam, France initiated efforts to recapture its Indochinese colonial holdings, particularly in southern Vietnam where its economic interests were strongest, DRV authority was weakest, and colonial forces were most deeply entrenched. In the immediate aftermath of World War II, French politicians came to an unprecedented imperial consensus, and the decision to press forward with the colonial project went virtually unquestioned.[69] Throughout World War II and especially in the final year, when Allied victory appeared increasingly certain, the Free French organization under General Charles de Gaulle became fixated on restoring its imperial claim on Indochina. French leaders bent on reasserting their traditional role as a global power aimed to preserve the nation's empire, particularly the crown jewel that was Indochina. They clung to the belief that this colony entitled France to participate in Far Eastern affairs, and that it held substantial economic value that could potentially aid the war-ravaged metropole in its recovery.

Thanks to the acquiescence of British occupation forces in the south, the French were able to move rapidly to reassert control over the southern half of the country. When British forces entered Saigon in September 1945 to oversee the Japanese surrender, they brought with them a detachment of French troops. The British refused to deal with the DRV committee, instead declaring martial law and promptly rearming fourteen hundred French soldiers who immediately launched a program to gain control of the capital city.[70] As southern Vietnam's disunited resistance forces struggled to push back French advances, Ho Chi Minh and the DRV negotiated with France in hopes of preserving national independence while avoiding war. In March 1946, the two sides reached a preliminary accord, but the status of southern Vietnam would remain the sticking point. The March accord, which called for a national referendum to determine whether the south would rejoin the rest of the country or remain a separate French territory, left the fate of former Cochin China in flux.

While Viet Minh cadres in the north gained an early advantage over their nationalist opponents and enjoyed a year's respite to consolidate power between the August Revolution and the outbreak of war, a much smaller number of southern cadres struggled from the outset to subdue intractable domestic opponents and to resist French reconquest.[71] Southern Viet Minh grew more intimidating, corrupt, and violent in their efforts to bring noncommunist nationalist leaders and organizations under their control. Such activities were most widespread in the south, where the DRV struggled to control local Viet Minh agents who defied official orders and resorted to terroristic tactics and assassinations in frustrated response to the stubborn resistance posed by their Vietnamese competitors. As Viet Minh prospects of uniting southern nationalist forces soured, so did Franco–Viet Minh negotiations. The two sides were unable to reach an agreement about the fate of southern Vietnam, causing negotiations in Da Lat and Fontainbleau in March 1946 to stall. In late November, the French seized the northern port city of Haiphong and on December 19, the DRV made the decision to abandon negotiations and go to war. The First Indochina War officially broke out largely as a result of the Franco–Viet Minh standoff over southern Vietnam, where war had effectively been raging since September 1945.

In spite of their early clashes with southern nationalist leaders, Viet Minh agents made every effort to seize leadership of the movement that emerged in September to resist the return of the French Army. Initially, the Hoa Hao, Cao Dai, and Binh Xuyen deployed the military forces they had built up during the course of their wartime relationships with the Japanese. They were aided by Vietnamese volunteers coming from Thailand, Laos, and Cambodia, as well as units from northern Vietnam. DRV leaders decided to send the charismatic and ruthless General Nguyen Binh to southern Vietnam with the charge of reining in these disparate forces and building up a unified army to fight the French. DRV leaders believed that Nguyen Binh's prewar experience in the south and the contacts he had developed during his time in prison, his military talents, his personal charisma, and his credentials as a noncommunist would enable him to unite southern Vietnamese nationalist forces under DRV military control. Certainly, they hoped, he would prove more adept at doing so than communist figures like Tran Van Giau, for whom the politico-religious organizations displayed an inherent mistrust.[72]

Nguyen Binh arrived in southern Vietnam in the middle of November 1945 and immediately initiated efforts to unify the diverse southern groups that had emerged to resist the French Expeditionary Corps as it advanced north toward the sixteenth parallel and west to the Cambodian border. Uniting these motley forces behind the Viet Minh in the wild south would be a great challenge, but DRV leaders hoped Nguyen Binh's unique personality, talents, and southern contacts, would enable him to accomplish the nearly impossible task. To this end, Nguyen Binh co-opted the exiting platform for cooperation between southern Vietnam's nationalists by forming a Front of National Unity (Mat Tran Quoc Gia Lien Hiep) designed to pull noncommunist nationalists, politico-religious figures, youth, and intellectuals in the south into the Viet Minh front.[73]

In the beginning, Ngyuen Binh had some success recruiting Hoa Hao, Cao Dai, and Binh Xuyen forces to fight with his army. At the same time, these organizations were scandalized by Viet Minh violence against noncommunist nationalists and by the communists' transparent efforts to dominate southern nationalist politics. Ongoing assassination attempts against noncommunist nationalist leaders not only alienated Viet Minh allies in the south, but also hampered united resistance against the French.[74] This fragile coalition of Viet Minh forces and politico-religious units held together to engage the French in guerilla warfare throughout 1946. But by the beginning of 1947, Nguyen Binh caught wind of discussions between politico-religious leaders and representatives of French military intelligence. He responded with the increasingly accepted Viet Minh repertoire of arson, kidnapping, targeted assassination, massacres, and small unit attacks to "cow any potential 'collaborators' into submission" and to promote allegiance to the DRV.[75] His efforts to control southern nationalist groups with terror backfired, igniting a low-level civil war in the south between the Viet Minh and the politico-religious organizations that would drive the Cao Dai and Hoa Hao to sign military conventions with France between January and May 1947 and compel the Binh Xuyen to join them by summer 1948.

Initially, however, it seemed as though Nguyen Binh would be able to count on support from the Binh Xuyen following the agreement brokered by Tran Van Giau in the midst of the August Revolution. During the summer of 1945, Binh Xuyen cooperation gave the Viet Minh a much needed foothold in southern Vietnam and the organization's support became even more critical once France initiated efforts to reconquer the country that fall. When French forces took control of all the buildings and public services in Saigon, forcing the Viet Minh's southern committee to abandon the city, Tran Van Giau put Binh Xuyen general Bay Vien in command of the troops in Saigon-Cholon, but assigned a Viet Minh official to monitor his activities. In an effort to unify the wide range of political factions active in Saigon-Cholon, the Binh Xuyen immediately forged an alliance with the city's nationalist youth movement, the Avant-Garde Youth (Thanh Nien Tien Phong), led by Lai Van Sang, future Binh Xuyen chief of police.[76] It was an odd marriage, as the Binh Xuyen, largely regarded as a band of ruthless criminals, asserted command over idealistic young students and intellectuals.[77]

Using its standard extortionist tactics, the Binh Xuyen drew in enough money to expand its forces to seven regiments, comprising ten thousand men, making it the largest force associated with the Viet Minh in the south. Yet despite the major Binh Xuyen contribution to the Viet Minh's southern cause, the alliance was not destined to last long. The Viet Minh's objective of unifying all national political movements under its control conflicted with the Binh Xuyen's desire for total autonomy within the territory under its purview.[78] This soon generated a clash that would tear apart the alliance and drive the Binh Xuyen into French arms.

In 1946, Nguyen Binh convened a military tribunal to investigate charges of murder and extortion against a minor Binh Xuyen chieftain, Ba Nho, who happened to be an intimate friend of the organization's leader, Ba Duong. The tribunal found Ba Nho guilty and condemned him to death, which provoked a heated argument between Ba Duong and Nguyen Binh, during which Ba Nho grabbed Nguyen Binh's pistol and shot himself in the head. Ba Duong blamed Nguyen Binh for his friend's suicide, asked to be relocated to get out from under Nguyen Binh's tight grip, and began organizing a movement to oust the general from his position in the Viet Minh hierarchy. But he was killed in combat just weeks later. In February 1946 the Binh Xuyen held an elaborate funeral in an area of mangrove swamps just outside of Saigon where the organization's chiefs unanimously selected Bay Vien as their next supreme commander.[79] Bay Vien continued his predecessor's vendetta against Nguyen Binh, though he nominally continued cooperating with the Viet Minh while conspiring surreptitiously with the Hoa Hao to form an anti-French, anti-Viet Minh coalition.

Like the Binh Xuyen, Hoa Hao and Cao Dai leaders at first proved willing to collaborate, however tentatively, with Nguyen Binh. But they were quickly alienated by the general's heavy-handed tactics and by Viet Minh demands that they relinquish their autonomy. After full-scale war broke out between France and the Viet Minh in the north at the end of 1946, French military intelligence officers developed a complex strategy to capitalize on dissension within the ranks of resistance forces. The French took steps to win over, buy off, or extort politico-religious organizations. They aimed to compel them to break with the Viet Minh in hopes of bolstering their defenses and avoiding the need to fight a unified bloc of nationalist forces in the south.[80] The Viet Minh determination to subordinate fiercely independent southern nationalist organizations under the DRV's centralized authority may have doomed the united front from the start, but Nguyen Binh's unpopular methods and France's skillful manipulation of the politico-religious organizations cemented the failure.

In spring 1946 French troops captured Tran Quang Vinh and the entire religious leadership of the Cao Dai, thus forcing him to sign an agreement with the French in June 1946. He pledged to surrender Cao Dai troops in exchange for the release of their dignitaries and the return of Pham

Cong Tac from his exile in Madagascar. On January 8, 1947, the Cao Dai signed an additional military convention with the French High command pledging "loyal collaboration" and respect for French laws and authority. In return, the French promised to arm and fund the Cao Dai forces, forty-five hundred of whom were charged with defending Tay Ninh against Viet Minh forces.[81] Although the January convention was secret, Nguyen Binh caught wind of the Cao Dai betrayal and flew into a rage. On January 24, 1947, he created a special military assault force to take on the "pro-French" Cao Dai and purge the organization of "reactionary" followers.[82]

Nguyen Binh also faced obstacles to his united front from the Hoa Hao. The organization was suspicious of the Viet Minh even before the clashes of August 1945, and undertook a number of measures early on to protect its freedom of action.[83] In September 1946, partly to counter the influence of Nguyen Binh's Front of National Unity, Huynh Phu So founded the Vietnamese Social Democratic Party (Viet Nam Dan Chu Xa Hoi Dang), with an eye toward uniting all of the noncommunist nationalist groups that had existed in Vietnam prior to the Japanese defeat behind a platform of peace, national independence, and socialist principles, including social security for the disabled. The party manifesto was focused primarily on the attainment of national independence but it also placed a great deal of emphasis on social welfare measures.[84] It brought the organization more squarely into the realm of contemporarily politics than it had ever been. At the same time, the Hoa Hao also bucked Viet Minh efforts to co-opt its armed forces by creating a new military branch under the direction of General Tran Van Soai.

Responding to Nguyen Binh's violent methods, the Hoa Hao quickly became more anticommunist than anti-French. Suspecting the Hoa Hao of disloyalty, the Viet Minh issued orders to arrest the organization's spiritual leader, Huynh Phu So, put him on trial, and punish his accomplices. Nguyen Binh's forces abducted and arrested him in Long Xuyen on his way to a "conciliation meeting." Most likely they executed him on the spot before issuing a statement in his name exhorting his followers to unify with other Vietnamese in support of Ho Chi Minh.[85] The decision to execute Huynh Phu So was approved by the DRV's Executive Committee of the southern resistance on April 25 for "the crime of treason towards the Nation and for having fomented a civil war in the West at a time when all the energy of the people must be unified for the resistance."[86] Some historians suggest that the Viet Minh targeted Huynh Phu So when they learned about his intentions to travel to Hong Kong to join other noncommunist nationalists in a nascent effort to install former emperor Bao Dai at the head of an alternative Vietnamese government.[87]

Hoa Hao authorities attempted unconvincingly to conceal their leader's demise by claiming he had gone into hiding and would return at a later date.[88] Not all believers accepted the news of his death, but some who did retaliated with a spate of rampages against the Viet Minh, who responded in kind, leading to several thousand deaths on both sides.[89] Meanwhile, Nguyen Binh, who suspected Hoa Hao military leaders Tran Van Soai, Ba Cut, and Nguyen Giac Ngo of contacts with French intelligence agents, prepared to strike Hoa Hao strongholds. Huynh Phu So's assassination and the violence that ensued cemented Tran Van Soai's decision to sign a military convention with France on May 18, 1947. The French recognized for the first time the Hoa Hao's right to exist, granted the organization the authority to protect its followers with its own armed forces and conceded its right to representation in the national administration. This was in exchange for Hoa Hao observance of national law, respect for French and other national authorities, and hostility against the Viet Minh.

By May a full-fledged civil war had ignited between the Viet Minh military and police forces and both the Cao Dai and Hoa Hao.[90] The Viet Minh's military, security, and intelligence apparatus sought to repress "reactionaries" within these two organizations. The Binh Xuyen remained neutral, officially still aligned with the Viet Minh, but working behind the scenes to forge alliances with the other politico-religious organizations while also exploring relations with the French. Nguyen Binh was furious over what he perceived to be acts of treason on the part of Cao Dai and Hoa Hao leaders; so furious that he lost sight of the fact that his violent responses to politico-religious accommodations with the French only further alienated southern nationalists from the Viet Minh cause, thereby facilitating French efforts to court them.[91] His heavy-handed reactions to Hoa Hao and Cao Dai betrayals, and his preemptive dissolution or heavy surveillance of other nationalist parties that he feared would defect, only heightened the level of anger and violence that pervaded the south. Yet he and his Viet Minh cadres were not the only sources of violence, as all sides committed their share of atrocities in this civil war.

The Binh Xuyen managed to stay out of the fray during the bloody year 1947, but watched carefully as the Viet Minh came to rely more and more heavily on terror as a means of maintaining and expanding state control.[92] The French were eager to rally this last of the three major politico-religious organizations to their cause and stepped up incentives to lure Bay Vien and the Binh Xuyen into the fold. In 1948, mutual fear and distrust between the Binh Xuyen and the Viet Minh drove the former to begin negotiating a secret alliance with the French. Viet Minh officials, upon learning of the organization's double cross, reopened the civil war in the south. To clear the way for Nguyen Binh's forces to attack Binh Xuyen military units in the mangrove swamps of Rung Sat just outside of Saigon, the Viet Minh invited Bay Vien to their camp at the Plain of Reeds further west toward the Cambodian border on May 19. Although the invitation was ostensibly for a celebration of Ho Chi Minh's fifty-eighth birthday, it was really a setup. Nguyen Binh's men intended to assassinate Bay Vien, but he recognized the trap and showed up to the meeting with two hundred armed attendants. While he was there, though, the Viet Minh military quickly swept into the Rung Sat area to arrest Binh Xuyen agents and seize the territory under its control. From May 24 to May 31, Viet Minh forces arrested and purged a number of Binh Xuyen "reactionaries" and captured documents that proved the organization's collusion with the French. They drove the Binh Xuyen out of its base in the Rung Sat region, but the organization clung to strongholds in Saigon-Cholon. At the same time, the Viet Minh initiated a propaganda campaign to undermine the Binh Xuyen politically, especially in the eyes of the Avant-Garde Youth, by publicizing Bay Vien's secret collaboration with the French.

After this clash with the Viet Minh, French agents were able to convince Bay Vien, who had been reluctant to collaborate openly with them, that signing on with the French Army was his last chance to preserve the Binh Xuyen organization and bolster his own power. On June 16 the Binh Xuyen leader signed a prepared declaration denouncing the communists as traitors and avowing his loyalty to the dethroned Emperor Bao Dai.[93] By this time, the French were engaged in serious discussions with Bao Dai with an eye toward forming an independent Vietnamese state allied with France. This enabled the Binh Xuyen to align with the French without compromising its nationalist credentials entirely. According to the June agreement, the French conceded to the Binh Xuyen control of the police and security of Saigon-Cholon in exchange for which Binh Xuyen forces helped the French conduct a thorough sweep of the cities to root out and expel Viet Minh cadres, cells, and agents.[94]

Viet Minh efforts, led by Nguyen Binh, to terrorize Cao Dai, Hoa Hao, and Binh Xuyen forces into submission backfired and made more difficult their war against the French in the south. Attempts to co-opt the south's autonomous politico-religious organizations, each firmly rooted in the daily culture and grassroots politics of the territory under its control, backed them into a corner and forced them to unite with the French and at times with each other in order to preserve their autonomy.[95] The resistance Hoa Hao, Cao Dai, and Binh Xuyen forces posed to Viet Minh domination in the years following the August Revolution was a harbinger of what Ngo Dinh Diem would later face as he sought to establish total control over a highly heterogeneous southern population in which the politico-religious organizations were so firmly entrenched.

During the French War, the wild south arguably grew even wilder. Viet Minh efforts to subordinate southern Vietnam's heterodox forces under centralized rule led to a period of civil war that, although most fierce in 1947, would continue throughout the war as the Cao Dai, Hoa Hao, and Binh Xuyen's military conventions with the French pitted them against Viet Minh forces. Furthermore, alliances between the French and the politico-religious organizations ensured that these groups received substantial monetary subsidies and military equipment, which they used to expand the territory under their control, enhance their political power and autonomy, and enlarge their armed forces. This served to rigidify and militarize the boundaries between southern Vietnam's distinct communities. Where the region had once been difficult to govern, toward the end of the French War it may have become impossible to subdue without a fight, or at least without granting substantial political and financial concessions to the politico-religious organizations that were so dominant there.

Politico-religious leaders even found the autonomous zones under their authority difficult to govern. During the French war, Hoa Hao and Cao Dai military leadership factionalized as several generals vied to bring ever greater territories under their control. Factional battles within and between organizations led to frequent episodes of violence in and around Hoa Hao and Cao Dai strongholds. This cost the politico-religious groups some ground, as the Viet Minh were able to take advantage of their infighting to make inroads into the Mekong Delta for a brief time in 1953 and 1954. However, Viet Minh efforts to win over the Hoa Hao, and to a lesser extent the Cao Dai, in an effort to split them off from their alliance with the French would ultimately prove unsuccessful.[96] All three organizations remained hostile to the Viet Minh, leaving the communists with a weak foothold in the south. Thus, as the end of the First Indochina War drew near, politico-religious power was vast, but tenuous. Hoa Hao, Cao Dai, and Binh Xuyen influence was rooted in their tumultuous relationships with the French colonial administration, the benefits of which would end with a cease-fire. Just as France was looking for a way out of its war in Indochina, the United States deepened its involvement in Vietnam as a part of its Cold War program of preventing communist expansion—a commitment that expanded profoundly in 1950 with the outbreak of the Korean War and the adoption of NSC-68. Thus politico-religious leaders began to realize that their futures depended largely on their ability to establish domestic political legitimacy and to win American favor.

Chapter 2

The Crucible of Southern Vietnamese Nationalism and America's Cold War

On February 1, 1950, a U.S. State Department working group penned the following justification for providing American military aid to France for its war in Indochina:

> Unavoidably the United States is, together with France, committed in Indochina. That is, failure of the French Bao Dai "experiment" would mean the communization of Indochina. It is Bao Dai (or a similar anti-communist successor) or Ho Chi Minh (or a similar communist successor); there is no other alternative. The choice confronting the United States is to support the French in Indochina or face the extension of Communism over the remainder of the continental area of Southeast Asia and, possibly, farther westward.[1]

This logic represented a sharp departure from that which informed previous American policy. Until then, the Truman administration had resisted getting involved directly in France's military effort to reclaim its former colony. Not only did the war carry the taint of traditional colonialism, odious to most Americas, but Indochina seemed far removed from Washington's Cold War national security concerns. However, that would change abruptly following the victory of Mao Zedong and the Chinese Communist Party in 1949, and even more so after both China and the Soviet Union recognized Ho Chi Minh's Democratic Republic of Vietnam in January 1950. Secretary of State Dean Acheson claimed that the Soviet recognition of Vietnam's communist movement "should remove any illusions as to the 'nationalist' nature of Ho Chi Minh's aims and reveals Ho in his true colors as the mortal enemy of native independence in Indochina."[2] The United States therefore saw no choice but to commit its support to the new French-backed State of Vietnam headed by former emperor Bao Dai.

Ironically, Washington reached the conclusion that Indochina was critical to its larger Cold War strategy of containment just as France began to grow tired of its protracted war against the Viet Minh. The outbreak of war in Korea in June 1950 heightened American anxieties about the spread of communism in Asia and helped France persuade the Truman administration that its war against the Viet Minh was a crucial battle against Sino-Soviet expansion.[3] Over the next four years, as the war-weary French moved steadily toward the conclusion that the conflict was not worth its financial or political cost, Washington increased its economic support to France and pressured it to continue the fight against falling dominoes in Southeast Asia.

In keeping with its longstanding objection to colonial rule, the United States pressed the French to grant greater independence to the noncommunist nationalist government they had established in Saigon. Yet Washington's reasons for doing so had much more to do with Vietnam's perceived strategic significance within the Cold War international system, and fears that the United States might be losing ground to the Soviet Union in a competition for the allegiance of the rapidly decolonizing world, than with any concern over Vietnam's internal affairs. American diplomats knew little, and cared little, about the long history of cultural, political, and social heterodoxy that led to the fractious composition of southern society by the early 1950s. Americans thus failed to recognize the perils inherent in trying to silence southern Vietnam's disparate voices and impose centralized control at the expense of independent power groups like the Cao Dai, Hoa Hoa, and Binh Xuyen, as the Viet Minh had tried and failed to do in the aftermath of the August Revolution. The more deeply American diplomats waded into Vietnam's domestic political milieu, the more frustrated they became with the divisive nature of southern Vietnamese politics. Rather than search for ways to cooperate with or even appease politico-religious leaders and their noncommunist nationalist allies, U.S. officials dismissed them as venal, inept, immoral, and politically immature.

Meanwhile, the Vietnamese politicians that U.S. officials so readily and repeatedly discounted were well aware of the international dimension of their domestic conflict and made efforts to manipulate it to their advantage. In 1947 they participated in a coalition that appealed to French and American political sensibilities in hopes of advancing their plan to install former emperor Bao Dai at the head of a noncommunist Vietnamese nationalist government. By 1953, they recognized that French domestic politics, combined with recent changes to the international system, would soon compel Paris to end the war. Moreover, they came to realize that a Franco–Viet Minh cease-fire would likely usher in an era of direct American involvement in Vietnamese affairs. That spring, France's decision to devalue the Indochinese piaster sent a clear signal that the end of the war was drawing near, prompting a spree of noncommunist Vietnamese political activity. At first, southern Vietnam's politicians merely clamored for greater independence in an effort to distance themselves from French colonial ties, but as the movement continued they would begin to articulate platforms designed explicitly to appeal to the United States.

Vietnam and Truman's Cold War

At the end of the Second World War, France's determination to reclaim its Indochinese colony butted up against a fundamental opposition to traditional imperialism prevalent in the United States. President Franklin Roosevelt objected to the imperial system much more fervently than his successor, Harry Truman. Yet in the early years of the French war Truman would walk a fine line as he strove to avoid breaking completely with his predecessor's Indochina policy without alienating Paris and imperiling French support for Washington's postwar policies in Europe. Thus, while the Truman administration remained officially neutral and was often quite critical of French actions in the early years of the war, the emerging Cold War environment prevented Washington from taking a firm stand against French reconquest. Eventually, the logic of the Cold War would lead Washington to bankroll the French war effort and become even more determined than Paris to defeat the Viet Minh.

During World War II the United States threatened to block France's colonial ambitions in Southeast Asia. By the war's end Roosevelt had become an increasingly outspoken proponent of extending independence and self-determination to colonized peoples. He trained his attention especially on Indochina, where in 1941 French colonial administrators loyal to the Vichy regime had given in to Japanese pressure to halt the flow of supplies to nationalist China and allowed Japanese troops to establish a staging area for their invasion of Southeast Asia, a move that contributed directly to the Japanese decision to attack Pearl Harbor.[4] In 1944 Roosevelt specifically recommended barring the resumption of French colonial rule in Indochina, proposing instead an international trusteeship to oversee the colony's gradual move toward independence. Americans largely supported this objective, as it not only conformed to their long held anticolonial ideology but promised to open up trading opportunities around the globe in places that had once been restricted by imperial preferences.

At Yalta, Roosevelt indicated some flexibility in France's favor by agreeing that trusteeships would be established only with consent from the imperial powers involved. American diplomats were torn over whether or not to subordinate their goal of establishing a new world order based on self-determination to the more urgent imperative of supporting European allies in order to foster postwar solidarity in matters of defense and economic recovery. Roosevelt's death and the inauguration of Harry Truman on April 12, 1945, settled the argument in favor of those who sought to allow French recolonization of Indochina for the purpose of promoting good relations with Paris.[5] The United States officially declared itself neutral—it would not aid France's recolonization of Indochina, nor would it pose any obstruction.

In the short term, this came as a relief to French officials. It enabled them to begin efforts to reassert imperial control almost immediately after the August Revolution.[6] However, they recognized that in the long term they would need explicit support and access to resources from the United States if they were to have any hope of successfully restoring French authority over Indochina.[7] In collaboration with Britain, which had its own imperial interests at heart, France worked during the early years of its war with the Viet Minh to convince Washington to provide it with direct material and economic aid. At first, Paris relied on the Truman administration's reluctance to alienate France, which stemmed from its need to secure French support for emerging Cold War defense policies in Europe.[8] This was enough to prevent Washington from obstructing the French war effort, but the Franco-American relationship over Indochina was strained throughout the late 1940s, as American officials consistently pressured the French to move in the direction of liberalizing their rule and granting independence to the people of Indochina.

The so-called "Bao Dai solution" that would begin to address Washington's concerns about the deleterious effects of colonialism and help France win American support for its ongoing war was largely a product of Vietnamese nationalist politics. In mid-1947 a group of Vietnamese nationalists helped devise a plan that they hoped would secure independence, or at the very least a greater degree of autonomy for Vietnam under noncommunist leadership. Hoa Hao and Cao Dai figures joined a broad-based coalition of Vietnam's noncommunist nationalist organizations, including the VNQDD and the Dai Viet ("Greater Vietnam") Party, to call for the former emperor Bao Dai to return to Vietnam and preside over a nationalist government within the French Union.[9] Many representatives of these nationalist parties, especially the Dai Viet, were working in exile following a wave of Viet Minh campaigns against them launched in summer 1946, after the withdrawal of Chinese troops that had been stationed in the north to oversee Japan's surrender. In support of their efforts to regain some political traction in Vietnam via Bao Dai, they formed a short-lived Third Force coalition, the National Union Front (Mat Tran Thong Nhut Quoc Gia).[10] Ngo Dinh Diem, at the time a fairly minor player in Vietnamese politics, participated in this movement in hopes that it might eventually lead to Vietnam's independence from both French colonial rule and Viet Minh domination.[11]

French leaders, who were struggling not only to gain American financial backing but also to shore up domestic political support for an increasingly unpopular war, jumped on the idea of a Bao Dai solution.[12] Paris hoped to manipulate Vietnamese politics in a manner that would satisfy nationalist demands by conforming to international trends of liberalization and decolonization while preserving the basis of French domination of Indochina. Furthermore, French leaders sought to justify their refusal to negotiate with Ho Chi Minh's government by pointing to Bao Dai as the country's true national leader.[13] France also hoped that the Bao Dai solution might shift domestic and international perceptions of the war as a colonial war, casting it instead as a Cold War struggle against the communist Viet Minh waged in conjunction with a nationalist Vietnamese government that was at least moving in the direction of independence.[14]

One major obstacle to this plan's success was Bao Dai's reputation as a playboy and a political flip-flopper.[15] Born in 1913, he became the immediate heir to the Nguyen dynasty. His illustrious ancestor, the Gia Long Emperor, had unified the modern territory of Vietnam for the first time in 1802, not long before the country endured the first convulsions of French colonization. Bao Dai was born under the colonial system and grew up in

France under the patronage of former colonial officials, a fact that was all-too-evident due to his preference for French culture, French food, and even French women over their Vietnamese counterparts. He was an excellent student and had ideas about how to help Vietnam navigate its path to independence. But circumstances combined with his passive personality to limit his opportunities to implement them. By the time he returned to the capital city of Hue to assume the throne in 1932, the monarchy had been stripped of all but symbolic authority, and he did little to restore gravity to the throne.[16]

For much of his career, it seemed that Bao Dai was most important as a figurehead, and one whose image a wide range of Vietnamese politicians would seek to appropriate in hopes of legitimizing their movements with reference to Vietnamese culture and tradition. In 1932–33, a group of Vietnamese nationalists, including a young Ngo Dinh Diem, started a campaign "to project the young Emperor Bao Dai as a moral exemplar, a model of East-West harmony, a Vietnamese appropriately 'dyed with the new but never forgetting the old.'"[17] Years later, following Bao Dai's abdication, Ho Chi Minh and the Viet Minh would appoint him first as Supreme Commander of the DRV and then head of the National Committee of Advisors.

In the latter case, Bao Dai quickly grew frustrated with the DRV and dissatisfied with his life in Hanoi. In the summer of 1946 he fled to China and then settled in Hong Kong. He chose not to return to Hanoi, but again was sought out by an array of noncommunist Vietnamese nationalists led by the Dai Viet who hoped to recruit him back to head an alternative government. The Dai Viet was an anticolonial, anticommunist party that grew out of the tradition of bourgeois reform movements such as the Constitutionalist Party that was active in 1920s southern Vietnam. The constitutionalists, a group of southern elites who aimed to work within the French system to secure greater rights for their own class, sought the gradual evolution of self-government along the model of British India. As a group, they were stamped out by the French in the repressions of the early 1930s, but a series of moderate, noncommunist Dai Viet parties emerged primarily in and around Hanoi to take their place as secular noncommunist nationalists during the popular front era later that decade. Dai Viet leaders attempted to collaborate with the Japanese during World War II but received little support from them until after the March coup. Even then they made little headway in their efforts to be included in the Vietnamese government that emerged briefly prior to the August Revolution.

The fiercely anticommunist Dai Viet would continue fighting against the Viet Minh in the north after Ho Chi Minh's declaration of independence, and in 1947 it reconstituted in Nanking and Hong Kong to organize support for Bao Dai. Much like the Cao Dai, Hoa Hao, and Binh Xuyen, the Dai Viet saw little choice but to compromise its anticolonial principles to work with the French, who remained unwilling to grant full independence.[18] Thus many Dai Viet politicians, including Dr. Phan Huy Quat and northern governor Nguyen Huu Tri, would soon come to play important roles in southern Vietnamese politics under Bao Dai's government and into the period of national division that would commence in 1954.

While Bao Dai was engaged in discussions with the Dai Viet and their noncommunist nationalist allies, French secret agents caught up with him and felt out his willingness to participate in their own nascent plans to utilize his royal claim as a political weapon in their fight against the Viet Minh. French leaders knew that for the Bao Dai solution to have its intended effect on domestic Vietnamese politics and international opinion, the former emperor needed support from the full range of southern Vietnam's noncommunist nationalists. They were able to secure support from many Dai Viet figures, and in January 1948 representatives of the Cao Dai and Hoa Hao signed a petition requesting that Bao Dai take the lead in bringing about national independence and unification.[19] These endorsements paved the way for French negotiators to strike a deal with Bao Dai, who was assured that his government would find basic acceptance on the ground.

Unsurprisingly, France's vision for Bao Dai's government differed substantially from that of the nationalists who initially conceived of the idea. In February 1948, nationalist leaders met in Saigon to establish a framework for negotiating with the French over the terms of Vietnamese independence. They were reluctant to grant Bao Dai the authority to reach agreements with France without first securing approval from a national assembly. Future South Vietnamese president Ngo Dinh Diem was among those who feared that Bao Dai would be too willing to negotiate on French terms. His apprehension turned out to be well founded, as Bao Dai announced in March that he intended to move forward on Paris's terms and proceeded to negotiate an agreement that granted the new Vietnamese state little true independence.[20]

Bao Dai and the French initialed an agreement on June 5, 1948, according to which Émile Bollaert, French High Commissioner for Vietnam, "solemnly recognized the independence of Vietnam, which was free to realize its complete unity."[21] But the pledge was little more than lip service. In March 1949 Bao Dai met with French president Vincent Auriol at the Élysée to hash out a final agreement. The Élysée accords of March 8 promised eventual independence to Vietnam, Laos, and Cambodia within the French Union and put Bao Dai in charge of the newly established State of Vietnam (SVN). In spite of the former emperor's overly simplified reputation in many nationalist circles as a French lackey and a self-indulgent playboy, those who brokered the agreement at Élysée hoped that his royal blood, and the strength of Vietnam's dynastic tradition, would confer on him a degree of legitimacy.

The Élysée accords were highly imperfect from the perspective of Vietnam's noncommunist nationalists. France handed over very little real power to Bao Dai's government, retaining control over areas of Vietnam populated by ethnic minorities, as well as the agencies concerned with foreign trade, customs, finance, immigration, and security. Yet the politico-religious organizations stuck to their pledge to support his government, and the Dai Viet Party and a wide range of other nationalists decided to back Bao Dai and the new SVN in hopes that the new state might serve as a vehicle for gradually gaining independence. Ngo Dinh Diem, at the time little more than a bit player in Vietnamese nationalist political circles, was furious with the way Bao Dai caved to French demands. He was outraged by what he perceived to be Bao Dai's willingness to pursue personal advancement at the expense of Vietnam's national good, and by the former emperor's apparent subservience to French colonialists. On June 16, 1949, he issued a public statement condemning the former emperor and rejecting the Élysée accords.[22] Ngo Dinh Diem's voice at the time was not sufficiently powerful to interrupt the events in motion, but his disillusionment with Bao Dai would play a huge role in his political decisions as prime minister a few years later.

The United States was at first reluctant to recognize the new State of Vietnam, largely on the grounds that Bao Dai and his cabinet were "naïve and incapable of governance."[23] And as Washington grew more concerned about the promise that Soviet communism held for many in the decolonizing world, and the damage that the continuation of colonial rule might do to its goal of containing communism in the Third World, it objected to the lack of real independence that the Bao Dai solution granted to the Vietnamese. Yet as Vietnam became more important in the Cold War, Truman's administration promptly tabled those concerns. The twin shocks of 1949—the "loss" of China to communism and the first Soviet detonation of an atomic bomb—heightened American anxieties about Soviet aggression, turned Washington's focus to Asia as an emerging Cold War hot spot, and ushered in a major shift in the U.S. position on France's war against the Viet Minh. After Mao Zedong's People's Republic of China (PRC) extended recognition to Ho Chi Minh's government on January 18, followed shortly thereafter by the Soviets on January 30, Washington responded by formally recognizing Bao Dai's government on February 7. This was the first in a series of steps that would bind the United States to both the French war effort and the SVN.[24]

The year 1950 marked a key turning point in the Cold War and signaled a sea change in Franco-American relations over Indochina. Heightened fears of Soviet and Chinese aggression in Europe and Asia prompted the Truman administration to authorize Paul Nitze and the Policy Planning Staff to conduct a comprehensive national security assessment aimed at identifying national interests, potential threats, and feasible responses to those threats in light of the intensifying and expanding Cold War. The resulting document, NSC-68, militarized Washington's containment strategy and expanded the purview of containment from key strategic areas to the entire globe, with a particular focus on Asia.[25]

The outbreak of the Korean War fueled this shift in America's approach to the Cold War. It prompted the Truman administration to increase dramatically its contributions to the French war effort in Indochina. It also impelled the State Department to look for ways to enhance West European security while freeing up sufficient manpower and resources to fight communism in Korea and wherever else it might rear its head. Washington began to pressure West Germany to rearm and contribute more to the defense of Western Europe and asked other NATO allies to bolster their contributions as well. This not only revived French anxieties about German militarism but also taxed France's economy just as it began to recover. France lacked the resources to continue the fight against the Viet Minh while meeting U.S. expectations that it build up its forces on the continent. The challenge of getting France to do both led to a growing entanglement between Washington's policies regarding Indochina and West European security.

In light of its recent history, France was loath to see men in German Army uniforms marching around Europe. In response to Washington's demands for West Germany to rearm and join NATO allies in providing for the defense of Western Europe, French officials came up with the Pleven Plan, which would become the European Defense Community (EDC). Paris proposed a supranational European Army as a means of securing West Germany's contribution to continental defense without creating a German national army.[26] But in short order the French would come to fear that the EDC might shift the balance of power in the Western alliance away from France and toward West Germany, especially as long as French troops and resources remained mired in Southeast Asia. Thus, once the United States bought into the EDC and embraced it as the key to its strategy for West European security, it would become an important bargaining chip for the French, who dangled promises of its ratification to secure additional American aid for Indochina.

By the end of 1950, even a significant increase in American aid for the war in Indochina was not enough to alleviate the strain to the French economy created by the dual imperatives of building up forces in Europe while continuing the fight against the Viet Minh. Just as its economy was recovering from the blight of World War II, France initiated a huge rearmament program that the nation could hardly afford. Between 1950 and 1952 France almost tripled its military expenditures.[27] The French military budget grew steadily to take up an ever increasing percentage of the nation's gross national product while public investment in the civil sector declined.[28] France was badly overstretched, and its leaders were forced to reevaluate whether possessing Indochina helped or hurt their chances of claiming equal status with Britain and the United States in the Western alliance.[29]

After 1950, as America's determination to keep Indochina out of communist hands hardened and France's commitment to retaining its empire in Southeast Asia dwindled, both sides looked for ways to exert leverage over each other.[30] A devastating military defeat at Cao Bang in 1950 signaled to the French that they had entered a new phase of the war in which they would face a better-organized, more vigorous Viet Minh enemy. That combined with the mounting cost of the war prompted National Assembly member and future prime minister Pierre Mendès-France to conclude that his country must choose between Europe and Indochina. Thereafter, French public opinion grew steadily opposed to the war, as did a number of leading French political figures. However, many of those who wanted out of Indochina hoped to exit in a manner that would avoid setting a precedent that could undermine French rule in North Africa.[31] French leaders aimed to accomplish this by building up a Vietnamese national army to take over more and more of the fighting while convincing the United States to finance an ever greater percentage of the war's cost. And in exchange for bearing the financial brunt of the war, Washington expected France to enhance the independence of the Associated States of Vietnam, Laos, and Cambodia and to go along with its plans for the EDC in Western Europe.

In July 1951 Truman's secretary of state Dean Acheson secured the National Security Council's support for the EDC as a means of pursuing West Germany's political and military evolution while reassuring France of its security and continued position of prominence within the Western alliance. In February 1952 NATO finally endorsed the concept, and three months later the EDC was signed in Paris by France, West Germany, and the Benelux countries.[32] Getting France to ratify the treaty would be a much more difficult challenge. It became increasingly evident to French leaders that their troops would need to return from Indochina to Europe before the country would be comfortable enough with the prospect of German rearmament even to consider ratification. By late 1952 and into 1953, then, French leaders privately acknowledged the necessity of withdrawal from Indochina. But they sought to exploit American aid to minimize the political cost of their retreat. The indecision surrounding the EDC would prove just the tool they needed to bring the United States along.[33]

In January 1953, Prime Minister George Bidault pledged that he intended to press through growing domestic political opposition to the EDC to get the treaty ratified. One of his key motivations for doing so was the war in Indochina, which was by then eating up one-third of the French defense budget and was expected to take up even more of the pie over the coming year. American aid represented France's only hope to continue the fight and secure an acceptable peace. This, in turn, enabled Washington to exert its own form of leverage on the French by insisting that its assistance was contingent on good faith efforts to secure ratification of the EDC.[34] But the EDC soon took another hit with Joseph Stalin's death in March 1953, making it even more difficult to sell to the French public.

Following Stalin's death, Soviet premier Georgi Malenkov initiated a "peace offensive" aimed at relaxing East-West tensions. Many in France were optimistic that this change in Soviet leadership, and the Kremlin's softer diplomatic tack, could result in a real easing of Cold War tensions and present new avenues for ending the war in Indochina and guaranteeing West European security without resort to the EDC. The new Eisenhower administration, on the other hand, remained deeply distrustful of the Kremlin and feared that its new, more flexible diplomatic approach might enable it to undermine Western security while making inroads into the Third World. The United States faced a great challenge in convincing France that the Cold War necessitated both the EDC and the continuation of war in Indochina. After much discussion, the Eisenhower administration agreed to attend a four-power conference in Berlin, including Britain, France, the Soviet Union, and the United States, to discuss the prospect of German reunification. Eisenhower and Dulles were hoping that the conference would expose the Malenkov peace offensive as a charade, thus paving the way for France to ratify the EDC as the best prospect for Western security.[35]

In the meantime, French leaders had determined by May 1953 that Indochina had become a marginal asset, and that they had to look for a way out of the war sooner rather than later if they hoped to preserve their fragile position within the Western alliance and cling to their empire in North Africa.[36] In early May the United States and France agreed on a new aggressive military strategy known as the Navarre Plan, to be led by General Henri Navarre. Along with a more forceful approach to fighting the Viet Minh, the plan included a major strengthening of the Vietnamese national army under General Nguyen Van Hinh. Washington welcomed this as a response to Eisenhower's increasing pressure over March and April for Paris to improve on the weak enforcement of the Élysée accords as a means of expediting the transfer of French military responsibilities to local troops. The United States, hoping that the Navarre Plan posed an opportunity to defeat the Viet Minh, stepped up its level of aid to cover fully one-half of the war's cost by the middle of the year.[37] Regardless of what the French told their American allies at this point, though, they had all but given up hope of defeating the Viet Minh and decided to draw the war to a close, and soon. Indeed, when Prime Minister Rene Mayer approved the Navarre Plan on May 7, he told Henri Navarre that its object was to facilitate France's "graceful exit" from Indochina.[38]

Political Crisis and Nationalist Awakening

Another of France's moves in May 1953 signaled to southern Vietnamese nationalists, who had been keeping a close eye on the deteriorating French war effort and taking note of Washington's growing interest in Vietnam, that the French retreat that they had long anticipated was now imminent. At the end of April and beginning of May 1953, exposés in *Le Monde* and *L'Observateur* revealed that certain French politicians were taking advantage of the artificially overvalued Indochinese piaster to engage in illegal currency exchanges. On May 8, just one day after the revelations in *L'Observateur*, French premier René Mayer moved to end the scandal and reduce the financial burden of France's military campaign in Indochina by devaluing the Indochinese piaster from seventeen francs to ten, provoking what one historian has called a "financial Dien Bien Phu."[39]

The devaluation stirred up political rivalries between southern Vietnam's most prominent noncommunist nationalists as they struggled to position themselves to claim power in the impending postwar government. In keeping with the Cao Dai's longstanding ambition to seize political leadership of Vietnam, Pope Pham Cong Tac headed major initiatives supported by southern Vietnam's three powerful politico-religious organizations, the Cao Dai, Hoa Hoa, and Binh Xuyen. Since he returned from exile in 1946, he had been working to establish the Cao Dai as a national political force and expected it to play a substantial role in Vietnam's government in the postcolonial era.[40] One of the greatest challenges to Pham Cong Tac's primacy among southern nationalists came from Ngo Dinh Nhu, one of future prime minister Ngo Dinh Diem's brothers. Ngo Dinh Nhu, a bookish intellectual, had only recently begun to establish a public profile in Vietnamese political circles. Always more comfortable working behind the scenes, he founded a small discussion group focused on labor organizing in 1948, and became more active politically only after Ngo Dinh Diem fled the country in fear of Viet Minh reprisals in 1950. He then entered a phase of more vigorous political engagement and by 1953 was openly involved in a quest to pave the way for his brother to take power in postwar southern Vietnam.

France's decision to devalue the piaster, which set off the competition between Pham Cong Tac, Ngo Dinh Nhu, and a range of other southern nationalists, was long overdue. The currency had been overvalued for some time, as the French established its exchange rate in 1945 after regaining control of Indochina and had not revised it since. Pioneering French and Indochinese businessmen and administrators, including the Viet Minh, took advantage of the imbalance between its official value of seventeen francs and the more realistic value of seven or eight francs assigned to it by international monetary markets. Trafficking in piasters had long been accepted as the status quo, but as the war turned sour, critics in Paris began to accuse elements within the French Army and the Indochinese colonial administration of prolonging the conflict intentionally to capitalize on its profitability.[41] Such rumors had increased dramatically following the Viet Minh invasion of Laos in April 1953, which had further highlighted France's military weakness.[42]

Diplomatic pressure from the United States compounded France's domestic pleas to reevaluate the piaster.[43] A crisis had been approaching for months as the United States assumed more and more of the mounting costs of France's war against the Viet Minh, and became less and less willing to countenance the exorbitant financial burden resulting from what U.S. ambassador to Saigon Donald Heath called the "unrealistic exchange rate of the piaster agreed to by the French some years ago."[44] United States officials recognized what French leaders knew all too well: that devaluing the piaster, and cutting Vietnamese purchasing power in half, would worsen Vietnam's "not too happy relations with France."[45] Nonetheless they insisted that such action would be necessary if Paris and Washington wished to carry on the fight against communism in Indochina.

True to French and American predictions, France's move to devalue Indochina's currency had lasting political ramifications within Vietnam. Perhaps most damaging was Mayer's failure to consult with local leaders before effecting the change, on the grounds that it could prompt a spree of speculation. His secrecy created a good deal of economic upheaval and undermined the fragile marriage of convenience that existed between France and the Associated States.[46] Though the Élysée accords of 1949 guaranteed France the right to adjust the value of the piaster at any time, Indochinese government officials, nationalists, and businessmen regarded the May devaluation as a flagrant violation of agreements between France and the Associated States. It struck a serious blow to noncommunist nationalists' already dwindling confidence in the French and prompted many to embark upon bolder political programs in preparation for the end of the French war.

As U.S. consul to Saigon Robert McClintock noted at the time, "Certain nationalists take [the] view that devaluation [is] not unfortunate since it [is] indicative of [the] inherent weakness of France and favors greater Vietnamese direction of [their] own affairs."[47] Indeed, this perceived French betrayal motivated and galvanized a broad swath of noncommunist nationalists and spurred them to demand total independence rather than the broken promises and half-measures that France had delivered since concluding the Élysée accords. One historian has claimed that the decision to devalue "was economically justifiable but politically inept, exposing, as it did, the artificiality of the independence of the Associated States."[48]

Among other things, the currency crisis highlighted widespread dissatisfaction with SVN prime minister Nguyen Van Tam among his Vietnamese constituents. Nguyen Van Tam, himself a Cao Dai follower and French citizen known as "the tiger of Cai Lay" for his role in the French repression of Vietnamese revolutionaries in 1940, replaced Tran Van Huu in 1952.[49] Due to Nguyen Van Tam's history of collaboration with the French, Paris expected him to be more malleable politically than his predecessor. On the surface, he struggled during his tenure as prime minister to shake his reputation as a French nationalist and strove to represent a balance of Vietnamese and French interests. He was able to convince many in the United States of his sincerity. General O'Daniel once observed, "Tam is a naturalized

French citizen, but he seems to be a sincere Vietnamese Nationalist."[50] The prime minister, however, never succeeded in winning the trust of his countrymen, and the events of spring 1953 only further diminished his popular support within Vietnam.[51] A growing recognition among politico-religious leaders that France would not be present much longer to provide them with subsidies and protection compelled them to oppose Nguyen Van Tam's French-sponsored regime overtly. In the coming months they would band together with other noncommunist nationalists to demand an end to French colonialism and total independence for the Associated States.

It was the Cao Dai pope Pham Cong Tac who initially asserted himself as the leader of this movement.[52] Immediately after the French government announced its decision to devalue the Indochinese currency, his Cao Dai–led Association for National Restoration (Viet Nam Phuc Quoc Hoi) held an emergency meeting of Saigon political leaders who concluded that it had become more necessary than ever to denounce the Élysée accords of 1949.[53] Even those who saw fit to cooperate with the French during the war had steadily demanded increased sovereignty in the years since the treaty was promulgated. In the wake of devaluation, noncommunist Vietnamese leaders across the board concluded that they must make a break from France in order to pave the way for political influence in postarmistice Vietnam. Given Washington's persistent advocacy of greater independence for the Associated States and its clear commitment to anticommunism, southern nationalists hoped they might find an ally in the United States.

On July 3, 1953, in response to increasing unrest among nationalists around Saigon, diplomatic pressure from Washington, and political crisis at home, France's new prime minister Joseph Laniel announced that France was willing to "perfect" the independence of France's Indochina colonies by transferring control over finance, justice, political, and military affairs to local administrators.[54] Under the circumstances, Laniel's announcement came as little surprise. Moreover, given France's record of promising independence and not delivering, many outside observers viewed the vague pledge with skepticism. Reggie Burrows, the British diplomat in charge of Indochina affairs in the Foreign Office, commented that Laniel's announcement "amounts to little more than a declaration that France will now, in 1953, implement the 1949 agreements."[55] Others, however, attached to it much greater significance, going so far as to claim that it "amounted to the death of the French Union."[56]

Laniel's pledge to perfect the independence of the Associated States presented Vietnamese leaders with the choice of remaining in or withdrawing from the French Union. French and American officials downplayed this provision, claiming that the State of Vietnam's reliance on France for support against the communists would obviate the possibility of withdrawal.[57] Almost immediately thereafter, though, Bao Dai and Nguyen Van Tam announced that they would soon take a delegation to Paris to open negotiations with France on the future of Vietnamese independence. Their government seemed amenable to continued cooperation with France, but Nguyen Van Tam insisted that in order for Vietnam to remain a part of the French Union, France would have to improve significantly on the frail and inadequate independence granted by the Élysée agreement of 1949 and the Pau agreement of 1950 that guaranteed Vietnam a voice in economic decisions.[58]

Bao Dai and Nguyen Van Tam made this move largely in response to pressure from southern Vietnam's increasingly vocal nationalists. However, American policymakers who remained unfamiliar with Vietnam's indigenous noncommunist movements failed to perceive the imperative and responded with bemusement. Ambassador Heath betrayed America's ignorance of the country's domestic political affairs, describing himself as "rather quizzical when [Bao Dai] mentioned Vietnamese 'political parties.'" The chief of state gently informed Heath that while these parties were "small and not really organized, they nevertheless had an influence on Vietnamese public opinion."[59] Among the most powerful groups of which he spoke were the Hoa Hao, Cao Dai, and Binh Xuyen organizations, and their affiliated political parties.[60] Washington's weak understanding of these organizations and their positions in southern Vietnamese politics and society would limit its ability to make sense of the events that ensued.

In September 1953, Pham Cong Tac led a revolt against the official Vietnamese delegation currently negotiating with France. After Nguyen Van Tam departed for Cannes to consult with Bao Dai, the Cao Dai pope joined together with Ngo Dinh Nhu to organize an unofficial Congress for National Union and Peace to be held in Cholon on September 6. Bao Dai, who wanted nongovernmental representatives to participate in his delegation, encouraged Pham Cong Tac and Ngo Dinh Nhu, perhaps as a means of undermining the increasingly unpopular Nguyen Van Tam and solidifying his connection with southern Vietnam's powerful nationalist groups. On September 4, the Cao Dai pope held a press conference announcing the congress and proclaiming, "The hour has come to realize the great union of all parties and nationalist elements in view of achieving the independence of our country."[61]

Under Pham Cong Tac and Ngo Dinh Nhu's direction, representatives from the politico-religious organizations, or "the big three organizations of South Vietnam," as French security agents referred to them, met with several other nationalist leaders at Binh Xuyen commander Bay Vien's headquarters to discuss plans for independence and future leadership. The Hoa Hao Social Democratic Party disseminated tracts explaining its motivations for participating in terms of patriotism, national unification, and resistance to outside invasion.[62] Nguyen Van Tam immediately cut his trip short and returned to Saigon in hopes of controlling the congress, which overtly opposed both him and the French.[63] According to Heath, the prime minister "thought the idea of a Congress was a bad one but, since [the] idea had been launched, he was confident he could organize and manage it so it did not go off the rails."[64]

Nguyen Van Tam's prediction that he could manage the national congress proved false. On October 16 it unexpectedly passed a unanimous resolution refusing to join the French Union.[65] Fed up with half-measures and illusions of self-determination, representatives of the "big five" noncommunist political groups, including the three politico-religious groups, the Dai Viet, and the northern Catholics demanded to be released from the French Union under several specific conditions. They requested unconditional independence, freedom of the press, an end to corruption, army and administrative reforms, and the immediate summoning of a national assembly.[66]

Only Nguyen Van Tam and Bao Dai possessed the real authority to withdraw from the union, and they had no intention of doing so. The chief of state claimed to be furious with the national congress resolution, criticizing it as "unwise, ill timed and contrary to Vietnam's interests which demand membership [in the] French Union."[67] He insisted that the resolution undercut his own negotiating position in France, diminished his authority within Vietnam, and undermined French support for noncommunist Vietnam. Bao Dai therefore threatened to take corrective steps including, if necessary, dissolving the congress.[68] He also removed Nguyen Van Tam from any connection or authority over the congress, presumably as a means of dissociating the State of Vietnam from its resolutions.[69] Ultimately, Bao Dai managed to extract from the group a fairly empty resolution placing confidence in his leadership and thanking the French Republic and the United States "for aid given [to] Vietnam in order to consolidate its national independence."[70] Yet the damage to Franco-Vietnamese diplomacy was already done.

Laniel and his political allies in Paris were concerned primarily about the effect that Vietnam's national congress announcement would have on the French National Assembly debates of that month. Vietnam's apparent unwillingness to remain within the French Union caused public support for the war to dwindle even further and fueled the October legislative conflict over France's future in Indochina. Bitter debate ensued between parties on the right and left over whether to withdraw French troops entirely or, alternatively, to launch an all-out assault on the Viet Minh. The assembly failed to reach a consensus, and France would continue down its gradual path to disengagement.

Meanwhile, the United States grew frustrated with the very Vietnamese nationalists that it expected to take over the war effort from France. Recent studies have demonstrated that Americans in the mid-twentieth century often approached Asians with a set of racially based preconceptions that prompted them to expect little in the way of competence or rationality.[71] Indeed, American officials responded to Vietnam's noncommunist nationalists as though they were irrational, childlike figures. Their frustrations were fueled by a general ignorance of Vietnamese history, culture, and politics. In contrast to France's impressions of Vietnamese affairs, tainted by its colonial lens but informed by years of intimate contact, the United States had almost no knowledge of Vietnamese political life. American policymakers lacked more than the most basic understanding of the historically fractious "wild" south into which they waded. The United States, focused on the international rather than local ramifications of Vietnam's political future, displayed a stubborn determination to simplify Vietnam's complicated political situation in hopes that it might be made to conform to Washington's strategy of containment.

Ambassador Heath, furious with Vietnamese politicians for taking a move that could jeopardize France's military and political programs for fighting the Viet Minh, lashed out at them in his missives to the State Department. "It was apparent," he claimed, "that [the] majority of delegates had honestly no idea of [the] import of [the] language in [the] resolution they had just passed." He claimed it was probable that the congress had been "cleverly sabotaged by pro-Viet Minh stooges in its midst," though he later backtracked to the position that, while the Viet Minh would have infiltrated if they could, this "motion appears rather the product of emotional, irresponsible nationalism."[72] Heath essentially concluded that responsible nationalists, in this case, should follow French and American directives unquestioningly in exchange for protection. To Dulles he wrote, "It is a matter of extraordinary difficulty to convey [the] degree of naiveté and childlike belief that no matter what defamatory language they use, the Vietnamese will still be safeguarded from [the] lethal Communist enemy by France and [the] US."[73] In subsequent telegrams the ambassador would refer to Vietnamese "leaders," "nationalists," and "intelligentsia," in scare quotes meant to convey that Vietnam had no such thing, or at the very least that the congress participants did not qualify as such.

Heath would later note the apparent contradiction between Hoa Hao, Cao Dai, and Binh Xuyen demands for independence from France and their dependence on French support payments for their armies.[74] In his view, this only supported the conclusion that Vietnamese nationalists were too ignorant to realize the consequences of their actions. Actually, though, politico-religious leaders did perceive the likelihood of a precipitous French withdrawal from the war effort and aimed to establish themselves as the successive leaders of the noncommunist Vietnam that they hoped would result from Franco–Viet Minh negotiations. Their current livelihoods depended on French support, but their futures rested on the ability to establish clear anticolonial and anticommunist credentials.

Officials within the State Department failed to recognize any such rational motivations on the part of Hoa Hao, Cao Dai, and Binh Xuyen leaders. John Foster Dulles and his subordinates echoed Heath's attitude toward southern Vietnam's key political actors. American diplomats would reluctantly follow the French lead and refer to Pham Cong Tac, Tran Van Soai, and others as "nationalists" throughout 1953, but would cease to apply this term altogether after Ngo Dinh Diem came to power in July 1954. At that point politico-religious leaders would become "warlords," "plotters," "confessional groups" or even "the Junta" in Washington's lexicon.

While politico-religious leaders struggled to win over the Americans, Pham Cong Tac persisted in his efforts to seize the political initiative in southern Vietnam. Cao Dai–led agitation crippled Nguyen Van Tam's government and forced Bao Dai to replace him in January 1954. The Movement for National Union, however, did not welcome Nguyen Van Tam's successor Buu Loc as an improvement. In fact, Cao Dai general Nguyen Thanh Phuong refused to participate in Buu Loc's inaugural ceremony and forbade other members of the movement from doing so. He claimed that the new prime minister's cabinet was composed almost exclusively of figures who had never involved themselves in Vietnam's struggle for independence, and that his administration provided no guarantee of political representation to the bloc of anticommunist nationalists when unity was most needed.[75] Spokesmen for the Cao Dai armed forces criticized Buu Loc for his failure to recognize the sacrifices of noncommunist nationalist combatants and his obliviousness to public opinion.[76] The Cao Dai journal *Tien*, in its special Tet holiday edition, claimed that Buu Loc was an affable enough fellow, but incapable of leading a government of national union. The organization predicted that he would not last longer than three or four months in office.[77]

The Cao Dai organization thus stepped up its propaganda efforts in hopes that Pham Cong Tac might fill the void Buu Loc's failed government could create. Cao Dai publications reflected heightened efforts by the organization's leaders to represent it as a progressive movement at the vanguard of Vietnamese anticolonialism and anticommunism. It published articles hailing Egypt's 1952 revolution to depose the monarchy and establish a republican government as a model that Vietnam should emulate. This reflected not only the Cao Dai's dissatisfaction with Bao Dai and his prime ministers' refusal to give full support to the national union movement, but also cast the organization as a forward looking prodemocracy movement rather than a mere band of feudal warlords, as detractors charged. To highlight its anticommunist credentials, the Cao Dai organized and publicized a grand celebration to commemorate the anniversary of its entry into the war against the Viet Minh.[78]

Nguyen Thanh Phuong spoke at the celebration for the seventh anniversary of the Cao Dai's anticommunist struggle on February 7, 1954, during which he described Cao Dai followers as authentic nationalists and the Viet Minh as imposters. He praised Cao Dai adepts for their great sacrifices and for performing all of their civic duties. On the other hand, he denounced the Viet Minh for its "obedience to the orders of a foreign power that aims to enslave the world, betraying our national sprit, our aspirations for independence, and our ardent desire for liberty."[79] He took pains to explain that the Cao Dai's wartime collaboration with France was a necessity brought on by Viet Minh threats to citizens' security and indeed to national survival. This arrangement, he claimed, contrasted sharply with the Viet Minh's willingness to do the bidding of Soviet and Chinese communists. Moreover, Nguyen Thanh Phuong sought to distance the Cao Dai from colonial ties by imploring the French government and its people to recognize that the moment for Vietnamese independence had arrived. He asked France to place its confidence in Vietnam's "true nationalists" to liberate the country from communism while preserving the Franco-Vietnamese friendship.

By early 1954, politico-religious leaders were making concerted efforts to align their political appeals with what they understood to be Washington's Cold War objectives in Vietnam, namely an end to colonial rule and the establishment of a stable anticommunist government in the south. The French war was winding down, and it had become clear that the ability of any southern nationalist to assert leadership in a postwar government would depend on American sanction. Hoa Hao, Cao Dai, and Binh Xuyen figures thus sharpened their critiques of French colonialism and made efforts to distance themselves from the French Army on which they had come to depend for subsidies and preferential treatment. They focused more and more on their ideological opposition to communism and their histories of violent opposition to the communist Viet Minh. These positions were by no means incompatible with their domestic political objectives, but they reflected a growing tendency among the politico-religious groups to target an international audience. Those tendencies would become much more pronounced during the Geneva accords and into the period of Vietnam's division.

During that transition, as Washington searched for anticommunist nationalist leadership for Vietnam that could inspire popular passion, politico-religious leaders hoped to provide the answer. However, U.S. officials remained wedded to their convictions that Hoa Hao, Cao Dai, and Binh Xuyen figures were backward, irrational, and incapable of providing effective national leadership. The more politico-religious figures clamored for influence, the more frustrated American officials would become with what they perceived to be petty acts of political subversion pursued for the sake of individual gain. Rather than winning American support as intended, politico-religious activities led the United States to support the new prime minister Ngo Dinh Diem's efforts to spurn their demands and exclude them from power. Yet they would prove much tougher to silence than both Ngo Dinh Diem and his American backers hoped.

Chapter 3

"Sink or Swim with Ngo Dinh Diem"

As the French war approached its denouement, the United States identified as one of its key objectives the "development of indigenous leadership which will be truly representative and symbolic of Indo-Chinese national aspirations and win the loyalty and support of the people."[1] Washington had long lamented Bao Dai's failure to inspire nationalist support and hoped to establish a noncommunist Vietnamese government that could do just that. Even as it pursued this objective, however, the United States remained focused more on the international Cold War that seemed to envelop Vietnam than the domestic political competition that was unfolding within its borders. Many U.S. officials agreed with the premise, "The war in Indo-China is merely an extension of the international Communist movement. The entire operation is directed, supervised, and supplied by the Soviets and their junior partners, the Chinese Communists."[2] According to President Dwight Eisenhower's domino theory, stemming the tide of communist expansion in Southeast Asia was critical. Therefore, strong anticommunist credentials were the most important criteria for any indigenous leader hoping to garner American backing.

Politico-religious figures and their noncommunist nationalist competitors recognized this, and in the weeks surrounding the Battle of Dien Bien

Phu and the Geneva Conference placed ever greater emphasis on platforms that would enable them to establish strong claims to legitimacy within Vietnamese political circles and court American support. The principle tenets of those platforms, honed and sharpened between the currency devaluation crisis in May 1953 and the Geneva Conference exactly one year later, were anticolonialism, antifeudalism, and especially anticommunism. Despite persistent appeals to those tropes, designed to overlap explicitly with Washington's objectives in Vietnam, the politico-religious organizations failed to attract American support. The United States continued to dismiss prominent Cao Dai, Hoa Hao, and Binh Xuyen figures as naïve, unpredictable, backward, and corrupt. American diplomats had already decided that the politico-religious organizations were the purveyors of "emotional, irresponsible nationalism" and would cling to the view that they were "anticommunist in orientation, but feudalistic and regressive in all other respects."[3]

Eisenhower's administration instead threw its support behind Ngo Dinh Diem, a familiar, anticommunist figure whom it deemed to be "a man of integrity and principle, worthy of American support."[4] Washington's backing for Ngo Dinh Diem, and its disdain for noncommunist nationalist alternatives, played a major role in Bao Dai's decision to appoint him prime minister amidst the Geneva Conference that resulted in a Franco–Viet Minh cease-fire. Yet, when the new prime minister proceeded to exclude politico-religious leaders from power, and target their organizations for elimination, they mobilized a response that would place the new South Vietnamese government in peril and with it the American project of containing communism in Southeast Asia.

Dien Bien Phu and the Geneva Conference

By the beginning of 1954, the increasingly anti-French tenor of southern Vietnamese nationalist activity combined with battlefield losses, high costs, and France's domestic political crises to fuel opposition to the war at home. French politicians of all stripes were crying out for a cease-fire. In January and February, Defense Minister René Pleven toured Indochina with a group of military leaders and concluded that, despite General Henri Navarre's increased military operations, only a negotiated settlement could retain for France any semblance of influence in the colonies of Indochina.[5]

The timing of France's resolution to pursue negotiations coincided with the Berlin Conference, the four-power talks stemming from Malenkov's peace offensive that finally kicked off on January 23, 1954. France, Britain, and the United States received Soviet foreign minister Vyacheslav Molotov's suggestions for the future of Europe as a poorly cloaked effort to torpedo the EDC and prevent West German rearmament. The most significant outcome of the Berlin Conference thus pertained not to Europe but to Indochina. French officials were able to convince a very reluctant John Foster Dulles to agree to a five-power conference to discuss both Indochina and Korea. They attempted to sway the American delegation by pointing out that the groundswell of French opposition to the war was compounded by Washington's apparent hypocrisy as it negotiated an armistice in Korea on July 27, 1953, but seemed to forbid France from doing the same in Indochina.[6] But Eisenhower and Dulles were only fully persuaded to put Indochina on the docket of a five-power conference to be held in Geneva once Bidault assured them that he would secure ratification of the EDC before the talks commenced that coming April.[7]

In anticipation of the Geneva Conference, French strategists planned to lure Viet Minh forces into battle at Dien Bien Phu, a valley in the northwest corner of Vietnam. Their scaled back goal was simply to strengthen their military position in hopes of improving their hand at the negotiating table, not to secure a total defeat of the Viet Minh army as Eisenhower's administration continued to hope. The plan quickly went awry as Viet Minh soldiers laid siege to French garrisons trapped in the valley, prompting French leaders to hope in vain that the United States would step in to provide relief in the form of massive air strikes. In response to French entreaties for military support, Eisenhower and Dulles devised a plan called "United Action" to ensure that any U.S. intervention would have international and domestic support. The plan stipulated that the United States would go to war only as part of a regional defense coalition including Great Britain, France, Australia, New Zealand, Thailand, and the Philippines.[8] Moreover, Eisenhower pledged not to intervene without a constitutional declaration of war from Congress. These two unattainable provisions obviated the possibility of American intervention and doomed the French Army to a devastating loss.[9] France's surrender to Viet Minh General Vo Nguyen Giap on May 7, the day before the Indochina phase of the Geneva Conference was scheduled to kick off, represented a major military and psychological defeat for France.[10]

Even before the battle turned sour for French commanders, southern Vietnam's nationalist politicians recognized that Dien Bien Phu would be the final act in the French war and made last ditch efforts to advance their positions. In early March, a group of nationalists led by the Cao Dai and some dissident Dai Viet politicians presented Bao Dai with an ultimatum demanding that he immediately hold elections for a national assembly.[11] American officials concluded that the "people behind the 'ultimatum' were in no way representative of [the] majority or general nationalist sentiment here in Vietnam."[12] Even if this were true, nationalist claims that Bao Dai's State of Vietnam was not responsive to the popular will served to complicate France's impending efforts to negotiate with the Viet Minh. The ultimatum therefore forced French and American officials to urge Bao Dai to take "some action which would convince Vietnamese people that his regime and government would become truly representative and responsible to Vietnamese public opinion."[13]

American ambassador Donald Heath quietly changed his perspective on nationalist requests without ever acknowledging their authors as legitimate political actors. By the end of March he encouraged France to accept the essence of Vietnamese proposals for independence in order to strengthen the Franco-American negotiating position at the upcoming Geneva Conference. He urged Paris to sign two treaties with Vietnamese nationalists: one clearly establishing Vietnam's independence and sovereignty, and the second invoking this sovereignty to establish the country's voluntary relationship within the French Union. This would serve to justify any economic, political, or military agreements with France into which the State of Vietnam might enter. Above all, Heath conceived of these measures as a means of convincing Vietnamese fence-sitters that the SVN had achieved a level of independence that Ho Chi Minh could never attain as "a puppet of Communist imperialism."[14]

In the end, France did not extend such treaties and Bao Dai did not convene a national assembly. Prime Minister Buu Loc responded to the nationalist outcry instead by forming a war cabinet "to insure a more determined and efficient prosecution of war."[15] Much like Ngo Dinh Diem later would, he sought to silence nationalist agitators rather than respond to their demands. His next move only exacerbated the government's ongoing difficulties with the Cao Dai, and to a lesser extent the Hoa Hao. On April 12, as French defeat drew near and negotiations to rally politico-religious troops to the national army dragged on, the SVN initiated a draft to mobilize all males between the ages of twenty and twenty-five. This was intended to gut politico-religious support, but ended up having the opposite effect. Of the expected 150,000 conscripts, only 9,000 came forward to join the national army. The rest apparently managed to avoid service by hiding, fleeing to Viet Minh territory, or enlisting in the Hoa Hao, Cao Dai, and Binh Xuyen militias.

In response to this, national army General Nguyen Van Hinh scorned the politico-religious militaries that would later support him in a feud with Ngo Dinh Diem. He charged that they served primarily as excuses for adepts to remain exempt from national military conscription, while providing "local satraps armed forces with which to exert influence." While politico-religious armies were certainly more than this, their appeal to draft dodgers was of no small concern, as French security agents estimated that the Cao Dai had an army of about 20,000 soldiers, and its Association for National Restoration boasted upward of 600,000 adherents prior to the Geneva accords.[16] To quell their growing influence, Buu Loc insisted that France must cease support payments to politico-religious troops before their leaders could be brought in line with the existing government. He even suggested that France and the United States turn over to the Vietnamese government the money they were paying to maintain those troops as a means of supporting the integration of supplementary politico-religious forces into the national army. But before any decisions about this could be made, the negotiators in Geneva turned their attention to hashing out a cease-fire for Indochina.

When the Indochina phase of the Geneva Conference opened on May 8, France still had not ratified the EDC, much to Dulles and Eisenhower's displeasure. Partly out of frustration with the French, and partly due to his fear that negotiating on equal terms with Chinese, Soviet, and Vietnamese communists would be tantamount to appeasement, John Foster Dulles departed Geneva before the talks turned to Indochina. He instructed his delegation to participate only as an "interested nation," rather than as a "belligerent or a principal in the negotiations."[17] Eisenhower, Dulles, and other top U.S. officials viewed events in Vietnam through Cold War–colored glasses. To them it was of paramount importance to keep the country out of communist hands in order to check Sino-Soviet expansion and protect Western trading interests in Southeast Asia. Also, intensely concerned with American credibility with both friend and foe, the secretary of state was determined that the United States should not bear responsibility for the loss of Indochina and the failure of the Geneva Conference. This prevented him and his delegation from engaging fully in the cease-fire negotiations in which southern Vietnam's politico-religious organizations played a vocal role.

France's military defeat and the prospect of a negotiated settlement of the Franco-Viet Minh War threw southern Vietnam's nationalists into a renewed frenzy of activity, focused increasingly on winning American favor. As the Geneva Conference unfolded, Saigon's political frontrunners scrambled to position themselves to play key roles in an independent Vietnamese state. Politico-religious leaders realized that the end of the French war would cut off the source of their subsidies, and that their very survival would then depend on their ability to assume a central position within the postwar political system. Southern Vietnamese nationalists who had been active throughout the previous year redoubled their efforts to assert their political relevance on the national stage. French intelligence sources noted that they made noticeable efforts to align their views publicly with those of the United States, which they recognized would be the SVN's most critical postwar ally.[18]

By the time the Indochina phase of the Geneva Conference opened, the politico-religious organizations had crystallized political platforms emphasizing their commitments to fighting communism, to modernizing the country's infrastructure and political system, and to liberating the country from outside control. Opposition to these three social ills—communism, feudalism, and colonialism—is often intimately associated with Ngo Dinh Diem, who would later identify them as the evil triad that his government was uniquely capable of destroying.[19] Yet the extent to which his political competitors spoke in these terms before he took office suggests that his well-known emphasis on eradicating this same villainous triad was actually part of a larger political discourse in which individuals or groups seeking to participate in southern Vietnam's noncommunist politics felt compelled to present themselves as committed to and capable of advancing the same goals.

Indeed, this language was a variation on the anticolonial rhetorical framework developed in large part by communists in the 1920s and 1930s that focused on liberating Vietnam from imperialist aggression and transforming society into one capable of surviving autonomously and competing in the modern world. The centrality of modernization, an end to colonial rule, and in some cases anticommunism as tropes in the larger tradition of Vietnamese anticolonial politics enabled southern Vietnam's politicians to mobilize those themes to appeal to a domestic audience even as they aimed to attract support from American diplomats with whom they shared key objectives. During the Geneva negotiations, they would place particular emphasis on their anticommunism, and on their awareness of the larger Cold War conflict, by taking a firm stand against dividing Vietnam and, especially, against ceding control of any portion of the country to the communists, whom they deemed to be agents of Chinese and Soviet imperialism.

On May 7, 1954, Pham Cong Tac and Binh Xuyen leader Bay Vien formed a new nationalist organization under Bao Dai's direction. The National Salvation Front (Mat Tran Quoc Gia Cuu Quoc) constituted the latest, but by no means the last effort to unite Vietnam's most powerful non-communist religious and political groups under one canopy. Pham Cong Tac and Bay Vien conceived of the body as a means of exerting some influence over the SVN's official delegation to the Geneva Conference. They also hoped that a strong alliance of Saigon's nationalists at this pivotal juncture would attract heretofore unaligned nationalists.[20] Hoa Hao generals Tran Van Soai and Lam Thanh Nguyen, and Catholic leader Le Huu Tu, along with several other key politicians, quickly became involved with the front. On May 10 they published a petition in support of Bao Dai's delegation, demanding that he resist making concessions to the communists, thereby enslaving "free Vietnam."[21] The group did little more than express nationalist solidarity, demand total independence, and protest national partition, but it did so in a way that reminded Bao Dai, Buu Loc, and their delegation in Geneva that southern Vietnam's many political voices could not be ignored.

By far the most vocal nationalist outcry from early May 1954 through the end of the Geneva Conference was against the division of Vietnam. Some historians claim that, despite their opposition to it, the politico-religious organizations hoped to benefit from partition. This is almost certainly true, given the history of violence and distrust between the politico-religious organizations and the Viet Minh. A unified Vietnam at this time most likely would have fallen under communist control, which at best would circumscribe Hoa Hao, Cao Dai, and Binh Xuyen autonomy and at worst would have subjected their leaders and followers to the targeted assassinations and violence that Viet Minh leaders exercised in early years of the French war. Indeed, these organizations thrived on a lack of centralized control, which largely explained their resistance to Viet Minh attempts at national unification after the August Revolution. Still, to accept national division without objections would have eviscerated politico-religious claims to nationalism, reinforced charges that they were nothing more than regional warlords, and crushed their aspirations to political leadership. And in the most practical terms, the very prospect of a cease-fire threatened to undermine their military, economic, and political power by bringing an end to the French subsidies on which they so depended. Thus Cao Dai and Hoa Hao leaders spearheaded protests against partition.[22]

Days before the Indochina phase of the Geneva Conference opened, Pham Cong Tac made overtures to Ho Chi Minh, noting that they were kindred spirits in the struggle for independence and urging him not to let soon-to-be independent Vietnam be divided by the influence of competing Soviet and American blocs.[23] The politico-religious groups signaled their ongoing support for the chief of state as the figure best suited to bring about national unity with public refrains such as, "Support chief-of-state Bao Dai!" and by imploring the Viet Minh to remember that the former emperor had initially collaborated with the DRV.[24] Not long after the Geneva negotiations started, Cao Dai propagandists began to levy charges that Ho Chi Minh was a pawn of China and the Soviet Union, and insisted that he would be to blame if the country were divided, given his refusal to work with Bao Dai to form a united government.[25]

On May 5, the Hoa Hao Vietnamese Social Democratic Party (Viet Nam Dan Chu Xa Hoi Dang), the Hoa Hao army, and sympathetic followers staged a march of more than fifteen thousand people in protest against partition. Demonstrators carried posters with such slogans as, "Struggle to the last drop of blood to protect the unity of Vietnam!" And Cao Dai radio broadcasts noted that national division would not only go against Vietnam's history but could subject it to the same sort of violent struggle that recently befell Korea.[26] This reference reflected the organization's awareness of the growing effort within the Third World to seek independence in terms that might avoid carving the newly decolonized world into the types of rigid fronts that the Cold War had already created in Korea and elsewhere.

Alongside these demonstrations, articles condemning the prospect of national partition appeared with increasing frequency in Saigon newspapers beginning in May 1954. "The Vietnamese people are all of one blood line, one language, one custom, and one culture," insisted one *Saigon Moi* editorial. The author claimed that Vietnam's history was formidable, awe inspiring, and marked by glorious, unifying struggle against foreign invasion. "Anybody plotting to divide this country and separate this people," he claimed, "must look again at the history of Vietnam."[27] These sorts of protests would continue unabated throughout the next two months, even into the early days following the Geneva peace agreement.[28] The SVN delegation to the Geneva Conference, which included Pham Cong Tac, also held a persistent public line emphasizing independence and hope for political unity in Vietnam under Bao Dai's leadership. Indeed, Saigon officials issued a communiqué at the beginning of the conference warning that a compromise agreement with communist "rebels" resulting in partition would never meet with government approval.[29]

By mid-June, France, which had initially promised the SVN delegation that it would not agree to a settlement that included partition, abandoned the pledge. The Geneva negotiations were by then deadlocked on the issues of partition, the composition of an international body to oversee the cease-fire, and the withdrawal of Viet Minh troops from Cambodia and Laos. On June 17, French voters elected Pierre Mendès-France to replace Joseph Laniel as prime minister. His ascendance was a blow to the United States, for Laniel had been relatively hawkish on the war and supportive of the European Defense Community (EDC), and Mendès-France was neither.[30] When Mendès-France assumed office, he immediately set out to expedite peace in Indochina and requested a mandate of one month to negotiate an armistice, promising to resign if he failed.[31]

On July 21, 1954, Mendès-France and DRV representatives signed an agreement that would divide Vietnam into two halves along the seventeenth parallel, to be reunited through countrywide elections scheduled for the summer of 1956. An International Control Commission (ICC), composed of representatives from Canada, Poland, and India, was appointed to supervise the elections and ensure that neither half of Vietnam entered into a military alliance in the meantime.[32] France and the DRV managed to conclude this peace agreement just a few hours after Mendès-France's self-imposed deadline had expired. In many respects, the results of Geneva were a diplomatic victory for the United States, France, and the State of Vietnam. In the end, the Viet Minh ceded substantial battlefield advances and bent to Soviet and Chinese pressure to compromise on the placement of the partition line and the timing of the reunification elections.[33] Although Dulles and Eisenhower decried the settlement as an act of communist appeasement, a U.S. Defense Department study later conceded that the SVN "received much more than they could have realistically expected from the Geneva Conference."[34] The United States pledged to uphold the agreements, but would not sign them, ostensibly since the policy of nonrecognition of the People's Republic of China barred any official interaction with Chinese diplomats.[35]

Ngo Dinh Diem, whom Bao Dai appointed prime minister of the SVN in the middle of the cease-fire negotiations, also refused to sign the Geneva agreements, claiming that the terms did not represent Vietnam's popular will. He insisted that the country would remain divided so long as communism "enslaved" the north. But he denounced national division, for which he roundly blamed the Hanoi government. Given the southern nationalist outcry against partition, to take any other position would have been political suicide. Thenceforth he would speak of his government as the one true government of Vietnam, and his policies as though they would one day extend both north and south of the seventeenth parallel. Yet, Ngo Dinh Diem came to power over a remarkably divided, almost anarchic south, amidst a sea of doubt about his capacity to lead. His ability to control even the territory south of the seventeenth parallel remained for some time an open question.

Ngo Dinh Diem and the New South Vietnamese Government

Bao Dai's decision to appoint Ngo Dinh Diem prime minister of South Vietnam's first postwar government was heavily influenced by the United States. Although the chief of state made his selection autonomously, he recognized that the SVN would need support from Washington in order to survive and appears to have chosen Ngo Dinh Diem largely in response to pressure from the State Department and the CIA.[36] By the end of the war, Ngo Dinh Nhu had maneuvered himself and by extension his brother into a primary position within South Vietnam's noncommunist political sphere. Equally, if not more important, though, were the activities Ngo Dinh Diem had undertaken in the preceding years to ingratiate himself with powerful religious and political leaders in the United States. This gave him a distinct advantage over politico-religious figures like Pham Cong Tac, who had earned a prominent position in South Vietnamese nationalist circles but failed to persuade the United States of his capacity to lead.

Much of Ngo Dinh Nhu's political activity took shadowy form, as he preferred to work behind the scenes rather than on the public stage. He enjoyed a close relationship with the CIA, especially during his tenure as its main political action contact in Vietnam between 1951 and 1953.[37] Newly declassified documentation of CIA activities in Vietnam reveals that in May 1954 Ngo Dinh Nhu was in contact with CIA agent Paul Harwood about the terms under which the U.S. would support his brother's bid to become prime minister, and that the CIA responded favorably to his requests.[38] In addition to his work with the CIA, Ngo Dinh Nhu's other efforts to make inroads into Vietnamese politics reflected a similar preference for secrecy. One historian has suggested that Ngo Dinh Nhu may have quietly founded the Can Lao Party (Personalist Labor Revolutionary Party, or Can Lao Nhan Vi Cach Mang Dang) as early as 1950. The party, formally acknowledged for the first time in 1954, was rooted in the philosophy of personalism with which Ngo Dinh Nhu had become acquainted while he was in Paris in the 1930s studying to be an archivist, and which would later emerge as the official state philosophy under Ngo Dinh Diem's Republic of Vietnam. During its early years, the Can Lao organization operated covertly, making it difficult to discern the exact nature of its activities. Still shadowy after 1954, it would become the central organ of South Vietnamese internal security and political organization.[39] Ngo Dinh Nhu's power and influence in southern Vietnam grew during the last half of the French war as his Can Lao organization took root, and as he became engaged more overtly in nationalist politics after the currency devaluation crisis in May 1953.

While Ngo Dinh Nhu worked to shore up a political foundation in Vietnam, Ngo Dinh Diem traveled to the United States where he courted American politicians, diplomats, and clergymen, and built up a base of political support in Washington with which no other Vietnamese figure would be able to compete.[40] As early as April 1953 American diplomats ranked him among the most likely suitable replacements for then prime minister Nguyen Van Tam.[41] Not only was he familiar to Americans and able to communicate in English in a way that his rivals were not, he seemed to possess the right character for the job. Diplomats like Donald Heath and Robert McClintock, though troubled by Ngo Dinh Diem's apparent political shortcomings, lauded his "unquestioned integrity," and his "sincerity, nationalism and honesty."[42]

American officials' positive assessments of Ngo Dinh Diem contrasted sharply with their negative opinions of the politico-religious leaders who struggled to outmaneuver the Ngos for primacy in Vietnam's noncommunist political milieu. Pham Cong Tac, who held one of the most prominent positions in southern Vietnamese politics at the end of the French war, failed to convince U.S. officials of his potential for national leadership. On the contrary, American observers deemed him reckless and incompetent. Following the October 1953 national congress statement renouncing the French Union, Ambassador Heath had informed Dulles that the "Caodaist Pope, although fond of strutting on the podium, in reality had no political judgment or control over his delegation."[43] He was, in McClintock's estimation, "politically naïve and unpredictable," despite his position as the "unquestioned spiritual leader at Tay Ninh."[44] McClintock would go so far as to call the Cao Dai Pope a "charlatan ... with no convictions ... who is lured by the will-of-the-wisp of neutralism."[45] Heath concluded that the

Cao Dai "were morally in a superior position to the other 'war lord sects' of Binh Xuyen and Hoa Hao," but this only highlighted the depth of his disdain for the latter two groups.[46]

By dismissing the politico-religious organizations in this manner, the United States wrote off the most influential political blocs and individuals in southern Vietnam aside from the Ngo brothers. This left Bao Dai with few options for prime minister that could both satisfy the United States and hopefully command some respect and cooperation from southern Vietnam's noncommunist nationalists. Thus, in late May 1954, with the Geneva Conference underway, the chief of state informed Buu Loc and Ngo Dinh Diem of his intention to place the latter in charge of forming a new government on the conclusion of the cease-fire negotiations.[47] On June 18, Bao Dai officially asked Ngo Dinh Diem to take the helm in South Vietnam. He agreed almost immediately, and announced during his acceptance speech that "the Vietnamese people, long deceived, are seeking a new path which will lead to their ardently desired ideals." He promised that he was "firmly determined to lead the way to this path, overcoming any and all obstacles."[48] His obstacles would be many, as he discovered on June 25 on arriving in Saigon to begin setting up his government, and even more so when he formally took office in early July.[49]

Throughout the preceding year, as Ngo Dinh Diem's name had been floated about as a potential leader for the State of Vietnam, spokesmen for the politico-religious organizations indicated that they knew too little about him to come out for or against him. Hoa Hao general Nguyen Giac Ngo expressed reservations about appointing a Catholic to rule over a predominantly Buddhist population. Others worried, presciently, that Ngo Dinh Diem's reputation for insularity and fence-sitting might limit his effectiveness and prompt him to exclude Vietnam's diverse political and religious groups from his government.[50]

Some of Ngo Dinh Diem's competitors took it on themselves to caution American officials about what they saw as his troubling shortcomings. Northern Dai Viet politician Nguyen Huu Tri confronted United States consul Turner Cameron in a manner Cameron deemed "oriental double-talk." He warned that Ngo Dinh Diem's "high moral character and personal integrity [did] not compensate for [his] almost total lack of professional competence and administrative experience." Nguyen Huu Tri feared that Ngo Dinh Diem's "narrow sectarian approach" would alienate Vietnam's other noncommunist nationalists. Moreover, since the potential prime minister was known to be arrogant and "intellectually opposed to practical approach," Nguyen Huu Tri worried that he might attempt to make rash changes to all levels of Vietnamese political life that could throw South Vietnamese society into chaos and confusion.[51] According to Dr. Phan Huy Quat, another Dai Viet politician who had held several high-ranking positions in the SVN, Ngo Dinh Diem was too "inexperienced, fanatic, and naïve" to accomplish the political feats required of him in the wake of France's withdrawal.[52] Even the bishop of Phat Diem province, a northern Catholic stronghold, advised Heath that Ngo Dinh Diem lacked popular appeal and was unsuited to leadership.[53]

Many French officials shared these concerns and strongly cautioned Bao Dai and the United States against pursuing Ngo Dinh Diem's appointment.[54] Maurice Dejean, French commissioner general in Indochina, complained to United States consul Robert McClintock that "Diem [was] too narrow, too rigid, too unworldly, and too pure to have any chance of creating an effective government in Vietnam."[55] But not all French officials opposed him. Indeed, in the days leading up to his appointment he enjoyed support from high-level figures who viewed him as South Vietnam's only chance for salvation. These included Deputy Prime Minister Paul Reynaud and French undersecretary for the associated states Marc Jacquet.[56] Despite these supporters, Eisenhower administration officials tended to assume the French were universally opposed to Ngo Dinh Diem.

During summer 1954 U.S. officials themselves had little more than a dim hope for Ngo Dinh Diem and for South Vietnam's noncommunist future. After Bao Dai formally solicited Ngo Dinh Diem to lead the country, McClintock wrote to inform Dulles that "Bao Dai's action in requesting [that] Ngo Dinh Diem form [a] government has totally failed to arouse [the] enthusiasm of the Vietnamese people so essential if [the] war effort and [the] National Army are to get necessary support." He worried that Ngo Dinh Diem was too proud and too unknown in Vietnam to form a representative government, and that, at any rate, there was little evidence that the religious and political groups that had opposed previous governments would be willing to cooperate with this one.[57] Ambassador Dillon met with what he identified as a "vague, rambling, and even unintelligible" Ngo Dinh Diem on June 24, and described him to Dulles with the following mixed review:

> As on past occasions, we were strongly impressed with Ngo's simplicity, naiveté and honesty. He impresses one as a mystic who has just emerged from a religious retreat into the cold world which is, in fact almost what he has done. He appears too unworldly and unsophisticated to be able to cope

with the grave problems and unscrupulous people he will find in Saigon. Yet his apparent sincerity, patriotic fervor and honesty are refreshing by comparison and we are led to think that these qualities may outweigh his other deficiencies. The grossly unrealistic attitude to current problems in past appears to have improved.... . On balance we are favorably impressed but only in the realization that we are prepared to accept the seemingly ridiculous prospect that this Yogi-like mystic could assume the charge he is apparently about to undertake only because the standard set by his predecessors is so low.[58]

American officials seriously doubted Ngo Dinh Diem's leadership abilities but embraced him nonetheless as the candidate most likely to unify South Vietnam and prevent communism from spreading there.[59]

However, the task of unifying and pacifying South Vietnam in the wake of the Geneva Conference would be a heady one for any leader, much less one with the limitations attributed to the new prime minister. Ngo Dinh Diem returned home to Vietnam in June 1954, after a long absence, to a site of near anarchy that sharply contrasted with the highly organized, consolidated North Vietnamese regime.[60] He took control of a weakly defined political entity that lacked the institutions and organization required to run an independent government.[61] French journalists Jean Lacouture and Philippe Devillers described the South Vietnam Ngo Dinh Diem came home to as "a country ruined, cancerous, stunned—a sentence in suspension."[62]

When Ngo Dinh Diem took power, the Cao Dai, Hoa Hao, and Binh Xuyen controlled substantial portions of the south, both in terms of population and geography. By summer 1954, the three politico-religious organizations collectively controlled approximately one-third of the territory and population below the seventeenth parallel. The Binh Xuyen had a monopoly over Saigon-Cholon vice industries, running prostitution rings and casinos, trading in opium, and imposing illegal "road safety taxes" in roadways in and out of Saigon, all to generate wealth even beyond the annual stipend of eighty-five thousand dollars paid to the organization by the French.[63] During the war Bay Vien had taken over directorship of one of Asia's largest gambling establishments, the Grand Monde (Dai The Gioi) Casino in Cholon, and received a commission from the French as a brigadier general in the auxiliary forces of Vietnam's national army.[64] In 1953, he purchased the Saigon-Cholon police concession from his ally Bao Dai for $1.2 million, thus enabling his forces to rove the twin cities without even nominal oversight. Also that year, the Binh Xuyen obtained nine seats in the

SVN's National Assembly. By 1954, the organization essentially controlled all government functions in the capital city.[65]

Beyond Saigon, the Hoa Hao and Cao Dai organizations controlled extensive autonomous zones in which they collected taxes, elected their own officials, and maintained their own militaries. Yet even those zones were fraught with conflict. By 1954, the Hoa Hao would claim more than 1 million followers, armed forces totaling over twenty thousand soldiers, and uncontested power and influence in the provinces of Chau Doc and Long Xuyen.[66] But the Hoa Hao military factionalized during the war, leaving four generals—Nguyen Giac Ngo, Ba Cut, Lam Thanh Nguyen, and the most dominant, Tran Van Soai—vying for control so viciously that one French military official labeled the organization a "brotherhood of enemies."[67] The Cao Dai had also struggled with bitter military and political infighting throughout the war. By 1954, Pham Cong Tac managed to restore the organization to a state of relative cohesion under his control.[68] The mainstream Cao Dai leadership was never sure, though, what to expect from its dissident military faction led by the anticommunist, anti-French "ultranationalist" Trinh Minh The, who had joined and broken with Tay Ninh several times over the preceding eight years.[69]

A number of other destabilizing factors compounded Ngo Dinh Diem's difficulty in consolidating power over a remarkably fractious South Vietnam. The national army rested under the independent control of the Francophile general Nguyen Van Hinh, the notoriously impetuous son of former prime minister Nguyen Van Tam who was by no means guaranteed to support Ngo Dinh Diem. French military withdrawals and the chaotic influx of Catholic refugees from north of the seventeenth parallel rendered the prime minister's task even more challenging. Over summer 1954, as the United States replaced France as the principal patron of the SVN, American advisors encouraged Ngo Dinh Diem to cooperate with other nationalist figures including politico-religious leaders, within limits, in order to bolster his power and forge a more solid political bloc against the communists. From the outset, however, Ngo Dinh Diem resisted this advice and exhibited a remarkably insular approach to governance that would provoke opposition almost immediately.

As Ngo Dinh Diem formally took office and announced the formation of his cabinet on July 7, 1954, his initial selection of government appointees spoke volumes of the manner in which he would shore up his administration by stonewalling and eventually eradicating all political opposition over the next two years. He packed his cabinet full of individuals with close ties to himself or his family, many of whom belonged to the country's Catholic minority. Their near total exclusion from real positions of power chilled politico-religious leaders, who had initially presented a façade of political unity in support Ngo Dinh Diem in hopes that he might help them to retain their military, economic, and political power in the wake of the cease-fire and the impending end of French subsidies.[70]

French General Paul Ely observed that "after the formation of the Ngo Dinh Diem government a growing malaise spread amongst sect leaders."[71] These groups would not have the luxury of nurturing this malaise for long, as they rapidly grew wise to the prime minister's plans to divide and conquer their organizations. Indeed, Ngo Dinh Diem's apparent desire to consolidate total authority by eliminating all political competition reminded southern nationalists of the Viet Minh in the first two years following the August Revolution. This time around they were well aware of the need to act quickly to safeguard their positions and to seek allies for support. By September, their antigovernment activities, pursued in conjunction with national army general Nguyen Van Hinh, would prompt Maurice Dejean, one of the prime minister's earliest and most consistent French detractors, to call Ngo Dinh Diem's cabinet a "total failure" and insist that the leader's departure had become inevitable.[72]

Within days of taking office, Ngo Dinh Diem began feeling out prospects for abolishing opposition elements south of the seventeenth parallel. He seized on the Binh Xuyen and national army general Nguyen Van Hinh as the two most pressing obstacles to establishing order in the south. He considered Bay Vien's men to be "gangsters of the worst sort" and freely expressed his intention to do away with the Binh Xuyen's gambling and police concessions, and eventually to eradicate the group entirely.[73] He also wished to purge Nguyen Van Hinh from his post at the helm of the national army. However, he recognized the need for caution in light of Saigon's perilous security situation. Crushing these two enemies would be no minor task. France remained a powerful player in the south and was not shy about its desire to see Ngo Dinh Diem's government replaced or significantly enlarged. France's sympathy often lay more with his enemies than it did with him. And as of July 1954, Bay Vien and Nguyen Van Hinh together controlled South Vietnam's police and military organizations, leaving Ngo Dinh Diem with little, if any, force to levy against them.

By the beginning of August 1954, Nguyen Van Hinh was conspiring with leaders of all three politico-religious organizations on a plan to corner the prime minister before he could seize the initiative against them. As intrigues against Ngo Dinh Diem mounted in Saigon, French general Paul Ely and American ambassador Donald Heath implored the prime minister to broaden his government to incorporate some of his challengers in hopes of forestalling an impending crisis. Ngo Dinh Diem refused and his recalcitrance encouraged Nguyen Van Hinh to proceed rapidly with an antigovernment plot.[74] On August 7, Cao Dai, Hoa Hao, and Binh Xuyen leaders and a few token anti–Ngo Dinh Diem Catholics joined league with the national army general in an effort to force the prime minister to enlarge his government on threat of ouster.[75]

Although the United States grew ever more pessimistic about Ngo Dinh Diem's chances to retain power absent a more inclusive government, it conveyed clear signals that he could count on Washington's support even should he fail to do so. This message, rooted perhaps as deeply in Washington's disdain for Ngo Dinh Diem's challengers as in their faith in his leadership abilities, came most clearly through undercover CIA agent Edward Lansdale, with whom the prime minister enjoyed a close relationship.[76] Lansdale referred to the Hinh Crisis dismissively as a "shallow melodrama … played out in slapstick style."[77] As much as anything, this was indicative of an ethnocentric worldview that frequently blinded him to the nuances of Vietnam's political affairs. As he saw it, "We are not dealing here with fully rational, educated, unbiased Westerners."[78]

However, a close reading of the crisis suggests that politico-religious leaders acted more rationally than Lansdale presumed. Hoa Hao, Cao Dai, and Binh Xuyen figures allied with Nguyen Van Hinh in an effort to shore up power within their regional zones of influence, but they were not blind to the broader international realities of the conflict. They recognized the importance of French and American sanction for carrying out a coup and establishing a viable alternative government. In fact, their vagueness throughout the crisis about the specific nature of their demands suggests that they may not have been seeking to overthrow Diem, but to put pressure on him to grant them serious government posts while winning international support, especially from Washington. Rebels therefore courted both the French and the Americans from the outset, to be embraced cautiously by the French and rebuffed wholly by the United States.

French generals Ely and La Chambre responded almost enthusiastically to this opportunity to rethink South Vietnam's leadership quandary. Some have even suggested that French agents fomented the rebellion in an effort to expel Ngo Dinh Diem.[79] Both Ely and La Chambre advocated replacing him with former prime minister Nguyen Van Tam, or at the very least restructuring a coalition government including both Nguyen Van Tam and Ngo Dinh Diem. They argued that Nguyen Van Hinh's father, Nguyen Van Tam would have the best chance of controlling the general, thereby keeping the politico-religious organizations in line.[80] Throughout the crisis they floated a number of options for a new or substantially enlarged government to include some combination of Ngo Dinh Diem, Nguyen Van Xuan, Buu Loc, Tran Van Huu, and invariably representatives of the Binh Xuyen, Cao Dai, and Hoa Hao.

The catch was that any solution would have to meet with American approval. Washington found fault with each of these figures, who were either too Francophile, too pro–Viet Minh, or simply not as capable nor as upstanding as Ngo Dinh Diem. One historian has argued that Dulles and the State Department seized on this as an opportunity to assert American autonomy from France's Indochina policy while reinforcing Washington's support for Ngo Dinh Diem.[81] However, the embassy's assessments of Diem would waver somewhat during the crisis, as Heath, whose views were growing ever closer to Ely's, submitted pessimistic reports about the prime minister and advocated for an enlarged government.[82] This prompted Lansdale and other figures in the CIA to express frustration over what they saw as embassy support for French interests over those of Ngo Dinh Diem. In spite of Heath's growing concern, though, both agencies stood by the prime minister, whom U.S. officials considered to be the only acceptable option among South Vietnam's potential leaders.

In hopes of deterring dissident activity, Heath assured Cao Dai general Nguyen Thanh Phuong, who frequently expressed a desire to see the Cao Dai pope preside over a new "Third Force" government, "that any action or agitation against [the] Diem government at this time would have a very bad reaction in the US and abroad."[83] On August 19, Secretary of State John Foster Dulles clarified his position on long-term U.S. policy through a letter to Pierre Mendès-France, insisting that Washington's overriding goal was to develop and support a strong nationalist government in South Vietnam under Ngo Dinh Diem's direction. Meanwhile, Washington encouraged Ngo Dinh Diem to pursue aggressive negotiations with all three politico-religious groups aimed at isolating Nguyen Van Hinh and staving off a potential coup attempt.

For a time, Ngo Dinh Diem seemed willing to pursue such negotiations, despite prognostications from French and Vietnamese figures, including French emissary Jacques Raphael-Leygues and Prince Buu Hoi, that his government would be unable to earn the allegiance of the Cao Dai, Hoa

Hao, and Binh Xuyen.[84] The extent to which elements within the French government sympathized with Nguyen Van Hinh and these three organizations became clear to Heath on August 25, when he arrived late to a cocktail party hosted by Raphael-Leygues. The ambassador walked in to find "that [the] so-called 'cocktail party' was instead [a] full dress meeting of chief plotters among confessional groups and [the] air of conspiracy was thick." The "plotters" included the Cao Dai pope, Hoa Hao general Tran Van Soai, General Nguyen Van Hinh, and a Binh Xuyen political counselor.

During the course of this meeting a Cao Dai colonel conveyed to Heath the depth of the politico-religious groups' dissatisfaction with Ngo Dinh Diem's government. He insisted that the prime minister's previously reported negotiations with these organizations "had not been negotiations at all as Diem's representatives had been obscure and inept and no practical political concessions or accommodations had been proffered." He made it clear that Nguyen Van Hinh and the three politico-religious organizations were in the advanced stages of planning to overthrow the prime minister and brazenly requested American permission to do so. In the end, though, he indicated that the Hoa Hao, Cao Dai, and Binh Xuyen could still be persuaded to cooperate with the prime minister if he would agree to broaden his government to include their representatives in sufficiently powerful positions.[85]

Though startled by the conspiratorial nature of the meeting, Heath admitted in his note to John Foster Dulles that these anti–Ngo Dinh Diem politicians displayed a "remarkable degree of harmony." The politico-religious organizations had a definite program for the government that would replace the prime minister and acknowledged that French and American support would be necessary for the success of the new regime. Politico-religious leaders appealed directly to Washington's anticommunist sensibilities, claiming that without a new government, the "cold war in Vietnam will be lost to the Viet Minh."[86]

By the next day it seemed that Heath was beginning to believe the dire predictions for Ngo Dinh Diem's fate, and he moved to convince Undersecretary of State Walter Bedell Smith that disaster was impeding in Saigon.[87] He lamented to Washington that French and Vietnamese criticisms of Ngo Dinh Diem's political incompetence were all too valid and questioned whether it was even still possible for the prime minister to build a strong, effective regime. Still, he insisted that "no successor government that we can envisage at this time would have any real appeal to nationalist or anticommunist sentiment."[88] The United States, by this time, had excluded the politico-religious organizations from the acceptable range of Vietnamese nationalist leadership and remained unwilling to consider a government made up of any combination of their leaders. Nor was it likely to countenance any of the names France put forward.

With assurances from Lansdale, Ngo Dinh Diem remained confident of Washington's continued support. He met with Nguyen Van Hinh on the afternoon of August 27 and disingenuously offered to relinquish his authority. His real message was that "the seat of power would not be a comfortable one," as the United States would withhold aid from the new government in the event of his ouster.[89] When Nguyen Van Hinh visited Heath two days later to feel out the U.S. position on replacing the current government in the event that Ngo Dinh Diem ultimately failed to present him and his allies with an acceptable agreement, he found that the prime minister's representation of Washington's attitude was dead on.

By the end of August it had become apparent to dissident politico-religious leaders that American support for a coup against Ngo Dinh Diem would be impossible to obtain, at least under the current circumstances. They began to back down, assuring Washington that a crisis was no longer imminent. The powerful Cao Dai dropped out of the group of plotters, critically weakening Nguyen Van Hinh's coalition and leading the State Department to conclude that a coup was no longer likely in the immediate term.[90] But the Cao Dai organization continued to stake out a firm anticommunist position, aimed both at the United States and its domestic audience, demonstrating that Cao Dai leaders had by no means abandoned their political ambitions. A September 4 Cao Dai radio broadcast issued a scathing rant against the Viet Minh regime, charging that it pretended to lead a revolution while deliberately selling the northern part of the country to the Chinese and Soviet communists. It claimed, "Under the communist regime of today, the people live in tyranny similar to that under the old feudal system," in the extent to which it deprived citizens of individual rights. The broadcast concluded with the proclamation, "We, the bloc of authentic nationalists, are ready to welcome and support the efforts of our compatriots in service of national Revolution, well-being, independence, and true liberty."[91]

Politico-religious leaders gave no indication that they were any more satisfied with Ngo Dinh Diem's rule than they had been prior to the stand-off and showed no signs of submission, but they changed tack and entered into negotiations with the prime minister in an effort to secure significant representation in his cabinet by less hostile means.[92] According to American observers, their initial demands were overambitious, but the crisis convinced U.S. officials that Ngo Dinh Diem should make more of an effort to accommodate the demands of his political competitors. Heath, in fact, concluded on September 14 that "there is no question *but that [Diem] must broaden support for his government if he is to survive.*"[93]

Even as the politico-religious groups suspended their efforts to overthrow the prime minister, they made clear their disgust with his government's conduct during the standoff. On September 16, the Cao Dai, Binh Xuyen, and Hoa Hao issued a joint declaration condemning Ngo Dinh Diem's exclusive, unresponsive leadership. They claimed that the conflict between the government and the army was "basically a rivalry for personal power and that it could result in bloody internal conflict," and blamed the government for failing to resolve it adequately. Spokesmen for the three organizations criticized Ngo Dinh Diem for thwarting the "legitimate aspirations of the people" and for pursuing policies that threatened to destroy Vietnam's nationalist base.[94]

Despite the dissolution of the anti–Ngo Dinh Diem bloc, Nguyen Van Hinh had not quite given up hope of using the national army to overthrow the current government. On September 19 he held a press conference to publicize an entreaty that he had just sent to Bao Dai condemning the prime minister and asking him to help settle the clash between the national army and the Saigon government.[95] But Bao Dai by this time seemed more inclined to support Bay Vien in a bid for power. The Binh Xuyen leader returned to Saigon claiming he had instructions from the chief of state to form a new cabinet, but he was unable to convince other politico-religious leaders of the veracity of his claims. Nor was he able to enlist support from the French who, despite their sympathy for efforts by the army and the politico-religious organizations to replace Ngo Dinh Diem, were unwilling to risk alienating the Americans completely.[96]

Ngo Dinh Diem shared a brief and caustic meeting with Bay Vien, but the two men found no grounds for cooperation. Meanwhile, the prime minister accused Nguyen Van Hinh of rebellion, after which the general barricaded himself in his palace to prepare for a final clash. Apparently convinced that the current government was doomed, nine of Ngo Dinh Diem's fifteen cabinet members resigned. But the national army did not move to overthrow him. Within a few days it became clear that a coup was not to be this time around. On September 24 several Hoa Hao and Cao Dai leaders agreed to join Ngo Dinh Diem's cabinet in exchange for financial compensation.[97] Tran Van Soai and Nguyen Thanh Phuong issued a joint statement

in French and English claiming that they agreed to "sacrifice personal objectives" to participate in Ngo Dinh Diem's government in order to shore
up "free Vietnam" against the "unified Viet Minh, Chinese, [and] Russian
Communist menace."[98] This stated objective conformed to the staunchly
anticommunist position that the Hoa Hao and Cao Dai held throughout
the French war and asserted most vehemently in the year leading up to the
Geneva Conference. Doubtless, they also intended this statement as an appeal to American observers, who were concerned first and foremost with
preventing South Vietnam from falling into communist hands.

The failure of these maneuvers in Saigon, particularly to compel Ngo
Dinh Diem to enlarge his government, appeared to be a success for the
Americans and a defeat for the French.[99] The crisis reinforced the fact that
the cease-fire, and France's subsequent failure to meet U.S. demands that
it ratify the EDC, radically diminished France's clout in negotiations with
Washington and, by extension, weakened its ability to influence events in
Vietnam. To obtain American funding, Paris was essentially bound to follow
Washington's lead. By the end of September, Ely reluctantly agreed to work
with the Americans to support Ngo Dinh Diem and attempt to fortify his
position in South Vietnam. He and La Chambre advised Bao Dai to accept
that Ngo Dinh Diem would remain in power and asked the prime minister
to demand that the national army and its leaders cooperate with him loyally.
By early October, Bao Dai seemed to accept that he had gone too far in his
support for the prime minister's adversaries and agreed to conform to the
Franco-American line.[100]

Washington's position on Ngo Dinh Diem remained rigid. During the
crisis, Eisenhower commissioned pro–Ngo Dinh Diem senator Mike Mansfield to draw up a report on South Vietnam's political future based on
observations made during a September study trip to Indochina. Mansfield
concluded in his October 15 report that, "in the event that the Diem government falls ... the United States should consider an immediate suspension of all aid to Vietnam and the French Union forces there."[101] While
the senator's report is often credited with forming the basis for American
support for Ngo Dinh Diem, it merely cemented Eisenhower's preexist-
ing inclination to do so.[102] However, it also limited the State Department's
range of options, as Dulles thenceforth feared that Mansfield might press
Congress to cut off funds for Vietnam in the event that Ngo Dinh Diem's
government should fall. Ambassador Heath would become one of the first
casualties of this report. He disagreed with Mansfield and Eisenhower's
conclusion that Ngo Dinh Diem was the only hope for South Vietnam,

causing Dulles to discharge him of his duties as rapidly as possible.[103] His replacement, "Lighting Joe" Lawton Collins arrived in Saigon on November 8 to undertake a mission aimed at strengthening Ngo Dinh Diem's government. In time, however, Collins would become even more pessimistic than Heath ever was about Ngo Dinh Diem's potential to maintain control of a noncommunist South Vietnam.

Meanwhile, in late October Dulles informed Mendès-France that the United States had developed a new plan to bolster Ngo Dinh Diem's authority, predicated at least partly on Mansfield's report. On October 25, Eisenhower sent the prime minister a letter reaffirming American support and expressing his intention to start channeling aid directly into South Vietnam. Two days later, the French ambassador to the United States registered his protest that Eisenhower's overture to Ngo Dinh Diem violated the terms of Franco-American cooperation in Indochina.[104] French officials lamented that "France now had *everyone* against her in Indochina." Moreover, they noted with reproach that Eisenhower's letter had given full support to Ngo Dinh Diem without the precondition that he form a strong and stable government.

While France and the United States focused on their disputes, the Nguyen Van Hinh crisis staggered to its denouement. Despite his isolation, Nguyen Van Hinh continued to speak publicly, with increasing bluster, of his plans to oust Ngo Dinh Diem and bragged that he could do so just by lifting the telephone. The crisis continued into November, but by then it was clear that Nguyen Van Hinh lacked the force the back his threats. By November 11 the prime minister finally appeared to have settled the crisis by firing the general and convincing him to take a six-month "study trip" to France.[105] Still, Nguyen Van Hinh would not simply roll over. Stubborn as always, he delayed his departure and refused to leave, claiming that only Bao Dai had the authority to remove him from his position as commander of the national army.[106]

In the end, Nguyen Van Hinh resigned from his post and fled to Paris, handing over command of the national army to Nguyen Van Vy on his way out. By mid-November, the Americans had finally convinced him that the United States would cut off its aid to the army if he went through with a coup.[107] Once in France, Nguyen Van Hinh would continue to work with Bao Dai and other Vietnamese expatriates to support the politico-religious organizations against Ngo Dinh Diem. While the general no longer posed an immediate threat to the South Vietnamese government, the prime minister's position was no less precarious.

By the end of the crisis, the major branches of the Cao Dai and Hoa Hao saw fit to align with Ngo Dinh Diem's government but insisted that they had not submitted to his authority, but simply agreed to advise him on how best to pursue Vietnam's security and prosperity. They continued to pressure him to reform and broaden his government in order to galvanize "authentic nationalists" against communist oppression and conquest. Their propaganda claimed diplomatically that Ngo Dinh Diem was above reproach, but condemned the corruption and injustices exercised by his subordinates on the ground. Politico-religious broadcasts reminded him that his task was not only to establish his prestige and secure foreign aid to fight the communists, but to reorganize society to provide his people with a better life. "Our enemies," they noted, "are Soviet, Chinese, and Vietnamese communists, corruption, and decay."[108] They implored Ngo Dinh Diem to let them assist him in combating these foes, but made clear that they intended to wage their struggle with or without him. Their lofty language surely obscured more parochial motives to retain and expand their own power, but it would be far too facile to dismiss their rhetoric as wholly disingenuous and outside the pale of legitimate nationalist politics, as American officials were wont to do.

The Hinh crisis and its resolution merely postponed both the Franco-American conflict over South Vietnam's leadership and the politico-religious challenge to Ngo Dinh Diem. French officials appeared relieved to have averted a more serious crisis, but remained skeptical about Ngo Dinh Diem's ability to govern South Vietnam in the long-term. One week after Nguyen Van Hinh's final stand, Ely noted that the prime minister's relations with the politico-religious organizations had already improved dramatically. But he warned that much still depended on Ngo Dinh Diem's ability to reshuffle his cabinet to his critics' satisfaction. Furthermore, Ely insisted that Bao Dai must be prepared to step in and replace the prime minister should those efforts ultimately fail.[109] A comprehensive French report on the status of Ngo Dinh Diem's government, issued in December 1954, concluded that his reforms would probably fall short of the mark if he continued on his current course.[110] According to the report, Ngo Dinh Diem did not possess the power to construct a strong, independent Vietnam with a unified sense of patriotism. Instead, he was most concerned with spreading an abstruse morality that appealed to few aside from the Catholic refuges flowing in from the north and proved particularly alienating to the Hoa Hao, Cao Dai, and Binh Xuyen.

The Nguyen Van Hinh episode awakened U.S. officials to the fragility of Ngo Dinh Diem's administration. Yet Washington still clung to the belief that the prime minster, while desperately in need of reform, represented the best leadership option for noncommunist Vietnam. Rather than searching for alternatives to the current prime minister or exerting real leverage to pressure him to accommodate his rivals, Eisenhower's administration assisted him in shoring up his power. As 1954 drew to a close, Washington's primary objectives in Vietnam were to keep Ngo Dinh Diem in office and to help him reorganize the national army so it would be loyal to him and capable of defending against future attacks from both communist and noncommunist challengers. Both of these goals would be severely tested in the early months of 1955.

Chapter 4

The "Sect" Crisis of 1955 and America's Miracle Man in Vietnam

The "sect" crisis of March and April 1955 was the culmination of the open conflict between politico-religious forces and Ngo Dinh Diem's government that began with the Hinh crisis the previous fall.[1] In the prior standoff, Cao Dai, Hoa Hao, and Binh Xuyen leaders had backed down on realizing that American sympathy for their cause would not be forthcoming, and that without it they had no hope of compelling the prime minister to meet their demands. In the interim, they temporarily eased pressure on Ngo Dinh Diem, hoping that they might secure positions of power in his government and perhaps even support for their armed forces by cooperating with rather than threatening to expel him. Yet Ngo Dinh Diem surged ahead with his plans to divide and conquer his domestic political enemies. The politico-religious organizations therefore faced ongoing exclusion from meaningful positions in Ngo Dinh Diem's government and increasingly bold efforts on his part to eliminate their existing power on the ground just as the deadline for the cessation of French subsidies to their armed forces drew near. In a desperate attempt to mobilize their existing power to preserve their endangered positions in the face of these mounting threats, the Hoa Hao, Cao Dai, and Binh Xuyen came together in a United Front of Nationalist Forces to engage in one last coordinated standoff with Ngo Dinh Diem.[2]

Throughout this clash, the United Front of Nationalist Forces continued previous efforts by politico-religious leaders to court French and American support. This would contribute to a growing rift between the French, who longed to see Ngo Dinh Diem replaced, and the United States, which remained committed to keeping him in power. The two powers had reached an entente in September 1954 predicated on a French pledge of support for Ngo Dinh Diem in exchange for assurances that the United States would consider alternatives if he faltered, but throughout the crisis both Paris and Washington would accuse each other of violating the agreement.[3] The French, as doubtful as ever about Ngo Dinh Diem's ability to retain power, were even more pessimistic about the future of French interests in Vietnam should he manage to do so.[4] They seized on the sect crisis as an opportunity to get the United States behind a plan to replace him with a new leader or a coalition government that might include politico-religious figures. American officials, however, persistently dismissed Cao Dai, Hoa Hao, and Binh Xuyen politicians as selfish warlords, incompetent politicians, and agents of French imperialism.[5] Washington also regarded a range of other nationalist politicians with suspicion, in most cases due to their histories of corruption, collaboration with the French, communication with the communists, or some combination thereof. Ngo Dinh Diem remained, to the Americans, the only palatable option for South Vietnamese leadership. However, as the crisis wore on, they would be forced to grapple with alternatives.

The Crisis in Context

Washington's frustration with the divisive nature of southern Vietnamese politics, so readily on display during the final year of the French war and in the early months of Ngo Dinh Diem's administration, continued unabated throughout the sect crisis. A *New York Times* article published at the zenith of Ngo Dinh Diem's clash with the Binh Xuyen army exemplified the Americans' quizzical attitude toward South Vietnam's politico-religious organizations. The April 29 headline proclaimed, "Struggle Weird in Vietnam." The author went on to explain, "The trouble in South Vietnam is one part volatile nationalism and one part bizarre and chaotic struggle for power."[6] He even quoted Eisenhower calling the situation "strange and inexplicable," a view the president seemed to share with most U.S. diplomats and politicians. Contrary to Eisenhower's assertion that the clash between the government and the politico-religious organizations was impossible to explain, some sort of showdown in spring 1955 was, in fact, quite predictable within the context of the country's recent political history.

Tensions between Ngo Dinh Diem and his politico-religious adversaries had been building even prior to summer 1954, when Bao Dai appointed him prime minister. When he arrived in Saigon to assume the premiership in July 1954, Hoa Hao, Cao Dai, and Binh Xuyen leaders vowed to set aside their differences with the Ngo family in the name of national unity and in hopes of securing privilege under the new government.[7] However, politico-religious figures from all factions were almost immediately disappointed when the new prime minister made his initial cabinet appointments. Ngo Dinh Diem's government roster consisted overwhelmingly of Catholics and of his own friends and family, many of whom lacked the requisite experience to perform their jobs effectively. Hoa Hao, Cao Dai, and Binh Xuyen leaders took up only a few token positions, and balked at their exclusion from the postarmistice administration. Binh Xuyen spokesmen claimed to be delighted by the prime minister's unpopular decisions, insisting that he could not possibly retain power for more than six months without incorporating a more representative array of nationalist figures into his cabinet.[8]

The timing of the French departure from Vietnam, and its related consequences for the politico-religious organizations, exacerbated Hoa Hao, Cao Dai, and Binh Xuyen dissatisfaction with Ngo Dinh Diem's political favoritism and drove them to increase their pressure on the prime minister to broaden his government. During the First Indochina War, French support payments for Cao Dai, Hoa Hao, and Binh Xuyen armed forces constituted the lifeblood of these organizations, enabling them to develop impressive infrastructures and expand their social, political, and military influence within their autonomous zones in the Mekong Delta. However, according to the terms of the 1954 ceasefire and subsequent agreements negotiated between France, the Saigon government, and the United States, France was to cease paying these subsidies in January 1955.[9] Politico-religious leaders were left with little choice but to turn to Ngo Dinh Diem in hopes that his government would provide them with outright financial support or, alternatively, integrate their troops into the national army and assume responsibility for paying and equipping them.

For two principle reasons, Ngo Dinh Diem proved unreceptive to these appeals. Quite simply, the prime minister lacked discretion over his own budget, which the United States supplied and therefore largely controlled.[10]

A reduction in French and American aid following the 1954 cease-fire made it necessary to cut the size of the existing army by more than half, a reality that severely hampered Ngo Dinh Diem's ability to integrate politico-religious troops.[11] More important, the Ngo brothers' approach to leadership precluded tolerance of what their French and American advisors called "loyal opposition" parties.[12] As would become increasingly evident in the coming years, Ngo Dinh Diem and Ngo Dinh Nhu strove to establish themselves as the sole stewards of a highly centralized government rooted in consensus and unconstrained by dissent. The brothers considered the vitiation of politico-religious influence to be an essential precursor to their broader goal of consolidating power by breaking free from Bao Dai's oversight, eliminating French influence in South Vietnam, and eventually subordinating all non-communist nationalist groups to a single government-sponsored party.[13]

Ngo Dinh Diem's virulently anti-French position was common knowledge by the time he came to power over South Vietnam. While in office, he came to believe that France was colluding with his enemies to remove him from power.[14] And this was not simply paranoid thinking. After signing the cease-fire agreement, France retained a strong presence south of Vietnam's seventeenth parallel, indirectly through its connections with Bao Dai and the politico-religious groups, and directly via several thousand French troops still stationed there. French officials in Paris and Saigon made no secret of their doubts about Ngo Dinh Diem's leadership abilities, claiming that he was too insular, too naïve, and temperamentally unsuited to the task of unifying and rebuilding war torn Vietnam. They also bristled at his past record of anti-French activity, and made clear their preference for a government run by Bao Dai, through whom they could continue to protect French political and economic interests in Vietnam. In fall 1954, during Ngo Dinh Diem's showdown with national army general Nguyen Van Hinh, French leaders made no secret of their desire to see the prime minister replaced. To prevent his own ouster, then, Ngo Dinh Diem set out to neutralize French influence in Saigon during his first year in office. Conquering Hoa Hao, Cao Dai, and Binh Xuyen challengers to his rule was but the first step in this process.

In early 1955 Ngo Dinh Diem took a number of steps designed to put an end to French meddling and to consolidate his own power by neutralizing intransigent politico-religious factions.[15] American special representative J. Lawton Collins agreed that it would be essential to do so, noting in January that the Cao Dai, Hoa Hao, and Binh Xuyen "have an effective veto power over government action. This power they use to block reforms which might threaten their preferred military, economic and political status."[16] Since taking power, Diem had pursued the goal of neutralizing these groups on a limited basis, with the help of General Edward Lansdale and U.S. government funds, by bribing certain politico-religious factions to join the national army.[17] Although the South Vietnamese government possessed neither the means nor the will to integrate the entire Hoa Hao and Cao Dai militaries into the national army, Ngo Dinh Diem aimed to draw "dissident" leaders away from the main forces in hopes of weakening politico-religious armies as a whole.

The prime minister stepped up his efforts at dividing and conquering these organizations in early January 1955, when he announced his intention to nationalize the Binh Xuyen owned and operated Saigon-Cholon police and security agency. He threatened to remove Binh Xuyen police chief Lai Van Sang from his post by February 1, although the ensuing stand-off would delay him from doing so until late April.[18] Shortly thereafter he further antagonized the Binh Xuyen by refusing to renew its license to operate the profitable Grand Monde Casino in Cholon.[19] Ngo Dinh Diem's crackdown served a troubling warning to all politico-religious leaders that he was prepared to risk confrontation rather than accommodate their existing power. In the short term this provoked hostility from the leaders of all three groups and bound them together in defiance against his government.[20]

Aside from the unreliable and potentially disloyal national army, support for Ngo Dinh Diem's government against these organizations came solely from the American government. France, of course, made clear its dissatisfaction with Ngo Dinh Diem's leadership and persistently tried to convince Washington to consider alternatives. Although Paris had reluctantly agreed to support Ngo Dinh Diem for the time being, Dulles and Eisenhower suspected that the French continued to undermine his regime whenever possible. Meanwhile, the United States remained committed to supporting the prime minister, but it was by no means confident that the limited backing it was prepared to give would prove enough to keep him in power in the event of a full-fledged politico-religious rebellion.[21] It was to find out whether this backing would be sufficient as the open clash between Ngo Dinh Diem and the politico-religious coalition to decide the future of South Vietnam's government came to a head with the formation of the United Front of Nationalist Forces (Mat Tran Thong Nhut Toan Luc Quoc Gia) on March 3, 1955.[22]

The Crisis Begins

Cao Dai pope Pham Cong Tac held a press conference the afternoon of March 4 to announce the front's existence and to publicize its intentions. He claimed that Ngo Dinh Diem had placed Vietnam in peril of communist conquest and vowed that despite the fragmentary nature of nationalist forces, front signatories would put aside their personal ideological differences in order to unite all of the country's noncommunist political and military forces under one effective leadership. The proclamation outlined front objectives as the defense of Vietnam, national independence and the protection of individual sovereignty, and the right to individual political participation. Politico-religious leaders pledged that once such a nationalist government was established, they would put their armed forces at its disposal to make Vietnam "a vanguard fighting unit of anti-communists in Southeast Asia."[23]

In a clear reference to Ngo Dinh Diem, the front denounced "dictatorship and sectarian policy which would provoke fratricidal war and cause [the] collapse of [the] nationalist cause." Pham Cong Tac insisted on behalf of the front that the prime minister's government apply its recommended program, but he said little about what that program entailed or what the consequences would be should Ngo Dinh Diem defy this pronouncement. Washington, already committed to Ngo Dinh Diem as the leader of "Free Vietnam," saw the United Front as a destabilizing element below the seventeenth parallel. At this time, however, both French and American observers perceived the politico-religious threat to be political and not military.

It is important to note that while the United Front represented leaders from all three organizations, not all of the most powerful generals endorsed the March 4 ultimatum. Hoa Hao generals Tran Van Soai, Lam Thanh Nguyen, and Ba Cut, Binh Xuyen leader Bay Vien, and Cao Dai pope Pham Cong Tac signed the pronouncement. But the signatures of several politico-religious generals who had recently rallied their troops to the national army were conspicuously absent from the document. This included both major Cao Dai generals Trinh Minh The and Nguyen Thanh Phuong, and the predominant Hoa Hao Generals Nguyen Giac Ngo and Nguyen Van Hue. Given the politico-religious organizations' strategy of playing powerful groups off one another, this did not necessarily represent a repudiation of the front's anti–Ngo Dinh Diem stance, but simply a refusal to align openly with the new organization. In fact, days later Hoa Hao major Nam, an emissary of Tran Van Soai, presented American officials with an earlier draft of the proclamation containing the signatures of Nguyen Thanh Phuong and Trinh Minh The, although he admitted that Nguyen Giac Ngo had refused all along to join the front.[24] Major Nam claimed that Nguyen Thanh Phuong and Trinh Minh The had joined the organization but requested that this fact be kept secret, as they "still had some business to do with the government." Some observers, including General Fernand Gambiez, commander of French forces in South Vietnam, suspected that the dissident politico-religious forces that had recently joined Ngo Dinh Diem's government and been integrated into the national army actually maintained covert loyalty to their respective organizations. He alleged that they were scheming to gain a preponderant representation in the armed forces in order to weaken the current government's defenses from within and would return to fight with the United Front in the event of armed conflict.[25]

American, French, and South Vietnamese officials recognized the increasing volatility of the political situation in Saigon and the likelihood of a violent crisis in the near future should Ngo Dinh Diem fail to manage the politico-religious threat diplomatically. But they almost uniformly discounted the possibility of an immediate uprising.[26] In the days following March 4, Collins and his French counterpart, Commissioner General Paul Ely, came to the cautious conclusion that the United Front was unlikely to take any violent action to back its declaration. In fact, observers in the CIA concluded that the front's decision to publicize its plans reflected the weakening position of the politico-religious groups in relation to the government. "The sects," according to a CIA report, "can be expected to explore every opportunity to check the growth of central government authority at the expense of their own, but they are probably realistic enough not to seek a forcible showdown."[27] On the contrary, U.S. officials perceived the United Front pronouncement as an instrument of blackmail designed to induce Ngo Dinh Diem to hasten the integration of politico-religious forces into the national army and to increase payments to the organizations' military leaders.

Ngo Dinh Diem accused the French of inciting the Hoa Hao, Cao Dai, and Binh Xuyen to found the United Front as part of a larger plan to overthrow his regime and replace him with Bay Vien.[28] While some French agents in Saigon did support Binh Xuyen activities, French policy was not aimed at facilitating Bay Vien's rise to power in Ngo Dinh Diem's stead.[29] Nonetheless, the prime minister insisted that opposing the supposed Franco–Binh Xuyen plot was the only way to free Vietnam from

French colonial bondage. Although determined to put down politico-religious affronts vigorously, he initially responded to nonmilitary United Front demands. In mid-March, CIA officials noted that his main tactic was to continue plying select politico-religious generals with lavish bribes rather than threatening the United Front with force.[30] Although he worried that politico-religious leaders might use his own funds to wage war against him, Ngo Dinh Diem attempted to placate willing collaborators by assuming responsibility for a portion of the support payments halted by the French in January.[31] Rather than trying to lure away the principle Hoa Hao faction led by Tran Van Soai or make concession to the Cao Dai spiritual leader Pham Cong Tac, he aimed to generate internal divisions within each organization by luring away "dissident" leaders with smaller followings. "By such means," ventured the CIA, "[Diem] hopes to weaken the sects as a whole to the extent that a military solution would be feasible."[32] He encountered some success with this approach, convincing a handful of minor politico-religious generals to rally to the government in the days after March 4.[33] But the prime minister's attempt to finesse the situation through bribery was not enough to force the front to back down.

On the afternoon of March 21, the United Front raised its threat against the southern government to a higher level. Pham Cong Tac issued a critique of Ngo Dinh Diem's leadership, claiming that "after nine months in power Diem has not been able to realize any program while [the] Vietnamese people are confused and communist forces continue [to] advance."[34] The front further attacked the prime minister's character, blaming him for obstructing unification movements deliberately in order to keep the public divided for his own personal advantage, and accusing him of governing through nepotism and favoritism with disastrous consequences for the nation. As for broader failures of the administration, the front claimed that refugee resettlement from north to south was tainted with odious favoritism, that government censorship of the press had prevented the media from fulfilling its role of guiding public opinion, and that the total control that the government exerted over the provisional assembly had rendered it entirely unresponsive to the will of the people.[35]

Pham Cong Tac concluded that "Diem, by his errors, has maintained his unpopular and ineffective policy ... which is leading the country inevitably into communist slavery." He issued an ultimatum demanding that the prime minister reorganize his government completely within five days or the United Front of Nationalist Forces would "appeal to the people for [a] decision." The declaration itself did not indicate specifically what actions the United Front was prepared to take in the face of Ngo Dinh Diem's noncompliance, but press reports indicated that some members of the coalition had hinted at an imminent attempt to overthrow the southern government. Binh Xuyen general Bay Vien openly vowed to use force to topple Ngo Dinh Diem's administration if the prime minister failed to reorganize his government immediately.[36]

Arguably, the March 4 and March 21 moves by the politico-religious organizations to publicize their discontent were above all for international political consumption. According to the French interpretation of events, "Not only do the sects wish Diem to come to terms, but [they] want [the] French and [the] US to realize that they exist and are important."[37] United Front rhetoric was at least partially directed toward the United States, to feel out American receptivity to an alternative South Vietnamese government in place of Ngo Dinh Diem's. The front's firm anticommunist stance sent a clear message to the United States that Washington's objective of preventing the spread of communism in Southeast Asia could be better achieved under an alternative nationalist government that included politico-religious representatives than by the current administration.

The American response to these overtures from the United Front was definitive and unfavorable. Immediately after the March 21 ultimatum, Collins met with Cao Dai generals Trinh Minh The and Nguyen Thanh Phuong to inform them and their allies that "any successful attempt by [the] sects to overthrow [the] government would probably lead to [the] cessation of all American aid."[38] The United States certainly was concerned by the growing state of crisis in Saigon but was not prepared to sanction the violent overthrow of its ally.

Collins chose to approach the United Front through Trinh Minh The and Nguyen Thanh Phuong for a number of reasons. The United States already had contacts with them, primarily due to Edward Lansdale's efforts to recruit them away from their parent organizations and into an alliance with Ngo Dinh Diem and the national army. Moreover, as recent allies of Ngo Dinh Diem's administration, they were the most likely of the politico-religious leaders to feel some remaining allegiance toward the existing government, or at least ambivalence about the United Front.[39] Aside from the increasing urgency of the situation generated by the five-day deadline, Collins's greatest concern over the March 21 declaration was that, unlike the first pronouncement, it bore the signatures of Trinh Minh The and Nguyen Thanh Phuong. "For the first time," Collins wrote to Dulles, "[the] United Front had managed to gain [the] public adherence of almost all significant elements of [the] sect groups."[40] Trinh Minh The's defection, in particular, dealt a serious blow to Ngo Dinh Diem, who had been relying heavily on the Cao Dai dissident and his troops to safeguard against Hoa Hao and Binh Xuyen forces in the area surrounding Saigon-Cholon.[41] Therefore, Collins wished to speak with Trinh Minh The and Nguyen Thanh Phuong directly in order to better understand the nature of the United Front and the extent of the threat it posed to Ngo Dinh Diem.

Despite their growing pessimism, American and French officials still deemed armed politico-religious activity unlikely and predicted that the front would continue to restrict its activity to the political and economic spheres. Ngo Dinh Diem, they agreed, could not cede to politico-religious demands without losing face but must continue to negotiate and buy time for the tenuous coalition to crumble from within.[42] Meanwhile, Collins felt it was necessary for the prime minister to issue some sort of tactful response to the United Front ultimatum that would neither alienate the front nor dignify its complaints.

Collins grew increasing frustrated by his inability to clarify politico-religious demands sufficiently to aid Ngo Dinh Diem in formulating an adequate reply. After his March 22 meeting with Nguyen Thanh Phuong and Trinh Minh The, Collins vented to Dulles that "discussing this problem with these generals was like trying to reason with two stubborn four year old children. They were either lying very ineptly or they are alarmingly stupid considering the influence and power they wield." He concluded, "Trying to determine from them exactly what they wanted was completely futile. I am convinced that their evasive answers to my questions were clumsy attempts to cover selfish motives."[43]

Collins failed to see that his frustrations stemmed neither from ineptitude nor stupidity on the part of the generals, but rather from their cunning, intentionally noncommittal political strategy. By making vague overtures to all sides while refusing to commit wholeheartedly to any, politico-religious leaders were able to lull American, French, and South Vietnamese officials alike into positions of defensiveness and indecision. The fragmentary nature of the politico-religious organizations only added to their advantage, as the United Front could make alliance overtures to Ngo Dinh Diem, the United States, France, and the Viet Minh simultaneously through different factions, all the while maintaining the unified objective of preserving and perhaps enhancing each organization's autonomy and power. Such an approach was typical of the politico-religious groups, which one Vietnam expert has described as "devious collaborators" due to their many divisions and frequent changes in tactics dating back to the mid-1940s.[44] Although frustratingly unpredictable, the United Front intentionally sought to manipulate the political environment to its advantage without committing irrevocably to any one side.[45]

Collins's inability to pin down a clear set of politico-religious objectives was only one of many obstacles emerging to prevent him from achieving his goals of fortifying Ngo Dinh Diem's government and ensuring its survival. Following the second United Front declaration, a noticeable rift began to emerge between France and the United States over how best to respond to the developing crisis. France had been looking for an excuse to call the "Diem experiment" a failure since the prime minister took office in July 1954, and its low regard for his leadership clashed with the American desire to see Ngo Dinh Diem succeed at any cost. Dulles chafed at the French tendency to put the politico-religious organizations on an equal plane with the prime minister owing to their actual military and political power. According to the secretary, the United States viewed these groups as rebels and therefore deemed them unworthy of serious consideration by Ngo Dinh Diem's legitimate government, regardless of whatever strength they might have displayed.[46]

Another point of Franco-American disagreement stemmed from Washington's determination that the crisis should be resolved without involving Bao Dai. Dulles claimed that to do so would undermine Ngo Dinh Diem's authority and hamper his ability to rule after the crisis was resolved. Contrary to Dulles's wishes, French officials in Saigon sent a telegram to diplomats in Paris recommending that they consider making arrangements for Bao Dai to return to Vietnam. Even Ely, Collins's staunchest collaborator amongst the French, concluded that no real settlement could be reached between Ngo Dinh Diem and the politico-religious groups without involving Bao Dai.[47] France's insistence on involving the absentee chief of state only fueled Washington's suspicions that its obstinate ally was out to sabotage Ngo Dinh Diem's government. Ensuing events quickly intensified the conflict of interests between France and the United States, but the prospect of a total collapse of the South Vietnamese government—an eventuality anathema to both powers—forced them to grapple with their differences and continue to seek a joint solution to the crisis.

In the days following the second United Front ultimatum it became increasingly clear that the Hoa Hao, Cao Dai, and Binh Xuyen were entrenched in their position of defiance against Ngo Dinh Diem's administration. South Vietnamese defense minister Ho Thong Minh lamented that the break between the prime minister and the politico-religious organizations was now complete and irreparable. He blamed Ngo Dinh Diem for failing to prevent the crisis, as he might have done by taking a more sensitive tack toward politico-religious leaders early in his administration. Moreover, he predicted that even if the prime minister did succeed in winning back some of the organizations' factions, the damage had already been done, and the atmosphere of suspicion and distrust could not be unraveled.[48]

Ngo Dinh Diem, although avowedly resigned to the likelihood of an imminent attack on his government, made some superficial efforts to negotiate with politico-religious leaders, welcoming them to attend the March 22 cabinet meeting and inviting them to his palace for consultations on multiple occasions. Although they did send emissaries, whom the prime minister reportedly received quite rudely, none of the politico-religious leaders appeared for talks, perhaps because they feared for their lives. On March 25, right before the ultimatum was due to expire, Ngo Dinh Diem requested one last time that United Front leaders visit him to discuss their grievances. That night, Bao Dai sent a message to the United Front and the prime minister urging both parties to seek a compromise solution.[49] However, the front remained confident of Bao Dai's support, and the following day it spurned Ngo Dinh Diem's invitation, reiterating its ultimatum and insisting that he accept the principle of reshuffling his government before the politico-religious groups would bring forth a definite program for consideration. It indicated that front members would continue to refuse further discussions until the prime minister agreed to its preliminary terms.[50]

On the night of March 27, Trinh Minh The defected from the front to rejoin the ranks of the national army, most likely in response to a substantial bribe.[51] This weakened the Cao Dai bloc and decreased the likelihood of the organization participating in an antigovernmental uprising, although Cao Dai spokesmen led by Pham Cong Tac continued to criticize Ngo Dinh Diem for his insularity and antidemocratic practices. Meanwhile, Hoa Hao and Binh Xuyen forces remained strong and entrenched in their positions against the prime minister. The Hoa Hao continued to use its control over river traffic in the Mekong Delta to hold up food supplies destined for Saigon-Cholon while Binh Xuyen forces buttressed themselves in the police headquarters and in other strategic locations around the capital. Both were determined to resist the prime minister's efforts to destroy their organizations bit by bit.

Ngo Dinh Diem was incensed by this intransigent behavior and refused to yield to pressure from the United Front. He disregarded Bao Dai's

March 25 appeal for unity between the government and the United Front, and on March 27 sent a letter to front leaders detailing the occasions on which he had invited them for consultations only to be refused. He accused the politico-religious organizations of driving South Vietnam into communist arms through their selfish pursuit of power and the protection of special positions. According to the prime minister, politico-religious military activities only weakened the national spirit and endangered the citizenry, and thus could not be considered patriotic.[52] He maintained that the only reasonable solution to the current problem was to form an impartial cabinet comprised of virtuous individuals interested solely in serving the will of the nation and the people of Vietnam. Needless to say, this would not include his politico-religious opponents.

While Ngo Dinh Diem claimed he was willing to cooperate, or at least communicate, with politico-religious leaders, he took additional steps to exacerbate the conflict between his government and the Binh Xuyen. On March 26 he attempted to give teeth to his January threat to replace the Binh Xuyen police chief by issuing a decree to establish a separate Saigon-Cholon prefectural police under which the existing municipal police was eventually to be transferred.[53] Bay Vien responded by notifying French officials that Binh Xuyen leaders not only desired a new government, but that they wanted Ngo Dinh Diem out of the picture completely. The Binh Xuyen general was emboldened by his belief that the United States was too invested in preserving South Vietnam as a noncommunist bastion to follow through on its threat to withdraw American aid in the event of a coup against the current government. Furthermore, France's refusal to commit its forces to fight against Ngo Dinh Diem's enemies gave Binh Xuyen leaders great confidence that a coup would succeed.[54]

Several members of the southern administration seemed to agree with Bay Vien's assessment. On March 29, Defense Minister Ho Thong Minh tendered his resignation upon learning that Ngo Dinh Diem had developed concrete plans to replace Binh Xuyen police chief Lai Van Sang with Colonel Nguyen Ngoc Le. Ho Thong Minh claimed that such a move would invite an open clash with the government's politico-religious adversaries, which government forces were likely to lose.[55] Collins agreed with Ho Thong Minh's assessment and notified Ngo Dinh Diem "that in my opinion he had succeeded in outmaneuvering sects to the present but was now risking open strife with them. I warned him that without Minh he might not secure loyal support of Army."[56] Some American intelligence officers were less sympathetic to Ho Thong Minh's criticisms and perceived them as evidence that he was colluding with the United Front and would rather resign his post than fire on the Binh Xuyen if ordered to do so.[57] Despite these suspicions, Collins and Ely pressured Ngo Dinh Diem to reinstate the defense minister in the coming days, in hopes that he could influence the southern leader to broaden his government and temper his response to the United Front.[58]

At exactly midnight on March 30, rifle and machine-gun fire broke out between Binh Xuyen and national army troops around the police prefectural building in Cholon. It is unclear who initiated the clash, although the southern government's forces had been harassing the Binh Xuyen for days leading up to the fight.[59] The national army quickly gained the upper hand, with assistance from twenty thousand French troops deployed throughout Saigon to separate the combatants, and the fighting ceased around 4:30 a.m.[60] Some American officials would later charge that French forces prevented the national government from wiping out the Binh Xuyen at this time by withholding fuel and critical supplies.[61] Ngo Dinh Diem went even further, claiming that it was the French who incited the Binh Xuyen to violence in the first place.[62] The prime minister's virulently anti-French attitude and Washington's increasing distrust of France's motives came to play an ever more dominant role in the sect crisis in the coming weeks.

The violence on March 29–30 further inflamed the conflict between French and American officials over Vietnam policy. This may have reflected the prime minister's strategy, as Ely warned Collins, "Diem would . . . no doubt try to drive a wedge between France and U.S."[63] Dulles and his underlings in the State Department believed that Ngo Dinh Diem should be allowed to reestablish his authority in Saigon with full support and no restrictions. French officials, however, maintained that the prime minister's continued leadership could provoke widespread conflict and insisted that his eventual replacement had become inevitable.[64] Moreover, the secretary of state and his colleagues in Washington continued to rankle at what they saw as French insistence on treating the southern government and the rebellious politico-religious organizations as political equals.[65] The Americans considered it a travesty that an established leader was forced to negotiate and sign truces with what they viewed as groups of illegal bandits.

Collins's Break with Ngo Dinh Diem

In many respects, Collins agreed with the overall French position rather than embracing Washington's line. Ely recognized this and seized the opportunity to use his longtime acquaintance Collins as a conduit to convince Dulles and the State Department of the urgent need to replace Ngo Dinh Diem.[66] One American journalist sympathetic to Ngo Dinh Diem has even gone so far as to write that, during this time, "Collins became engaged in what can only be described as plotting in collusion with the French."[67] Although this statement is hyperbolic, Collins often did concur with French assessments and, in spite of the widening gap between their governments, Collins and Ely maintained a cooperative relationship in Saigon throughout the sect crisis.

On the afternoon of March 30, once the fighting had died down, Ely reported to Collins that Ngo Dinh Diem had finally promised not to use force to take over the headquarters of the national police and security agency, although he continued to insist on dismissing Lai Van Sang immediately despite French and American advice to the contrary.[68] For the time being, though, Ely had secured a fragile truce between the prime minister and the Binh Xuyen that would hold up for almost a month.[69] After Ely left Ngo Dinh Diem that afternoon, Collins paid the prime minister a visit to warn him that he was making it very difficult for the U.S. Embassy to continue supporting his government. "If he continued his present course," Collins noted, "we would be under heavy pressure to support a change in the government."[70]

The very next day, Collins cabled Dulles a telegram insisting that the time had come for the United States to consider possible alternatives to continuing support for Ngo Dinh Diem. "In light of recent developments," he wrote, "we must now squarely face [the] fact that Diem is operating practically [a] one-man government with his two brothers Luyen and Nhu as [his] principle advisors. I seriously doubt this can last long."[71] He explained that the prime minister was almost entirely isolated as a result of recent resignations by four Hoa Hao ministers, defense minister Ho Thong Minh, and four Cao Dai members of government. These Cao Dai representatives resigned on March 30 despite the integration of Nguyen Thanh Phuong's Cao Dai forces into the national army that took place the very same day.[72] About this seeming contradiction, Collins remarked with exasperation, "Please don't expect me to explain this gobble-de-gook!" When Nguyen Thanh Phuong returned to join the national army, U.S. intelligence officers concluded, "The permanence of any single rallié is dubious and probably depends on the amount of his subsidy and his estimate of Diem's power position."[73] Nguyen Thanh Phuong and Trinh Minh The's rallying of Cao Dai troops to the national army certainly was not a marker of total loyalty to Ngo Dinh Diem's government. On the contrary, the emerging international consensus by the end of March 1955 was that the prime minister had burned his final bridges to reconciliation with the United Front, and his administration, by all accounts, teetered on the brink of collapse.

By the end of March, Collins concluded that Ngo Dinh Diem had been given more than a fair chance to establish an effective government, but that he had accumulated little or no positive achievements during his brief administration. "We have found it necessary," he claimed, "to assist him in proposing, drafting, and attempting to breathe life into most of his programs." Collins insisted that France and the United States had consistently maintained positive efforts to help the prime minister, but that the he had failed to capitalize on the support. Collins therefore placed the blame for South Vietnamese government failures fully on Ngo Dinh Diem's shoulders.

Having made the leap to suggest that the prime minister be replaced, Collins provided Dulles with a few brief suggestions for possible leadership alternatives. These included a familiar litany of options that the French had proposed on several occasions during Ngo Dinh Diem's first ten months in office: a new government to be formed with Tran Van Do or Phan Huy Quat as president, the return of Bao Dai to preside over a new government to be led by Ngo Dinh Diem, or the return of Bao Dai to assume the presidency of an entirely new government. Although the problem of the politico-religious organizations would remain the primary obstacle for any new government, Collins believed it was essential to break the present impasse immediately if there was to be any hope of preserving an independent noncommunist South Vietnam. His suggestions to include Bao Dai in the solution clearly reflected Ely's influence, and this overt nod to French preferences may have prejudiced Washington against his recommendations.

Dulles rejected Collins's appeal immediately. "We do not think a switch would be desirable or practicable at [the] present time," he wrote the very next day. "We doubt that there is any acceptable alternative which we could back on the scale necessary for success."[74] The secretary authorized Collins to convey frankly to Ngo Dinh Diem that, unless he could greatly improve his administration, the United States would be forced to withdraw its support for Vietnam, which would jeopardize not only the current southern government, but would place the entire nation at risk of falling under communist control. But for the time being, replacing the premier remained out of the question for Washington officials. One U.S. intelligence report concluded, incorrectly, that the politico-religious organizations were "primarily the creation of the French," and predicted that "if . . . Diem resigns or is removed during this crisis, many Vietnamese will almost certainly conclude that the French are still the arbiters of political action in South Vietnam."[75] Indeed, Dulles and his staff perceived Bao Dai as a symbol of French power in Vietnam and Ngo Dinh Diem as a symbol of American influence. To U.S. policymakers, then, Ngo Dinh Diem's replacement by Bao Dai would represent a blatant diplomatic defeat for the United States and a victory for France.[76]

As France and the United States debated his removal, Ngo Dinh Diem and his small band of supporters attempted to validate Washington's support, and stake out the public position that his government represented the best possibility for democracy in Vietnam. The United Front's demands on the government, conversely, reflected an attempt by minority groups to impede mass political participation. An article in the progovernment daily *Thoi Luan* (Commentary) exhorted, "There is no individual and no group that has the particular right to determine state affairs."[77] Author Nguyen Van An invoked the memory of Louis XVI to remind readers of the treacherous fate reserved for individuals who sacrifice the rights of the many for the privileges of the few. His clear implication was that Ngo Dinh Diem represented the Vietnamese masses, while the politico-religious groups promoted selfish private interests.

Another article attributed to Cao Dai general Nguyen Thanh Phuong, but likely orchestrated by the southern government, condemned the United Front as an opportunistic ploy stemming naturally from the unstable political situation following the Geneva accords.[78] He asserted that the front was not the indigenous political movement that it claimed to be, but the result of sedition on the part of French colonialists who could not admit defeat. Nguyen Thanh Phuong explained that his Cao Dai army had decided to rally to the national army in order to avoid spilling any more Vietnamese blood on French initiative. Although the current government may not have been ideal, he claimed, it represented Vietnam's best prospect for peace and true independence. This sort of patriotic sentiment appeared often in the South Vietnamese press; expressed in a particular kind of clichéd language, it strongly suggests it was penned by government propagandists and adopted by prominent political figures like Nguyen Thanh Phuong under pressure from Ngo Dinh Diem's administration.

The prime minister's righteous indignation coincided with the sentiments expressed in the above articles and drove him to frustrate already tense Franco-American efforts to forestall a greater crisis in South Vietnam. He clung to his resolve to use force if necessary to wrest control of the national police and security agency from the Binh Xuyen. Ngo Dinh Diem justified his position with claims that the people of Vietnam did not understand his delay in removing Lai Van Sang as chief of police and asserting governmental authority, and that failing to exert military muscle at this critical moment would damage his government's reputation, perhaps irreparably. Ngo Dinh Diem's conviction that the Binh Xuyen was acting under French direction in an effort to undermine his government drove him to take firm, immediate steps to challenge the organization's power and influence in Saigon-Cholon.[79]

Meanwhile, American and French officials alike believed that Ngo Dinh Diem's belligerent approach to the Binh Xuyen was tantamount to suicide. They judged that the national army, even if joined by the French, would be capable only of solving the problem in Saigon, and that "those Binh Xuyen elements not smashed would go underground, fall under Viet Minh influence . . . and form [the] nucleus of [an] anti-government force in [a] civil war." International observers feared that even capturing and killing politico-religious chiefs such as Bay Vien would have little effect, as they would simply be martyred and replaced from the ranks of politico-religious armies. The United States agreed with Ngo Dinh Diem that control of the police should be removed from the hands of the Binh Xuyen and nationalized, but insisted that it must be done gradually through negotiations and legitimate channels of power, possibly including an official decree from Bao Dai. By April 6, though, both Ely and Collins concurred that despite American and French pleas for moderation, "Diem [was] determined to take over control of [the] Police without regard to consequences."[80]

Ely and Collins also fretted over Ngo Dinh Diem's increasing political isolation and his dogged unwillingness to broaden his cabinet and consider the input of individuals outside his immediate family and a dwindling number of close advisers. As Vietnam expert Joseph Buttinger put it, the prime minister "no longer had a government, not even as window dressing."[81] On the evening of April 6, Ely noted in his diary that he had changed his thinking on the "Diem question." Up to that point, he was willing to consider retaining Ngo Dinh Diem in a coalition government for the sake of Franco-American cooperation. But he had come to believe that the prime minister must go and decided to increase pressure on the United States to abandon the prime minister and appeal to Bao Dai to salvage Saigon from the brink of civil war.[82] On April 7, Ely warned Collins that "Diem can no longer be saved except at [the] cost of overcoming enormous difficulties, and if he is saved, we shall have spared for Vietnam the worst Prime

Minister it ever had."[83] He insisted that an alternative leader, and Bao Dai's involvement, was desperately needed to carry out major reforms and to prepare for the 1956 nationwide elections mandated by the Geneva agreements if South Vietnam was to have any chance of remaining outside the communist sphere.

Collins dutifully toed the official American line, responding to Ely that "we have not gone far enough in our support of Diem to make a change acceptable now."[84] But he turned around immediately to pen another request for Dulles to consider replacing what he had come to regard as the utterly incompetent Ngo Dinh Diem. "His lack of practical political sense," wrote Collins, "his inability to compromise, his inherent incapacity to get along with other able men, and his tendency to be suspicious of the motives of anyone who disagrees with him, make him practically incapable of holding this government together."[85] Collins assured Dulles that Ngo Dinh Diem was by no means indispensable to America's goal of preventing a communist takeover of South Vietnam. He reiterated his argument from a few days before; that the United States should refrain from adopting too rigid a stance in support of the current government against all other alternatives, since such a position would allow no room for maneuver in the event that a change in South Vietnamese leadership became absolutely necessary.[86]

A Last Ditch Search for Alternatives

On April 9, Dulles replied to Collins's telegram with the first indication that he was willing to consider replacing Ngo Dinh Diem, albeit grudgingly.[87] The secretary claimed that Washington was disposed to back Collins's final decision, but that he should consider a number of factors before reaching any conclusions. First, Dulles questioned whether any of the prime minister's potential successors would have any greater success at handling the sect crisis than Ngo Dinh Diem. Second, he advised Collins to consider the effects on American prestige should the southern administration fail. "It is widely known," wrote Dulles, "that Diem has so far existed by reason of US support despite French reluctance. If, however, when the showdown comes the French view prevails then that will gravely weaken our influence for the future both in Vietnam and elsewhere."[88] Thereafter, the secretary feared, any successor to Ngo Dinh Diem would know that the real authority rested with the French and not the Americans.[89] Moreover, Washington's Cold

War allies throughout the world might lose confidence in the United States. Last, perhaps the most important factor militating against a U.S. decision to replace the prime minister was the force of American domestic politics. Dulles reminded Collins that Congress would be likely to oppose continuing its economic support for Vietnam if Ngo Dinh Diem's government was replaced under the current circumstances. Indeed, Mike Mansfield (D-Montana), one of Ngo Dinh Diem's most vocal supporters in the Senate, had recently responded to Collins's report on the prime minister's failure by insisting that the United States continue to back him to the very end. According to Mansfield and the "Vietnam lobby," anything less would serve to hand all of Vietnam over to Ho Chi Minh and the Communist Party.[90]

Despite their grave concerns, policymakers in Washington seemed to be coming around to the necessity of regime change in Saigon. On April 11, Dulles considered authorizing Collins to acquiesce in plans to replace Ngo Dinh Diem but decided to delay this move after a last-minute meeting with his staff. Instead the secretary plied Collins for specific information on the timing of the proposed change and the political implications of a new government. "We do not," he asserted, "wish to make a commitment in principle on replacement before we are certain [a] candidate acceptable to us can be agreed upon."[91]

On April 12, Dulles delivered to the Quay d'Orsay a questionnaire asking the French to clarify their intentions regarding whom would replace Ngo Dinh Diem, when the succession would occur, what would be the fate of the Saigon police force, and how France intended to guarantee politico-religious support for the new government.[92] French officials chaffed at this request, which seemed like little more than a delay tactic, and grew more frustrated the next day when Washington made clear that it had intentions neither of participating in planning Ngo Dinh Diem's ouster nor in naming his successors. In his instructions to U.S. diplomats in Paris and Saigon, Dulles noted, "We have recognized [the] . . . French proposal that the US agree to join with [the] French in discussing replacing Diem. We wish to preserve this perspective and avoid [the] issue being described as arising out of US initiative."[93] Dulles insisted that the French must first set a plan before the United States would consider whether or not to support it.[94] Dulles's position placed the full burden of South Vietnam's future on France's shoulders. In the event that Ngo Dinh Diem's government failed, Paris would be accountable for the success or failure of his successor.[95]

French officials, of course, resented Dulles's insistence on saddling them with all of the responsibility for making essential decisions about South

Vietnam's future, much less bearing sole liability for their consequences. United States Ambassador to Paris Douglas Dillon met with French diplomats on April 16 to discuss the crisis, only to face French apprehension over "the apparent lack of desire on the part of the US to seek [a] solution [to the] crisis [in] Saigon within [the] Franco-American context."[96] According to the French, the U.S. position in this instance seemed to represent a blatant departure from the established principle of Franco-American cooperation over all Indochina matters, and a break from the policy of both parties to avoid unilateral action. Ely conveyed to Collins on April 19 that, due to Washington's unyielding position, the French government had decided to withhold specific names of potential prime ministers and cabinet members in order to prevent the United States from manipulating the eventual solution to appear unilaterally French.[97]

Although neither side was willing to endorse any specific candidates or outline a concrete blueprint for a new South Vietnamese government, both the French and the Americans generally agreed on the available options, limited though they were. By this time, virtually all notable political actors in Saigon had concluded that Ngo Dinh Diem's leadership mandate had expired, that he would be unable to convince able men to join his cabinet, and that his government would thus be incapable of resolving the present crisis. One of the prime minister's former cabinet ministers, Nguyen Van Thoai, outlined a proposal for a South Vietnamese interim government which both French and American diplomats supported. He suggested that he, Phan Huy Quat, Tran Van Do, Ho Thong Minh, Tran Van Van, and other Vietnamese figures with reasonable nationalist credentials form a provisional coalition government under Ngo Dinh Diem, most likely with Phan Huy Quat eventually assuming the role of prime minister.[98] Phan Huy Quat and a number of other names floated about had connections to the Dai Viet Party and had served in various SVN cabinets since the government's formation in 1949. Some, like Phan Huy Quat and Tran Van Do, had become disillusioned with the prime minister as they served in his government, and they would continue to oppose Ngo Dinh Diem's oppressive, insular ways long after this crisis was over.[99] Nguyen Van Thoai suggested that a provisional assembly be formed once a coalition of these individuals took power to assist the interim government in establishing a permanent regime.

The advantage of this plan, as French and American officials perceived it, was that Vietnamese figures had developed and proposed it all of their own accord.[100] But its success was contingent on Ngo Dinh Diem's acceptance as well as the concurrence of those politicians expected to constitute the new cabinet. Tran Van Do, Ho Thong Minh, Phan Huy Quat, and Tran Van Van told Collins on April 19 that they were unlikely to risk participating in such an interim government since Ngo Dinh Diem had so entirely lost the support of the country and proven that he was incapable of change. They remarked that Nguyen Van Thoai's solution had been "overtaken by events" and that any resolution to the crisis gripping Saigon would have to begin with removing Ngo Dinh Diem from power.[101]

The prime minister was nearly as sour on the idea of working with these men as they were on the prospect of laboring under him. He told Collins that the proposed cabinet members were "men from small opposition parties who only represent a handful of people [and were not] in accord with the principle of having the great majority of the people represented in the government."[102] However, he claimed to be in favor of a coalition, in theory, if it were geared toward including all citizens in Vietnam's political life. With this goal in mind, he suggested that his government organize a general election in three or four months to select a national assembly charged with determining South Vietnam's political future. Meanwhile, he asserted his right to use military pressure to defend the country against what he regarded as the villainous triad of communism, feudalism, and colonialism. He described his crusade against the Binh Xuyen and its allies as an essential move against all three of these evils, since he regarded the politico-religious organizations as feudalistic relics in the employ of the French, whom he had come to suspect of conspiring with the communist government in the north to bring down his administration.

After hearing Ngo Dinh Diem's justifications for provoking the Binh Xuyen, Collins warned the prime minister that Bao Dai was likely to remove him from power if he continued on his present course. Back in his office that evening, Collins once again notified Dulles, "I see no repeat no alternative to the early replacement of Diem." Early the next morning Collins and Ely agreed with exasperation that the Nguyen Van Thoai proposal was dead, and that they must devise another solution right away. To make matters worse, reports of shooting incidents and kidnappings between Binh Xuyen and national army troops threatened to ignite the powder keg before a back-channel political resolution to the crisis could be achieved.[103] Collins, scheduled to fly to Washington for consultations later that same day, pondered delaying his departure in light of the recent increase in violent clashes. Ultimately he decided to stick to his schedule in hopes that the crisis would not erupt into armed conflict for another week.

Ely, meanwhile, took it on himself to make one last-ditch effort to re-
vive Bao Dai's solution by sending a telegram to the chief of state asking
him to intervene at once to prevent the outbreak of war in Saigon. On
April 21 Bao Dai's emissary Nguyen De delivered to the U.S. Embassy in
Paris a comprehensive plan for resolving the current crisis in Vietnam. The
chief of state declared his intention to bring Phan Huy Quat to France to
receive instructions for forming a new government. He would then remove
Ngo Dinh Diem as quietly as possible while the new prime minister commenced negotiations with all anticommunist political and religious factions
to form a new Council of Ministers and "Council of National Union."[104]
Bao Dai insisted that these steps must be carried out rapidly and without
foreign interference "beyond [the] initial Franco–United States approval of
main features." Nguyen De emphasized that the chief of state was present-
ing this as the "last and possibly only plan" to prevent all of Vietnam from
falling to communism. The "prolongation of the present crisis," he claimed,
"is driving [the] country into [the] hands of the Vietminh without their
lifting a finger."[105]

Back in Washington, Collins reinforced the work Ely was doing in Saigon. He delivered his message in person to the Department of State that
Ngo Dinh Diem must be removed immediately if South Vietnam was to be
saved, and indicated his support for Phan Huy Quat as a possible successor,
especially in light of Bao Dai's formal proposal and France's likely endorsement.[106] Some State Department officials suspected a French plot behind
Bao Dai's plan. A few days later, though, the United States Embassy in Paris
communicated to Dulles that the chief of state had most likely selected
Phan Huy Quat as the flag bearer out of his desire to please the United
States and to retain American support for South Vietnam. "In our opinion,"
wrote Ambassador C. Douglas Dillon, "if Bao Dai and [the] French were
not to take US views into account they would each choose [a] man other
than Quat."[107]

While the United States remained mired in indecision and suspicious of
French motives, much of the world concluded that Ngo Dinh Diem's days
were numbered. The international press reported the impending demise of
his regime, and it seemed that the prime minister alone was not convinced.
Choosing the possibility of civil war over capitulation, he brought the crisis
to a head. On April 26, after months of temporizing, he finally issued a
decree removing the Binh Xuyen police chief and installing his own man,
Nguyen Ngoc Le, as successor. The prime minister made no precipitous
move to seize the national police building, but issued an order for all Binh

Xuyen security agents to report to Nguyen Ngoc Le within forty-eight hours upon threat of court-martial.[108] Binh Xuyen officials, meanwhile, refused to relinquish their power on the grounds that only Bao Dai had the authority to revoke the organization's police concession. Binh Xuyen police chief Lai Van Sang went on the United Front radio station that night to assert his uninterrupted authority and to warn that "any use of force by Diem will have disastrous consequences for which Diem alone will bear [the] blame."[109] According to French general Gambiez, Binh Xuyen leaders implored France and the United States to "withdraw support from Diem, thus causing [the] ripe fruit to fall without [the] Binh Xuyen having to shake [the] tree."[110]

Meanwhile, Bao Dai informed the United States that he intended to take action to remove Ngo Dinh Diem no later than April 28.[111] Even in the midst of this face-off, the Americans warned him against doing so, threatening him again with the cessation of U.S. aid to Vietnam if he removed the prime minister without the official go-ahead from Collins.[112] Dulles remained deeply concerned about the domestic political repercussions of backing away from Ngo Dinh Diem. In a letter Dulles penned to Collins on April 20, in response to Collins's insistence that the prime minister be replaced, he expressed the following worry:

> Among other things that need to be explored . . . is the question of what change can obtain financial backing from the United States comparable to that which we are prepared to give Diem. This is not a matter just for the Executive but for the Congress and those who have leadership in this matter, such as Mansfield in the Senate and Walter Judd in the House, are strongly opposed to any shift. As things stand now, they would, I think, throw their influence, perhaps decisively, against backing any substitute that now seems in sight.[113]

Despite these domestic political concerns, Dulles was inching closer to pulling the plug on Ngo Dinh Diem. "It seems," he conveyed to U.S. Embassy officials in Saigon and Paris on April 27, "that some change in political arrangements in Vietnam may be inevitable." Still unwilling to commit American prestige to a change, he added, "Our general position remains that we continue [to] support the legal government under Prime Minister Diem until Vietnamese nationalist elements evolve another formula warranting continued US assistance and support."[114] The secretary lamented, "Situation disturbing and disappointing in Vietnam . . . people have concluded it confirms estimate it is hopeless to try to build anything there."[115] He indicated that officials in Washington would consider backing Bao Dai in removing Ngo Dinh Diem under certain circumstances, but that "the US is not interested in continuing to seek to give support to Viet-Nam under the current ambiguous conditions." Dulles assured diplomats in Paris and Saigon, "We will not continue to engage our prestige and furnish our resources for a project which is certain to fail."[116] He maintained that for the United States even to consider supporting a new government, Bao Dai would need to guarantee that he would confirm the new prime minister's authority over police officials and that he would remove the Binh Xuyen from all police functions. Dulles also demanded concrete assurances of France's future support for the Saigon regime, to dispel any ambiguity surrounding Paris's recent overtures to North Vietnam through Jean Sainteny. The secretary feared it would complicate his efforts to secure continued congressional support for South Vietnam and the French Expeditionary Corps if French intentions remained unclear.

The Battle of Saigon and the End of the United Front

On April 28, a military clash between the Binh Xuyen and the Vietnamese National Army finally interrupted this diplomatic quagmire. At first, a series of small firefights much like those of the preceding days broke out throughout Saigon-Cholon, particularly in the area surrounding the Binh Xuyen headquarters. The organization's increasingly aggressive stance provoked the national army to turn these minor incidents into a full-fledged battle. At about noon, government paratroopers launched attacks on Binh Xuyen soldiers around the capital, prompting Bay Vien's men to fire mortars into the grounds of Ngo Dinh Diem's palace. Chaos reigned in Saigon that day as hundreds of civilians perished in the fighting and thousands lost their homes to fires that raged throughout the city. Duong Van Mai Elliott, who observed the battle from her home in Cholon, claims that Binh Xuyen soldiers set the fires "to sow panic among the people."[117]

Ely and other French diplomats blamed Ngo Dinh Diem for the outbreak of violence. But they also claimed that the United States had precipitated the clash by failing to agree to some political solution two or three weeks earlier.[118] To make matters worse, Collins was still in Washington when the fighting broke out, leaving Ely alone with the job of attempting to arrange a cease-fire. Once Ngo Dinh Diem refused Ely's overtures, French officials limited their activity to protecting Saigon's European population. French forces stood by while the Vietnamese National Army performed surprising well against Binh Xuyen forces, who some speculated had been counting on French forces to defend them.[119] By dawn on April 30, Bay Vien's troops fled Saigon-Cholon and over the next few days a coalition of national army forces and Trinh Minh The's men forced the Binh Xuyen army into retreat. What remained of the organization's decimated army retracted into the jungles of Rung Sat, about ten miles south of Saigon, where national army forces would pursue it to annihilation throughout the coming year.

As events unfolded in Ngo Dinh Diem's favor the United States backed off its willingness to consider alternative leadership for South Vietnam. Throughout the crisis, Washington had refused to join forces with France to replace the prime minister due to a combination of domestic political pressures from America's "Vietnam lobby," perceived links between Ngo Dinh Diem's success and U.S. prestige, negative assessments of Bao Dai and politico-religious leaders, and a desire to keep the Saigon government free of the taint of French colonialism. The seemingly miraculous last-minute success of the national army in defending the prime minister spared American officials from making the difficult choice to participate in a leadership change. On the contrary, on April 30, State Department officer Kenneth Young observed, "As this crisis develops we are being forced to take a more and more unequivocal and strong stand for Diem."[120] And Dulles wrote to Collins on May 1, "Diem rightly or wrongly is becoming a symbol of Vietnamese nationalism struggling against French colonialism and corrupt backward elements."[121]

France, meanwhile, recognized that its last opportunity to work through Bao Dai to replace Ngo Dinh Diem had slipped away. Indeed, the political atmosphere in Saigon turned markedly more anti-French and anti–Bao Dai in the hours and days following Ngo Dinh Diem's clash with the Binh Xuyen army. As the crisis came to an end, French officials concluded that Washington's support for Ngo Dinh Diem was an "addiction" resulting from the belief that he was "the only Vietnamese politician who would absolutely never enter into contact with the Vietminh under any circumstances."[122] French politicians and journalists warned the United States that the stubborn, brutal manner in which Ngo Dinh Diem suppressed his opponents during the crisis boded ill for his ability to win popular support and retain control of South Vietnam down the line. The State Department, however, dismissed those warnings and pointed to the fractious nature of the United Front, compared with the apparent unity of the national army, as evidence that the prime minister's determination to eradicate his enemies was both brave and wise.

The fact that the Binh Xuyen stood alone in the Battle of Saigon, even against some of the recently rallied Cao Dai troops, is often cited as evidence that the United Front lacked solidarity and that its constituent organizations were unwilling to take risks in opposing Ngo Dinh Diem's leadership. Indeed, South Vietnam's politico-religious organizations were highly fragmented and often at odds despite their common antipathy to the prime minister. By the end of the crisis, Hoa Hao and Cao Dai factions had split between those who rallied to the national army and those who continued to oppose Ngo Dinh Diem's government. Even the rebellious factions proved unwilling to risk total annihilation to defend Binh Xuyen interests. However, on witnessing the Binh Xuyen defeat, Cao Dai and Hoa Hao leaders did not simply rescind the demands they had made on the prime minister under the auspices of the United Front. On the contrary, politico-religious leaders continued to seize opportunities to manipulate South Vietnam's volatile political environment to their advantage.

In the throes of the fighting, Cao Dai generals Nguyen Thanh Phuong and Trinh Minh The, and Hoa Hao General Nguyen Giac Ngo, all of whom had defected from the United Front to join the national army in late March, seized the political stage to denounce Binh Xuyen activities as inspired by and beneficial for French colonialists. The French, they alleged, had been conducting subversive activities in the south while conspiring with the communists in the north to destabilize Vietnam, all in order to preserve their colonial interests. Bao Dai's attempt to unseat Ngo Dinh Diem in the middle of the battle through a letter from France only ratified this suspicion.[123]

These politico-religious leaders called on Vietnamese of all classes to sacrifice their lives to fight against anyone who continued to wage war against the government.[124] Nguyen Thanh Phuong and Trinh Minh The's troops met the challenge, fighting alongside the national army against Binh Xuyen forces, although Nguyen Giac Ngo lacked the requisite power against neighboring antigovernment Hoa Hao forces to commit his men. Nguyen Thanh Phuong and Trinh Minh The were certainly less resolute in their opposition to Ngo Dinh Diem than the other politico-religious factions discussed here, especially those led by Bay Vien, Ba Cut, Tran Van Soai, and Pham Cong Tac. The activities of rallied politico-religious leaders described above might, at first glance, seem to indicate sycophantic support for Ngo Dinh Diem's government, but were in fact quite empowering. By making themselves essential to his defense and necessary for the survival and health of his regime, these leaders continued their efforts to manipulate the prime minister into meeting their demands for powerful roles in his government.

The primary instrument through which the Cao Dai and Hoa Hao leadership attempted to exert pressure on Ngo Dinh Diem following the Battle of Saigon was the Revolutionary Council. On the afternoon of April 30 approximately two hundred people gathered at the Saigon Town Hall, constituting the "General Assembly of Democratic and Revolutionary Forces of the Nation."[125] It was clear from the events of the previous three days that the Binh Xuyen, Bao Dai, and the French had lost substantial ground in South Vietnam in the face of Ngo Dinh Diem's eleventh-hour victory, inspiring Saigon's nationalist leaders to jump behind the winning horse. Eighteen parties in all, spearheaded by Cao Dai generals Trinh Minh The and Nguyen Thanh Phuong and Hoa Hao general Nguyen Giac Ngo, met briefly before issuing a public demand for Bao Dai to step down as chief of state and calling on Ngo Dinh Diem to form a new government.[126] The general assembly concluded by electing a thirty-one member Revolutionary Council to oversee this process. In all likelihood Ngo Dinh Nhu orchestrated the council's formation, but he would quickly lose control of its members who refused to be used as tools to lend legitimacy to what they still saw as a nepotistic, undemocratic administration.

That same evening the Revolutionary Council marched to Ngo Dinh Diem's palace to press him to renounce Bao Dai and dispose of the chief of state's new appointee to command the national army.[127] After a few hours of disorder, Nguyen Thanh Phuong and Trinh Minh The vacated the grounds, but the council soon returned to install itself in the palace with every intention of exerting direct influence over the prime minister's policies. Many of its members clearly expected to play a prominent role in the government they had directed Ngo Dinh Diem to form. In fact, U.S. officials speculated that certain factions the Cao Dai and the Hoa Hao may have been aiming to use the council as a means of seizing control of the South Vietnamese government, meanwhile assuring continued American support by retaining Ngo Dinh Diem as a figurehead.[128] These politico-religious factions, then, had not crumbled in the face of the Binh Xuyen rout, but rechanneled their political energies into the Revolutionary Council to seek the same concessions that they had demanded all along. Still other politico-religious factions, including Tran Van Soai and Ba Cut's Hoa Hao armies and Bay Vien's weakened Binh Xuyen forces, continued to stage armed resistance against Ngo Dinh Diem and the national army in southwest Vietnam. Even well on their way to defeat, the politico-religious organizations continued to factor much more heavily into South Vietnamese political and military concerns than scholars have previously recognized. Indeed, many of Ngo Dinh Diem's harsh policies against dissidents formulated in the coming year would be designed to subdue and control the Hoa Hao, Cao Dai, and Binh Xuyen, although they were pitched in terms of anticommunism.

The sect crisis was a key turning point in Ngo Dinh Diem's administration and its connection to the United States. The prime minister entered the conflict on the brink of collapse and emerged from it with what seemed to be uncontested control over South Vietnam and full support from Washington. The United States came out of the crisis more committed than ever to Ngo Dinh Diem as the sole nationalist capable of governing noncommunist South Vietnam. The "Diem lobby" in Washington was stronger than ever before, and many Americans who had once doubted the prime minister's leadership abilities laid their concerns to rest. As Ngo Dinh Diem consolidated his power in the coming months, observers in the United States hailed him as Vietnam's "Miracle Man" for pulling off the seemingly impossible task of defeating his formidable politico-religious opponents and establishing a viable government south of the seventeenth parallel.[129] In the wake of the sect crisis, Washington facilitated this process with increased monetary aid to South Vietnam's national army and new advisory programs to assist with the country's infrastructure and political development. In short order, the United States committed huge amounts of money—and more important, American prestige—to maintaining Ngo Dinh Diem's South Vietnamese government.

During and immediately after the crisis, Ngo Dinh Diem came to see just how reliant the United States was on his regime in particular and realized that he had a great deal of latitude to accept or reject American proposals in the future. Henceforth he settled into a pattern of accepting Washington's aid while resisting its advice—a practice that endlessly frustrated U.S. officials.[130] The prime minister's victory over the United Front also reaffirmed his belief that his political goals would be best served by totally suppressing dissent. Rather than broadening his government to include "loyal opposition" as his French and American advisors suggested, he concluded that his political future depended on his ability to root out and destroy potential challengers, both political and military.

It was in this vein that in May 1955, he launched the brutal Nguyen Hue operation against the remaining politico-religious armies, which he joined with a propaganda campaign designed to discredit politico-religious leaders. His government instituted a related program to identify anti–Ngo Dinh Diem figures throughout South Vietnam, brand them communists, and have them arrested or killed.[131] He would lump together the politico-religious groups, which he regarded as backward feudal warlords, with colonialists and communists as enemies of the state, and in so doing leave them with little alternative but to join forces against him. The prime minister would pair this broad campaign of oppression against anyone perceived to represent the triad of feudalism, colonialism, and communism with a political campaign through which he promised to modernize and democratize Vietnam, a hypocrisy that would not be lost on his opponents.[132]

Chapter 5

Destroying the Sources of Demoralization

Ngo Dinh Diem's National Revolution

In the aftermath of Ngo Dinh Diem's dramatic and unexpected victory in the sect crisis, American observers celebrated his leadership as nothing less than a miracle.[1] Pressmen and politicians alike were awed by his unlikely triumph over what they viewed as forces of chaos, greed, and depravity. Any doubt Eisenhower's administration might have entertained about whether Ngo Dinh Diem should be Washington's man in Vietnam was put to rest. Above all, the outcome of the sect crisis reassured Americans that Ngo Dinh Diem had what it took to maintain order in the face of major political and military challenges to his government, an ability that boded well for his capacity to fend off what they saw as the even more dire looming threat of communist subversion. Secretary of State John Foster Dulles and the U.S. State Department hoped to see some semblance of order and the trappings of democracy emerge within South Vietnam sooner rather than later, but Washington's primary concern was to secure the country's position as a noncommunist power within the region. On May 5, 1955, Dulles wrote to Collins:

I am somewhat concerned lest our position become too rigid on fundamental political questions regarding the future of Vietnam. The ultimate form and organization of the state and the government must be left to the Vietnamese to decide in an orderly manner. . . . It strikes me that this is not the time to declare for or against any particular form of the state. . . . Of course we would like to preserve basis of legitimacy of the government by some orderly process rather than by revolutionary action. . . . We are primarily concerned with whether government effectively controls country and has genuine anti-communist and nationalist support.[2]

Following the Battle of Saigon, the United States committed substantial economic aid and advisory support to assist Ngo Dinh Diem in the process of establishing both control over and legitimacy among his constituents. Washington focused on the need to restructure and retrain the South Vietnamese military, to complete the process of establishing a fully functioning, nominally democratic government, and to modernize civil administration throughout the country. Ngo Dinh Diem's American advisors wanted him to move past the struggles with politico-religious leaders that had defined his first year in office and begin building a state that could repel more persistent, coordinated communist attacks that they expected might emerge down the line.

Ngo Dinh Diem, however, had his own agenda. He was determined to make sure all of his challengers—chief among them the remaining antigovernment Hoa Hao, Cao Dai, and Binh Xuyen forces—were fully annihilated before he could commit himself to the nation-building projects his American patrons envisioned. He perceived the south to be in a state of chaos and moral decay after years of colonialism and war, and strove to restore not only political and military stability, but also moral order. To this end, he launched a military campaign to root out and destroy politico-religious rebels that was accompanied closely by a propaganda campaign designed to discredit them. He would manipulate the lives and reputations of his most prominent noncommunist foes, and in one notable case a noncommunist ally, in a deliberate effort to neutralize his enemies' appeal, legitimize his leadership, and spread the basic principles of his governing philosophy.

The prime minister maintained that eradicating despicable politico-religious leaders and their corrupting effects on South Vietnamese society was an essential first step toward the establishment of a stable government and a functioning polity. "In order to meet the external threat," he believed, "Viet-Nam must first be strong internally."[3] According to his administration's information agents, his goal was to give "Vietnam a strong moral basis [with] which to rebuild a strong, healthy, democratic State." Ngo Dinh Diem's officials warned, "To think of the form before the substance is certainly to run into failure." His main concern was "to destroy the sources of demoralization, however powerful, before getting down to the problem of endowing Vietnam with a democratic apparatus in the Western sense of the word."[4]

Ngo Dinh Diem would thenceforth conflate communists, colonialists, and feudalists—by which he meant politico-religious rebels—as "sources of demoralization" and enemies of the people. He attempted to convey to the citizens of South Vietnam a vision for "national revolution," rooted in the arcane philosophy of personalism, that cast his administration as that best suited to lead the country toward modernity, independence, and re-unification in a manner that would preserve the nation's traditions and moral foundations. He also aimed to use his national revolution construct to justify even the most extreme measures to silence his opponents among the evil triad mentioned above.[5]

National Revolution and Good Citizenship

After Ngo Dinh Diem established basic control over the capital city and the national army by putting down the United Front coup attempt in early 1955, he considered the dual tasks of neutralizing his enemies and legitimizing his leadership to be urgent. If he hoped to avoid participating in the Geneva mandated countrywide elections that threatened to reunite Vietnam under communist rule as early as summer 1956, he needed to establish a stable government with some semblance of popular support. To justify his refusal to negotiate with DRV representatives on plans for those elections, he challenged the communists' claims to represent authentic Vietnamese nationalism, instead depicting them as traitors and agents of foreign aggression. He insisted that they were marionettes of Moscow and Beijing who had exploited Vietnam's vulnerability to hijack the extreme nationalist movement.[6]

Indeed, anticommunism was at the heart of Ngo Dinh Diem's national revolution. Given the fact that he had remained above the fray while the Viet Minh sacrificed their lives during a grueling nine-year war to expel the French, he had to chisel an argument to convince his constituents that he and his administration represented genuine Vietnamese nationalism while the communists were traitors. To this end, he drew a distinction between resistance, which was righteous, and communism, an externally inspired and directed ideology that had tainted the resistance movement and needed to be eradicated in order to save Vietnam.[7] His emphasis on opposing communism as a means of combating foreign subversion was, in part, an attempt to counter charges levied by communists and "loyal opposition" leaders that he and his administration were former French collaborators cum lackeys of the United States, and that his government invited the recolonization of South Vietnam by Western powers.[8] Ngo Dinh Diem fired back against these claims with charges that it was, in fact, the communists who intended to hand over Vietnam to China, the nation's age-old oppressor, if given half a chance.[9] This helped justify Ngo Dinh Diem's resort to aid and support from the United States as a necessary measure to stave off conquest by the real threat to Vietnamese sovereignty emanating from the north. It also rationalized the Ngo brothers' violent and repressive campaigns against communists and their supposed conspirators.

Relative to the communist threat, Ngo Dinh Diem's administration defined its national revolution and the Vietnam that would emerge from it in overwhelmingly negative and reactive terms. RVN officials penned the following in 1956:

> In the present task of national revolution and reconstruction it is the anti-Communist spirit that counts. It is the strongest and most comprehensive spirit, because it includes all others. Those who have the anti-Communist spirit are well-qualified to be entrusted with the noble mission of liberating the people from oppression and slavery. So the main factor in our national revolution is the spirit, the will to fight Communism.[10]

This definition permitted the southern government to identify anything less than overt anticommunism as counterrevolutionary and treasonous. Indeed, one of the first tasks the government assigned to the Denounce the Communists Campaign on its inception on July 20, 1955, was "to condemn indifferent, reactionary and pro-Communist attitudes."[11] By classifying anyone who was not actively anticommunist as a procommunist saboteur by default, the RVN justified rooting out and punishing all those who failed to fall lock step with its national revolution.

The Denounce the Communists Campaign operated under the canopy of the newly formed Ministry of Information and Youth, which was charged with purging the south of communist and other antigovernment elements.[12] Ngo Dinh Diem's brother Ngo Dinh Nhu, head of the government's Can

Lao Party (Personalist Labor Revolutionary Party, or Can Lao Nhan Vi Cach Mang Dang), spearheaded the ground operations of the Denounce the Communists Campaign. Although the campaign commenced during summer 1955, after which finding and neutralizing communist agents in South Vietnamese villages quickly emerged as one of the administrations putative goals, through the summer 1956 Ngo Dinh Diem remained preoccupied with eradicating politico-religious opposition. Even after his landmark victory in the Battle of Saigon, he insisted that the politico-religious organizations still posed a substantial threat to stability in the countryside and served as an obstacle to political consolidation in South Vietnam.

While U.S. military advisors lamented Ngo Dinh Diem's determination to destroy politico-religious military power completely, as it delayed the training and reorganization of many South Vietnamese army units and siphoned off American aid dollars, the prime minister insisted that the task was integral to shoring up his government against communist subversion.[13] A report on the achievements of the Denounce the Communists Campaign, produced by the RVN in May 1956 revealed the administration's preoccupation with the link between communists and the politico-religious groups. In a list of "Crimes of the Communist Vietminh," the first two charges were: "In connivance with the colonialists, they have sowed dissension among the religious sects, instigated the rebels to fight against the Government, causing death and destruction in the country"; and, "They have mixed with the rebels to pull strings and give evil advice, disturbing order and security."[14]

Such fears of linkages and collusion between his enemies consumed Ngo Dinh Diem's administration. He identified the triad of feudalism, colonialism, and communism as "enemies of the people," and his insistence that they were interrelated and interdependent forces served as the premise of his programs to subdue resistance and consolidate his power throughout the countryside.[15] Conflating these three groups served to justify violent action against any of them as a noble defense of Vietnam's national integrity. It presupposed that targeting one of these forces would inherently weaken all of them. Furthermore, through his iterative identification of communists, French agents, and politico-religious leaders as innate conspirators against the nation, Ngo Dinh Diem obviated the need to prove concrete connections between them. Any evidence of collusion he could find would provide useful fodder for propaganda, but even without it he could tar them all with the same brush. In his view, they were all "enemies of the people" because they were all communists or communist sympathizers by definition. By extension, any crimes committed or harm done to society by any of them served as further evidence of the insidiousness of communism and justified violent efforts to combat its agents.

While anticommunism was by far the clearest and most widely recognized aspect of Ngo Dinh Diem's national revolution, he certainly strove to create a more positive sense of what he and his administration could offer the people of Vietnam. His effort to construct a Vietnamese national identity revolving around himself and his government in Saigon was rooted in the philosophy of personalism, a fairly obscure ideology unknown to most of his countrymen. Ngo Dinh Diem would not officially embrace personalism as South Vietnam's governing doctrine until October 1956, when he inaugurated a "Personalist Training Center" under the direction of his older brother Ngo Dinh Thuc.[16] And he infrequently spoke of it by name prior to spring 1957, when the National Cultural Council consolidated personalist and traditional Vietnamese Confucian values into a new national culture, which it then disseminated through public lectures and provincial outreach groups.[17] Nonetheless, Ngo Dinh Diem's policies and rhetoric during his first two years in office bear clear makings of personalist influence.

Ngo Dinh Nhu introduced his brother to personalist philosophy, which he first encountered in the 1930s as a student in Paris at the École des Chartes.[18] The Ngo brothers found in personalism, popularized by Emmanuel Mounier and other French humanist philosophers during the interwar period, several concepts that fit their needs perfectly. As they seized on the philosophy to provide a coherent cultural basis for anticommunist nation building, they appeared willing to manipulate or disregard aspects of the philosophy that did not serve their objectives.[19] At heart, personalism proposed a middle ground between communism and capitalism that could protect society from the threats to individual dignity posed by both systems. Whereas communism required individuals to sacrifice everything for the common good, and capitalism corrupted individuals and weakened the social fabric by encouraging greed and materialism, personalism, according to its adherents, struck a balance by which the state could respect individual dignity while also ensuring the common good of society.[20] In an effort to disseminate this ideology and establish his connection to it, Ngo Dinh Diem spoke often about the importance of "respect for human dignity," which he claimed his government alone could provide the people of Vietnam.[21]

Perhaps the most important aspect of personalism that the Ngos borrowed from their French forerunners was their approach to national leadership. All French personalists shared an opposition to the democratic status quo in the West, on the grounds that mass politics dehumanized men by treating them all the same and by neglecting spirituality.[22] Mounier's view was especially useful for Ngo Dinh Diem who sought to respond to domestic and international calls for representative government and democratic reforms while avoiding relinquishing any of his power to competing groups. Unlike his peers, Mounier continued to use the word *democracy* to describe his vision for government, even as he criticized existing forms of democracy in the West.[23] He envisioned a "personalist democracy" that promoted a stable and satisfying life for its citizens without necessarily giving them a voice in national politics. Much like the model the Ngo brothers would pursue, Mounier advocated leadership by an elite cadre, drawn from all social classes, but comprising only those who subscribed to the personalist program.[24] The influence of personalism on Ngo Dinh Diem's political thought thus helps explain the gaping chasm between his understanding of democracy and that of his American patrons. In his view, citizens had great responsibilities under a personalist democratic system, but they rested more in the realms of personal conduct and communal responsibility than in the arena of political engagement.

In Ngo Dinh Diem's view, a personalist system—indeed any free society—could only function if the citizens recognized and fulfilled their social obligations. And this, he feared, was something the people of Vietnam were woefully unprepared to do. Indeed, the Ngo brothers believed that the legacies of colonialism and the depredations of war left their country backward and its citizens unprepared to assume the responsibilities of modern citizenship. In their estimation, rural peoples especially needed to be tutored slowly in the ways of democratic participation and good citizenship. In the meantime, it might be necessary to force them to perform the social functions necessary to advance the common good.[25] In viewing peasants and workers as "people who were not quite full citizens in that they needed to be educated in the habits and manners of citizens," Ngo Dinh Diem was not alone among postcolonial ruling elites. Indeed, one scholar has identified this as a key factor contributing to a "pedagogical style of politics" typical of the decolonizing and decolonized world at the time.[26]

Ngo Dinh Diem, then, set out to foster a sense of South Vietnamese citizenship that he believed would enable him to build a state capable of ushering the country out of its feudal and colonial heritage and past the threat of communist enslavement. The term *citizenship*, so central to our understanding of politics in the modern nation-state, carries several meanings. On one hand, it refers to the process and the criteria by which an individual is included fully in the body politic of a nation, and connotes the corresponding rights and responsibilities. On the other, as one scholar explains, citizenship "refers to a person's moral quality as exemplified by his or her behavior: thus, one is a good citizen if one is 'civic-minded,' that is, one acts responsibly and honestly, obeys the law, makes demands upon the social and political system that are reasonable, and is cognizant of the interests of society at large."[27]

Ngo Dinh Diem's promotion of ideal citizenship focused largely on the latter definition. During the early years of his administration, his descriptions of good citizenship centered on moral and ethical behavior, and on respect for humankind. His ideal citizens would embrace virtue and eschew vice in their personal lives—in his words he sought "to rearm the citizen morally."[28] In their public lives, they would demonstrate their loyalty to his government and patriotism to the nation of Vietnam by resisting communism and condemning all those who attempted to criticize or subvert the Saigon government. According to the prime minister, it was his own scrupulous morality and "strong sense of public duty and responsibility to the people," key elements in both personalist and Confucian standards for leadership, that merited such allegiance.

Theoretically at least, his broadly defined and inclusive notion of the rights and responsibilities of citizenship in "Free Vietnam" extended to all Vietnamese people, both north and south of the seventeenth parallel. Indeed, Ngo Dinh Diem cast his notion of citizenship as the antithesis of the communist vision put forth by the Hanoi government that, in his view, required citizens to relinquish their rights and submit to the tyranny of a foreign-dominated state. Thus he claimed that freedom for Vietnam could not be attained, and the Saigon government could not fulfill its promises to the Vietnamese people, until the country was reunited under noncommunist rule. A citizen's paramount duty under this paradigm was to resist vice in general, and the corruptions and perversions inherent in communism, colonialism, and feudalism in particular, in order to maintain a strong, united opposition to communist onslaughts.

The Ngo brothers encountered a number of obstacles in their quest to establish personalism as the rallying point for Vietnamese nationalism and as the basis of a noncommunist citizenship ideal. Most important, it was not widely known in Vietnam or elsewhere as a proven revolutionary or political ideology, and it was not linked with any of the major anticolonial movements that had so pervaded Vietnamese society in the first half of the twentieth century. While Ho Chi Minh and the Viet Minh, via the 1945

August Revolution and the ensuing struggle against French reconquest, had made Vietnamese communism synonymous with Vietnamese nationalism in many circles, personalism carried no such connotations. On top of this, Ngo Dinh Diem's inability to explain personalist philosophy to his constituents in a clear, inspiring, or even penetrable way rendered it meaningless to most. But he had far greater success in clarifying the moral principles underpinning his politics when he spoke in concrete terms about opponents of his government. During the year after the sect crisis, he waged a propaganda campaign against some of the key politico-religious leaders through which he illustrated the core tenets of personalist citizenship. This propaganda offensive went hand-in-hand with the national army's military operations against rebel politico-religious armies.

Mopping Up Resistance

In spring 1955 Ngo Dinh Diem defied the counsel of French, American, and Vietnamese advisors to launch a military campaign against Hoa Hao, Cao Dai, and Binh Xuyen armies. While his supporters in Washington argued that the national army's victory over Bay Vien's forces had resolved the politico-religious problem, and that Saigon should focus its attention and American aid money on reforming the military and building a strong state apparatus, Ngo Dinh Diem was determined to root out and defeat remaining rebel politico-religious forces in order to preempt future challenges to his government. The Binh Xuyen loss and the dissolution of the United Front forced armies led by Hoa Hao generals Tran Van Soai and Ba Cut, and Binh Xuyen commander Bay Vien to flee their secure positions and stake out new guerrilla hideouts in South Vietnam. Ngo Dinh Diem wanted to press his military advantage while he could.

By April 30 the national army had driven Binh Xuyen rebel forces completely out of their urban stronghold in Saigon-Cholon. Ngo Dinh Diem immediately placed Cao Dai general Trinh Minh The, who had just abandoned the United Front and rejoined the national army, in charge of the operation to chase down and destroy Bay Vien's remaining troops, only to see him perish in battle on May 3.[29] Trinh Minh The's death might have been a loss for the government forces, but they won the battle and forced the Binh Xuyen to withdraw to the jungles of Rung Sat just days later. Ngo Dinh Diem decided not to go after them immediately but ordered his army to seal off all points of entry and exit to the jungle in order to hamper their military intelligence, and in hopes that they would succumb to malaria and malnutrition.

While the Saigon government waited for the Binh Xuyen to crumble from within, it turned its attention to eliminating the Hoa Hao threat once-and-for-all. Ba Cut's army had been fighting government forces in Long Xuyen from the beginning of Ngo Dinh Diem's administration. By this time he was joined by the leading Hoa Hao general, Tran Van Soai, whom the national army had declared in late March to be in open rebellion against the government due to his leading role in the United Front.[30] On May 24, Ngo Dinh Diem sought to undercut this bloc of resistance by offering the four dominant Hoa Hao generals a substantial bribe if they would relinquish their autonomy and surrender their troops to the government. As *Time* magazine reported, "Premier Diem first offered the Hoa Hao a chance to integrate themselves into the national army and form a peaceful political party, but the Hoa Hao replied by raiding Diem's outposts and blowing up bridges."[31] Indeed, just prior to the prime minister's overture all of the Hoa Hao leaders had met with former national army general Nguyen Van Hinh and resolved to continue their resistance against the government.[32] Tran Van Soai, Lam Thanh Nguyen, Nguyen Giac Ngo, and Ba Cut therefore rejected Ngo Dinh Diem's offer and declared war on the national army. Yet the Hoa Hao rebels, like the Binh Xuyen before them, quickly realized that they could not compete with the government forces in conventional fighting. On May 25, they abandoned their positions and bases, set fire to their stockpiles of food and supplies, and took to the jungles to prepare for the impending guerilla war.

Tran Van Soai almost immediately turned back on his decision to defy Ngo Dinh Diem. On May 29 he announced that he was ready to surrender, but by then it was too late. According to one observer, "Premier Diem needed a military victory more than a surrender and he was in a position to fight the demoralized sects to the finish."[33] Therefore, the prime minister rejected the Hoa Hao olive branch and condemned Tran Van Soai as a criminal. Ngo Dinh Diem had just issued orders for seven thousand men, led by Duong Van Minh ("Big Minh"), to pursue politico-religious rebels into the area of southwest Vietnam where Tran Van Soai and Ba Cut's armies remained active, and he intended to annihilate them.

Ngo Dinh Diem had every reason to be optimistic about the national army's chances against Hoa Hao troops. In early June, American Embassy officials in Saigon discounted the prospects of France resupplying Hoa Hao forces and estimated that the national army should be able to reduce the rebels to "traditional small banditry" through a three-month "starve-out" campaign.[34] CIA analysts likewise concluded that "the [National] Army's superiority in numbers and weapons leaves little doubt of [the] eventual outcome."[35] Ngo Dinh Diem, who shared this assessment, appointed Duong Van Minh to lead the national army's offensive against the remaining politico-religious forces throughout the next year. Duong Van Minh's Nguyen Hue operation opened its offensive with an amphibious attack against the Hoa Hao in Can Tho on June 5, 1955. Almost immediately after the fighting broke out, five Hoa Hao battalions surrendered, and General Nguyen Giac Ngo rallied his forces to the government, this time for good. To gain favor with Ngo Dinh Diem he publicly condemned Tran Van Soai and Ba Cut for contravening Hoa Hao religious principles explicated by founder Huynh Phu So and accused Ba Cut of fighting alongside communist battalions.[36]

Meanwhile, Tran Van Soai teamed up with outcast Generals Nguyen Van Hinh and Nguyen Van Vy to challenge Duong Van Minh's army along the Vietnam-Cambodia border. In mid-June, however, Tran Van Soai was injured and nearly captured. He managed to escape to Cambodia with help from Nguyen Van Hinh, but not before voicing his request for a cease-fire to begin in forty-eight hours. He hoped that this would convince Ngo Dinh Diem to open negotiations on integrating Hoa Hao troops into the national army.[37] But Ngo Dinh Diem once again denied Tran Van Soai's request, opting instead to brand the Hoa Hao general a traitor and an outlaw.

Shortly after Tran Van Soai's exodus to Cambodia, Lam Thanh Nguyen decided to surrender, leaving Ba Cut as the only Hoa Hao general in active defiance of the Saigon regime. Tran Van Soai remained adversarial toward the government but could not command his troops into battle from afar. Duong Van Minh's forces soldiered on in opposition to Ba Cut's guerillas, but in September 1955 they returned their attention to the Binh Xuyen troops that had been languishing in the Rung Sat region since early May. The national army wiped out Bay Vien's remaining forces by the end of October in an intense four-week siege. Binh Xuyen troops were killed, captured, or disbursed, while Bay Vien eventually succeeded in escaping to France where, according to one source, "He settled down to enjoy the riches he had amassed while serving the French and Bao Dai."[38]

While the army dealt with the Binh Xuyen, progovernment Cao Dai general Nguyen Thanh Phuong worked in conjunction with the national army to undermine Cao Dai dissidents in Tay Ninh. On the night of October 5–6 he invaded the Holy See to disarm the three-hundred man papal guard and arrest Pham Cong Tac's two daughters on charges of corruption and exploitation of the people. A few days later Nguyen Thanh Phuong completed his coup against conventional Cao Dai authority by proclaiming the pope deposed.[39]

Pham Cong Tac clung to his position at the Holy See until February 1956 when the approach of government troops forced him to flee to Cambodia. That same month, Tran Van Soai finally convinced Ngo Dinh Diem to accept his surrender. Until then, the prime minister had continued to reject Tran Van Soai's pleas to integrate Hoa Hao troops into the national army, as evidenced by the commander of the army's announcement in November 1955 of a 1 million dong reward for the capture of Tran Van Soai and Ba Cut, dead or alive, or a 200,000 dong reward for information leading directly to their capture.[40] The incentive, announced in *Thoi Dai*, emphasized that the army was enacting this measure to ensure the safety of citizens in areas where the two men and their armies operated. It was accompanied by thorough physical descriptions of both Tran Van Soai and Ba Cut as well as clear, close-up head shots of the two men looking clean and well dressed.

THÔNG CÁO

Bộ Tổng Tham-mưu Quân-đội Quốc gia Việt-Nam thông cáo :
1') Bất cứ một ai, thường d n cũng như quân nhân, mà giết chết hoặc bắt sống được 1 trong 2 tên cầm đầu phiến loạn BA CỤT và NĂM LỬA thì sẽ được thưởng MỘT TRIỆU ĐỒNG (1.000.000 đồng).
Việc giết chết phải được chứng minh bằng cách mang xác về nạp cho các nhà chức trách hữu quyền (quân sự hoặc hành chánh).
2') Nếu chỉ điểm cho các nhà chức trách quân sự bay hành chánh giết chết hoặc bắt sống được 1 trong 2 tên giặc nói trên thì người chỉ điểm sẽ được thưởng HAI TRĂM ngàn đồng (200.000 đồng)
TIỀN THƯỞNG NÀY SẼ ĐƯỢC CẤP một cách rải nhanh chóng và dễ dàng, và hơn nữa:
CHÍNH PHỦ SẼ DÙNG MỌI BIỆN PHÁP CẦN THIẾT ĐỂ ĐẢM BẢO SỰ AN NINH CHO NHỮNG NGƯỜI CÓ CÔNG TRÊN.

HÌNH NĂM LỬA
Đặc điểm của Năm Lửa :
— có bộ râu cảnh trẻ (nhưng khi có thể y đã cạo đi)
— cao 1 th, 65, giả, nhưng rắn rỏi.

HÌNH BA CỤT
Đặc điểm của Ba Cụt :
— tóc bồ phồ vai
— cao 1 th, 70
— người gầy mình khỏe
— mặt xương.

Figure 5.1. Wanted poster for Ba Cut and Tran Van Soai, November 23, 1955 (*Thoi Dai*)

The reward for capture clearly stepped up the pressure on these two Hoa Hao generals to surrender themselves to the national army, and by mid-February the increasingly desperate Tran Van Soai managed to do so on terms he found acceptable. He rallied approximately twenty-nine hundred troops to the national army, many of whom the U.S. embassy reported to be children between the ages of ten and twelve years old that might have been strays picked up on the way to Saigon rather than troops actively engaged in the struggle against the government. In a futile attempt to save face, Tran Van Soai insisted that his ragged Hoa Hao soldiers were not "surrendering" to the government, but "rejoining" the national army.[41]

Once Tran Van Soai had submitted to Ngo Dinh Diem's authority, Ba Cut's army was the only politico-religious front still capable of posing organized violent resistance to the government forces. The Nguyen Hue operation thus turned its full attention to capturing the Hoa Hao rebel and eliminating his troops. On April 13, 1956, government forces captured him in Long Xuyen, confiscated more than 1 million piasters, and took him to Saigon to await his fate.[42] As it turned out, he was to become the last South Vietnamese citizen to lose his head on the guillotine.

The blade falling upon Ba Cut's neck seemed to signal Ngo Dinh Diem's final defeat of the noncommunist opposition that just two years earlier appeared destined to sabotage his rule. Although politico-religious forces would continue to serve as key elements of antigovernment activity in the coming years, they appeared to be nothing but memories as of summer 1956. But how would they be remembered? As with every aspect of South Vietnamese political life, the Ngo brothers sought total control over their enemies' legacies.

Representations of Politico-Religious Leaders

Concomitant with the national army's military operations against the politico-religious organizations, the Saigon government, with help from a compliant press corps, waged a propaganda campaign revolving around the reputations of several key politico-religious leaders. Ngo Dinh Diem's administration identified this as the third phase of the Denounce the Communists Campaign, in which the government would "wage a violent psychological attack on the adversary, denounce reactionary elements, in order to purge our own people's rank, annihilate the remaining political influence of the feudal rebels, colonialists and Communists." Government spokesmen described their program as an "attack on the fields of culture and morals," designed to condemn crimes, "campaign against social plagues," and develop sound patriotism.[43]

This was part of a broader effort by the Ministry of Information and Youth and the National Revolutionary Movement (NRM) to organize South Vietnam's information and propaganda programs. The overarching objective of the ministry and the NRM, both run by personalist politician Tran Chanh Tranh, was to propagate a national identity for Vietnam centered on Ngo Dinh Diem's leadership and rooted in his ideals.[44] The NRM, established in October 1954, spearheaded public efforts to bring the peasantry under government control via propaganda programs, public works projects, and campaigns to root out subversives. The movement borrowed heavily from Viet Minh organizing tactics, coupled with Vichyite indoctrination practices by which government officials repeated to the peasants lectures given by the Ngo brothers on personalist principles of government and citizenship. The NRM operated in plain sight, as opposed to Ngo Dinh Nhu's smaller Can Lao Party, which operated entirely out of the public view.[45] Nonetheless, despite its efforts to build grassroots community support, the NRM was by all accounts overwhelmingly oppressive, relying more on intimidation than inspiration to win peasant support.[46]

In 1955 Ngo Dinh Diem created the Ministry of Information and Youth under the canopy of the NRM to oversee national propaganda efforts designed to win the loyalties of both communist and politico-religious sympathizers while military operations targeted their leadership structures. Tran Chanh Tranh coordinated the ministry's efforts to distribute propaganda throughout South Vietnam via pamphlets and books, radio broadcasts, and propaganda films. Starting in late 1955, his team launched a campaign to "win the hearts" (*tranh thu nhan tam*) of the people in areas that had, until recently, been dominated by the politico-religious organizations and the Viet Minh. In part, the organization aimed to build a cult of personality for Ngo Dinh Diem akin to that of "Uncle Ho." It cited the narrative of his life, especially his staunch refusal to compromise Vietnamese autonomy, to establish him as an "enlightened sovereign" who could improve the lot of all Vietnamese by creating "economic and social stability for all" within a personalist framework.[47] The Ministry of Information and Youth not only spread its own propaganda, but also controlled the information put out by independent sources by means of the Vietnam Press Agency, which supplied press releases to South Vietnamese newspapers and magazines, kept watch over the media, and censored its content.[48]

This bourgeoning government control over the press helped ensure that South Vietnam's print media would facilitate Ngo Dinh Diem's politically motivated invocations against politico-religious leaders. But his allies in the press, most notably the editors of *Thoi Dai* (the Era) and *Thoi Luan* (Commentary), supported the southern government for a number of other reasons. To some extent they made common cause with Ngo Dinh Diem and Ngo Dinh Nhu out of shared opposition to Bao Dai, which stemmed from suppression that had occurred under the Nguyen Van Tam and Buu Loc governments toward the end of the Franco–Viet Minh War. One scholar has demonstrated that *Thoi Luan* was led by a faction of Cao Dai dissidents who had aligned themselves with Ngo Dinh Nhu's Movement for National Union and Peace in spring of 1954, before Ngo Dinh Diem even assumed power. The paper would not become critical of the southern government until 1958, by which time Ngo Dinh Diem's administration, especially Ngo Dinh Nhu's Can Lao Party, had become markedly more organized and oppressive. The paper was shut down that year after it published "a broadside attack against nearly every aspect of the regime."[49]

In 1955 and 1956 the newspapers discussed here operated at least somewhat independent of government direction, and often opposed politico-religious military activities for their own reasons. At heart, though, they faced powerful incentives to conform to the administration's line after the Battle of Saigon. Ngo Dinh Diem had just begun the process of asserting control over the South Vietnamese press, which would be nearly complete within a few years. And the Ministry of Information and Youth was less coercive during the year after the sect crisis than it would be by the decade's end. But the national army's loyal performance against the Binh Xuyen was a huge political and military victory for Ngo Dinh Diem and set up his administration to control events in South Vietnam as never before. The prime minister had finally displayed his strength, made clear his intolerance for dissent, and begun to demonstrate the violent and oppressive means by which he would combat it, thereby narrowing the range of acceptable political discourse in South Vietnam. Therefore, while the newspapers discussed here were not merely mouthpieces of the administration, neither were they free from government influence.

Unsurprisingly, Ngo Dinh Diem's government and the press cast most politico-religious leaders in a negative light. Chief amongst these were Binh Xuyen commander Bay Vien and Hoa Hao general Ba Cut, and to a lesser degree Cao Dai pope Pham Cong Tac and Hoa Hao general Tran Van Soai. The recently deceased Cao Dai general Trinh Minh The proved a notable exception, as Ngo Dinh Diem sought to canonize him as a martyr of the administration and an exemplar of all for which it stood.

The southern government's manipulation of its politico-religious adversaries' images drew heavily on Catholic and Confucian hagiographic traditions in which the lives of saints—and in this case sinners as well—were mobilized by the church and the state to serve current political circumstances. In both traditions, saints and heroes had long been used to justify policies, unify and pacify populations, establish behavioral norms, and legitimate governments. Along those same lines, Ngo Dinh Diem's political exploitation of his enemies' reputations served several specific purposes. Most fundamentally, demonizing these figures as scourges on society and enemies of the Vietnamese nation helped justify the violent measures the Ngos undertook to eradicate them and helped to build a case for harsh, ongoing antisubversive programs like Denounce the Communists. At the same time, by decrying the predatory, corrosive nature of notable opponents that it had forced into exile, executed, or subdued, the government publicized its ability and will to protect the citizens of South Vietnam from villainy and to pave the way for a safer, more virtuous society.

In a related vein, by discussing and condemning specific actions taken by various politico-religious leaders, Ngo Dinh Diem's administration disseminated in concrete terms some of the key tenets of personalism that remained abstract and inaccessible to most South Vietnamese citizens. The politico-religious leaders discussed most often by Ngo Dinh Diem and the South Vietnamese press served as object lessons of the potentially catastrophic consequences that could result from public figures shirking their responsibilities to the nation of Vietnam, and even of private citizens behaving degenerately. By exiling Bay Vien and Tran Van Soai—just as he had exiled Nguyen Van Hinh and Pham Cong Tac and was working to cast out Bao Dai—and by executing Ba Cut, Ngo Dinh Diem sent a dual message to the citizens of South Vietnam: first, they were obligated to place the health of the nation as defined by Ngo Dinh Diem above personal gain and pleasure; and second, the South Vietnamese government, with support from a loyal army, was prepared to go to great lengths to punish or expel those who failed to do so.

In the Ministry of Information and Youth's telling, Trinh Minh The stood alone among politico-religious figures as a symbol of virtue and patriotism. He seemed to exemplify the balance personalist philosophers advocated between respect for individual dignity and the duty to forfeit self-interest for the good of society. Indeed, he embodied the Vietnamese tradition of resistance and self-sacrifice.

Relying largely on these politico-religious figures, Ngo Dinh Diem's administration created a public cast of characters to fit the morality play he wished for his first two years in office to tell. In the words of his own Ministry of Information and Youth, "President Ngo Dinh Diem's Weltan-schauung . . . is essentially an ethical one. He judges men and things from a moral standpoint. For him a thing is either good or evil."[50] The prime minister envisioned himself as a nationalist hero, fighting for good, who strove to save Vietnam from evil foreign predators and internal forces of backwardness and social decay.

Trinh Minh The

When the smoke cleared in Saigon in early May 1955, Cao Dai general Trinh Minh The had perished in battle on behalf of the national army. He met his death on May 3 along the Saigon River during the course of his mission to destroy Bay Vien's forces. He supposedly died at the hands of Binh Xuyen gunmen, but some historians and observers have since argued that Ngo Dinh Diem himself ordered the general's murder.[51] According to correspondent Donald Lancaster, "Although The's death was officially ascribed to Binh Xuyen marksmanship, the fact that he had been shot from behind and that the wound was powder-blackened gave rise to a belief that he had in fact been assassinated at point-blank range by one of his entourage."[52]

By many accounts Trinh Minh The posed the greatest challenge to Ngo Dinh Diem's authority at this time, a claim supported by his ongoing, independent political leadership and by his self-presentation as "a champion of the people and a fighter against corruption."[53] Trinh Minh The may well have been planning to use his talents in a competition for power with Ngo Dinh Diem, which would have given the prime minister ample motive to eliminate the Cao Dai leader while he had the chance. "Whether it shocked or pleased him," writes one Vietnam expert, "[Trinh Minh The's death] must be considered as a stroke of luck for the man who was beginning to be convinced that his government could be strong only if he did not have to share his powers with anyone, be it enemy or friend."[54] Some American observers, however, contested the view that Ngo Dinh Diem was at best relieved by Trinh Minh The's death and at worst responsible. On the contrary, some recall Ngo Dinh Diem spontaneously breaking into tears when he learned of Trinh Minh The's demise, suggesting that he was genuinely surprised and grief-stricken by the loss.[55]

Whether or not Ngo Dinh Diem was truly saddened by Trinh Minh The's passing, his administration immediately made pageantry of its mourning. Ngo Dinh Diem publicly blamed the Binh Xuyen and the French for Trinh Minh The's murder, a charge which coincided with an overall increase in anti-French sentiment that surfaced in Saigon in the wake of the sect crisis.[56] Without any solid evidence, South Vietnam's defense minister Dung reported to his contacts in the U.S. Embassy that the French had most likely deliberately assassinated Trinh Minh The.[57] This accusation served a far greater purpose than simply to deflect suspicion from Ngo Dinh Diem and fuel the tide of anti-French public opinion that helped generate short-term support for his government.

By casting Trinh Minh The as a martyr who sacrificed his life in a heroic struggle to defeat internal saboteurs and expel French colonizers, the Saigon government associated him with Vietnam's historic "spirit of resistance against foreign aggression," dating back to the Trung sisters in 40 CE and carrying through to the recent anticolonial struggle.[58] According to this vision of the country's past, prevalent within anticolonial narratives from at least the 1920s, the Vietnamese had defined and distinguished themselves for generations by their fierce determination to resist subjugation by greater powers.[59] The Hanoi government made concerted efforts to mobilize this narrative as a rallying point, and at the Fourth National Assembly of the DRV in February 1955, historians were formally instructed to emphasize the "fighting spirit of the Vietnamese."[60] Ngo Dinh Diem aimed to challenge DRV claims to represent that fighting spirit and to legitimize his rule by casting his government, with the support of Trinh Minh The's martyrdom, as the natural standard-bearer of Vietnam's tradition of self-sacrifice and resistance against foreign invaders.

Trinh Minh The possessed the perfect pedigree by which Ngo Dinh Diem could dispute Ho Chi Minh and the DRV's claims to represent the true spirit of resistance against foreign aggression. His reputation as an "ultranationalist," who had long refused to collaborate with both the communists and the French on the grounds that they each represented predatory outside forces, made him the perfect martyr for the southern government.[61] Ngo Dinh Diem claimed that the DRV was under China's thumb, and to a lesser degree Moscow's, and that it therefore was facilitating rather than resisting another wave of foreign aggression.[62] By contrast, Trinh Minh The earned his reputation as an unflappable patriot during the Franco–Viet Minh War, when he emerged as the only politico-religious military leader who refused to ally with both the French and the communists.

As American Embassy officials observed, "The has always been among [the] most rabid anti-French leaders and has been hated and feared by the French."[63] And he shared with his fellow politico-religious leaders a hatred for the communists, who had violently betrayed their politico-religious allies immediately following the 1945 August Revolution. Trinh Minh The thus possessed a strong record of fighting feudalism and colonialism, two of Ngo Dinh Diem's trifecta of enemies. And he had apparently rejected the third evil, feudalism, by breaking with the United Front and rallying to the national army during the sect crisis. The prime minister therefore took pains to claim Trinh Minh The as a martyr for his administration. Moreover, he highlighted similarities between the Cao Dai leader's extreme nationalism and his own record of rejecting overtures to collaborate with France, Bao Dai, and the communists.

Ngo Dinh Diem, with help from a sympathetic press corps in Saigon, set out to enshrine Trinh Minh The as the first national hero of his independent, noncommunist South Vietnam. In a May 5 article entitled "We Must Study General Trinh Minh The's Fighting Example," *Thoi Dai* editorialist Nguyen Thanh Danh proclaimed, "Generals who have died in this glorious fashion deserve to be heroes of the nation of Vietnam." He went on to praise Trinh Minh The for his genuine patriotism and promised that the general would always be remembered among Vietnam's pantheon of heroes.[64] Furthermore, he juxtaposed Trinh Minh The's heroism with the perfidy of dissident Hoa Hao and Binh Xuyen leaders, claiming that the Cao Dai general would serve as a role model for the Vietnamese people and as an eye-opener to the "gangs of scoundrels" who had been sponging off the French colonial regime and intriguing for personal gain. Contrary to these criminals, Trinh Minh The's sacrifice embodied the proverb, "To die gloriously is better than to live in disgrace." Nguyen Thanh Danh claimed that Trinh Minh The's martyrdom had been essential for the national army's defeat of the "French invaders" and "feudalist scoundrels" in the late April battle in Saigon-Cholon. To ensure Vietnam's future independence and unification, he called on citizens of the south to emulate Trinh Minh The's spirit of self-sacrifice and follow him down the path to glory, even should it demand their lives.[65]

A brief biographical sketch of Trinh Minh The published in *Thoi Dai* two days after his death traced the general's life from boyhood in Tay Ninh to his brutal demise along the Saigon River as a demonstration of the archetypical life of nationalist sacrifice. According to this account, Trinh Minh The was born to a fervently nationalist father and, as a schoolboy at the

Cao Dai Holy See, banded together with a handful of schoolmates to resist the tyranny of local village officials who had sullied their honor by bowing to the French. As he grew older his revolutionary reputation spread, and "people everywhere admired his indomitable will and publicly or privately supported his revolution against the nation's two enemies: Communists and Feudalist scoundrels."[66] Trinh Minh The was among the founders of the Cao Dai army in 1943, though he broke from the organization's ranks and took to the hills to continue his resistance against the French in 1951. From there he led his forces in campaigns against the French, the communists, and even against other politico-religious factions like Ba Cut's Hoa Hao troops who reportedly terrorized the innocent villagers of Chau Doc Province. This biographer noted that throughout his years of hardship and struggle, Trinh Minh The remained ever honorable and refused to accept even the smallest bribe from Bao Dai.

In this telling, after his many years of noble nationalist resistance, Trinh Minh The finally returned to cooperate with the national army on February 13, 1955, "because he realized that the forces of the national army were struggling for the country."[67] In fact, Trinh Minh The's decision was influenced in part by substantial American bribes channeled through Edward Lansdale, a CIA agent assigned to collaborate with Ngo Dinh Diem on psychological warfare strategies.[68] Lansdale regarded Trinh Minh The as a true patriot, whose allegiance could lend credibility to the Saigon government, and spared no expense to get him on the prime minister's side.[69] In the public eye, however, Trinh Minh The retained his reputation as an ultranationalist who could not be bought off so easily. Thus the author of this *Thoi Dai* editorial pledged that his countrymen would repay the Cao Dai martyr by recording his name eternally in the history of Vietnam's struggle for independence.

Saigon press accounts of Trinh Minh The's memorial service demonstrate that the government wasted no time enshrining him as a hero—and ensuring that the citizens of Vietnam recognized that he had given his life in defense of Ngo Dinh Diem's government. On May 4 the state gave Trinh Minh The an official funeral, including a somber procession from his home to his temporary resting place in front of the Saigon Town Hall.[70] Above his casket hung a black banner with silver lettering proclaiming, "State funeral of General Trinh Minh The, national hero." To reinforce the general's connection with the state, four high-level national army soldiers stood somber watch over his body day and night. And to further guarantee that mourners recognized that Trinh Minh The's primary allegiance had been to Ngo

Dinh Diem's government and not to the Cao Dai organization, they hung a South Vietnamese flag next to an old portrait in front of his casket.

Saigon newspapers reported that Vietnamese citizens came from near and far, from Saigon-Cholon and distant provinces, to pay their respects to Trinh Minh The.[71] A number of high-ranking government and army officials took the podium to extol his virtues and seized the opportunity to call for the people of Vietnam to join the struggle for independence and reunification. Ngo Dinh Diem even showed up to mourn Trinh Minh The and to link the public memory of the fallen hero to the national army and the southern government by promoting him to division general and conferring upon him a posthumous medal of honor.[72] At some point during the service Ngo Dinh Diem collapsed, perhaps out of grief or perhaps from exhaustion following the Battle of Saigon and its tense political aftermath. Regardless of the cause, his fainting spell enhanced the dramatic tone of Trinh Minh The's funeral and helped cement the link between the prime minister and the Cao Dai general as kindred revolutionary spirits.

Meanwhile, as this memorial took place in the capital, rumor had it that national army soldiers gathered in their camps to discuss the demise of the great Cao Dai martyr. One *Thoi Dai* reporter claimed, "They all feel a constant, limitless vindictive hatred for the enemies of the nation, the French colonialists and the insurrectionary Binh Xuyen who assassinated the general."[73] This is a perfect example of the pro–Ngo Dinh Diem, anti–Bao Dai position that *Thoi Dai* and *Thoi Luan* editors adopted following the sect crisis. Such embellished reporting of the widespread reaction to Trinh Minh The's death might well have been an independent effort by the editors to memorialize the fallen Cao Dai hero, but they simultaneously played into the government's goal of representing the event as a crime against the nation committed by foreigners and traitors.

Although *Thoi Luan* was run by a progovernment faction of the Cao Dai, the paper only briefly noted Trinh Minh The's affiliation with the organization. Upon the conclusion of the state ceremony several soldiers embarked on a journey to Tay Ninh to deliver Trinh Minh The's body for burial. Some accounts depict Trinh Minh The as a Cao Dai reject, claiming that he was denied burial within the Holy See. Pope Pham Cong Tac reportedly attributed Trinh Minh The's death to his insubordination within the Cao Dai organization and refused to admit the general's body into the main temple to receive the organization's preburial rites.[74] American CIA officer Edward Lansdale recalls attending a somber and respectful interment ceremony held on May 8 on Nui Ba Den (Ba Den Mountain), attended primarily by Trinh Minh The's loyal Cao Dai Lien Minh soldiers.[75] Presumably this took the place of an official, Cao Dai–sponsored burial.

Ngo Dinh Diem and his allies went to great lengths to ensure that Trinh Minh The's legend was not buried with his body. On July 13, 1955, the Saigon General Assembly announced its decision to commemorate "the national hero Trinh Minh The" by naming a boulevard in his honor. It resolved "to commend the nation's hero who laid down his life on the battlefield." At first the assemblymen decided simply to rename Eyriaud des Vergenes Street, which ran directly in front of Trinh Minh The's old house, but after further discussion they named a bridge after the fallen hero as well.[76] Trinh Minh The thus became an important aspect of the government's plan to superimpose its authority over the capital city by naming streets after Vietnamese heroes perceived to exemplify the causes of freedom, independence, and even anticommunism.

Ngo Dinh Diem and Ho Chi Minh's governments both employed this tactic, which they may have drawn from the Japanese-sponsored Tran Trong Kim government, which renamed a number of streets in Hanoi after anti-French martyrs during its brief period of control between the Japanese coup in March 1945 and the August Revolution a few months later.[77] Indeed, this was part of an ongoing Vietnamese project to establish legitimacy by linking state power with a heroic national past, and after the war, Hanoi leaders would change Saigon to Ho Chi Minh City and rename its streets after national heroes, many of whom never set foot in the south.[78] In addition to naming these streets after Trinh Minh The, Ngo Dinh Diem organized a battalion of the national army in his name a few months later, thereby cementing the general's link with South Vietnam's most powerful institution.

Of course, Ngo Dinh Diem's efforts to manipulate the images of his allies and enemies to foster public support were not entirely unique, and his rightful claim to Trinh Minh The's legacy remained open to debate. Critics in the DRV contested Ngo Dinh Diem's self-serving representation of Trinh Minh The as a hero of the noncommunist nationalist cause. During a broadcast of "The Voice of Vietnam" ("Tieng Noi Viet Nam") on the one-year anniversary of Trinh Minh The's death, DRV spokesmen accused Ngo Dinh Diem of misappropriating the general's memory to manipulate his former allies into supporting the government. Like Donald Lancaster, they claimed that Ngo Dinh Diem arranged to have Trinh Minh The murdered when the Binh Xuyen "rose up against the fascist southern regime." DRV representatives insisted that Ngo Dinh Diem had become paranoid that Trinh Minh The was lurking in the shadows, waiting for the right moment to pounce on his weak administration. "Because of this," they claimed, "Diem delegated The to mop up the wooded areas and then killed him." DRV critics claimed that the Saigon press, though seemingly loyal to the southern government, had leaked portions of this story over the preceding year, and that the truth had gradually driven Cao Dai and Hoa Hao armies to join the Binh Xuyen's struggle against Ngo Dinh Diem's tyranny. Further, they insisted that many of Trinh Minh The's old allies had been forced by Ngo Dinh Diem's "blood-stained policies" to renounce the Saigon government and seek refuge in foreign lands.[79]

This claim that Trinh Minh The's forces had gradually turned against Ngo Dinh Diem is supported by the exodus of Cao Dai troops back into the antigovernmental resistance movement. By November 1955, the director of South Vietnam's police and security agency noted an upsurge in public outrage against progovernment general Nguyen Thanh Phuong amongst Cao Dai believers. Large numbers of Cao Dai soldiers were reportedly deserting Nguyen Thanh Phuong's rallied army to form an organized force in opposition to his acceptance of bribes and his violent activities. Pham Cong Tac encouraged desertion from Nguyen Thanh Phuong's ranks by means of propaganda campaigns conducted in Cao Dai villages and temples. On December 30, three thousand Cao Dai troops officially turned against Ngo Dinh Diem and joined Trinh Minh The's successor General Van Thanh Cao's opposition forces.[80]

Van Thanh Cao explained this as a reaction to two specific government acts. First, Ngo Dinh Diem ordered the demobilization of Trinh Minh The's Cao Dai Lien Minh front rather than integrating it into the national army as promised. And second, the Saigon government proposed to dissolve the National Resistance Front (Mat Tran Quoc Gia Khang Chien), the Cao Dai party led by Van Thanh Cao. Ngo Dinh Diem aimed to fuse this Cao Dai organization with an existing government-controlled party, Ngo Dinh Nhu's Can Lao. Van Thanh Cao responded to these government efforts to undercut Cao Dai autonomy by circulating in Saigon a series of letters characterizing the government as "a despotic and feudal regime of terror comparable to the former French regime, a government of religion and family, a dictatorship of Diem and his brother Nhu." He accused Ngo Dinh Diem of eliminating all legitimate political parties, dividing the country, and creating opportunities for increased communist subversion below the seventeenth parallel. Van Thanh Cao and his fellow Cao Dai generals thus announced that they could no longer support Ngo

Dinh Diem's government, "since this would be a betrayal of their fallen comrades and of the late General The's National Salvation Program calling for the annihilation of colonialists, communists and the feudal regime." By highlighting Trinh Minh The's legacy and announcing their willingness to collaborate with "all true nationalist parties which share the basic aims of The's program," these Cao Dai leaders sought to establish themselves as nationalist revolutionaries rather than the "feudalist scoundrels" Ngo Dinh Diem made them out to be.[81] In the process, they also undermined the prime minister's representation of Trinh Minh The as a hero of the South Vietnamese state and attempted to reclaim him as a martyr for the Cao Dai organization.

American Foreign Service officers interpreted this Cao Dai desertion as an attempt to pressure Ngo Dinh Diem's government into extending full democratic freedoms to nongovernmental parties in the national assembly elections scheduled for March 1956. At the same time, U.S. diplomat Daniel Anderson noted that Cao Dai leaders were probably "serving notice on Diem that if government-controlled elections result in the elimination of effective opposition in the government and solidification of Diem's 'one-man-rule,' they are preserving a military nucleus which they might, at a later date, bring into active military opposition to the government."[82] This evidence all suggests that Ngo Dinh Diem's efforts to manipulate Trinh Minh The's image to promote loyalty to the southern regime in particular and moral rectitude in general, fell short of the mark.

Bay Vien

If Ngo Dinh Diem had attempted to turn Trinh Minh The into his government's first modern hero, he applied the same rationale to depict Binh Xuyen commander Le Van Vien (alias Bay Vien) as one of the nation's principal villains. Bay Vien was perhaps the weakest threat to the Saigon government following the Binh Xuyen rout in late-April 1955, but he remained the most obvious target of Ngo Dinh Diem's opprobrium. Following the showdown between the Binh Xuyen and the national army, Bay Vien's forces posed less of a peril to the southern regime than either of the other two politico-religious organizations. The Binh Xuyen had played its hand and lost. As CIA officials noted in early May, "The Binh Xuyen will probably prove a long-term police problem, but it is no longer a serious threat to the stability of the Diem government."[83]

In addition to annihilating Bay Vien's military, though, Ngo Dinh Diem sought to utilize the commander's thuggish image to advance the government's personalist citizenship ideals. The Binh Xuyen chief headed up the only one of South Vietnam's three powerful organizations with no claim to religious underpinnings; it was an organization that Vietnamese leaders and outside observers had long condemned as a rapacious gang of criminals. To prove that Bay Vien posed a significant threat to the nation of Vietnam as a whole, Ngo Dinh Diem publicized his suspicions that the Binh Xuyen attack on national army forces at the end of April 1955 was all a part of the commander's plan to coerce Bao Dai into elevating him to the post of prime minister.[84] Of course, Ngo Dinh Diem claimed that Bay Vien was motivated not by nationalism, but by a desire to prey on the nation's postwar weakness and social disorder for personal gain. To prevent such an eventuality from ever again threatening the state, the southern administration and its allies in the press waged a campaign of derision against Bay Vien as both a public and private figure. In Ngo Dinh Diem's view, it was just as important to condemn the Binh Xuyen leader for his personal degeneracy as for his military actions against the government. Within the personalist framework, Bay Vien's personal and political behaviors each constituted forms of treason, as they threatened Vietnam's moral fabric, undermined the prime minister's state-building efforts, and paved the way for communist advances.

Thoi Dai journalists Phuong Ha and Pham Con Son exposed "the scoundrel" Bay Vien's lurid secret love life with the claim that he had accrued no less than thirty-three wives by May 1955.[85] In a moralistic article series much like the exposé of Bao Dai's love life that would appear in the lead-up to the October 1955 referendum, they accused him of kidnapping young girls and enslaving in them in a manner unbefitting of human beings. Phuong Ha and Pham Con Son insisted that Bay Vien conducted himself as a sullied, impure, dishonorable monster.[86] Allegedly, he abused his position of power in Saigon-Cholon to seduce young, pure, moral women only to cast them aside in short order to cope unassisted with their ruined lives. One of his victims reportedly committed suicide to escape her shame, while another was forced to seek treatment in a mental hospital subsequent to delivering a "premature" baby to her husband after being released from Bay Vien's captivity.[87] Phuong Ha and Pham Con Son even accused Bay Vien of providing Binh Xuyen leaders Lai Van Sang and Lai Huu Tai with young girls to rape viciously at the magnificent Nghia Hiep guesthouse in the midst of the organization's late-April clash with the national army.[88]

On top of accusing Bay Vien of sexual perversion and predation, Ngo Dinh Diem's administration highlighted his record of dealing opium while heading up the Saigon-Cholon police force.[89] After the national army drove Binh Xuyen forces out of the capital in late-April, Ngo Dinh Diem's police and security forces unearthed evidence of Bay Vien's opium network and charged many of his associates with illegal drug trafficking.[90] The commander himself escaped prosecution, as he had fled to Paris shortly after his army's defeat, but the press all but tried him in absentia.

Media condemnations focused not only on Bay Vien's criminal acts but also on his propensity to pursue personal gain at the nation's expense. Journalists described him as a spineless rogue who had aligned himself first with the Japanese, then the Viet Minh, then the French. When Ngo Dinh Diem took office after the French defeat at Dien Bien Phu, journalists alleged, Bay Vien bribed Bao Dai with outrageous sums of tainted drug money to protect his network of vice industries and, by extension, his own political power and privilege. Even after the Battle of Saigon, he continued to try to secure his position through the emperor, but this ultimately failed when the South Vietnamese electorate deposed Bao Dai in October 1955.[91] The commander then allied with Vietnamese politicians in Parisian exile, including Bao Dai, Tran Van Huu, Nguyen Van Hinh, and other anti–Ngo Dinh Diem politicians who had been driven from Saigon during the prime minister's first two years in office.[92] This group lacked any real power but continued to lobby persistently for influence in South Vietnam and for international support for its objective of driving Ngo Dinh Diem from power and forming an alternative, noncommunist government south of the seventeenth parallel.

Ba Cut

In terms of armed resistance in the countryside, Ba Cut's Hoa Hao army posed the most persistent challenge to the Saigon administration in the months before and after the sect crisis. Of the four top Hoa Hao generals, Ba Cut was the most resolute in his opposition to Ngo Dinh Diem's government. Whereas Tran Van Soai, Lam Thanh Nguyen, and Nguyen Giac Ngo had vacillated between opposing the government and rallying to the national army in response to bribes throughout the first year of Ngo Dinh Diem's rule, Ba Cut had refused to align with Ngo Dinh Diem under any circumstances. Instead, almost before the ink had dried on the 1954 Geneva accords, he withdrew his troops into the Ca Mau region in the western

territory of South Vietnam and established himself as the southern government's principal military opposition within the organization.[93] When the
standoff between the United Front of Nationalist Forces and the national
army came to a head in March and April of 1955, politico-religious leaders
who had once disparaged Ba Cut recast his defiance as heroism. The United
Front blamed Ngo Dinh Diem for provoking Ba Cut's forces into battle
and insisted that his regime bore sole responsibility for the Hoa Hao insurrection.

Ba Cut's eventual capture in April 1956 served as an important symbolic
victory for the Saigon regime. Political commentators in Paris and Saigon
concluded that his apprehension "practically marked the end of all armed
opposition against the Government of President Ngo Dinh Diem."[94] As
Daniel Anderson of the U.S. Embassy in Saigon put it, the arrest of Ba Cut,
"the most able and spectacular leader of the Hoa Hao sect forces . . . was
one of the signal successes of the efforts to pacify the [southwest] region,
and may well lead to the virtual elimination of noncommunist armed opposition to the Diem government."[95]

American observers speculated on Ba Cut's capture that Ngo Dinh
Diem might seek to integrate him into the government rather than punish
him harshly for his antigovernmental activities. They noted that he possessed uncommon military ability and talent for leadership that could serve
the administration well. "Another factor which might operate in his favor,"
ventured one U.S. diplomat in Saigon, "is his apparently high degree of
popularity in South Vietnam, where he is widely viewed as a Robin Hood
type, personifying, in its good and bad aspects, the Vietnamese ideal of 'resistance.'" Washington feared that executing him could provoke anti–Ngo
Dinh Diem elements to exploit the Hoa Hao leader as a martyr for their
cause.[96] Even Lansdale, whose overall assessment of Ba Cut was far from
flattering, claims to have pleaded with Ngo Dinh Diem for clemency on
the Hoa Hao leader's behalf.[97]

For Ngo Dinh Diem, however, Ba Cut's popularity provided an argument for severity rather than leniency. He considered it imperative to
counter the notion that Ba Cut's resistance against the Saigon government
exemplified the Vietnamese tradition of struggle and self-sacrifice that Ngo
Dinh Diem himself claimed to represent. Thus South Vietnamese officials
immediately charged the Hoa Hao rebel with treason by virtue of Article
146 of the Republic of Vietnam's military code.[98] Ngo Dinh Diem alleged
that Ba Cut had rallied to the government and deserted a total of four times
between 1945 and 1954, after which he ended up commanding a battalion

of Hoa Hao soldiers in Thot Not.[99] By July 30, 1954, the administration claimed, Ba Cut had gone underground with thirty-five hundred soldiers and thirty-two hundred guns to stage a protracted campaign against Ngo Dinh Diem's national army. Perhaps most damningly, Ba Cut's Hoa Hao troops had for a time cooperated with communist forces. A rift quickly developed in that alliance, but nonetheless, it proved to Ngo Dinh Diem that Ba Cut was willing to align his forces with communists despite old animosities.[100]

In the end, the South Vietnamese government accused Ba Cut of committing several independent attacks on national army battalions, officers, and vehicles between July 1954 and April 1956, which added up to the grand charge of treason.[101] The government sought the death penalty for Ba Cut, armed with petitions from the people of My Tho, Long Xuyen, and more generally from the citizens of southwest Vietnam heralding the democratic underpinnings of Ngo Dinh Diem's regime and calling for the total annihilation of Ba Cut and his forces.[102] According to American sources, these petitions originated largely in official circles and were publicized in the government controlled press, and therefore could not be taken to represent genuine popular outrage against the Hoa Hao dissident.[103]

On June 11 a court in Can Tho sentenced Ba Cut to death for murder and arson, and a court of appeals confirmed this sentence on June 27. On July 4, 1956, the government tried him again in a military court, which issued a verdict condemning him to capital punishment with military degradation and the confiscation of his property.[104] Ngo Dinh Diem followed this up with an edict denying Ba Cut's request for amnesty and ordering the Minister of Justice of South Vietnam to carry out his execution.[105]

The Hoa Hao organization condemned Ba Cut's trial as shameful and unjust. On June 15 the Vietnamese Social Democratic Party (Viet Nam Dan Chu Xa Hoi Dang), the political arm of the Hoa Hao, issued an appeal to Vietnamese at home and abroad accusing Ngo Dinh Diem's Ministry of Justice of arbitrarily conferring the death sentence on Ba Cut out of spite and without sufficient evidence. The party's lawyer Dinh Van Cac, who had defended Ba Cut, asserted that the trial in Can Tho was a wasted opportunity for the court to set a noble precedent for future generations and for South Vietnam's judges to establish themselves as wise, discriminating, and righteous.[106] He claimed that Ngo Dinh Diem's administration had applied a double standard by convicting Ba Cut of the nebulous crime of treason while averting its eyes when the soldiers of General Duong Van Minh's Nguyen Hue operation raped the women and plundered the property of southwest Vietnam. "South Vietnam has no democracy and no freedom," declared Dinh Van Cac. "It has only shamelessness and foolishness, and only exercises the brand of justice applied by Diem's strongmen everywhere and in every case."[107] Ba Cut's lawyer threatened that 2 million members of the Vietnamese Social Democratic Party and three thousand Hoa Hao soldiers would continue to oppose Ngo Dinh Diem's regime as a result of his dictatorial policies.

Ba Cut's legal team continued to challenge these civilian and military verdicts to the very end. On July 9 another Hoa Hao lawyer, Vuong Quang Nhuong, appealed the previous judgments in the Supreme Appeals Court in Saigon and asked Ngo Dinh Diem to issue a pardon or clemency for his client. The court rejected the appeal within hours, on the same day that Ngo Dinh Diem rejected Ba Cut's personal plea for a pardon. The Hoa Hao dissident's fate to die at the hands of the state was sealed.[108]

At exactly 5:40 a.m. on July 13, Ba Cut met his destiny in a Can Tho cemetery.[109] Several hundred were on hand to observe his beheading, including his captor, General Duong Van Minh, as well as national assembly members, provincial officials, and a handful of South Vietnamese and foreign correspondents. American diplomat Daniel Anderson noted that Ba Cut's civilian style execution on the guillotine, in place of a military death in front of the firing squad, "was clearly intended to emphasize that Ba Cut was executed primarily as a civilian who had committed murders rather than as a rebel military chieftain."[110] This explains the dual civilian and military trials confirming his death sentence. By condemning Ba Cut first for his crimes committed as a private citizen before trying him for leading the government's political and military opposition, Ngo Dinh Diem's government made it clear that he was being punished for his personal degeneracy as much as he was for his political dissidence. At once this underscored Ngo Dinh Diem's personalist vision of good and bad citizenship and sent a broad warning about the grave consequences of attempting to subvert his government.

Observers in the CIA highlighted the significance of Ba Cut's demise in a January 1957 intelligence report. During Phase I of South Vietnam's history, according to this document, Ngo Dinh Diem concentrated his efforts on building a strong central government and obtaining security for South Vietnamese citizens. "The recent execution of Ba Cut, notorious leader of the dissident Hoa Hao sect, may be cited as a symbol of Diem's success on nearing the completion of Phase I." CIA officials claimed that Ngo Dinh Diem was then poised to turn his attention to Phase II, which would entail attempts to modernize the national army and revitalize South Vietnam's economy through land reform and resettlement.[111]

Dispatching the politico-religious military threat to his government was one of Ngo Dinh Diem's principal goals between 1954 and 1956. His army's success in doing so was critical to the total consolidation of political and military power, achieved by fall 1956, that enabled him to pursue his political objectives unchecked and to launch increasingly repressive anti-subversive programs in ensuing years. Through the attendant propaganda campaign, the Ministry of Information and Youth attempted to maximize the political mileage of the Battle of Saigon and the ensuing Nguyen Hue operation by discrediting pillars of the politico-religious communities, clarifying the Ngos' message about how a personalist Vietnamese society should and should not operate, and warning off potential critics of the Saigon government.

Another of Ngo Dinh Diem's most pressing objectives in his early administration was to eliminate French influence over South Vietnamese affairs. Defeating the politico-religious armies, many factions of which boasted close ties with France carried over from the war years, contributed to this goal. Equally critical was the challenge of removing chief-of-state Bao Dai from office in a manner that served Ngo Dinh Diem's political aims. He hoped to distance his administration from Vietnam's French co-lonial past, assert his uncontested authority south of the seventeenth paral-lel, and set himself up to create whatever form of government he chose. Deposing the chief of state by popular mandate rather than decree would better justify his refusal to take part in preparations for the countrywide elections slated by the ceasefire agreement to take place in summer 1956, and in which he never intended to participate. Moreover, a nationwide campaign against Bao Dai would present a perfect opportunity for the Ministry of Information and Youth to spread the Ngos' political message and build a case for the legitimacy of the South Vietnamese state under their direction.

Chapter 6

A Different Democracy

South Vietnam's Referendum to Depose Bao Dai

On October 23, 1955, amid the government's military and propaganda campaigns against the politico-religious organizations, South Vietnam's citizens took to the polls to choose between the country's obsolete emperor Bao Dai and its far-from-popular prime minister Ngo Dinh Diem.[1] Government propaganda told them that Bao Dai was a treacherous, slovenly womanizer who amounted to nothing more than a shackle on Vietnam's development. Ngo Dinh Diem, on the other hand, promised to usher in a new and glorious era in the nation's history marked by democracy, self-determination, and individual rights.

This referendum is often dismissed as a simple rigged election with little relevance to South Vietnam's larger cultural and political trajectory.[2] Yet Ngo Dinh Diem's campaign and its outcome exerted a lasting influence on politics below the seventeenth parallel and on the diplomatic relationship between the United States and South Vietnam. Like the propaganda offensive against politico-religious leadership, Ngo Dinh Diem intended his government's campaign against Bao Dai to help eradicate opposition and define "Free Vietnam's" political and moral boundaries. The character of Ngo Dinh Diem's government was relatively unimportant to his American patrons, who concerned themselves more with how it would be perceived by outside powers than by South Vietnam's own citizens.

Examined from within the South Vietnamese political context, the plebiscite represents far more than the simple removal of an unpopular emperor by authoritarian means. A close look at Ngo Dinh Diem's campaign rhetoric illuminates the changing nature of South Vietnam's political culture as he attempted to navigate the country's transition from what he viewed as its traditional past to a modernized future[3] in direct competition with the communist regime in the north.[4] Ngo Dinh Diem's approach to the campaign, and indeed to winning political legitimacy in South Vietnam, revealed the influence of his mandarin background from central, rather than the more heterogeneous southern, Vietnam. His appeals to the electorate combined somewhat veiled references to conventional Confucian notions of moral leadership—which he hoped would underscore his personalist ideas about social responsibility—with Western ideas about democracy and liberty to justify removing the emperor, and replacing the 1956 country-wide elections stipulated by the Geneva accords with his own national assembly elections to be held early that same year. Although Ngo Dinh Diem is traditionally represented as an authoritarian leader with no real interest in democracy, he issued broad promises of democratic rights and self-determination in this campaign that would inform South Vietnam's future political conflicts. The prime minister's opponents would thenceforth respond to his lofty promises of equal rights and self-rule by criticizing his regime for failing to live up to the democratic ideals that it espoused.

The referendum was also a significant event in the early days of the U.S.–South Vietnamese relationship. In keeping with the diplomatic trend one scholar refers to as "liberal democratic capitalism," the United States supported the election as a means of spreading democracy to Southeast Asia.[5] American officials from Secretary of State John Foster Dulles to ambassador to Saigon Frederick Reinhardt, however, were more concerned with how the referendum would be perceived internationally than they were with how it would be experienced within South Vietnam. By turning a blind eye to the contradictions between Ngo Dinh Diem's democratic rhetoric and his undemocratic practices, and by discounting the breadth and endurance of his political opposition, the United States helped generate the popular discontent that would plague the prime minister's administration until his assassination in November 1963. Since Bao Dai's removal from power dealt the final blow to France's already diminished influence in

Vietnam, the United States would reap these future consequences without support from European allies.[6] In short, the October referendum shaped the South Vietnamese political climate and the U.S.–South Vietnamese relationship in enduring ways and should be considered as both a formative event in the early history of the Republic of Vietnam and as an important moment in American foreign relations.

The Path to South Vietnam's First Election

Ngo Dinh Diem had been angling to liberate himself from Bao Dai's oversight since the emperor first appointed him to lead South Vietnam in June 1954. The sect crisis of March and April 1955 reinforced his hatred and suspicion of the French, and cemented his resolve to depose Bao Dai, whom he accused of colluding with French colonialist agents and rebellious politico-religious leaders to incite the crisis and attempt to remove him from power. Indeed, in the throes of the standoff, Bao Dai had been working with the French government to create an alternative nationalist government to replace the prime minister.[7] This act of subversion guaranteed that Ngo Dinh Diem would seek to unseat the emperor upon regaining a modicum of control over South Vietnamese politics. Ngo Dinh Diem was by no means alone in renouncing Bao Dai, as evidenced by a April 30, 1955 demand, issued by the newly formed Revolutionary Council, that the Saigon government should immediately remove the emperor from power. The council, however, was only an ostensibly pro–Ngo Dinh Diem body that was in fact dominated by Cao Dai elements and angling to seize control of the government by making the prime minister dependent on its support.[8] The prime minister therefore resisted the council's immediate pressures but went on to unseat Bao Dai and ratify his own authority by means of a popular referendum eight months later.

Historians have offered several explanations for Ngo Dinh Diem's refusal to go along with the Revolutionary Council's plan to depose Bao Dai immediately in the spring of 1955. Some have claimed that the prime minister was making good on his pledge not to use his grant of full powers to oust the emperor arbitrarily, but to submit Bao Dai's fate to the will of the people.[9] Others have argued that had Ngo Dinh Diem bowed to the council's demands and proclaimed Bao Dai's overthrow, he would have been accused by his constituents of committing an illegal coup d'état, which would have undermined his already fragile authority.[10] Beyond these considerations, though, Ngo Dinh Diem wanted not only to be rid of Bao Dai but also to assert himself as the one true liberator of Vietnam. He sought to validate his right to preside over the formation of a new government for the south, and could only do this by resisting the political pressure applied by the Revolutionary Council. He was determined to invest the demise of the monarchy and his own rise to power with an air of legality and legitimacy, and a popular referendum seemed the perfect means of accomplishing this.[11]

To regain control of South Vietnamese political momentum, Ngo Dinh Diem waited for the chaos of the sect crisis to abate before acting on the Revolutionary Council's demands for a new government. The prime minister then sought to legitimate his mission to depose the emperor by seeking a repudiation of Bao Dai and his heirs by the imperial Nguyen Phuoc family. Probably to shield itself from further defamation and to protect the sanctity of royal properties, the royal family eagerly complied on June 15, 1955.[12] The supreme body of the Nguyen Phuoc family denounced Bao Dai on the grounds that his decision to cede the throne to the Viet Minh in 1945 was a crime against Vietnam's citizens, and that he had plotted with French colonialists, the Binh Xuyen, and Hoa Hao generals Ba Cut and Nam Lua (Tran Van Soai) to threaten the nation's independence. The royal family thus pledged that it would no longer recognize Bao Dai's claims to rule and formally solicited Ngo Dinh Diem to become Vietnam's provisional president. It asked him to lead the "national revolution" through the difficult upcoming phase. In return, the Nguyen Phuocs requested that he cease his campaign against Bao Dai's private life and continue to protect the royal mausoleums, tombs, and shrines.

Even after this royal endorsement of Ngo Dinh Diem, the Revolutionary Council hoped to use Bao Dai's ouster as an opportunity to move against the current administration. By late June, observers in the U.S. Embassy noted, "Recent trends within [the] 'Revolutionary Council' indicate [a] serious cleavage between Diem and Cao Dai elements." To be sure, the two groups were united in their desire for Bao Dai's deposal, but their remaining objectives were almost diametrically opposed. Ngo Dinh Diem, on one hand, envisioned only minor postelection cabinet changes to bring in additional individuals who supported his leadership. And he sought to ensure his own victory in the elections by arresting pro–Bao Dai elements and keeping extremists in line through force. United States ambassador Reinhardt noted that Cao Dai representatives, on the other hand, "wished to see drastic reorganization [of the] cabinet resulting in replacement [of] many if not most incumbents by 'revolutionary' elements."[13] According to

Reinhardt, Cao Dai members of the Revolutionary Council continued to go along with Ngo Dinh Diem's programs in hopes of preventing him from moving against them and as part of a larger plot eventually to seize control of the government.

On July 7, the prime minister captured the initiative from the Cao Dai by announcing plans for a referendum that would remove the emperor from power and authorize him to found a new republic in the southern half of Vietnam. He made this announcement at least partly in response to messages from the United States that continued American support for his regime would depend on his ability to depose Bao Dai by legal, popular means. American diplomats considered this to be an essential move to forestall future challenges from the Viet Minh and the politico-religious organizations.[14] It was not until October 6, following what American diplomats in Saigon identified as a "three-week long government inspired press campaign against Bao Dai," that Ngo Dinh Diem set the referendum date for October 23, 1955.[15] This left little time for the Revolutionary Council, overall lacking in significant media channels,[16] to commandeer the prime minister's move for total authority over South Vietnam's political future. Bao Dai, living in luxury on the French Riviera, also had little time to formulate a response and initiate a campaign to defend his throne. At any rate, by this time he had minimal claim to political effectiveness or moral authority and stood virtually no chance of defeating Ngo Dinh Diem at the polls, even if given a fair chance to campaign.

The chief of state responded to the referendum announcement from his home in Cannes on October 13, accusing Ngo Dinh Diem of impeding peaceful reunification of South and North Vietnam. He implored his people not to support or encourage "a governmental activity which conforms neither to the profound sentiment of the Vietnamese people nor to the common cause of peace."[17] He issued his plea not to Vietnamese voters, but to French, British, and American leaders, since he had no outlet for propaganda in Saigon's tightly censored media.[18] Finally recognizing the inevitability of electoral defeat, Bao Dai made one last-ditch effort to salvage his authority on October 18, 1955. Accusing Ngo Dinh Diem of using the referendum to reestablish his personal dictatorship and to encourage renewed conflict between France and the United States, Bao Dai revoked his appointment as prime minister.[19]

Though American diplomats feared that Bao Dai's messages were designed to promote national reunification under communist leadership, his efforts to undermine the referendum registered hardly a ripple in South

Vietnam's political arena.[20] Ngo Dinh Diem continued with a vigorous campaign against the emperor during the week prior to the vote. His tenacity, combined with more than a little bit of rancor, was rewarded with just more than a 98 percent margin of victory.[21] On October 26, just moments after officially declaring triumph over Bao Dai, the prime minister announced the establishment of the Republic of Vietnam. "The October 23rd plebiscite," he exhorted, "in which [the people of South Vietnam] took such as enthusiastic part, constitutes an approval of the policies pursued thus far and at the same time augurs a whole new era for the future of our country."[22] Although this was a vast overstatement of the level of public support the prime minister enjoyed, the referendum and Ngo Dinh Diem's ensuing proclamation of the RVN did usher in a new era for the country. It was at this moment that South Vietnam was transformed from a temporary regroupment zone into a distinct, semipermanent political entity under Ngo Dinh Diem's control.

Campaigning through Tradition and Modernity

Although the public campaign leading up to the October 23 vote was almost completely one-sided, and the outcome of the referendum was hardly in doubt, it nevertheless reveals a great deal about Ngo Dinh Diem's efforts to establish a sense of nationhood in South Vietnam to rival the northern communist ideal. The campaign rhetoric the prime minister employed throughout fall 1955 provides a lens into what scholars have recently identified as his broader inclination to draw deeply on older ideas and customs in his quest to build a modern, postcolonial Vietnamese nation.[23] As Ngo Dinh Diem's rhetorical treatment of his politico-religious rivals demonstrated, he lamented the decay of traditional morals wrought by subjugation to French colonial rule and years of savage warfare. He hoped to restore the moral foundation of Vietnamese society; indeed he considered such moral recovery to be an essential precursor to the success of national modernization and reunification projects. His pledge "to destroy the sources of demoralization, however powerful, before getting down to the problem of endowing Vietnam with a democratic apparatus in the Western sense of the word" was as relevant to the referendum to depose Bao Dai as it was to his concurrent efforts to eradicate politico-religious opposition.[24]

Many of the ethical appeals Ngo Dinh Diem's issued during his campaign conformed to the basic principles of the "mandate of heaven" (*thien menh*), a Confucian notion inherited from the Chinese intellectual tradition, which Western scholars since the 1950s have identified as the driving force behind traditional Vietnamese political behavior.[25] The mandate of heaven endowed leaders with a responsibility to uphold strict moral and ethical standards, lest they lose the divine sanction to rule. Immoral conduct, whether it be personal or political, could cause a leader to lose his heavenly mandate and subject the entire society to heaven's wrath in the form of lost crops, wars, corruption, and other blights. Under the Confucian system, then, the people possessed a duty to rebel against corrupt leaders in order to restore heavenly sanction and with it social order.

The extent to which such Confucian beliefs and imperatives actually influenced Vietnamese political behavior remains open to debate, but recently historians have grown more and more skeptical of the power of the philosophy to shape political choices and outcomes in twentieth-century Vietnam. One claims that the influence of Confucianism in Vietnam has often been misunderstood and overstated, as it acted more as "a cluster of practices and ideas that appear to have some recognizable coherence," rather than a rigid political system.[26] And, of course, Confucianism was weakest in the frontier communities in the south, where Nguyen lords in the eighteenth century resorted to syncretic Buddhism rather than Confucianism as a mechanism for justifying their authority.[27] However, the notion of a virtuous ruler was also an important element of Vietnam's Buddhist tradition.[28]

An analysis of available campaign rhetoric and imagery suggests that the prime minister appealed somewhat vaguely to the concept of a heavenly mandate and the moral principles associated with it even as he attempted to modernize Vietnamese politics through a more overt emphasis on democracy and popular participation.[29] Indeed, the way that he emphasized the importance of virtuous leadership for Vietnam's future peace and prosperity, and insisted that citizens possessed a moral duty to cast off a leader who had proven himself corrupt, seemed to be an effort to mobilize Confucian principles of leadership precisely as a loose "cluster of practices and ideas" that he hoped would have some cultural resonance among Vietnamese voters.

Furthermore, by highlighting the moral responsibilities of both leaders and citizens, Ngo Dinh Diem also hoped to meld longstanding Vietnamese Confucian traditions with the foreign-inspired personalist philosophy on which he hoped to construct his government's legitimacy. Long before taking power in South Vietnam, Ngo Dinh Diem wrote that "a sacred respect is due to the person of the sovereign. . . . He is the mediator between the people and Heaven as he celebrates the national cult."[30] The father of French personalism, Emmanuel Mounier, articulated a justification for political leadership that sounded remarkably similar to Ngo Dinh Diem's: "Authority ... taken politically, is a vocation which the person receives from God (in the case of a Christian) or from his personalist mission which rises out of his social function (in the case of a non-Christian). . . . Personalism is an effort and a technique for constantly selecting from all social ranks a spiritual elite that is capable of authority."[31] During the campaign, the prime minister cast his personalist political appeals within a familiar, time-honored ethical framework while seeking to build a new, modern social order that could simultaneously provide for the collective good and protect the rights of individual citizens. Although Ngo Dinh Diem would ultimately fail to convey to his constituents the essence of personalist philosophy and its relevance to Vietnam's postcolonial future, it rested at the heart of his attempts to construct a popularly elected, modern government atop traditional tenets of Vietnamese ethical and political thought.[32]

A wide range of printed materials from Ngo Dinh Diem's campaign illuminates how he sought to utilize the concepts of virtuous leadership and the ethical duties of citizenship to persuade voters to jettison the chief of state and throw their support behind him and his new democratic form of government. Two strains of persuasion, one relatively traditional and the other clearly inspired by the West, permeated Ngo Dinh Diem's October 1955 crusade against Bao Dai. First, the South Vietnamese government and the Saigon press went to great lengths to discredit Bao Dai's morality in ways that made clear that heaven had stripped him and the royal family of the mandate and conferred it on Ngo Dinh Diem, a leader of great moral fortitude.[33] Responsibility, then, rested with the people, who possessed the power to salvage society by transferring power from Bao Dai to Ngo Dinh Diem. Second, newspaper articles and government statements extolled the merits of democratic government and self-determination. Conversely, they renounced Vietnam's old system of rule as feudalistic, authoritarian, and generally harmful to the nation's spirit.

The Debauched Emperor

In the first strain of this campaign, Ngo Dinh Diem and his supporters depicted Bao Dai as a debauched emperor in both the personal and political arenas. Though Bao Dai was actually a savvy politician with nationalist convictions of his own, the South Vietnamese regime reduced him to a caricature of evil and incompetence. He was, according to most accounts, a womanizer, a drunk, a glutton, and a slob. Observers viewed these attributes as contributing directly to his acquiescence with France's plots to recolonize Vietnam, his collusion with the communists, and his support for the "degenerate," "feudalistic" politico-religious warlords. Ngo Dinh Diem's agents and the Saigon media spared the emperor no fury in communicating these moral failings, and left no room for doubt that he had been stripped of heaven's mandate.

During the weeks preceding the referendum, the streets of Saigon and other provinces were littered with posters, streamers, effigies of Bao Dai, and a creative variety of other tools to denounce the chief of state and encourage citizens to cast their lot with Ngo Dinh Diem. The newspaper *Thoi Dai* published a photograph of a larger-than-life puppet of the former emperor in front of Saigon's central Ben Thanh market along with a poem that mocked his pale, puffy, ostentatious appearance and condemned his heartless promiscuity. The Bao Dai effigy, donning dark glasses and literally dripping women, was unmistakably aloof and out of touch. The lyrics to a song entitled "Depose Bao Dai," published in the same daily paper, beseeched the people of South Vietnam to join in condemning the chief of state for his record of selling out the country to colonial control so that he could more easily indulge his depraved, wanton ways.

Some of Ngo Dinh Diem's typical campaign slogans included "Bao Dai, puppet king selling his country," "Bao Dai, master keeper of gambling dens and brothels," "Being aware of vicious Bao Dai's preference for gambling, girls, wine, milk, and butter, those who vote for him will betray their country and despoil their people." On the other hand, "To vote for the revolutionary man Ngo Dinh Diem is to build a society of welfare and justice," and "Welcome Ngo Dinh Diem, the savior of the people. To kill communists, depose the king, [and] struggle against colonialists is a citizen's duty in Free Vietnam."[34]

Newspapers provided an opportunity for Ngo Dinh Diem's supporters to develop their condemnations of the emperor more thoroughly than they could on the aforementioned campaign posters. In August 1955 the daily paper *Thoi Dai* attacked Bao Dai's moral authority with a scathing three-week series on his sensational love life by editorialist Hong Van. He started out by condemning Bao Dai's devious attempts to depict himself as a national hero when he was in fact "a dung beetle who sold his country for personal glory."[35] According to this author, Bao Dai, born with the name Vinh Thuy, was not actually the legitimate son of King Khai Dinh.[36] Instead

Vịnh thằng nộm Bảo Đại trước Chợ Bến Thành

Áo vàng, đai đỏ, mặt bầu bầu
Mặt trắng, kính đen, cằm không râu...
Gát dựa cổ tay, nhìn nhớn nhác
Tiền treo dưới mắt, ngắm đi đâu...

Ông nghè thằng lảm ? Không người dốn !
Thằng nộm vườn dưa ? Chẳng kẻ cần !
Thiên hạ si sào : Kìa, Bảo Đại
Suốt đời chim gái với đi câu !

HÀN-CÔNG.KỊCH

Figure 6.1. Effigy of Bao Dai in front of Saigon's Ben Thanh Market, October 1955 (*Thoi Dai*). Ode to the effigy of Bao Dai in front of Ben Thanh Market (English translation): Yellow shirt, red sash, round face / Pale face, black shades, hairless chin . . . / Girls wrapped around his arms, searching / Dollar signs in his eyes, look no farther . . . / A doctor in name only? No one respected! / A scarecrow in the garden? No one needed! / People whisper: "Look, it's Bao Dai / Womanizing and wasting his whole life!"

he came into the royal family through a stroke of sheer luck. Khai Dinh was apparently known by many to be infertile, a fact which gravely affected his birthright to assume the throne as two others vied for control of the royal court at Hue. The author vaguely claims that the royal court might have issued an edict declaring that no childless man would be accepted as king. At any rate, Khai Dinh took a maidservant by the name of Cuc (later Hue Phi) as his imperial concubine and Bao Dai was born a prince soon after on October 22, 1913. Though Hong Van claimed that there was some evidence to prove Bao Dai's illegitimacy, including Khai Dinh's reputed scheme to bribe the boy's real father to keep quiet, it was not enough to negate the king's own testimony and Bao Dai's claims of legitimacy went officially unchallenged.

Hong Van described Khai Dinh and his brother Dong Khanh as feeble, thin, childless, and generally disinterested in women. Bao Dai, on the contrary, was "big like a lubber, had many children, and was very fond of

Figure 6.2. "A Song to Depose Bao Dai," October 1955 (*Thoi Dai*). Written to commemorate the day the Vietnamese deposed Bao Dai the puppet, music and lyrics by Minh Huy. English translation: 1) Yo-heave-ho, Yo-heave-ho. / Vietnam is shining bright. All of its people are arm in arm. / Let's sing: / "Depose Bao Dai, who betrayed our country. He is only good at self-indulgence and wantonness. / He gave our nation Vietnam to the stinking Colonialists. / He spends his time in dancing clubs with flashing lights. He is addicted to gambling and wastes people's money on himself only." / Oh, my wretched body! Yo-heave-ho. / 2) Yo-heave-ho, Yo-heave-ho. / Vietnam is shining bright. All of its people are arm in arm. / Let's sing: / "Bao Dai relies on the Colonialists while befriending the Communists to divide Vietnam into North and South. / People of our free nation should stand up to depose Bao Dai from his throne and support Ngo the Righteous Scholar. / Let's build a life full of glory, and a tomorrow when the whole nation prospers in peace." / Yo-heave-ho.

women."[37] On one hand, the author invoked this comparison to highlight the differences between Bao Dai and Khai Dinh that could have stemmed from their lack of a shared lineage. On the other, it implied that Bao Dai's lascivious behavior was not becoming of royalty, and that he would better have served the country as a weakling like his father rather than as the playboy he turned out to be.

Consistent with the anti-French feeling that quickly blossomed in South Vietnam under Ngo Dinh Diem's authority,[38] Hong Van blamed Bao Dai's French upbringing for his loose morality in the realm of love. He was essentially raised in Paris by the former governor general of Vietnam and his wife, and stayed there even after he ascended the Vietnamese throne on January 8, 1926, at the age of thirteen. By the time Bao Dai reached his late-teens, his mother began to hear rumors that he was learning the ways of love in France, a prospect that filled her with horror. According to these articles, she fretted over who would continue to worship and leave offerings for the former kings of Vietnam if her son should marry a French woman and spawn a flock of mixed-race children.[39] She allegedly wrote immediately to Bao Dai's guardians informing them of her wish to marry him to a Vietnamese woman, and to guard him from corrupting experiences during his stay in France. To her dismay, however, her son had apparently fallen in love with a French national by the name of Marie Jeanne Henriette Nguyen Huu Hao, who Hong Van described as "a Vietnamese girl, but like a French girl and loyal to France."[40] That she was a Christian made the union all the more deplorable to Bao Dai's elders in the royal court at Hue, as they were certain that he and his family would turn their attention away from Buddhist tradition and toward the Christian church, thus shirking their duties to attend to their ancestors' needs in the afterlife.[41]

Despite family concerns, the two were married on March 24, 1934, and Henriette took the name Nam Phuong. She proved to be an even less filial daughter-in-law than the Queen Mother expected, but revenge was quick in coming. After she bore Bao Dai three sons and two daughters in quick succession, Hong Van claimed, Nam Phuong's slender figure became wide and her luster dimmed considerably in her husband's eyes. After a few years, the emperor forgot his vows of everlasting love for Nam Phuong and took off to France to debauch and fulfill his lust for beautiful women, particularly French women.[42] He took up next with a French bar girl by the name of Evelyn Riva, after which he floated from one woman to another, taking some as mistresses and some as concubines, all the while neglecting his one legitimate wife.

Hong Van invoked the memory of former Vietnamese monarchs Le Thanh Ton and Mong Miep to assess the propriety of Bao Dai's behavior. Le Thanh Ton took a total of six concubines during his life, one of whom was Chinese. And Mong Miep had a whopping seventy-eight sons and forty-six daughters with several different women. According to Vietnamese tradition and rule of law, then, Bao Dai could not be faulted for taking multiple brides, even foreign ones. His real crime, according to Hong Van, was the mean, fickle way in which he used women and tossed them aside with no attention to his responsibilities as Vietnam's moral and political leader. Unlike Le Thanh Ton and Mong Miep, the author alleged that "Bao Dai was a depraved gambler, alcoholic, and womanizer who had a succession of fleeting love affairs that greatly damaged Vietnam's national honor."[43] Moreover, his penchant for French women, coupled with his lack of political acuity, made him vulnerable to manipulation by cunning French colonial officials. "You must agree with us on this point," wrote Hong Van, "Bao Dai is a playing card of the French—or more accurately—of a number of French colonists."[44]

Just four days prior to the referendum, the editors of *Thoi Dai* reminded their readers of Bao Dai's debauched upbringing, as it was exposed by Hong Van in August, with a cartoon rendition of his vapid youth and his consequent life of lewd and avaricious behavior. Anyone who saw the cartoon would be hard-pressed to forget the vivid images of the chief of state gorging himself on sex, food, alcohol, and gambling. And they would certainly understand the meaning of the last panel of the cartoon which depicted a photograph of Bao Dai with a sword through his eye printed next to "23–10," the date of the referendum.

As persuasive as this assault was, painting Bao Dai as depraved was only part of Ngo Dinh Diem's programmatic campaign to defame the emperor. He was also a traitor. Above all, as Hong Van implied by calling Bao Dai a French playing card, Ngo Dinh Diem insisted that he was guilty of falling into the role of France's lackey and of enabling French colonialists to reassert their authority in Vietnam after the Second World War.[45] The Committee for the Popular Referendum published an announcement claiming, "Bao Dai, the puppet emperor, the chief of state who divided the people, divided the country, and sold the entire nation to France and Japan is now plotting to join hands with the colonialists and the communists to sell the country once again."[46] Bao Dai, in turn, blamed the Chinese, the Russians, and the general outcome of the Geneva Conference for "selling" the northern half of the country into slavery. But his critics simply used this as

Figure 6.3. "The Story of Bao Dai," October 19, 1955 (*Thoi Dai*)

evidence that he was not only an inept leader but a leader unwilling and incapable of taking responsibility for his failures.[47]

As the above indictment indicates, Bao Dai's alleged transgressions against Vietnam did not cease with the Geneva accords. Individuals, soldiers, governmental agencies, and a variety of South Vietnamese political groups submitted piles of petitions imploring Ngo Dinh Diem to remove Bao Dai as chief of state of Vietnam.[48] Though these petitions were likely coerced, rather than spontaneous expressions of outrage, they called for Bao Dai's removal on the basis of his connection with various antigovernmental activities that had taken place throughout the preceding year. Petitioners accused him of conspiring with rogue Vietnam national army General Nguyen Van

Hinh to overthrow Ngo Dinh Diem in late 1954.[49] Moreover, they charged
Bao Dai with supporting the Hoa Hao, Cao Dai, and Binh Xuyen in their
efforts to sabotage Ngo Dinh Diem's administration in March and April
1955.[50] Some claimed that Bao Dai joined this group of traitors simply
because he did not possess the wisdom to use his power to appoint men of
virtue.[51] Instead, he ended up filling the ranks of government with political scoundrels interested only in stuffing their pockets with money. At any
rate, charges of pro-French, anti–Ngo Dinh Diem activities required little
imagination, since the emperor had in fact cooperated with the French attempt to replace the prime minister with an alternative nationalist government in the midst of the spring sect crisis.[52] But it did take some revisionist
thinking to represent this as treacherous behavior, and not just astute politics
in the face of Ngo Dinh Diem's faltering regime.

According to Ngo Dinh Diem's supporters, Bao Dai's most unforgiv-
able act of treason was not his collaboration with French colonialists nor his
conspiring with politico-religious leaders, but his collusion with northern
communists. In September 1955, by which point the national army had
subdued all but a few politico-religious rebels, he admitted in an interview
with *Collier's* magazine to ongoing contact with the Viet Cong. This was
widely interpreted within pro–Ngo Dinh Diem political circles as a sign
of Bao Dai's impending plans to subject the entire country once again to
foreign enslavement.[53] The emperor had often found himself on the wrong
side of South Vietnamese political conflicts, but to the prime minister his
conspiracy with communists was too nefarious to bear. Therefore Ngo
Dinh Diem insisted that Bao Dai be divested of his authority immediately.

Heralding Democracy

Without a doubt, Ngo Dinh Diem's assault on Bao Dai's character described
above followed the model established by Confucian political thought and
conformed to his personalist vision of social responsibility and individual
morality. He accused Bao Dai of being profoundly immoral and unethical, a fact that contributed to Vietnam's weakness and enslavement. While
his constituents may have interpreted these assertions within the familiar
Confucian framework, it appears that Ngo Dinh Diem and his allies never
claimed overtly that Bao Dai had lost the mandate of heaven. As one postcolonial theorist has written, "Even the most undemocratic of modern regimes must claim its legitimacy not from divine right or dynastic succession

or the right of conquest but from the will of the people."[54] Indeed, the prime minister was out to prove that his leadership and Bao Dai's deposal represented the popular will.

If Bao Dai as an individual had lost the mandate of heaven, then one could conclude from the prime minister's campaign that the institution of the monarchy had also fallen out of favor. Ngo Dinh Diem and his allies represented a modern democratic government, with himself at the helm, as the antithesis of the disgraced imperial system. While historians have traditionally claimed that the prime minister's democratic rhetoric was primarily directed at the United States, Vietnamese sources demonstrate that he disseminated these ideas broadly amongst the population below the seventeenth parallel.[55] The prime minister used the referendum as an opportunity to initiate a widespread drive to educate South Vietnamese citizens about the virtues of his own brand of personalist democracy and the malignancy of the old feudalistic imperial system.

On October 6, when the prime minister announced formal plans for the referendum, he portrayed it as a response to popular outcry against Bao Dai. He referred to countless motions submitted to the government by all manner of political, religious, and popular groups imploring him to organize a referendum to depose the emperor and to stabilize South Vietnam's political situation. The prime minister therefore billed the October 23 referendum as a response to these "legitimate and democratic" motions.[56]

Ngo Dinh Diem, however, envisioned the referendum as much more than a simple formality. It would be the country's inauguration into the free world. "This shall be but the first step," he claimed, "made by our people in the free use of our political rights."[57] A government declaration issued on October 19, 1955, passionately rallied citizens to seize these new democratic rights: "Dear compatriots, proclaim your will forcefully! Go forward firmly in the path of Freedom, Independence and Democracy!"[58] And on the eve of the election he announced over the radio, "This 23 October, for the first time in our country's history, our men and women will exercise one of many basic civil rights of a democracy, the right to vote."[59]

Since Vietnam had no real tradition of electoral politics, the South Vietnamese Ministry of Information and Youth had its work cut out for it if Ngo Dinh Diem truly expected citizens to exercise their right to vote. The administration initiated its campaign with extremely basic descriptions of a democratic government and its component parts. An educational pamphlet issued by the government addressed the question of why it was necessary to organize a popular referendum to depose Bao Dai even though the people and their political parties had already demanded his abdication in April and May. "Deposing a chief of state is a vital act," it explained, "and must follow a democratic procedure and send a clear order to the opponent that he cannot deny."[60]

The rest of this pamphlet revealed just how little some Vietnamese must have understood about the democratic process and even the role of central government. "A popular referendum," it explained, "is an extremely democratic method whereby citizens can directly reveal their ideas by voting to determine the fate of many important national issues like choosing the political regime, choosing the chief of state, etc." It went on to describe the important stabilizing role of a chief of state, especially in Vietnam where half the country was enslaved by communism, and the free half had not yet devised a constitution or elected a national assembly. Bao Dai, hated by his people and scorned abroad, could not possibly meet the country's needs for a strong and able chief of state.[61] For that reason, according to Ngo Dinh Diem's agents, the people should take it on themselves to remove Vietnam's last emperor from power on October 23.

In the months prior to the election, Saigon newspapers joined the Ministry of Information and Youth in broadcasting the appeal of a democratic system. "Under a dictatorial regime, communism or fascism, people do not speak of loyalty to the king or filial piety to their parents but of fidelity to the party," expounded one *Thoi Luan* editorial. "The citizens are merely the property of the party. Therefore, the people cannot speak of individual rights or demand that their basic needs be met."[62] The author went on to explain that, in a democracy, individual rights are exalted above all else. Democracies enjoy free elections, encourage criticism, and demand sacrifice only when it benefits the citizens. Democracy, then, represented a step forward from the old imperial system, whereas communism signaled a huge step back.

Ngo Dinh Diem and his supporters always spoke of this democratic revolution as a nationwide movement. Both the DRV and the RVN government each claimed to be the legitimate government of all Vietnam, both above and below the seventeenth parallel. According to northern communists, the southern government was nothing more than a neocolonial entity controlled by the United States.[63] Ngo Dinh Diem countered this argument with similar logic: communism was inherently totalitarian and unresponsive to the popular will. And to make matters worse, North Vietnam clearly rested under the thumb of Chinese and Soviet colonialists. Saigon newspapers published horror stories about communist atrocities in the north, as told by refugees living in resettlement camps, to demonstrate the tyrannical nature of the DRV. Ngo Dinh Diem's administration, then, asserted the right to establish a government for all of Vietnam while waiting for a chance to emancipate the north and reunify the country.

Indeed, an article in the Saigon daily *Lua Song* maintained that communism posed the primary obstacle to establishing a real democratic government, one that would serve and protect the rights of the people.[64] Anyone, especially Bao Dai in this case, who willfully cooperated with communists, colonialists, or feudalists, was acting contrary to the interests of the nation and endangering Vietnam's future stability and happiness. The only way to rid the nation of its backward, corrupt regime, then, was to vote in favor of elevating the proven anticommunist Ngo Dinh Diem to chief of state on October 23.

The prime minister's rhetoric of democracy and his condemnation of communism served a purpose in the context of the referendum far greater than discrediting Bao Dai. Aside from ridding South Vietnam of French influence via the emperor, Ngo Dinh Diem envisioned the referendum as a means of legitimating his refusal to hold the 1956 countrywide elections stipulated by the Geneva accords.[65] By depicting the southern regime as a democracy, and condemning the northern government for its authoritarianism, he hoped to gain domestic and international support for his unwillingness to negotiate with the communists.

As far back as late June, South Vietnamese foreign minister Vu Van Mau communicated to the United States that his government sought to unify the country through free, democratic elections. He insisted, however, that the South Vietnamese government was the "sole legal government in the country," and that it would pursue unification through its own national assembly elections rather than by participating in the countrywide elections promoted by the International Control Council.[66] While the United States quietly supported South Vietnamese efforts to avoid reunification elections, it urged Ngo Dinh Diem to begin consultations with the north to create at least the appearance of complying with the Geneva agreements.

On July 16, 1955, though, just ten days after publicizing plans for the referendum to depose Bao Dai, Ngo Dinh Diem personally announced his refusal to negotiate with the DRV over countrywide elections.[67] "We will not be tied down," he declared, "by the [Geneva] treaty that was signed against the wishes of the Vietnamese people." He thus called for all citizens below the seventeenth parallel to support his mission to establish a free, independent, democratic government to rival Ho Chi Minh's government.[68] The Saigon press, which was by then subject to increasing government censorship and intimidation, consistently supported his position, referring to the accords as "the Geneva treaty to sell the country," and insisting that South Vietnam's forced participation in the scheduled elections would be a huge step backward, tantamount to national enslavement.[69]

According to southern anticommunists, the very basis of communism was inherently antidemocratic, and it logically followed that the northern government was incapable of hosting a truly free election. On August 15, 1955, Nghiem Thi Xuan, the staunchly anticommunist, pro–Ngo Dinh Diem editor of Saigon's largest weekly, *Thoi Luan,*[70] defended this argument in an article entitled "How to Hold a Free Election in Vietnam." She charged that communist soldiers had visited voters' homes prior to the 1946 Viet Minh election and ordered them to cast their ballots for preselected communist candidates. On the day of the election, these soldiers allegedly followed people to the polls and watched closely to make sure they followed instructions. Nghiem Thi Xuan insisted that "no national government, nor any free citizen, can accept another such meaningless election."[71]

During his October campaign, then, Ngo Dinh Diem attempted to shift the focus away from reunification elections and toward both the national assembly elections scheduled for early 1956 and the constitution that newly elected representatives would be appointed to draft. He repeatedly billed the October 23 referendum as merely the first of several steps necessary to form a democratic polity. The process would only be complete once the constitution was ratified.[72]

American officials fully supported the prime minister's efforts to avoid reunification elections by establishing a popularly elected national assembly in the south, but held some reservations about the procedures he set in place.[73] State Department official Kenneth Young claimed, "A national assembly in Free Viet-Nam is a prerequisite to any Vietnamese consideration of consultations and all-Vietnamese elections." But he was concerned about the unpredictability of democratic elections in newly independent states and the potential for undermining Ngo Dinh Diem's fragile regime. Young therefore warned, "I am reluctant for the United States and its friends to start pressing the Vietnamese down this path from which there is no return."[74]

Ambassador Reinhardt, moreover, expressed reservations about the public relations problem that could result from Ngo Dinh Diem's plans to remove Bao Dai and to ratify a South Vietnamese constitution by a popular vote. "[The] referendum procedure," he claimed, was "clearly less democratic than having [an] elected assembly decide on questions of Bao Dai and [the] new constitution."[75] Reinhardt's concerns reflected the broader

American preoccupation with the negative publicity the White House anticipated in response to Ngo Dinh Diem's blatantly undemocratic referendum.
"Government control of [the] referendum," warned the ambassador, "and
[the] absence [of] opportunity [for] opposition elements [to] obtain hearing
as well as other undemocratic elements of this exercise have not been lost
upon representatives [of the] foreign press [in Saigon]."[76] He insisted that it
would be unwise for U.S. officials to imply publicly that the referendum was
a free and democratic expression of the Vietnamese popular will. Reinhardt
advised instead that they maintain simply that the future government of
Vietnam was an internal matter that should be left to its citizens to decide.
The State Department agreed and on October 20 Dulles's press spokes-
man issued a public statement along these very lines.[77] The United States, it
seems, opted to downplay the democratic nature of the referendum to avoid
political embarrassment when it became clear to international observers that
Ngo Dinh Diem's veil of democracy was wearing thin.

October 23

By the time the South Vietnamese electorate arrived at the polls on October 23, Ngo Dinh Diem's administration had devised a very specific mechanism by which to conduct and record the vote. Shortly after the prime
minister officially announced the date of the referendum on October 6, his
government publicized important logistical information for the election.
Though some of these provisions may appear mundane to twenty-first-
century Western eyes, they were novel and important to Vietnamese voters
in 1955.

In an effort to guarantee universal suffrage, or at least to create that appearance, all men and women over the age of eighteen who had registered
in the recent census would have the right to cast a secret ballot. According to
the final government count, registered voters tallied 5,335,688.[78] To ensure
accuracy and prevent fraud, government regulations required provincial officials to organize a separate polling station for every one thousand voters.[79]

Upon entering the polls, voters would be asked to present their identity
cards before receiving a ballot and an envelope. They were instructed to tear
off the half representing their candidate of choice, place it in the envelope,
and present it to the commission chief for inspection before inserting it into
the ballot box. Voters would then discard the rejected half onto the floor or
some other receptacle. Despite the appearance of impartiality generated by

these electoral regulations, the ballot sent an unmistakable signal that Ngo Dinh Diem was the only real choice. The left side, with an inauspicious green border, showed a bloated, somber, traditionally clad Bao Dai above the text, "I do not depose Bao Dai and do not recognize Ngo Dinh Diem as the chief of state of Vietnam with the duty to organize a democratic government." The right side, bordered by the lucky color red, showed a smiling, vibrant, modern clad Ngo Dinh Diem making his way through an adoring throng, above the text, "I depose Bao Dai and recognize Ngo Dinh Diem as chief of state of Vietnam with the duty to organize a democratic government."[80] CIA officer and Ngo Dinh Diem confidant Edward Lansdale recalls advising the prime minister to use color on the ballot to send a subliminal message to voters without appealing directly to superstition or custom. He claims, however, that he urged Ngo Dinh Diem to use a good photograph of Bao Dai in order to confirm the validity of the vote.[81] Beyond this, there is little evidence that the United States took significant interest in Ngo Dinh Diem's polling procedures prior to the referendum.

Tôi không truất-phế (không bỏ) Ong Bảo-Đại và không công nhận (không bằng lòng) Ông Ngô-Đinh-Diệm làm Quốc-Trưởng Việt-Nam với nhiệm-vụ tổ-chức một chính-thể dân-chủ.

Tôi truất-phế (bỏ) Ông Bảo-Đại và công nhận (bằng lòng) Ông Ngô-Đinh-Diệm làm Quốc-Trưởng Việt-Nam với nhiệm-vụ tổ-chức một chính-thể dân-chủ.

Figure 6.4. Ballot for South Vietnamese referendum, October 23, 1955 (Vietnamese National Archives #2)

In any case, despite the suggestive nature of the ballot, Ngo Dinh Diem's administration represented the process of recording the vote to be impartial. Once all votes were cast, poll workers had specific instructions for counting and reporting the returns. Government regulations dictated exactly how to determine whether or not a ballot was valid, and detailed to whom returns should be reported and when. Extensive steps had been taken, at least on paper, to prevent electoral fraud. In truth, however, no amount of unilateral campaigning, anti–Bao Dai sentiment, or Confucian political restraint could explain Ngo Dinh Diem's 98 percent margin of victory in a politically heterogeneous South Vietnam. Corruption and intimidation must have played a significant role.

Assessing the Results

A 1966 CIA review of election processes in South Vietnam concluded that the October 1955 referendum was the most heavily predetermined of the six elections held in the south since the Geneva accords. "Both the voting procedures," it claimed, "and the atmosphere in advance of the balloting, were calculated to produce the desired results."[82] Ngo Dinh Diem, it claimed, used the Ministry of Information and Youth's voter education campaign to publicize the government's candidates, "while seldom going so far as to explain to the people the meaning of elections or the power of the ballot." This is perhaps an unfair critique, as the South Vietnamese government did go to some effort to illuminate the process of democracy. However, these educational efforts were always slanted heavily in favor of the prime minister. Beyond these manipulations, the CIA noted that military pressure, ballot tampering, and a lack of genuine secrecy might have contributed to Ngo Dinh Diem's overwhelming victory. The U.S. government concluded in 1955, though, that propaganda was of greater consequence than voter irregularities in determining the outcome of the referendum. "With Bao Dai in Paris and unable to plead his case," noted U.S. intelligence analysts, "the government-controlled press and radio had a monopoly on all campaigning."[83]

Despite this skewed campaign that had worried American officials in the days leading up to the vote, Washington welcomed Ngo Dinh Diem's victory. After the prime minister announced his triumph on October 26, Reinhardt edged away from his earlier concerns and concluded that the "referendum proved [a] resounding success for [the] Diem government."

The results, he claimed, did not prove that the prime minister commanded majority support in South Vietnam but that the government was able to carry out a nearly unchallenged popular referendum.[84] Aside from scattered attacks on Can Tho polling places by Hoa Hao soldiers, visible resistance to Ngo Dinh Diem's controlled election was nil.[85] In absence of a true show of democracy, American officials enthusiastically greeted the southern leader's ability to suppress dissent from the politico-religious organizations, communists, and Bao Dai sympathizers.

Moreover, in spite of Reinhardt's preelection concerns, much of the American press hailed the vote in Vietnam as a great victory for democracy and a blow to communism worldwide. One Midwest newspaper interpreted the results as "an overwhelming vote of confidence" for Ngo Dinh Diem and "wholehearted backing for the democratic principles for which he is known to stand."[86] According to one Ohio paper, "A people most inexperienced in the ways of democracy went to the polls Sunday and returned a verdict loaded with sound philosophical instincts."[87] Commentators on the east coast, however, remained more skeptical. "The heavy referendum vote throughout South Vietnam," wrote Henry Lieberman of the *New York Times*, "makes Diem's administrative control look more pervasive than is thought to be the case by a number of observers here."[88]

Both pessimists and optimists noted that the prime minister's victory in the referendum would likely preclude national reunification elections scheduled for the following spring, just as he intended. The *Los Angeles Times* pointed out on October 24, "The overwhelming Diem victory virtually eliminated any possibility there will be a Viet-Nam unification election next July as provided by the Geneva armistice accords."[89] Ngo Dinh Diem verified this suspicion on October 25 when he announced that he would not proceed with negotiations in preparation for countrywide elections until "true liberty" was established in the communist north.[90] This result came as a relief to Americans who, by and large, feared the cascade of red dominoes throughout Southeast Asia.

For many American journalists, though, the referendum was notable foremost for its role in solidifying South Vietnam's political move away from France and toward the United States.[91] Americans saw the October vote as a slap in the face and yet another deep humiliation for France. Since France had gambled on opposing Ngo Dinh Diem and promoting Bao Dai as the supreme leader of South Vietnam, the emperor's final ouster signaled the end of any lingering French efforts to assert authority in Saigon.[92] Though many Americans heralded this as a positive development, one that would

enable the competent Ngo Dinh Diem to carry on an effective government once and for all, others were wary of the future implications.[93] They
recognized that France's expulsion isolated the United States as the sole
Western power in South Vietnam, a fact that could haunt Washington in
years to come.

French diplomats and journalists naturally interpreted the referendum
as more than a simple slap in the face. Though France officially recognized
Ngo Dinh Diem's RVN almost immediately, the French media betrayed the
nation's unease with his victory. In the days leading up to the vote, French
officials in Saigon feared that Ngo Dinh Diem's administration would take
the referendum as evidence that it was no longer bound to previous international agreements, thus enabling it to call for the immediate dissolution
of the French High Command. Such a move, France feared, would make
it impossible to implement the Geneva agreements below the seventeenth
parallel.[94] Some journalists claimed that the plot to depose Bao Dai was a
part of the American plan to undermine the Geneva elections by sponsor-
ing a separate vote in the south.[95] They described the referendum as the
first of two stages in Ngo Dinh Diem's strategy to sabotage the peaceful
reestablishment of national unity, and to eliminate opposition in general and
French influence in particular. The election of a national assembly for South
Vietnam would complete Ngo Dinh Diem's devious plan. Many French
observers worried that this would severely damage Franco-American relations and obviate any possibility for rapprochement between North and
South Vietnam.[96]

Though *Le Monde* remained cautiously hopeful about the democratic
potential of Ngo Dinh Diem's government, several other French newspapers insisted that the election procedures were fundamentally undemocratic
and called the election results into question. Some claimed that the lack of
vocal opposition in Saigon provided evidence of oppression rather than
unanimity.[97] Approximately 50 percent of voters abstained, according to
the Paris press, thus explaining Ngo Dinh Diem's overwhelming victory.
He garnered all the votes simply because none of his detractors bothered
to show up at the polls.[98]

Seeds of Dissent

Even more important than French and American responses to Ngo Dinh
Diem's campaign were the reactions of Vietnamese opposition leaders.[99]

Because the prime minister promoted the referendum as the great demo-cratic moment in Vietnam's history, his opponents attacked him on the grounds that his commitment to democratic ideals was largely rhetorical. In fact, the election was, by design, anything but democratic. Ngo Dinh Diem's former cabinet member Cao Van Luan recalls a 1955 conversation dur-ing which the prime minister complained that too many seedling parties threatened to generate chaos in the south. The country, Ngo Dinh Diem insisted, should have but one national revolutionary movement (*phong trao cach mang quoc gia*) and one political party, the Personalist Labor Revolu-tionary Party (Can Lao Nhan Vi Cach Mang Dang) controlled by Ngo Dinh Nhu.[100] The government thus liquidated opposing parties by force and eliminated any real prospect for open political competition. According to one northern historian's statistics the *My-Diem*, or American sponsored Ngo Dinh Diem regime, killed or imprisoned 93,362 opposition soldiers, party members, and patriots between July 1955 and February 1956 during a violent campaign to eradicate rivals.[101] This figure is likely exaggerated, but certainly denotes a culture of fear that would have impeded the democratic process.

There was, indeed, little public opposition to Ngo Dinh Diem prior to the referendum. Several powerful Cao Dai and Hoa Hao leaders were still working within the Revolutionary Council to wrest power from the government, while those who opposed the prime minister overtly were en-gaged in battles against the national army for their very survival.[102] Disgrun-tled politico-religious leaders did pose some resistance, but were limited by their lack of access to the press. On October 22 Hoa Hao general Tran Van Soai, who would not rally his forces to the government for another month, announced that he would prefer a truly democratic regime to Ngo Dinh Diem's sham of a government, and declared the referendum illegal, and its results null and void. He invited "friendly countries and the people of Vietnam to distrust this political maneuver."[103]

Ba Cut's Hoa Hao forces, still engaged in battle with the national army in the western region of South Vietnam, raised similar criticisms against the prime minister's intrigues. In a pamphlet dated October 3, 1955, Ba Cut charged that the referendum was a time "for Diem to gather the people from all towns and force them to demonstrate one goal: to depose Bao Dai and proclaim the puppet Diem as the chief of state of Vietnam."[104] This, he claimed, was proof of the American plot to "Catholicize" Vietnam, as Ngo Dinh Diem reportedly used not only $2 million dollars of American aid, but also $2 million in aid from American Catholic organizations to support the referendum. According to the Vietnamese Social Democratic Party, also a Hoa Hao organ, the prime minister put this American aid money to less than honorable use. Its spokesmen claimed that he "bribed the world of laborers and young students to petition in support of Diem's rise to chief of state and to petition in favor of deposing Bao Dai."[105]

By the time the national assembly elections rolled around in March 1956, these scattered criticisms would blossom into full-fledged opposition. This was due, at least in part, to Ngo Dinh Diem's dissolution of the Revolutionary Council on January 15, 1956, by a series of police raids that forced most of its members into exile or back into the militarized jungles of southwest Vietnam.[106] These leaders understandably felt double-crossed and responded by joining other disenfranchised Vietnamese nationalists in vigorously denouncing Ngo Dinh Diem's pseudodemocratic means of securing his authority. Come March, they would mimic the communists in labeling his government *My-Diem*, and would add some new and enduring slurs to the political dialogue, including *ton giao tri* (religious government) and *gia dinh tri* (family government).

This reinterpretation of the October 23 referendum reveals that Ngo Dinh Diem made sweeping promises of democracy and self-determination to his constituents throughout South Vietnam. To date, historians have overwhelmingly concluded that Ngo Dinh Diem merely paid lip service to democratic ideals in the international arena to please his American sponsors, but the campaign rhetoric discussed here demonstrates that the prime minister himself believed in the virtues of his particular brand of democracy. His democratic ideal, rooted in personalism, reflected a critique of the Western model and was based less on citizens' participation in government than citizens' moral participation in society at the local level. Promoting his version of democracy, while eliminating opposition, was all a part of the personalist revolution through which the Ngo brothers sought to transform Vietnam into a modern state with strong ethical foundations. It is critical to remember that democracy within the context of a personalist revolution had its own unique meaning, and the Ngos did not endorse the "one-man, one-vote" approach that underpinned democratic systems in the West.

However, the Ngo brothers failed to explain personalism fully, much less win mass converts to the approach. Therefore, the unfulfilled promises of equal rights and individual freedoms issued in this campaign, and perpetuated in future political contests, can help to explain the outrage with which South Vietnamese citizens would respond to Ngo Dinh Diem's oppressive reign in subsequent years. In October 1955 the prime minister claimed to revolutionize Vietnamese society by emancipating it from its backward imperial past and ridding it of an unethical leader. But he failed to replace the old system with a more popular regime, and his rhetoric of democracy provided his opponents with a ready vocabulary to propagandize against him. From October 1955 on, South Vietnamese opposition groups would accuse Ngo Dinh Diem not only of poor leadership but also of hypocrisy. In the short term, he succeeded in forestalling the 1956 unification elections and establishing South Vietnam as an autonomous state, but in the process he planted some of the seeds of dissent that would ultimately lead to his downfall and to the failure of the RVN.

On the flip side, American sources reveal that U.S. officials devoted much more attention to international public opinion in this case than they did to internal Vietnamese political affairs. Policymakers in Washington and Saigon were concerned about the undemocratic nature of this October referendum only to the extent that it would damage Ngo Dinh Diem's international reputation and tarnish America's image by extension. Dulles, Reinhardt, and their colleagues were not particularly concerned with how the referendum was experienced by South Vietnam's citizens and by the country's competing political factions like the Hoa Hao, Binh Xuyen, and Cao Dai. American officials' lack of attention to South Vietnam's complex domestic political environment permitted the United States to stand idly by as Ngo Dinh Diem undermined his own authority, and left Washington ill-equipped to interpret and respond to the negative fallout that would eventually result from Ngo Dinh Diem's broken promises and repressive policies. In the months and years that followed, Ngo Dinh Diem's opponents sought to warn the United States of the backlash that was building against the Saigon government, but for the remainder of the decade most in Washington would remain wedded to the myth of their client's miraculous leadership.

Chapter 7

The Making of a Revolution
in South Vietnam

The government of Ngo Dinh Diem reached a critical turning point at the beginning of 1956. He had deposed Bao Dai, established a new republican government in South Vietnam, and validated his leadership through an ostensibly democratic referendum. He held firm to his refusal to participate in preparations for the countrywide reunification elections mandated by the 1954 Geneva agreements that he had not signed and to which he did not feel bound. Instead, he looked forward to RVN national assembly elections, confident of his ability to influence the results thanks largely to the success of military operations against politico-religious rebels that his army was just wrapping up. Moreover, the Denounce the Communists Campaign and its attendant security apparatus under Ngo Dinh Nhu's supervision provided Ngo Dinh Diem with the means and the justification he needed to suppress opponents of his government, violently if necessary.

After his victory in the sect crisis of spring 1955, observers in the U.S. government and the American press celebrated Ngo Dinh Diem's consolidation of power as nothing short of a miracle. Ngo Dinh Diem's supporters in the United States, liberal and conservative alike, praised him for his "dynamic leadership," his "hatred of tyranny," and his "stubborn patriotism and honesty."[1] While Washington's allies in France, Britain, and even Australia were taken aback by the oppressive means by which they saw Diem prevail against his politico-religious adversaries during and after the Battle of Saigon, Americans overlooked the growing police state he was building and instead focused on the blows he dealt to communism in Southeast Asia and praised him for wrapping his government in the trappings of democracy.

Thereafter, the United States committed itself fully to working with Ngo Dinh Diem on a program of nation-building in South Vietnam. Between fiscal years 1955 and 1961, the United States funneled more than $1.5 billion in economic and $500 million in military aid to the RVN.[2] American advisors took over France's role of training and equipping the Army of the Republic of Vietnam (ARVN) and busied themselves assisting Ngo Dinh Diem with the task of establishing a fully functioning government along democratic lines. They consulted with his administration on land reform, civil service reform, and most important to the Ngos, internal security. In the coming years, the U.S.–RVN relationship would be strained by ongoing conflicts over competing visions for how best to modernize South Vietnam.[3]

Even as American officials complained about Ngo Dinh Diem's stubborn refusal to follow their advice to combat his enemies less through violence and oppression and more through democratizing political reforms, they discounted his opponents' charges that his authoritarian methods were fueling the communist cause and undermining South Vietnam's long-term stability. After all, he managed to establish a high degree of order out of the anarchy that prevailed when he took power. True democracy might come more slowly, indeed perhaps only after strong centralized authority was firmly established, reasoned his American backers. In the meantime, as South Vietnam became more stable, it faded from American attention and became a backburner diplomatic issue. For a few short years after 1956, South Vietnam seemed to stand out as a great American success in the global struggle to contain communism and promote democracy.

However, while Ngo Dinh Diem's rapid and near total consolidation of power by 1956 appeared at the time to signal success, its real significance lay in how it set the stage for his ultimate failure and for the failure of the American nation-building project in Vietnam. The structure and professed ideology of the South Vietnamese state that he established during his first two years in office came about in direct response to challenges posed by his noncommunist domestic political rivals. In turn, the insular, oppressive nature of his state paved the way for the Hanoi-backed resistance movement against the *My-Diem* (American-Diem) government that would emerge by the decade's end. Despite persistent claims that his government's highest purpose was to combat communism, his first two years in office were dominated by struggles with noncommunist politico-religious rivals, and those rivals would continue to pose the most immediate threats to government control in various parts of the countryside in the years just after 1956. South Vietnam's oppressive security apparatus thus developed not only in response to a largely anticipated communist threat, but as a means of identifying and neutralizing other challenges to the Saigon government, the most prominent of which originated with the politico-religious organizations.

The timing and justification for all of Ngo Dinh Diem's major early political moves also emerged in reaction to challenges from the Cao Dai, Hoa Hao, Binh Xuyen, and other noncommunist nationalists who aligned themselves with these groups. His tight control over political participation, which ultimately led to widespread dissatisfaction with his nepotism and the glaring emptiness of his democratic rhetoric, resulted from his desire to shut politico-religious figures and other noncommunist nationalists out of his government, a goal only fueled by his paranoid, insular personality. The Ngo brothers' insistence on lumping all critics of their administration into the category of "communists," or what they called Viet Cong after 1956—a category they defined as treasonous—isolated discontented politico-religious figures and other anti-Diem nationalists and encouraged them to collaborate with communists in the coming years. Indeed, by excluding them from the political process and targeting them as enemies of the state, Ngo Dinh Diem left them with little choice. His own policies, the trajectory of which was cemented during his consolidation of power in 1955 and 1956, contributed as much as anything to fulfilling his prophecy that all who opposed his government were communists or communist collaborators. The backlash against those policies would come home to roost with the formation of the broad-based, communist-directed National Liberation Front for South Vietnam (NLF) in 1960.

Electing a National Assembly and Drafting a Constitution

In early 1956, Ngo Dinh Diem aimed to flesh out the structure and foundation of his government and solidify his refusal to hold reunification elections.

During his campaign against Bao Dai he had promised the citizens of South Vietnam that by the end of 1955 he would complete the country's transition from an oppressed colony to a representative democracy by holding popular elections for a national assembly. And on October 26, as he announced his victory over the chief of state and the formation of the RVN, he reiterated his intention to broaden the country's democratic base by drafting a constitution and holding elections for a national assembly.[4] He frustrated American officials by dragging his feet on setting a date for the elections, but justified the delay on the grounds that the country's "many main parties" had requested a postponement to allow them time to mount effective campaigns.[5] More likely, however, the Ngos wanted more time to complete their military campaign against the politico-religious rebel armies and to better establish government parties in the countryside in order to ensure that they could control the election results. On January 23, 1956, Ngo Dinh Diem finally issued Presidential Ordinances 8 and 9, which called for an election on March 4, 1956, to select 123 national assembly members from districts approximately equal in voting strength. The assembly would then have forty-five days from its first meeting to prepare a draft constitution to submit to the president for consideration and amendment.[6]

The president and his Ministry of Information and Youth disseminated propaganda touting the democratic nature of the elections, even as they set out to ensure the victory of government approved candidates. A January 1956 *Saigon Moi* article promised that the RVN assembly would include people from all classes and represent every political leaning and every philosophy aside from communism. The author juxtaposed it with both the Viet Minh Assembly of 1946, which allegedly was controlled by a small band of military leaders, and Bao Dai's SVN Assembly, which had not been popularly elected and failed to represent majority interests.[7]

In truth, the RVN's first national assembly election was democratic in name only.[8] As early as December 1955 Ambassador Reinhardt warned Dulles that whenever elections did occur, "genuine noncommunist opposition elements will have very limited scope, if any." But he hastened to add that this was not necessarily something the United States should worry about. In his judgment, few leaders in Vietnam were truly motivated by sincere democratic principles and, aside from Ngo Dinh Diem, the country lacked legitimate political players worth accommodating. Reinhardt advised Dulles, "It is clearly undesirable at this time to risk upsetting [the] stability of [the] government by permitting too great a degree of political freedom." Moreover, he recognized that American "influence over [the] course of government action is obviously limited by Ngo Dinh Diem's realization that we have committed ourselves to backing him fully, and his conviction that our aid and support can be taken for granted."[9]

Meanwhile, Ngo Dinh Diem's domestic political opponents criticized his increasing authoritarianism. In late November 1955, Revolutionary Council president Nguyen Bao Toan, who had yet to break with the president, lamented South Vietnam's increasing trend toward a "completely totalitarian regime with terroristic repression [of] all national elements outside [the] small clique in Ngo Dinh Diem's immediate entourage."[10] The government put him under strong pressure to disband the Revolutionary Council in advance of the national assembly elections, and when he resisted, the Ngo brothers proceeded on their own. Breaking up the council and dismantling the parties it comprised was a critical step in their overall plan to organize all progovernment and "loyal opposition" groups into one official government party under Ngo Dinh Nhu's direction.[11] Politico-religious parties, including the Cao Dai's Viet Nam Phuc Quoc Hoi (Association for National Restoration) and Mat Tran Quoc Gia Khang Chien (National Resistance Front), and the Hoa Hao's Dan Chu Xa Hoi Dang (Social Democratic Party), refused to comply. Nguyen Bao Toan led the resistance, which prompted Ngo Dinh Diem to cast him out of government circles entirely by the end of 1955. Then, with nothing left to lose, Nguyen Bao Toan openly defied the RVN, insisting that majority support in the council gave him the right and the power to ignore the president's orders to disband.[12] Ngo Dinh Diem responded by ordering ARVN troops to occupy Revolutionary Council headquarters to expel Nguyen Bao Toan and his supporters by force.

This political battle between Nguyen Bao Toan and the government coincided with increasing Cao Dai restiveness, which culminated in the defection of about three thousand of Trinh Minh The's former Lien Minh soldiers from the national army. Moreover, it occasioned yet another key instance of cooperation between disparate politico-religious leaders united in opposition to Ngo Dinh Diem's exclusivity. In late January 1956, Ngo Khai Minh, a high-ranking Cao Dai representative in Paris, led an anti–Ngo Dinh Diem meeting of nearly twenty expatriated Vietnamese military and political personalities. The group, including Buu Loc, Buu Hoi, Nguyen Van Tam, Nguyen Van Hinh, Tran Van Huu, and Bay Vien, condemned the dictatorial nature of Ngo Dinh Diem's regime, particularly in reference to recent measures taken against anti–Ngo Dinh Diem, anti–Viet Minh nationalists. They referred, of course, to the Nguyen Hue operation, the Denounce the Communists Campaign, and related instances of violence, intimidation, and propaganda directed against the Ngos' political challengers. The group listed a number of what they considered to be the government's victims, which included Bao Dai, Nguyen Van Hinh, Bay Vien, Ba Cut, and Tran Van Soai. Furthermore, it vowed to boycott the elections unless the Saigon government allowed for fair and open campaign and voting procedures.[13]

Ngo Dinh Diem's administration ignored these dissenting voices as it kicked off its campaign. On January 22, 1956, the National Revolutionary Movement held a press conference to present its platform, which consisted of a pro-forma endorsement of a multiparty system, an invitation for France to withdraw its Expeditionary Corps, and promises of equality of the sexes, agrarian reform, and social insurance laws. Regarding domestic political opposition, the NRM covered its bases with the announcement that "democratic liberties [were] to be guaranteed to all except traitors, agents of communism, and feudalists."[14]

In keeping with the fundamental anticommunist premise of Ngo Dinh Diem's national revolution, government vitriol in the national assembly campaign was directed overwhelmingly at communists. The Ngo brothers continued their strategy of lumping all antigovernment figures into the communist camp, thereby branding them as criminals, in order to justify excluding them from the democratic process. This task was made easier by the fact that disaffected Hoa Hao, Cao Dai, Binh Xuyen, and other noncommunist nationalists, having been fully excluded from Ngo Dinh Diem's government, were left with little alternative but to begin cooperating with the communist figures they had once despised.

In the end, the democratic façade of this election was no more convincing than that of the previous October. The government bore all campaign expenses, but rather than serving to equalize the race, this proved to be just another means of controlling information. This time the government-run Candidates' Campaign Committee (CCC) joined the Ministry of Information and Youth in getting out the vote. Ngo Dinh Diem charged the CCC with allocating funds, selecting and printing campaign literature, allotting radio time, and apportioning sound trucks. Though the stated purpose of the committee was to oversee "electoral preparations for the candidates on a basis of absolute equality among all candidates," its composition overwhelmingly favored government-sponsored aspirants.[15] The CCC contained one representative from each of the political groups running candidates—almost all of which were government-sponsored—as well as one representative from each independent candidate. There was little to distinguish most independents from progovernment candidates, and indeed, a number of government-sponsored candidates ran as independents. The few truly independent candidates were thus grossly outnumbered, and their campaigns suffered tremendously.

"With the campaign committee weighted by progovernment representatives," noted one CIA report, "the printing of literature for non-government candidates was often delayed until well into the campaign."[16] This was especially devastating since open campaigning was already limited to the period from February 20 to March 2, 1956. Moreover, although Ngo Dinh Diem technically suspended censorship of the press during the campaign, the publication of anything favoring "communist or anti-national activities," remained punishable by six months to five years in prison. Dr. Pham Quang Dan, leader of the Cao Dai's Republican Party, was arrested for distributing leaflets protesting the newly devised electoral law.

Instead of attempting to run a campaign in the face of such blatant censorship, most of Ngo Dinh Diem's opponents reaffirmed their decision to boycott the election on the grounds that no genuine freedom of speech or the press existed.[17] They opted to abstain from the election process rather than lending legitimacy to the results by participating in what they viewed as an undemocratic farce. Cao Dai, Hoa Hao, and Binh Xuyen leaders led the charge against Ngo Dinh Diem's unfair election practices, which provided communists in the north with evidence to critique the RVN as a cruel, oppressive state.[18] In a February 10 Hanoi radio broadcast, for instance, Viet Minh propagandists condemned the elections and urged South Vietnamese citizens to oppose them violently, thereby transforming them into "a bloody reply to the Americans and their lackeys." But no such uprising transpired. With the politico-religious organizations in disarray and Ngo Dinh Nhu's clandestine security apparatus in place, there was no one in South Vietnam capable of posing a serious challenge to the president and his preferred candidates.

In the end, of some 450 candidates only 50, including Ngo Dinh Nhu and his wife, received any real attention from the Saigon media.[19] Press space that could have been devoted to the remaining 400 candidates was used instead to glorify Ngo Dinh Diem's administration and to vilify communists as tyrannical and insensitive to popular needs and demands. The daily paper *Saigon Moi* carried a propaganda banner on the bottom of every front page with the following question and answer format: "Who brought rice fields to the tillers? President Ngo Dinh Diem"; "Who protected workers' rights in the plantations and factories? President Ngo Dinh Diem"; "Who participated in the colonial plot to divide northern and southern allies and stirred up revolt, in league with Bao Dai? The Viet Cong"; "Who destroys temples and churches? The Viet Cong"; and "Where is the highest salary of the workers just 45 kilos of rice? In the Viet Cong region."[20] This litany of progovernment, anticommunist propaganda continued for months leading up to the election.

As in the October referendum, what Ngo Dinh Diem did manage to publicize widely through pamphlets, posters, and the press were guidelines for voter eligibility and procedures for the national assembly elections. The rules in March 1956 were almost identical to those for the referendum to depose Bao Dai, and the conduct of the national assembly polling bore the same democratic façade. Again, the outcome was almost entirely predetermined. "The voting," wrote one Michigan State advisor, "was carried on in fairness and secrecy . . . [but] the Government did interfere at every other stage in the electoral process."[21] This included everything from screening candidates and controlling political parties, to preventing nationalist opposition from organizing aboveground by setting off small bombs outside Saigon printing presses to dissuade merchants from producing campaign materials for nongovernment candidates. After the election, Ngo Dinh Diem's opponents accused the government of using arrests, intimidation, and even kidnapping to control the voting populace. According to one representative of the Hanoi press, "The farcical election revealed Ngo Dinh Diem's true face of fascism."[22]

RVN tactics in the 1956 national assembly election served as a prototype for the more organized system of oppression and control that Ngo Dinh Diem would unveil in the 1959 campaign. In the meantime, the Saigon government had set in place a series of controls to circumscribe all political activity and criticism not sanctioned by the Ngos. This included shutting down the free press in March 1958, threatening and impeding with bureaucratic red tape anyone who attempted to form opposition parties to run for positions in the national assembly, and by 1959 bringing a halt to all independent political activity.[23] Nguyen Tuyet Mai, a candidate in the 1959 national assembly race, recalls government intimidation and disruption ranging from tearing down her posters and misprinting her pamphlets to branding her a communist, accusing her of electoral violations, and pressuring her to withdraw from the race to allow for a friend of Madame Nhu to claim victory.[24] Though a 1966 CIA report identified the 1959 vote as the "dirtiest and most openly rigged of all" South Vietnamese elections, it varied from the events of March 1956 only by degree.[25]

The fact that most Vietnamese opposition parties and antigovernment politicians boycotted the 1956 election had little effect on its outcome. Had they campaigned, they would have stood little chance of success due to the extreme bias imposed by the CCC. The assembly election results, heavily favoring government-sponsored candidates and government controlled parties, surprised no one. Of the 123 seats, about 50 went to the government's NRM party, and more than 35 were claimed by other government-sponsored parties. Of the 36 victorious independents, 18 were easily identified as pro–Ngo Dinh Diem, and only 3 could lay any genuine claim to independent status. Even these supposed mavericks considered themselves to be loyal "watchdog" opposition, rather than true opponents of the government.[26] American diplomats in the Saigon embassy therefore noted that "party lines in the new assembly were likely to be subordinate to the overwhelmingly pro–Ngo Dinh Diem orientation of the body as a whole."[27] Nonetheless, U.S. officials were pleased with the outcome, which amounted to the appearance, if not the reality, of a representative government in Saigon.[28]

On March 15, 1956, the national assembly held its inaugural session. Though its main charge was to draft a constitution for the fledgling RVN, it was "an institution of form, hardly of power."[29] Ngo Dinh Diem's government exercised a heavy hand over the assembly, and little real political debate visited South Vietnam's legislative halls. A fifteen-member committee within the assembly, comprising several of the president's close friends and cabinet members, took charge of drawing up the constitution. By the time the committee handed Ngo Dinh Diem a draft for review he had already exercised a great deal of influence over its content. It represented the work of an eleven-member Constitutional Commission appointed by Ngo Dinh Diem in November 1955 more than it did the independent will of South Vietnam's legislature. The RVN president therefore accepted the document in October 1956 without substantial changes, and the national assembly ratified it with just one dissenting vote.

The nuts and bolts of the 1956 constitution reflected the president's desire to harness total control over the government. Its central theme, as American legal expert J. A. C. Grant observed at the time, was executive leadership and control.[30] Ngo Dinh Diem sought to aggrandize presidential powers and to limit those of the legislature and the judiciary. The document resulted from a mixture of Western influences. Following the U.S. system, it called for a president without a prime minister, but its complicated, multi-cameral judiciary system resembled that of France. The RVN constitution placed a much stronger emphasis on a strong executive than the United States would consider proper, giving Ngo Dinh Diem the right to declare states of emergency or to rule by decree in the event of a disagreement with the legislature.[31] "The vital issue," claimed Ngo Dinh Diem, "is to establish an effective state apparatus." He argued that "a weak and powerless executive will bring about discontent and indignation. . . . This might pave the way to revolution."[32]

A Cycle of Repression and Revolt

Ironically, the very manner in which Ngo Dinh Diem organized his state and exerted his authority as a powerful executive would contribute to the rising discontent and indignation that paved the way for a revolutionary movement against his government. He implemented draconian policies that targeted, terrorized, and punished anyone who was not fully on board with his leadership. This contributed to a cyclical pattern of repression and resistance that intensified between 1956 and 1960, at which point Hanoi stepped in to organize South Vietnam's disaffected citizens into an insurgency against the RVN.[33] Ngo Dinh Diem's indiscriminate offensive against former Viet Minh cadres, politico-religious figures, and anyone else with views or associations deemed threatening to the state created a backlash that generated more enemies than it suppressed.[34]

Following Ngo Dinh Diem's consolidation of power, differences of opinion between the RVN and the United States quickly emerged over how best to combat threats to internal security while building support for the government. Ngo Dinh Diem sought an increase in American aid, primarily for his military and police forces, which he considered vital elements of his program to destroy the regime's enemies. He intended to couple this with a positive program of propaganda and economic development, but those programs were always secondary to his quest for internal security. Meanwhile, Washington was determined to curtail the amount of aid it sent to the RVN and urged Ngo Dinh Diem to focus on economic development, land reform, and political liberalization. Nonetheless, Washington continued to pour aid into South Vietnam until it was surpassed only by the American commitment to South Korea.[35] Meanwhile, U.S. advisors cautioned Ngo Dinh Diem against pursuing repressive measures that could stir up resentment against his administration and risk fueling the communist rebellion, but exerted little leverage to prevent such policies.

Ngo Dinh Diem's triumphant trip to the United States in 1957 highlighted the divergence between Washington and Saigon's approaches to
shoring up South Vietnam as a beacon of freedom in contrast to the communist north. On the surface, the trip marked a celebration of Ngo Dinh
Diem's successes and a show of U.S.–RVN unity, but the RVN president
grew frustrated as his behind-the-scenes pleas for increased economic support fell on deaf ears. Eisenhower and Dulles seemed satisfied with the
progress Ngo Dinh Diem's administration had made toward establishing
security and political order in Vietnam, and were inclined to turn their
attention to more pressing issues, including the civil rights crisis in Little
Rock, anxiety over the space race spurred by Sputnik, and the showdown
with China in the Taiwan Straits. Ngo Dinh Diem would have to accept
that Vietnam no longer occupied the White House's attention as a top-tier
diplomatic issue. He returned to Vietnam deeply concerned that Washington's perception of him as a miracle worker had made it complacent about
the very real challenges that his government still faced.[36]

Ngo Dinh Diem proceeded to confront those challenges as he was
wont to do, by rooting out and suppressing all of his government's critics.
In 1956 and into 1957 he took aggressive steps to assert RVN control over
the countryside and silence all remaining forms of opposition to government authority. Ten months after the Saigon government established the
Denounce the Communists Campaign, just as the Nguyen Hue operation
was winding to a close, the RVN claimed to have rallied nearly 100,000
former Viet Minh agents to the government, captured massive weapons
stockpiles and secret document caches, and "entirely destroyed the predominant communist influence of the previous nine years."[37] It seems as though
all opponents of the Diem regime, including communist cadres, nonparty
sympathizers, and politico-religious followers were included in this count.[38]

Ngo Dinh Diem followed this avowed success by imposing a number of
antitreason laws that permitted armed agents of his administration to terrorize anyone who demonstrated the inclination to challenge or criticize
his government. Ordinance Number 6 called for the arrest and detention
of all persons deemed dangerous to the state and provided legal justification
for creating political prison camps throughout the country and suspending
all habeas corpus laws. Ordinance 47 established being a communist—as
broadly defined by the Ngos—or working for them, as a capital crime.[39]
Ngo Dinh Diem's administration intentionally wrote these laws in the most
general terms possible in order to broaden the definition of crimes against
the state and define all of the government's critics as criminals.[40] By the end

of 1956, then, the prison camps ostensibly intended for communist subversives housed approximately twenty thousand—and perhaps as many as fifty thousand—prisoners, including the leaders of the politico-religious groups and nonstate political parties, as well as uncooperative members of the press and trade unions.[41] Arguably, rather than quarantining and neutralizing communists as intended, this practice of physically lumping together all critics of the state encouraged Ngo Dinh Diem's communist and noncommunist enemies to cooperate. As Peter Zinoman has demonstrated, French colonial prisons served as effective recruiting grounds for the Communist Party, and this was no doubt true of the South Vietnamese prison system as well.[42]

By 1956, Vietnam Workers Party (VWP) leaders in Hanoi had lost hope in reunifying the country through countrywide elections. As Ngo Dinh Diem tightened his grip over South Vietnam with the help of the Americans, the promise of Geneva faded. Communist cadres in the south were operating under instructions from Hanoi to restrict themselves to political agitation under a repressive regime that answered such activities with arrests, imprisonment, and torture. Southern communists led by Le Duan, author of the 1956 pamphlet "The Path to Revolution in the South" and future party general secretary, agitated the VWP for permission to resume armed struggle in the south. Yet party leaders in Hanoi were reluctant to provoke the United States, especially while they were preoccupied with postwar recovery in the north and consumed by their own land reform debacle. They hoped to wear away at the southern government through propaganda and political subversion while building international sympathy for the plight of southern revolutionaries.

After Le Duan was appointed to the Politburo in 1957, the party introduced a policy sanctioning armed anti-Diem propaganda teams and permitting them to use their weapons in self-defense, but continued to forbid violent resistance under any other circumstances.[43] As the government continued its violent crackdown in 1957, fighting between government officials and communist agents flared. Communist cadres began to skirt Hanoi's orders, assassinating hated local officials, attacking local garrisons, and collaborating with other armed antigovernment groups.[44] For the most part, party discipline was maintained. But the Ngos ever-tightening grip on communist and other antigovernment activity in the south forced Hanoi's hand. As repression thinned the ranks of the party in the south while discontent with Ngo Dinh Diem's policies in the countryside grew, it became increasingly challenging for leaders in Hanoi to insist that southern party members restrict themselves to political struggle.[45]

The Denounce the Communists Campaign placed the RVN's communist and noncommunist opponents desperately on the defensive. By 1956, Ngo Dinh Diem had made it clear to his enemies that he regarded them as a coordinated antigovernment bloc and that he would target them all with the same high level of vengeance. Even the secret Defense Department study commissioned by Robert McNamara in 1967 known as the Pentagon Papers acknowledged, "There is little doubt that Diem and his government applied the term Viet Cong somewhat loosely within South Vietnam to mean all persons or groups who resorted to clandestine political activity or armed opposition against his government."[46] In so doing, he pitted them against the government in a desperate struggle to survive and provided the impetus to galvanize them into reluctant cooperation. Many elements of the Cao Dai, Hoa Hao, and Binh Xuyen left standing after the Nguyen Hue Operation joined with a handful of dissident Catholics to form a force that could continue opposing Ngo Dinh Diem. A number of former Viet Minh cadres who had stayed behind in the south during the regroupment period were eager to join up with these antigovernment forces.[47] The party organization in the south focused its attention on the day-to-day abuses of Ngo Dinh Diem's government, many stemming from the indiscriminate Denounce the Communists Campaign, to win over frustrated southerners.[48]

By 1958 a loose coalition of communists, remnants of the politico-religious armies, and other disaffected members of southern society emerged in opposition to Ngo Dinh Diem's administration.[49] In coming years, the party continued its strategy of actively cultivating the Cao Dai, Hoa Hao, and Binh Xuyen for inclusion in an anti-Diem bloc. Meanwhile, the politico-religious organizations could challenge the RVN without constraint by the limitations on armed struggle that Hanoi imposed on communist cadres operating under its purview. By this time, the politico-religious organizations were highly fragmented, and only some factions joined in militant opposition to the Saigon government. Those who did faced few restrictions and, as they were already targets of government repression, had little to lose. Thus they often posed the most violent threats to South Vietnamese internal security during 1957 and 1958.

Yet, as of late 1956 and into 1957, at least some leaders of the politico-religious organizations and their noncommunist nationalist allies, many of who were by then in exile, worked to achieve a political solution that might avert the need for violent conflict and enable them to avoid cooperating with communist cadres. Some continued to clamor for concessions from

Ngo Dinh Diem and inclusion in the Saigon government. They persisted in their efforts to persuade American officials that a more broad-based Saigon-government would be necessary to avoid total disaffection among South Vietnam's nationalist intelligentsia. Further, they insisted that a loss of support from those nationalist intellectuals would compromise the RVN's long-term security and play into communist schemes to swallow up the south. Washington, however, remained wedded to the perception of Ngo Dinh Diem as a "Miracle Man" in South Vietnam and to the judgment that his critics were bandits, warlords, and rubes unworthy of serious attention.

In early November 1956, the anticommunist, pro-American Le Tung Nghia, who was initially one of Ngo Dinh Diem's most ardent supporters, insisted to U.S. ambassador Daniel Anderson that Diem had made a mistake by forcing Pham Cong Tac to flee to Cambodia rather than granting him a position in the government. The result of that decision, he claimed, was that "thousands of potential supporters in Tay-Ninh are hostile or lukewarm toward the national government." In turn, government suspicion of the province's residents led to the shutdown of local sawmills, which carried serious consequences for the local economy and further alienated Cao Dai followers. Meanwhile, Le Tung Nghia warned, Pham Cong Tac was engaged in talks with Bao Dai, Tran Van Huu, and others in Phnom Penh to create a neutralist movement for Vietnam along the lines advocated by Nehru. He warned that by encouraging a negotiated settlement between Hanoi and Saigon, such a movement could undermine Ngo Dinh Diem's government and result in significant communist advances in the south. He suggested that Ngo Dinh Diem establish a High Council to ensure nationalist figures like the Cao Dai Pope a place in government, while sending his controversial brothers abroad on diplomatic missions. Anderson commented in his notes to Washington, "It hardly seems possible that an intelligent and experienced intellectual, who is also an active and prosperous businessman could still seriously suggest at the end of 1956 that President Diem banish his brothers, attempt to bring back 'Pope' Tac, and reshuffle his cabinet." However, he noted, "Ideas such as these continue to circulate in certain intellectual milieu in Saigon."[50]

A month later, when a group of Vietnamese nationalist expats approached the American embassy in Paris about their hope to return home to play a role in Ngo Dinh Diem's government, Douglas Dillon dismissed their suggestions as "the latest variation on a very old chestnut" and noted that they were living in a "never-never land."[51] Dulles, for his part, replied that the "doubtful value [of] their possible contribution to free Viet-Nam would not justify [the] risk [of] damaging US-GVN relations by provoking

Diem's irritation."[52] Over the next year American officials continued to shrug off appeals from nationalist Vietnamese figures abroad who made every effort to hammer home the point that Ngo Dinh Diem's failure to allow the nationalist opposition to participate freely in politics prevented him from winning the support of the nationalist intelligentsia. These individuals insisted that such support, and the broad willingness of nationalists to make common cause against the communists, would be crucial to the long-term security of South Vietnam. To the Department of State, the figures making these pleas were ignoring "clear evidence of recent history as to the near miraculous recovery which has taken place in Vietnam since the accession of Ngo Dinh Diem to power."[53]

In the spring of 1957, American officials in Saigon noted an increase in unrest and antigovernment activity among the Cao Dai that belied the notion that Ngo Dinh Diem's quest to vanquish his opposition was altogether miraculous, much less complete. "The Cao Dai still claim several hundred thousand adherents," noted Anderson, "who look for guidance to their Holy See at Tay Ninh, and undoubtedly hope for a return to happier times when the Cao Dai, riding high, had a well-equipped army and high-ranking officials and foreign ambassadors would come from Saigon to pay homage to his holiness Pope Pham Cong Tac." Anderson cited the February 8 demonstration for the return of the pope occasioned by Joseph Mankiewicz's filming of *The Quiet American* outside the Holy See in Tay Ninh as one minor manifestation of this unrest. He also pointed to rumors that the attempted assassination of Ngo Dinh Diem at Ban Me Thuot on February 22 may have been a Cao Dai plot, carried out perhaps by an assailant with both Cao Dai and communist connections. Some American observers concluded that Ngo Dinh Diem, in the wake of this incident, "displayed an inordinate concern with internal security at the expense of all other programs." Furthermore, regarding a Cao Dai attack on a village in Tay Ninh Province that overpowered Auto Defense units and resulted in the deaths of five Civic Action cadres, the perpetrators were rumored to have been communists posing as Cao Dai. The Saigon government was concerned enough about this upsurge in antigovernment activity among the Cao Dai and its possible connections to communism to form a special mission to examine the problem.[54]

Regarding Vietnam's southernmost provinces, the American embassy in Saigon observed an improving security situation that spring, but indicated that "communist and sect activities are still a problem." According to Anderson's report, "In most cases, officials expressed the opinion that the sect bandits are a more immediate problem than the communists."[55] By June, American officials were reporting a much higher level of cooperation between communists, politico-religious figures, and other disaffected nationalists. A report on the internal security situation in June 1957 indicated, "The communists are said to support and abet rebel activities and to be the motivating force behind the so-called Cao Thien Dai Hao Xuyen." That grouping, the name of which was made up of parts of the names Cao Dai, Hoa Hao, Binh Xuyen, Dai Viet, and Thien ("Christian"), was most likely a convenient way for government officials to lump together all "otherwise unidentifiable dissident elements," but reflected a growing tendency among these groups to cooperate in the common cause of opposition to Ngo Dinh Diem's administration.[56]

By 1958, Ngo Dinh Diem's intense focus on internal security at the expense of political and economic progress, and the oppressive and venal manner with which many civil servants carried out government policy, inspired widespread apathy and resentment among the southern populace. Even many influential Vietnamese who had once supported Ngo Dinh Diem, including military officers, cabinet members, and even his own vice president Nguyen Ngoc Tho, grew increasingly critical of his refusal to delegate authority and to broaden the base of his government. They worried that his terroristic police state, along with widespread corruption, ineffective land reform and resettlement policies, and favoritism toward Catholic refugees from the north could lend legitimacy to the communist cause and fuel the antigovernment movement.[57]

Army of the Republic of Vietnam (ARVN) general Lam Quang Thi would later comment that the problem was that Ngo Dinh Diem "acted like an emperor. He tolerated no organized opposition; his critics were harassed or arrested. His decrees became laws. He gradually transformed South Vietnam into a quasi-police state where the security apparatus was rigidly controlled by his brother Ngo Dinh Nhu."[58] Truong Nhu Tang, one of the founding members of the NLF, wrote after the war, "Had Ngo Dinh Diem been a man of breadth and vision, the core of people who filled the NLF and its sister organizations would have rallied to him. As it was, the South Vietnamese nationalists were driven to action by his contempt for the principles of independence and social progress in which they believed."[5] Such complaints embattled Ngo Dinh Diem's administration from within and without. They mounted to compel ARVN officers to stage an unsuccessful coup against the Ngo brothers in 1960 and ultimately a successful one in 1963, but not before the brothers' unpopular policies spurred

Hanoi to take charge of organizing South Vietnam's disparate antigovernment forces into a unified insurgency against RVN.

The Formation of the National Liberation Front

Ngo Dinh Diem's increasingly violent repression of his opponents, and the responses of his politico-religious adversaries, were key factors contributing to the emergence of an organized insurgency against the RVN. Official communist accounts of the foundation of the NLF, written in retrospect of the war, note that "many officers and troops of the religious sects became cadres of the Liberation Army."[60] Much of its early support indeed came from several antigovernment branches of the Cao Dai and Hoa Hao organizations. According to one U.S. Foreign Service officer, "Many of the original participants in the NLF had turned to it because they had been denied participation in South Vietnam's political process even in the role of loyal opposition."[61] The participants of which he spoke were drawn largely from politico-religious ranks, but also included members of several ethnic minority groups, idealistic youths recruited from universities and technical schools, representatives of farmers' organizations in parts of the Mekong delta plagued by serious land tenure problems, military deserters, leaders of small parties or groups, and intellectuals who had been alienated from Ngo Dinh Diem's government.[62] Not only did members of the politico-religious organizations and their fellow disaffected citizens join the NLF in quantity, their antigovernment activity contributed to Hanoi's decision to found the insurgent group.

Recent research into original sources from the Vietnamese Worker's Party illuminates Hanoi's decision finally to respond to the persistent pleas of southern revolutionaries who had been clamoring for northern support for a resumption of armed struggle in the south since the ink was barely dry on the Geneva agreements.[63] The January 1959 meeting of the VWP Central Committee was the first occasion seized by Hanoi's leadership since 1954 to reassess the course of the revolution. With socialist consolidation well underway in the north and the Geneva agreements no longer worth the paper on which they were written, Hanoi turned its attention to the south, where deteriorating conditions merited concern. United States support had allowed Ngo Dinh Diem to consolidate and project his power to a far greater degree than anticipated. The most active period of RVN activity against antigovernment elements under the auspices of the Denounce the Communists Campaign came between November 1957 and February 1959.[64] And in 1959 Ngo Dinh Diem upped the ante against his challengers with Law 10/59, which charged the enforcement of Ordinance 47—which defined being or working for communists as a capital crime—to special military tribunals whose decisions could not be appealed.[65] As one former revolutionary recalls, "Party members felt that it was no longer possible to talk of political struggle while looking down the gun barrels of the government."[66]

Such brazen examples of violent repression on the part of the Ngos led Politburo members to conclude that they must somehow intervene to curtail the operations of the Saigon government. "The Politburo," writes one historian, "now acknowledged that the 'most fundamental policy of the enemy' was annihilation of all revolutionary elements in the South in the furtherance of American objectives."[67] Thus the first factor behind Hanoi's decision to authorize a resumption of armed struggle in the south was the fact that southern communist cadres faced increasingly draconian policies and mounting challenges from Ngo Dinh Diem's government. Southern revolutionaries persuaded Hanoi that if they did not respond with coordinated force, the movement would face possible eradication.

Another key consideration behind Hanoi's decision stemmed from the fear that, in the absence of bold action, southern communists would cede the revolutionary initiative to other anti-Diem forces. Most notable among the noncommunist movements in the south with aspirations to lead the resistance movement against Ngo Dinh Diem and the Americans were the politico-religious organizations. They attracted to their military wings increasing numbers of frustrated party cadres, members, and sympathizers, along with other disaffected citizens.[68] Hanoi determined that organizations such as these could hijack the revolutionary movement in the south if it did not provide southern communists with the support they needed to lead the movement against Ngo Dinh Diem's government on both the military and political fronts.

In an effort to unite disparate anti-Diem forces behind a single revolutionary movement, Hanoi authorized the formation of a "truly broad" peoples' movement for reunification and opposition to Ngo Dinh Diem and the Americans. The Central Committee proclaimed, "We must unite all people who can be united."[69] Among those expected to provide support for the project, which was to appear as a truly southern force to facilitate recruitment, were ethnic minorities, petty bourgeois, intellectuals, and most promisingly, the Hoa Hao and the Cao Dai.[70] The Politburo was insistent through 1963 that military struggle should remain subordinate to political struggle, but southern revolutionaries increasingly took matters into their own hands and met violent repression with violent resistance. Thus the VWP's December 1960 decision to form the NLF was largely an effort to exert more effective control over the revolutionary movement in the south and to prevent ceding the revolutionary vanguard to Hoa Hao or Cao Dai resistance movements.

The cycle of violence between Ngo Dinh Diem's government and his enemies intensified dramatically in the months following the formation of the NLF. He continued to opt for repression over reform, even when pressed to moderate his approach by his American patrons, noncommunist opposition, and members of his own army. The United States would come to recognize belatedly the ways in which Ngo Dinh Diem wrote the script for the insurgency that mounted against his government by 1960. The Pentagon Papers concluded that, for all of Ngo Dinh Diem's preoccupation with rural security, he failed to provide adequate resources for rural police and intelligence operations. He lavished American aid dollars on the ARVN while placing responsibility for security in the countryside in the hands of the poorly trained, ill equipped, and woefully led Civil Guard and Self-Defense Corps. The Defense Department concluded that Ngo Dinh Diem's efforts at winning over rural constituents were squandered by "the corrupt, arrogant, and overbearing men the people knew as the GVN." Likewise, the Americans concluded that Ngo Dinh Diem's own policies inhibited his efforts to win over urban intellectuals: "Just as Diem and his brothers made the mistake of considering all former Viet Minh communists, they erred in condemning all non-Diemist nationalists as tools of Bao Dai or the French."[71]

The Defense Department acknowledged that the repression Ngo Dinh Diem's government implemented in electoral politics, the press, and the countryside as a result of those paranoid assumptions fueled the opposition to his government that would be summed up in the spring 1960 Caravelle Manifesto. That statement of grievances against Ngo Dinh Diem's regime was signed by eighteen noncommunist nationalists, including many former government officials and representatives of the politico-religious organizations. Their complaints against the Saigon government included the repression in recent years that had "provoked the discouragement and resentment of the people" and the tendency to use "as a criterion for promotion fidelity to the party in blind submission to its leaders." American officials noted that the manifesto scared Ngo Dinh Diem, but prompted him to further

measures to quell noncommunist opposition. "In brief," the Defense Department study concluded, "Diem's policies virtually assured that political
challenges to him would have to be extra-legal. Ultimately, these emerged
from the traditional sources of power in South Vietnam—the armed forces,
the religious sects, and the armed peasantry."[72]

The Ngo brothers' authoritarian approach to governance and the violently oppressive police state they implemented in an attempt to guarantee loyalty amongst the population backfired to create the conditions that
encouraged and enabled the VWP to seize control of the revolutionary
movement in the south. This outcome resulted from the brothers' refusal
to allow broad participation in the RVN's ostensibly democratic political
process, their brutal suppression of the government's opposition, and their
insistence on lumping together all critics of the state under the "communist" canopy. Washington facilitated all of these policies, as it continued its
aid program to the RVN unabated despite growing concerns over the Ngo
brother's tyrannical style of leadership. From cities to villages, peasant farmers to nationalist intelligentsia, politico-religious figures to students and
trade unionists, the people of South Vietnam grew ever more alienated and
convinced that the Ngos were their greatest enemies. By the decade's end,
even many among the Hoa Hao and Cao Dai, which had long histories
of vicious antagonism toward Vietnam's communists, saw fit to cooperate
with communist cadres in order to mount the strongest possible opposition
to Ngo Dinh Diem. Hanoi, well aware of the grave distrust between the
Vietnam Workers Party and southern Vietnam's noncommunist nationalists, made the collaboration easier by distancing itself from the NLF and
charging the front's leaders with the task of representing it as a broad-based
coalition of southern forces rather than a communist-directed organization
controlled by Hanoi.

Once the NLF was in place, an increasingly violent conflict ensued
to determine the future of South Vietnam's leadership. It would quickly
escalate to crisis proportions, as the Ngo brothers ramped up their repressive
tactics, thereby encouraging Hanoi to authorize more openly violent resistance to the RVN and encouraging more and more of the southern populace to join the fray against Ngo Dinh Diem's government. As critiques of
his government's conduct emerged from new quarters including the Buddhist population and his own army generals, the South Vietnamese leader
would resort to even greater violence and a more dogged determination
to cast all opposition as communist conspiracy. In the end, that approach
only further antagonized his domestic critics as well as his increasingly

disillusioned American backers, a combination that would soon lead to his demise.

Meanwhile, those among the Hoa Hao and Cao Dai that aligned with the communists in opposition to Ngo Dinh Diem's government again failed to attain the freedom and autonomy they sought. The uneasy alliance would ultimately wither, subjecting the politico-religious organizations to yet another round of severe repression—one that continues in moderated form to the present day. During the final years of Ngo Dinh Diem's administration and into the early years of the American war, many Cao Dai and Hoa Hao figures would continue to participate in the NLF in an effort to establish the southern insurgency as a broad-based nationalist movement inclusive of a wide range of organizations and perspectives. At first they expected that doing so would enable them to reclaim freedoms they had lost under the RVN and perhaps earn them a role in a postwar coalition government. However, as the war dragged on, Hanoi took increasing control over the war effort and appeared less and less willing to accommodate its noncommunist allies.

After northern forces toppled the U.S.–backed RVN government in 1975, communist leaders regarded the proliferation of religious groups, beliefs, images, and practices in the wild south as grave obstacles to their consolidation of power. The unfamiliar religious forms they encountered in and around the Mekong delta seemed to be obsolete relics of the feudal past that would both impede postcolonial modernization efforts and facilitate foreign attempts to subvert Vietnam's socialist revolution. All religions, including Catholicism, Buddhism, Protestantism, and Islam were severely restricted and subjected to close monitoring and control after 1975, but the most serious repression was reserved for indigenous religious movements like the Hoa Hao and Cao Dai. Hanoi's inclination to marginalize and oppress the politico-religious organizations was due largely to its perception that they were relics of medieval sociopolitical relations or tools of colonial powers.[73] It was also fueled by the fact that while some Hoa Hao and Cao Dai members had fought with the Viet Cong, others had maintained staunchly anticommunist stances—most notably the Cao Dai Holy See at Tay Ninh, which remained an anticommunist outpost throughout the war.

Leaders of the newly established Socialist Republic of Vietnam (SRV) insisted that superstition had no place in the modern state they sought to build. They enacted bans on religious organization and practice, targeting the politico-religious organizations most violently, claiming that their political activities were inconsistent with the parameters of religion. After toppling the Saigon government in 1975, communist forces seized almost all of the buildings at the Cao Dai Holy See, arrested more than a thousand Cao Dai religious leaders, killed thirty-nine in clashes, and sent several thousand of the organization's dignitaries to reeducation camps. They closed the Great Temple at Tay Ninh, suspended ritual séances and other important religious practices, and forced Cao Dai leaders to accept being ruled by a communist-appointed Steering Committee rather than following their own constitution.[74] The Hoa Hoa, members of which also fought on both sides during the American war, faced similar repression after reunification. All of their administrative offices, places of worship, and cultural institutions were shut down, effectively eliminating public gathering places. Those who did seek to gather were arrested and imprisoned. Such policies caused the Cao Dai, Hoa Hao, and other religious organizations under the SVN to become fragmented and isolated.[75]

Many Hoa Hao and Cao Dai followers fled what they considered to be intolerable conditions in postwar Vietnam and during the 1980s and 1990s rebuilt their religious communities in diaspora.[76] Drawing on their longstanding rhetorical commitments to liberating Vietnam and their deep histories of political engagement, those diasporic organizations quickly became active in advocating for reforms in Vietnam. Hoa Hao and Cao Dai religious communities outside of Vietnam organized information campaigns and raised money to support organizations within Vietnam that agitate for human rights, democratization, and religious freedom.

The SRV began easing restrictions on religious practices after implementing the reform program known as *Doi Moi* in 1986 and normalizing relations with the United States in 1993. As the government embraced a program of economic liberalism, it came to see Vietnam's unique religious traditions as vehicles for building national identity and pride, and ceremonial and ritual practices as ways to provide cultural grounding and psychological comfort in an era of rapidly changing material conditions.[77] Yet even in this era of relative religious revival, the state exerted a great deal of control over the religious sphere and the regulation of religious practices. In 1992, the SRV promulgated a new constitution and eased restrictions on religious worship and social work, but it made clear that the government would retain control over almost all aspects of religion. This slight easing emboldened religious leaders to press for more, primarily through the Unified Buddhist Church of Vietnam, which is supported by overseas Vietnamese Buddhist churches, including the sizable Hoa Hao and Cao Dai organizations in exile.[78]

Since the early 1990s, agitation for greater religious freedom has led to ongoing clashes between religious figures and the government. Recently, however, human rights, prodemocracy, and religious freedom groups, once compartmentalized from each other, have coordinated activities with unprecedented support from overseas Vietnamese.[79] This has led to a renewed outburst of religious participation in Vietnam, yet Vietnamese Buddhists at home and abroad remain unsatisfied with restrictions on their autonomy and on their ability to participate in Vietnam's one-party political system.[80] Thus the liberation of Vietnam from oppressive control and the reclamation of full rights—objectives that have motivated Hoa Hao and Cao Dai political engagement for most of their existence—remain central to these organizations even today.

Conclusion

When Washington replaced France as the predominant Western power in Vietnam in 1954, it stepped into the middle of a civil struggle over the nature of Vietnam's postcolonial political order, the lines of which had already been contorted by French intervention. One historian has written, "Rather than simply signaling a linear, diplomatic transfer of power from colonial to postcolonial status, decolonization equally constitutes a complex dialectical intersection of competing views and claims over colonial pasts, transitional presents, and inchoate futures."[1] Indeed, Vietnam's route to decolonization was more of a multisided tug-of-war than it was a tide moving steadily in one direction. This was especially true in the "wild" south where the communist organization was weakest, and the Cao Dai, Hoa Hao, and Binh Xuyen politico-religious organizations were firmly entrenched. They competed with the Vietnamese communists for influence over the country's anticolonial movement for decades prior to the August Revolution and shortly thereafter waged war against the Viet Minh to avoid being subordinated to its leadership. They allied with the French, and then contemplated allying with Ngo Dinh Diem and the Americans if it would enable them to retain and perhaps enhance their national political power. Only after that avenue was firmly closed to them, and once their ability to engage in national politics was cut off and their very lives threatened by RVN policies, did they see fit to enter into sustained collaboration with their former communist foes.

These nationalist organizations operated in the interstices between Ngo Dinh Diem's southern government and Ho Chi Minh's communist organization, and between France and the United States. In the decades leading up to the American war in Vietnam, they shifted allegiances often to work with the Japanese, the communists, the French, Ngo Dinh Diem, and each other, all the while refusing to relinquish their autonomy. They represented a substantial power bloc in southern Vietnam that might have been exploited to shore up the Saigon government against encroachment from its northern neighbor or, at the very least, appeased sufficiently to make the communist task of organizing a largely native southern insurgency against the RVN more difficult. Instead, Ngo Dinh Diem set out to destroy them, to exclude them from his government, and to terrorize them as a part of his Denounce the Communists Campaign. He could not have done so without Washington's aid and acquiescence. By disregarding southern Vietnam's most powerful noncommunist nationalists and downplaying the authoritarian, terroristic, indiscriminate methods Ngo Dinh Diem used to combat them, the United States fueled support for Ho Chi Minh and the DRV and facilitated Ngo Dinh Diem's dictatorship in ways that channeled Vietnam's disparate nationalist organizations into a two-sided struggle.

That the two sides in the ensuing struggle were, in overarching terms, communist and anticommunist, suggests that the Vietnam War was indeed a Cold War struggle, a proxy war between the Soviet Union and China on one side and the United States on the other. It was that, but not only that. For the superpowers involved, the stakes were obviously geostrategic, and the battle lines between communist internationalism and democratic capitalism seemed clear. Yet Washington's interest in South Vietnam was significantly greater than that of either of its Cold War rivals. And for the Vietnamese players involved, the objective of liberating Vietnam from foreign domination and tyranny was crystal clear, but the role of communism and the Cold War in that process was often somewhat murkier. For decades, scholars have mused over whether Ho Chi Minh was a nationalist or a communist, and most have long since reached the conclusion that he was both, that the duality posed no contradiction. The Vietnamese communist leader and his comrades were deeply motivated by national pride and an overwhelming desire for independence. Likewise, they were committed Marxist-Leninists with strong ties to Moscow and Beijing.[2] Although by no means subservient to these foreign powers, they were aided and often heavily influenced by them. Those who joined with them, however, frequently boasted no Marxist-Leninist ties and were often deeply suspicious of the social and diplomatic implications of communist government.

Ngo Dinh Diem, for his part, was a virulent anticommunist. He deplored Marxist-Leninist philosophy and the associated efforts by Vietnamese communists to displace the mandarin class to which he belonged. He railed against communist plots to sell his country to Moscow and Beijing, but he also resented Vietnamese communists for the brutal tactics they employed during the French war to try to subordinate the country's noncommunist nationalists under VWP leadership, which included assassinating one of his brothers and forcing him into exile. Ironically, however, Ngo Dinh Diem would employ similar tactics, justified in terms of anticommunism, to shore up his own power over the politically fractious south. When his government targeted Viet Cong—the term he used to describe Vietnamese communists after 1956—it went after all of his opponents, regardless of political creed or affiliation. Thus, in some important ways, Ngo Dinh Diem's anticommunism was related more to his quest to protect his own class interests and establish uncontested control than it was about any principled objection to Marxist-Leninism or even Sino-Soviet domination.

Likewise, for southern Vietnam's noncommunist nationalists, the term *communism* generally stood less for a system of government based on Marxist-Leninist philosophy than for the VWP, a competing Vietnamese power group against which they had struggled viciously and to which they refused to be subordinated. When viewed this way, it becomes easier to understand the decisions by Cao Dai, Hoa Hao, and Binh Xuyen adherents to give up their efforts to cooperate with Ngo Dinh Diem and the United States and shift their weight into the communist-led anti-RVN insurgency. Once their militaries were hunted down and decimated by Ngo Dinh Diem's armed forces, their political leaders deprived of their rights to open political participation, and their adherents targeted and terrorized as enemies of the state, the communists came to represent a vehicle rather than an obstacle to reclaiming their power, avenging their organizations, and protecting themselves and their interests.

Ironically, Ngo Dinh Diem supplanted the communists as the politico-religious organizations' greatest enemy by targeting them in the same manner that the Viet Minh had attacked them in the early years of the French War. Ngo Dinh Diem's campaign of terror had the same effect as that of the Viet Minh—to drive the politico-religious groups to cooperate with an entity that was once their primary foe. In the 1940s, they turned away from the communists and toward the French; in the 1950s, they turned away from Ngo Dinh Diem and the Americans and back into association with the communists. From the perspective of politico-religious figures, the United States, not the Soviet Union or China, came to represent the foreign power most determined to enslave Vietnam, thus justifying the choice to join ranks with the communists to oppose it and what they viewed as its South Vietnamese puppet.

Many of southern Vietnam's nationalists, including both Ngo Dinh Diem and the politico-religious organizations that opposed him, sought a "third way" to decolonization by which they could attract international support for their quest to gain independence and modernize the country without succumbing to the stark battle lines of the Cold War. Yet American policymakers in the 1950s viewed Vietnam's domestic political affairs through a distorting Cold War lens. As Matthew Connelly notes in his work on Algeria, that Cold War lens encompassed more than just the superpower conflict between the Soviet and American blocs.[3] The rapid process of decolonization that gripped much of the globe following World War II stirred long-standing American fears of international anarchy and disorder to fuel that superpower conflict. United States officials were especially fearful of unrest amongst nonwhite peoples, whom they sometimes deemed to be incapable of self-government, especially vulnerable to communist manipulation, and perhaps even prone to launch racially motivated wars against the colonizing countries of Western Europe, with which the United States was so closely aligned.[4] Furthermore, unrest in the decolonizing world threatened American economic interests around the globe just as the United States was becoming more dependent on foreign resources and markets and fearful that the Soviet Union would block access.

Testifying before Congress in 1953, John Foster Dulles admitted, "There are plenty of social problems and unrest which would exist if there were no such thing as Soviet communism in the world." But he concluded that "what makes this a very dangerous problem for us is that wherever those things exist . . . the forces of unrest are captured by the Soviets."[5] American concerns about Soviet designs on the Third World only intensified in 1955 and 1956, as the Kremlin's post-Stalin leadership maneuvered to gain allies among decolonizing countries. Washington perceived this as a grave threat to U.S. security, as any Soviet inroads into the decolonizing world would amount to American losses in the zero-sum Cold War competition.[6]

The Cold War lens that obscured American vision into Vietnam was hyperopic. It blurred vision of close objects and encouraged Washington to focus on the international forest rather than the local trees. Vietnam was important to the United States not for what happened inside its borders but for how it might affect the alignment of the region of which it was a part, and thus how it might affect the balance of power between the democratic West and the communist East. Dulles was particularly concerned about the region's fate given the strain that blocked access to Chinese trade posed to Japan's economy, and he hoped that Southeast Asia—and particularly a noncommunist South Vietnam—might become a reasonable substitute for Japanese trade and investment. Thus, despite rhetoric to the contrary, Washington considered it far less important that South Vietnam be free and democratic than for it to align with the United States geopolitically and remain strong enough to resist encroachment from the enemy camp.

This goes a long way toward explaining Washington's support for Ngo Dinh Diem, who was familiar, deeply anticommunist, and appeared far more malleable and predictable than any of his noncommunist challengers. By defining the stakes in Vietnam exclusively in geopolitical terms, and by failing to alter its perception when faced with evidence of a more complicated internal political struggle within Vietnam's borders, the United States locked itself into a rigid policy of support for Ngo Dinh Diem that worked against its avowed preference for democratic forms of government and ultimately subverted its objective of establishing a stable, legitimate noncommunist state in South Vietnam. Perhaps most important, Washington's outlook encouraged policymakers to ignore evidence that such an objective would have been difficult to attain in politically fractious South Vietnam even for a leader without Ngo Dinh Diem's shortcomings.

During the two critical years following the French war in which Ngo Dinh Diem shored up his power and established the basic character and mechanisms of his state, Dulles and the U.S. Department of State insisted that no acceptable alternative noncommunist leadership for South Vietnam existed. While they may not have been acceptable to Washington, alternatives did exist. They ranged from the installation of a coalition government representing the gamut of southern Vietnam's noncommunist nationalists to a total U.S. exit from Vietnam. What would have happened had Washington pursued these alternatives is a counterfactual question, and therefore an unanswerable one. It is clear that the American War would not have happened, at least not as it did. A more broad-based South Vietnamese government may have had greater success at staving off communist-led opposition, expelling the Americans, or some combination thereof. The VWP may have succeeded in unifying Vietnam and gone on to establish a collation government including a wide range of Vietnamese nationalists, including former Viet Minh, Dai Viet politicians, and politico-religious figures, among others. Even in absence of foreign intervention, Vietnam's political future likely would have been determined by fighting amongst Vietnam's political and military factions.

The United States lost its war in Vietnam because it picked its battles based on a worldview that downplayed the importance of local political conditions to the detriment of good strategy. The outcome of Vietnam's complex struggle for independence was contingent. Direct American involvement in Vietnam for more than twenty years—including, of course, a major war—did not simply stave off the country's inevitable reunification under communist rule until 1975, it contributed a great deal to shaping the domestic political conditions under which that reunification would occur and helped mold the Communist Party in Hanoi into something very different in 1975 than it was in 1954. We will never know exactly what would have happened in Vietnam in absence of American intervention. Yet we do know that the alternative would have been less costly for both the United States and Vietnam in diplomatic, political, economic, social, and ethical terms. The Vietnamese landscape would not be pocked by bomb craters, the country would have been spared the crippling legacies of Agent Orange, and the tally of more than 2 million dead would never have been approached. Had it not waged war in Vietnam, the United States could have avoided squandering diplomatic credibility in an effort to preserve it and prevented the emergence of enduring fault lines in its own domestic politics.

Washington's determination to fit Vietnam's complicated internal struggle for independence into its Cold War paradigm, and the consequences of doing so, holds lessons that pertain not just to America's Vietnam War, or even to its Cold War strategy, but to the conduct of U.S. foreign policy more generally. By viewing Vietnam as a pawn in its geopolitical chess match, U.S. officials blinded themselves to the nuances of Vietnamese politics that gave lie to the belief that its internal competitions represented a struggle between communism and capitalism, or even heavy-handed Sino-Soviet influence. And by judging and dismissing a range of influential Vietnamese political actors while applying that Cold War rubric to the country's conflicts, the United States unwittingly channeled many with whom it did not ally reluctantly into the enemy camp. This reflected Washington's characteristic tendency to try to fit, however awkwardly, complicated local conflicts into overly general geopolitical narratives. From waging war against Mexico in the name of Manifest Destiny, fighting communism in Vietnam to win the Cold War, or invading and occupying Iraq to win the war on terror, the United States has often ignored complexities on the ground in pursuit of goals that could not be attained by the methods employed. In the process, Washington has altered the course of events in starkly polarizing ways that have created more chaos, more violence, and graver consequences than would have resulted from a failure to intervene at all.

This examination of southern Vietnam in the mid-1950s, when Washington made the commitment to that country that served as the basis for a major war a decade later, suggests that American foreign policy could benefit from a healthy dose of flexibility and contingent thinking. Rather than viewing events around the globe as mere components in whatever geopolitical struggle currently defines its overarching national security strategy, the United States might be better served by analyzing what it has identified as "trouble spots" first as local conflicts with their own unique contours and range of actors, and only then by asking whether and how they fit into larger geopolitical patterns. In many cases, doing so might well lead to the conclusion that U.S. intervention to support a stalwart ally, such as Ngo Dinh Diem in 1950s Vietnam, Augusto Pinochet in 1970s Chile, Saddam Hussein in 1980s Iraq, or Hamid Karzai in present day Afghanistan would be unlikely to serve America's long-term national security objectives. Indeed, such an approach may lead Washington to conclude that some conflicts that appear on the surface to factor directly into American national security do so only indirectly or not at all.

During the Cold War, the United States was hardly alone in its failure to think locally. Its tendency to privilege geostrategic concerns over attention to local conditions was often matched by its superpower rivals. Starting in 1979, the Soviet Union squandered its own superpower status with a military overstretch in Afghanistan, where it remained mired in stalemated conflict for ten years. Moscow's commitment to Afghanistan and its decision to stay was, in the words of one scholar, rooted in "ignorance, ideological prejudice, muddled thinking, inadequate intelligence, divided counsel, and the sheer pressure of events."[7] Soviet policymakers, concerned that failing to intervene on behalf of Afghanistan's communists would undermine Moscow's status as the liberator of the Third World, ignored the voices of its own experts who warned that local conditions would thwart efforts to stabilize and modernize the government in Kabul. And for a decade the Kremlin, focused on domestic political crises and Cold War imperatives, doggedly refused to acknowledge evidence of failure on the ground.[8] More than twenty years later, the United States faces similar challenges in Afghanistan, where it intervened to fight the war on terror without full consideration of local conditions. All of these examples call into question the wisdom of intervening militarily into local conflicts in pursuit of larger geostrategic objectives. Indeed, each of these interventions ended up doing more to set back than to advance the objectives they were designed to serve.

In Vietnam, the battle between the forces of communism and those in support of American-style liberal democratic capitalism was long ago decided in favor of the communists. Yet Hanoi's victory over the south in 1975 and its subsequent reunification of Vietnam under communist rule left much of the country's religious and political conflict unresolved. The *Doi Moi* reform program initiated in the mid-1980s wrought a series of postsocialist economic and political changes that reverberate to the present day. Those changes allowed for a revival of religious activity that has once again generated an inextricable connection between politics and religion in Vietnamese civil society. While the U.S. government, international human rights organizations, and a host of Vietnamese religious groups at home and in exile criticize Vietnam's government for its violations of religious freedom, religious organizations within Vietnam continue to gain strength and put increasing pressure on the state to meet their demands not only for religious freedom, but also for an enlarged stake in the country's politics.[9] In the south, where these trends are most pronounced, the intersection between politics and religion remains wild, and many of the conflicts that animated Vietnam's civil struggles prior to American military intervention still simmer.

Select Vietnamese Names with Diacritics

Ba Cụt
Bảo Đạ
Bảy Viễn (Lê Văn Viễn)
Bình Xuyên
Bưu Lọc
Bửu Sơn Kỳ Hương
Cần Lao Nhân Vị Cách Mạng Đảng (Personalist Labor Revolutionary Party)
Cao Đài
Đại Việt Quốc Dan Đảng (Great Viet Party)
Dân Chủ Xã Hội Đảng (Social Democratic Party)
Duong Văn Minh ("Big Minh")
Hồ Chí Minh
Hồ Thông Minh
Hòa Hảo
Huỳnh Phú Sổ
Lai Văn Sang
Mặt Trận Quốc Gia Kháng Chiến (National Resistance Front)
Mặt Trận Thống Nhứt Toàn Lực Quốc Gia (United Front of Nationalist Forces)
Minh Mạng

Ngô Đình Cẩn

Ngô Đình Diệm

Ngô Đình Luyện

Ngô Đình Nhu

Ngô Đình Thục

Ngô Khải Minh

Nguyễn Bình

Nguyen Giác Ngộ

Nguyễn Hữu Trí

Nguyễn Ngọc Lễ

Nguyễn Thành Phuong

Nguyễn Văn An

Nguyễn Van Tâm

Nguyễn Van Thoại

Phạm Công Tắc

Trần Chánh Trành

Trần Quang Vinh

Trần Văn Hữu

Trình Minh Thế

Việt Minh

Việt Nam Phục Quốc Hội (Association for National Restoration)

Việt Nam Quốc Dan Đảng (Vietnamese Nationalist Party or VNQDD)

Võ Nguyên Giáp

Notes

Introduction

1. "South Vietnam: The Disquieted Americans," *Time*, 25 February 1957, 34–37; Arthur J. Dommen, *The Indochinese Experience of the French and the Americans: Nationalism and Communism in Cambodia, Laos, and Vietnam* (Bloomington: Indiana University Press, 2001), 362.

2. See Seth Jacobs, *America's Miracle Man in Vietnam: Ngo Dinh Diem, Religion, Race, and U.S. Intervention in Southeast Asia, 1950–1957* (Durham: Duke University Press, 2004).

3. Mark Philip Bradley, "Making Sense of the French War: The Postcolonial Moment and the First Vietnam War: 1945–1954," in Mark Atwood Lawrence and Fredrik Logevall, eds., *The First Vietnam War: Colonial Conflict and Cold War Crisis* (Cambridge: Harvard University Press, 2007), 39.

4. "McClintock to Department of State," 4 July 1954, *Foreign Relations of the United States* (Hereafter *FRUS*), 1952–1954, Indochina, Vol. 13, 1783–1784.

5. See Carlyle A. Thayer, *War by Other Means: National Liberation and Revolution in Vietnam 1954–1960* (Sydney: Allen and Unwin, 1989), esp. 1–67; and Pierre Asselin, "Choosing Peace: Hanoi and the Geneva Agreement on Vietnam, 1954–1955," *Journal of Cold War Studies* 9:2 (spring 2007), 95–126.

6. See David F. Schmitz, *Thank God They're on Our Side: The United States and Right-Wing Dictatorships, 1921–1965* (Chapel Hill: The University of North Carolina Press, 1999).

7. Gabriel Kolko, *Anatomy of a War: Vietnam, the United States, and the Modern Historical Experience* (New York: Pantheon Books, 1985), 95; Dommen, *The Indochinese Experience*, 406–423; David W. P. Elliott, *The Vietnamese War: Revolution and Social Change in the Mekong Delta, 1930–1975* (New York: M. E. Sharpe, 2003), 147.

8. See Frances Fitzgerald, *Fire in the Lake: The Vietnamese and the Americans in Vietnam* (New York: Vintage Books, 1972), 90–172; Kolko, *Anatomy of A War*; Robert Mann, *A Grand Delusion: America's Descent into Vietnam* (New York: Basic Books, 2001); Robert D. Schulzinger, *A Time for War: The United States and Vietnam, 1941–1975* (New York: Oxford University Press), 96. Schulzinger credits Ngo Dinh Diem with being honest and a sincere nationalist, but personally unsuited to lead the nation. Moreover, he claims that the U.S. strategy of nation building in Vietnam was doomed from the outset because it would be impossible to create a separate state in what was a single nation; James M. Carter, *Inventing Vietnam: The United States and State Building, 1954–1968* (Cambridge: Cambridge University Press, 2008). Carter discounts Ngo Dinh Diem's role entirely and claims that American state building in Vietnam was destined to fail, arguing, "In reality, 'South Vietnam,' to the extent that it came into being at all, was a failed American invention" (13).

9. Bradley, "Making Sense of the French War," 20.

10. Brian VanDeMark and Robert McNamara, *In Retrospect: The Tragedy and Lessons of Vietnam* (New York: Vintage Books, 1996). Prominent historians of the Vietnam Wars echo McNamara's claims about the failure among both policymakers and scholars to uncover the Vietnamese sides of the story, and note that historians have only recently begun to take up the task. See George Herring, "'Peoples Quite Apart': Americans, South Vietnamese, and the War in Vietnam," *Diplomatic History* 14:1 (January 1990), 1–23; Fredrik Logevall, "Bringing in the 'Other Side': New Scholarship on the Vietnam Wars," *Journal of Cold War Studies* 3:3 (fall 2001), 77–93; and Edward Miller, "War Stories: The Taylor-Buzzanco Debate and How We Think about the Vietnam War," *Journal of Vietnamese Studies* 1:1–2 (2006), 453–484.

11. Andrew J. Rotter, "Chronicle of a War Foretold: The United States and Vietnam, 1945–1954," in Lawrence and Logevall, *The First Vietnam War*, 284.

12. Mark Moyar, *Triumph Forsaken: The Vietnam War, 1954–1965* (Cambridge: Cambridge University Press, 2006).

13. Mark Bradley and Robert K. Brigham, "Vietnamese Archives and Scholarship on the Cold War Period: Two Reports," Cold War International History Project (CWIHP) Working Paper #7 (Washington, DC, September 1993); for an updated overview of archives in South Vietnam see Matthew Masur and Edward Miller, "Saigon Revisited: Researching South Vietnam's Republican Era (1954–1975) at Archives and Libraries in Ho Chi Minh City," CWIHP (September 5, 2006).

14. Among this first cut are Thayer, *War by Other Means*; Robert K. Brigham, *Guerrilla Diplomacy: The NLF's Foreign Relations and the Vietnam War* (Ithaca: Cornell University Press, 1999); Mark Philip Bradley, *Imagining Vietnam and America: The Making of Postcolonial Vietnam 1919–1950* (Chapel Hill: The University of North Carolina Press, 2000).

15. Edward Garvey Miller, "Grand Designs: Vision, Power, and Nation Building in America's Alliance with Ngo Dinh Diem," Ph.D. diss., Harvard University, 2004; Edward Miller, "Vision, Power, and Agency: The Ascent of Ngo Dinh Diem, 1945–1954," *Journal of Southeast Asian Studies* 3:35 (October 2004), 433–458. See also Matthew B. Masur, "Hearts and Minds: Cultural Nation Building in South Vietnam, 1954–1963," Ph.D. diss., Ohio State University, 2004; For a review of this newly "Vietnamized" literature on the war, see Edward Miller and Tuong Vu, "The Vietnam War as a Vietnamese War: Agency and Society in the Study of the Second Indochina War," *Journal of Vietnamese Studies* 4:3 (fall 2009), 1–16.

16. Mark Moyar, in *Triumph Forsaken*, has gone so far as to claim that by 1963 Ngo Dinh Diem had established his legitimacy and was on the verge of defeating the insurgency against his government, only to be subverted by fickle American allies who allowed themselves to be convinced otherwise by a misguided press corps. Sympathetic to this view, though more

critical of Diem, is Ronald B. Frankum, "Vietnam during the Rule of Ngo Dinh Diem, 1954–63," in David L. Anderson and John Ernst, eds., *The War that Never Ends: New Perspectives on the Vietnam War* (Lexington: University Press of Kentucky, 2007), 121–142. According to Keith Taylor, arguments that Diem was a lackey of the United States are hard to sustain. See K. W. Taylor, "How I Began to Teach about the Vietnam War," *Michigan Quarterly Review* 43:4 (fall 2004), 637–647; K. W. Taylor, "Robert Buzzanco's 'Fear and (Self) Loathing in Lubbock,'" *Journal of Vietnamese Studies* 1:1–2 (2006), 463–452. For other works sympathetic to Ngo Dinh Diem see Anthony Bouscaren, *The Last of the Mandarins: Diem of Vietnam* (Pittsburgh: Duquesne University Press, 1965); Denis Warner, *The Last Confucian* (New York: Macmillan, 1963).

Chapter 1

1. David Biggs, *Quagmire: Nation Building and Nature in the Mekong Delta* (Seattle: University of Washington Press, 2010), 26–28.

2. This 1936 quote by Pierre Gourou appears in Victor Lieberman, *Strange Parallels: Southeast Asia in Global Context, c. 800–1830*, vol. 1, *Integration on the Mainland* (Cambridge: Cambridge University Press, 2003), 343. See also David W. P. Elliott, "Official History, Revisionist History, and Wild History," in Mark Philip Bradley and Marilyn B. Young, eds. *Making Sense of the Vietnam Wars: Local, National, and Transnational Perspectives* (New York: Oxford University Press, 2008), 289.

3. The Mekong delta's diversity, and the individualistic pioneer spirit exhibited by its residents, gives lie to prevalent notions of Vietnam as a homogeneous society, united behind a singular national identity and a shared sense of nationalism. Such perceptions have undergirded official Vietnamese histories of the modern era and dominated the first wave of Western historiography about the American war in Vietnam. More recently, however, scholars have begun to explore the inchoate nature of Vietnamese identity and the high degree of contestation over anticolonial objectives that existed within southern Vietnam during the colonial and revolutionary periods. For example, see Pierre Brocheaux, *The Mekong Delta: Ecology, Economy, and Revolution, 1860–1960* (Madison: University of Wisconsin-Madison Center for Southeast Asian Studies Monograph Number 12, 1995); Hue Tam Ho Tai, *Millenarianism and Peasant Politics in Vietnam* (Cambridge: Harvard University Press, 1983); Hue Tam Ho Tai, *Passion, Betrayal, and Revolution in Colonial Saigon: The Memoirs of Bao Luong* (Berkeley: The University of California Press, 2010); Li Tana, *Nguyen Cochinchina: Southern Vietnam in the Seventeenth and Eighteenth Centuries* (Ithaca: Cornell University Press, 1998); Shawn McHale, "Understanding the Fanatic Mind? The Viet Minh and Race Hatred in the First Indochina War (1945–1954)," *Journal of Vietnamese Studies* 4:3 (fall 2009), 98–138.

4. Biggs, *Quagmire*, 127–130.

5. François Guillemot, "Autopsy of a Massacre: On a Political Purge in the Early Days of the Indochina War (Nam Bo 1947)," *European Journal of East Asian Studies* 9:2 (2010), 232.

6. R. B. Smith, "An Introduction to Caodaism II: Beliefs and Organization," *Bulletin of the School of Oriental and African Studies* 33:3 (1970), 586–589; Jérémy Jammes, "Divination and Politics in Southern Vietnam: Roots of Caodaism," *Social Compass* 57:3 (2010), 368.

7. Gabriel Gobron, *History and Philosophy of Caodaism* (Saigon: Le Van Tan Printing House, 1950), 31.

8. Gobron, *History and Philosophy of Caodaism,* 41; See also Bernard B. Fall, "The Political-Religious Sects of Viet-Nam," *Pacific Affairs* 28 (September 1955), 235–253. Much of Fall's

information on the Cao Dai comes from interviews conducted with Pope Pham Cong Tac during an extended stay at the Holy See in Tay Ninh.

9. A. M. Savani, "Notes sur le Phat Giao Hoa Hao," (mimeographed, n.p., n.d.), 5–9; see also Pascal Bourdeaux, "Approaches statistiques de la communauté du bouddhisme Hoà Hao (1939–1954)," in Christopher E. Goscha and Benoît de Tréglodé, eds. *Naissance d'un État-Parti: Le Viet Nam depuis 1945* (Paris: Les Indes Savantes, 2004), 280.

10. Fall, "The Political-Religious Sects of Viet-Nam," 244.

11. See *Biography and Teachings of Prophet Huynh Phu So* (Santa Fe Springs, CA: Hoa Hao Buddhist Church, 1983). "Prophet Huynh was among the first to discard the futile rituals and ceremonials never mentioned in the original teachings of Buddha. Furthermore, he set out to modernize the methods of self-improvement which remained unchanged through centuries of Buddhism," 6; See also Philip Taylor, "Apocalypse Now? Hoa Hao Buddhism Emerging from the Shadows of War," *Australian Journal of Anthropology* 12:3 (2001), 349. Taylor explains that "one of the four injunctions of the Hoa Hao faith is to recognize one's debt to humanity."

12. Alfred W. McCoy, *The Politics of Heroin in Southeast Asia* (New York: Harper and Row, 1972), 110.

13. Li Tana, *Nguyen Cochinchina,* 102–111.

14. Biggs, *Quagmire,* 16.

15. Hue Tam Ho Tai, *Millenarianism and Peasant Politics,* vii–38; Fall, "The Political-Religious Sects of Viet-Nam," 243.

16. Savani, "Notes sur le Phat Giao Hoa Hao" (mimeographed, n.p., n.d.) 1–2.

17. Hue Tam Ho Tai, *Millenarianism and Peasant Politics,* 76; Biggs, *Quagmire,* 28.

18. Brocheux, *The Mekong Delta,* 144.

19. Philip Taylor, "Apocalypse Now," 344.

20. For more on the syncretic nature of the Cao Dai, see Victor L. Oliver, *Caodai Spiritism: A Study of Religion in Vietnamese Society* (Leiden, Netherlands: E. J. Brill, 1976), 1–24. On the importance of print culture and transportation for the spread of modern nationalism, see Benedict Anderson, *Imagined Communities: Reflections on the Origin and Spread of Nationalism* (New York: Verso Press, 1983); For more on print culture in modern Vietnam, particularly as it pertained to the Cao Dai and its critics, see Shawn Fredrick McHale, *Print and Power: Confucianism, Communism, and Buddhism in the Making of Modern Vietnam* (Honolulu: University of Hawai'i Press, 2004), especially 157–158.

21. See Hue Tam Ho Tai, *Radicalism and the Origins of the Vietnamese Revolution* (Cambridge: Harvard University Press, 1992), 262; William J. Duiker, *The Rise of Nationalism in Vietnam, 1900–1941* (Ithaca: Cornell University Press, 1976), 149; David Marr, *Vietnamese Tradition on Trial, 1020–1941* (Berkeley: University of California Press, 1981); Frances FitzGerald, *Fire in the Lake: The Vietnamese and the Americans in Vietnam* (New York: Vintage Books, 1972). FitzGerald, though dismissive of the long-term significance of the Cao Dai and Hoa Hao, makes a similar point. She claims, "The main achievement of the sects was to fill in the social and religious gaps the French had left open in substituting their colonial administration and economic empire for that of the old system" (74).

22. See Hue Tam Ho Tai, *Radicalism and the Origins.* Hue Tam Ho Tai provides a detailed analysis of the era of radical nationalism in Vietnam, beginning in the 1920s and lasting into the 1930s. The movement began as a generational backlash against colonial collaboration, marked by a series of strikes in 1926, but quickly developed into a more ideological attack on the colonial state.

23. Hue Tam Ho Tai, *Radicalism and the Origins,* especially 172 and 262.

24. Jayne Susan Werner, *Peasant Politics and Religious Sectarianism: Peasant and Priest in the Cao Dai in Viet Nam* (New Haven: Yale University Southeast Asian Studies, 1981), 7; Oliver, *Caodai Spiritism*, 9; R. B. Smith, "An Introduction to Caodaism II," 580–582.

25. Jammes, "Divination and Politics," 357.

26. R. B. Smith, "An Introduction to Caodaism I. Origins and Early History." *Bulletin of the School of Oriental and African Studies* 33:2 (1970), 335–349.

27. Werner, *Peasant Politics*, 39.

28. Savani, "Notes sur le Caodaisme," (mimeographed, n.p., n.d.), 123.

29. Hue Tam Ho Tai, *Millenarianism and Peasant Politics*, 97.

30. Hoang Van Dao, *Viet-Nam Quoc-Dan Dang* (Hanoi: n.p., 1970).

31. Hue Tam Ho Tai, *Millenarianism and Peasant Politics,* 91.

32. Werner, *Peasant Politics*, 2 and 36.

33. Frances R. Hill, "Millenarian Machines in South Vietnam," *Comparative Studies in Society and History* 13:3 (July 1971), 335.

34. Werner, *Peasant Politics*, 15; Michael Adas, *Prophets of Rebellion: Millenarian Protest Movements against the European Colonial Order* (Chapel Hill: University of North Carolina Press, 1979), 136. Adas claims that peasant movements, especially when focused on protest actions that extend beyond short-lived outbursts of violence, often borrow leaders from different social groups.

35. Werner, *Peasant Politics*, 1.

36. Quoted in Fall, "The Political-Religious Sects of Viet-Nam," 239.

37. Savani, "Notes Sur les Binh Xuyen" (mimeographed, n.p., n.d.), 68.

38. McCoy, *Politics of Heroin*, 112. For more on anticolonial political activity within the French colonial prison system, see Peter Zinoman, *The Colonial Bastille: A History of Imprisonment in Vietnam, 1862–1940* (Berkeley: University of California Press, 2001).

39. Savani, "Notes Sur les Binh Xuyen," 67 and 94–95.

40. Hill, "Millenarian Machines in South Vietnam," 331.

41. Hue Tam Ho Tai, *Millenarianism and Peasant Politics*, 109–110 and 129–130.

42. David W. P. Elliott, *The Vietnamese War: Revolution and Social Change in the Mekong Delta, 1930–1975* (New York: M. E. Sharpe, 2003), 29–32.

43. Hue Tam Ho Tai, *Millenarianism and Peasant Politics*, 120.

44. According to one U.S. government study, which reveals America's parochial understanding of Vietnamese politics as much as it does the increasingly anticolonial bent of Hoa Hao political activity, Huynh Phu So and his Hoa Hao organization had taken on an "almost fanatically nationalistic" orientation. Joann L. Schrock, William Stockton Jr., Elaine M. Murphy, and Marilou Fromme, eds., *Minority Groups in the Republic of Vietnam* (Washington: Cultural Information Analysis Center, Ethnographic Study Series, 1966), 1021.

45. See Oliver, *Caodai Spiritism*, 85.

46. Tran My-Van, "Japan and Vietnam's Caodaists: A Wartime Relationship (1939–45)," *Journal of Southeast Asian Studies* 27:1 (March 1996), 181; Tran Quang Vinh, *Hoi Ky Tran Quang Vinh va Lich Su Quan Doi Cao Dai* (n.p., 1997); Vu Ngu Chieu, "The Other Side of the 1945 Vietnamese Revolution: The Empire of Viet-Nam (March–August 1945)," *Journal of Asian Studies* 45:2 (February 1986), 300; Ralph Smith, "The Japanese Period in Indochina and the Coup of 9 March 1945," *Journal of Southeast Asian Studies* 9:2 (September 1978), 268–301.

47. Tran My-Van, "Japan and Vietnam's Caodaists," 182.

48. Ibid., 183.

49. Tran Quang Vinh, *Hoi Ky Tran Quang Vinh*, 198–201.

50. See Elliott, *The Vietnamese War*, 70–71; Savani, "Notes sur le Caodaisme," 166–169; see also Huynh Kim Khanh, *Vietnamese Communism, 1925–1945* (Ithaca: Cornell University Press, 1982), 242–243.

51. Tran My-Van, "Japan and Vietnam's Caodaists," 186.

52. Schrock et al., *Minority Groups,* 1024.

53. Nguyen Long Thanh Nam, *Hoa Hao Buddhism in the Course of Vietnam's History* (New York: Nova Science Publishers, Inc., 2003), 60–66.

54. Tran Quang Vinh, *Hoi Ky Tran Quang Vinh*, 232.

55. David G. Marr, *Vietnam 1945: The Quest for Power* (Los Angeles: University of California Press, 1995), 347.

56. Tran My-Van, "Japan and Vietnam's Caodaists," 188; Tran Quang Vinh, *Hoi Ky Tran Quang Vinh*, 226–229.

57. Generally speaking, Viet Minh seizures of power in northern and central Vietnam were relatively bloodless. See Tuong Vu, "'It's Time for the Indochinese Revolution to Show Its True Colors': The Radical Turn of Vietnamese Politics in 1948," *Journal of Southeast Asian Studies* 40:3 (October 2009), 519–542.

58. Marr, *Vietnam 1945*, 402–471.

59. Shawn McHale, "Understanding the Fanatic Mind? 106; François Guillemot, "Autopsy of a Massacre, 232.

60. Vu Ngu Chieu, "The Other Side of the 1945 Vietnamese Revolution," 312.

61. Marr, *Vietnam 1945*, 456.

62. Nguyen Long Thanh Nam, *Hoa Hao Buddhism*, 66–67.

63. Tran My-Van, "Japan and Vietnam's Caodaists," 191–192; Tran Quang Vinh, *Hoi Ky Tran Quang Vinh*, 257–259.

64. Elliott, *The Vietnamese War*, 49.

65. Marr, *Vietnam 1945*, 467.

66. Nguyen Long Thanh Nam, *Hoa Hao Buddhism*, 70–71.

67. Marr, *Vietnam 1945*, 467–468.

68. Savani, "Notes Sur les Binh Xuyen," 9.

69. Martin Thomas, "French Imperial Reconstruction and the Development of the Indochina War, 1945–1950," in Mark Atwood Lawrence and Fredrik Logevall, eds., *The First Indochina War: Colonial Conflict and Cold War Crisis* (Cambridge: Harvard University Press, 2007), 130–131.

70. Bradley, *Vietnam at War*, 44.

71. Elliott, *The Vietnamese War*, 57.

72. Christopher E. Goscha, "A 'Popular' Side of the Vietnamese Army: General Nguyen Binh and War in the South," in Christopher E. Goscha and Benoît de Tréglodé, eds., *Naissance d'un État-Parti: Le Viêt Nam depuis 1945* (Paris: Les Indes Savantes, 2004), 335; Christopher E. Goscha, "La Guerre par d'Autres Moyens: Réflexions sur la Guerre du Viet Minh dans le Sud-Vietnam de 1945 à 1951," *Guerres Mondiales et Conflits Contemporains* 206 (April–June 2002), 29–57.

73. Goscha, "A 'Popular' Side of the Vietnamese Army," 336; Stein Tønnesson, *Vietnam 1946: How the War Began* (Berkeley: University of California Press, 2010), 75.

74. Guillemot, "Anatomy of a Massacre," 236–237.

75. Goscha, "A 'Popular' Side of the Vietnamese Army," 338; McHale, "Understanding the Fanatic Mind?" 109.

76. Savani, "Notes Sur les Binh Xuyen," 12.

77. McCoy, *The Politics of Heroin*, 114.

78. Savani, "Notes Sur les Binh Xuyen," 72.

79. Ibid., 37–38.

80. Bordeaux, "Approaches statistiques de la communauté du bouddhisme Hoà Hao," 290.

81. "Accords du 8 Janvier 1947 avec les Caodaistes," (Accords of 8 January 1947 with the Cao Dai), VNA2, Phu Thu Tuong (Hereafter PTT), Folder 14685; see also Fall, "The Political-Religious Sects of Viet-Nam," 240.

82. Guillemot, "Anatomy of a Massacre," 240.

83. Fall, "The Political-Religious Sects of Viet-Nam," 246. Fall writes, "Politically the Hoa Hao, with their wonderfully simple social-religious program and their good record of nationalism presented a serious danger to the Viet-Minh in its attempt to monopolize the nationalist label for itself and for the northern parties in the Viet-Minh government coalition."

84. Hill, "Millenarian Machines in South Vietnam," 337–338.

85. Savani, "Notes sur le Phat Giao Hoa Hao," 37–38.

86. Translation of a document from the southern resistance committee quoted in Goscha, "A 'Popular' Side of the Vietnamese Army," 344.

87. François Guillemot, "Révolution Nationale et Lutte pour l'Independence au Vietnam: L'Echec de la Troisieme Voie 'Dai Viet'"—Dai Viet Quoc Dan Dang—(1938–1955)," Thése doctorat, École Practique des Hautes Études, 2003, 487.

88. Schrock et al., *Minority Groups in the Republic of Vietnam*, 1027.

89. McHale, "Understanding the Fanatic Mind?" 112.

90. Goscha, "A 'Popular' Side of the Vietnamese Army," 342–343.

91. Ibid., 344.

92. Ibid., 345.

93. Savani, "Notes Sur les Binh Xuyen," 118–119.

94. McCoy, *Politics of Heroin*, 110–117; Hill, "Millenarian Machines in South Vietnam," 341–342; Fall, "The Political-Religious Sects of Viet-Nam," 250; Savani, "Notes Sur les Binh Xuyen, 121.

95. Guillemot, "Anatomy of a Massacre," 256.

96. See Elliott, *The Vietnamese War*, esp. 146–159.

Chapter 2

1. "Problem Paper Prepared by a Working Group in the Department of State," 1 February 1950, *Foreign Relations of the United States* (Hereafter *FRUS*), 1950, East Asia and the Pacific, 714.

2. "Editorial Note," *FRUS*, 1950, East Asia and the Pacific, 711.

3. Marilyn B. Young, "'The Same Struggle for Liberty': Korea and Vietnam," in Mark Atwood Lawrence and Fredrik Logevall, eds., *The First Indochina War: Colonial Conflict and Cold War Crisis* (Cambridge: Harvard University Press, 2007), 196–214.

4. Stein Tønnesson, "Franklin Roosevelt, Trusteeship, and Indochina: A Reassessment" in Lawrence and Logevall, *The First Indochina War*, 64.

5. For more on the divisions within U.S. policymaking circles over this issue see Mark Atwood Lawrence, *Assuming the Burden: Europe and the American Commitment to War in Vietnam* (Los Angeles: University of California Press, 2005), 45–74.

6. David G. Marr, *Vietnam 1945: The Quest for Power* (Berkeley: The University of California Press, 1997).

7. Lawrence, *Assuming the Burden,* 30.

8. Stein Tønnesson, *Vietnam 1946: How the War Began* (Berkeley: The University of California Press, 2011), 237.

9. Mark Atwood Lawrence, "Recasting Vietnam: The Bao Dai Solution and the Outbreak of the Cold War in Southeast Asia," in Christopher E. Goscha and Christian Ostermann, eds., *Connecting Histories: Decolonization and the Cold War in Southeast Asia, 1945–1962* (Washington, DC: Woodrow Wilson Center Press, 2009), 18. The Dai Viet was a prime target of the Viet Minh following the August Revolution and throughout the French War, and therefore conducted its political operations largely in exile. The party aimed to link its destiny to that of Bao Dai's state, but the effort ultimately failed. See François Guillemot, "Révolution Nationale et Lutte pour l'Independence au Vietnam: L'Echec de la Troisieme Voie 'Dai Viet' "—Dai Viet Quoc Dan Dang—(1938–1955)," Thèse doctorat, École Practique des Hautes Études, 2003.

10. Guillemot, "Révolution Nationale," 476; Miller, "Vision, Power, and Agency: The Ascent of Ngo Dinh Diem, 1945–1954," *Journal of Southeast Asian Studies* 3:35 (October 2004), 438.

11. Miller, "Vision, Power, and Agency," 437–440.

12. Martin Thomas, "People's War and the Collapse of French Indochina, 1945–1954," in Martin Thomas, Bob More, and L. J. Bulter, eds., *Crises of Empire: Decolonization and Europe's Imperial States, 1918–1975* (London: Hodder Education, 2008), 194.

13. Lawrence, "Recasting Vietnam," 24.

14. Laurent Cesari, *L'Indochine en guerres 1945–1993* (Paris: Éditions Belin, 1995), 57–64.

15. See Oscar Chapuis, *The Last Emperors of Vietnam: From Tu Duc to Bao Dai* (Westport, CT: Greenwood Press, 2000). Chapuis writes, "In spite of his concern for reforms, Bao Dai was by no means a political leader" (28); for Bao Dai's recollections of his own political involvement see S. M. Bao Dai, *Le Dragon d'Annam* (Paris: Plon, 1980).

16. See Chapuis, *Last Emperors*, 27–29.

17. David Marr, *Vietnamese Tradition on Trial, 1020–1941* (Berkeley: University of California Press, 1981), 69. Ngo Dinh Diem was minister of interior under Bao Dai in 1933 but resigned in protest against France's refusal to implement reforms.

18. See Francois Guillemot, "Vietnamese Nationalist Revolutionaries and the Japanese Occupation: The Case of the Dai Viet Parties (1936–1946)," in Li Narangoa and Robert Cribb, eds., *Imperial Japan and National Identities in Asia, 1895–1945* (New York: Routledge Curzon, 2003), 221–248.

19. Ellen J. Hammer, *The Struggle for Indochina* (Stanford: Stanford University Press, 1954), 211; Hans Antlöv, "Rulers in Imperial Policy: Sultan Ibrahim, Emperor Bao Dai, and Sultan Hamengku Buwono IX," in Hans Antlöv and Stein Tønnesson, eds., *Imperial Policy and Southeast Asian Nationalism, 1930–1957* (Richmond, Surrey, UK: Curzon Press, 1995), 247.

20. Miller, "Vision, Power, and Agency," 440.

21. Quoted in Pierre Brocheux and Daniel Hémery, *Indochina: An Ambiguous Colonization, 1858–1954* (Berkeley: The University of California Press, 2009), 364; Cesari, *L'Indochine en guerres*, 62–63.

22. Miller, "Vision, Power, and Agency, " 440.

23. Mark Philip Bradley, *Imagining Vietnam and America: The Making of Postcolonial Vietnam, 1919–1950* (Chapel Hill: The University of North Carolina Press, 2000), 179.

24. Lawrence, *Assuming the Burden*, 247–261. Lawrence details the debates in the United States, as well as Britain and France, over the question of recognition. His study concludes that Mao's recognition of the DRV led Washington officials to shelve concerns with Bao Dai's lack of political legitimacy and the insufficiency of France's grant of autonomy to the Associated States; see also Gary R. Hess, "The First American Commitment to Indochina: The Acceptance of the 'Bao Dai Solution,' in 1950," *Diplomatic History* 2:4 (fall 1978), 331–350.

25. See John Lewis Gaddis, *Strategies of Containment: A Critical Appraisal of American National Security Policy* (New York: Oxford University Press, 1982), 89–126.

26. William I. Hitchcock, *France Restored: Cold War Diplomacy and the Quest for Leadership in Europe, 1944–1954* (Chapel Hill: University of North Carolina Press, 1998), 134; Laurent Cesari, "The Declining Value of Indochina: France and the Economics of Empire, 1950–1955," in Mark Atwood Lawrence and Fredrik Logevall, eds., *The First Vietnam War: Colonial Conflict and Cold War Crisis* (Cambridge: Harvard University Press, 2007), 183.

27. Hitchcock, *France Restored*, 148.

28. Cesari, "The Declining Value of Indochina," 178.

29. Ibid., 175.

30. Kathryn C. Statler, *Replacing France: The Origins of American Intervention in Vietnam* (Lexington: University Press of Kentucky, 2007), 19.

31. Cesari, "The Declining Value of Indochina," 179.

32. Hitchcock, *France Restored*, 155 and 166; Statler, *Replacing France*, 47.

33. Cesari, "The Declining Value of Indochina," 183 and 188.

34. Hitchcock, *France Restored*, 179.

35. Ibid., 183–184.

36. Cesari, "The Declining Value of Indochina," 179.

37. See "Proposed Strategic Plan for the Successful Conclusion of the War in Indochina," Memorandum by the Joint Chiefs of Staff to the Secretary of Defense (Wilson), 21 April 1953, *FRUS,* 1952–1954, Indochina (vol. 13), 493–495; "Current Situation in Indochina," Memorandum by Ambassador Donald Heath to the Secretary of State, 28 April 1953, *FRUS,* 1952–1954, Indochina (vol. 13), 521–527; George C. Herring, "Franco-American Conflict in Indochina, 1950–1954," in Lawrence S. Kaplan, Denise Artaud, and Mark R. Rubin, eds., *Dien Bien Phu and the Crisis of Franco-American Relations* (Wilmington, DE: Scholarly Resources, 1990), 34.

38. Cesari, "The Declining Value of Indochina," 189.

39. Ibid., 189; Hugues Tertrais, *La Piastre et le Fusil: Le Coûte de la Guerre d'Indochine, 1945–1954* (Paris: Ministère de l'Economie des Finances et de l'Industrie, 2002) ; Pierre Journoud, "Au cœur de la décolonisation: la politique française en Indochine, entre continuités et ruptures (1954–1963)," in Christopher E. Goscha and Karine Laplante, eds., *L'Échec de la paix en Indochine (The Failure of Peace in Indochina), 1954–1962* (Paris: Les Indes Savantes, 2010), 133.

40. Savani, "Notes sur le Caodaisme," Mimeographed, no publisher, no date, 120–121 and 148; Nguyen Thanh Xuan, "Tim Hieu Cac Cuoc Van Dong Thong Nhat Dao Cao Dai Truoc Nam 1975," *Nghien Cuu Lich Su* (2003), 48–56.

41. For French reactions to trafficking in the piaster, see Jacques Despeuch, *Le Traffic de Piastres* (Paris: Deux-Rives, 1953); Arthur Laurent, *La Banque de l'Indochine et la Piastre* (Paris: Deux Rives, 1954); Tertrais, *La Piastre et le Fusil.*

42. Henry Giniger, "France Reduces Value of Indochinese Piaster," *New York Times,* 11 May 1953; Irwin M. Wall, *The United States and the Making of Postwar France, 1945–1954* (New York: Cambridge University Press, 1991), 252; Frank Giles, *The Locust Years: The Story of the Fourth French Republic, 1946–1958* (New York: Carroll and Graf, 1991), 195–196.

43. R. E. M. Irving, *The First Indochina War: French and American Policy, 1945–1954* (New York: Croom Helm, 1975), 105–111.

44. "The Ambassador at Saigon (Heath) to the Department of State," 12 March 1953, *FRUS,* 1952–1954, Indochina (vol. 13), 402–406; "The Charge at Saigon (McClintock) to the Department of State," 15 May 1953, *FRUS,* 1952–1954, Indochina (vol. 13), 566.

45. "The Ambassador at Saigon (Heath) to the Department of State," 12 March 1953, *FRUS,* 1952–1954, Indochina (vol. 13), 402–406.

46. Jaques Dalloz, *The War in Indochina, 1945–1954* (Dublin: Barnes and Noble, 1987), 153.

47. "The Charge at Saigon (McClintock) to the Department of State," 13 May 1953, *FRUS,* 1952–1954, Indochina (vol. 13), 562–563.

48. Irving, *The First Indochina War,* 107; see also Joseph Buttinger, *Vietnam: A Dragon Embattled,* vol. 2, *Vietnam at War* (London: Pall Mall Press, 1967), 780.

49. Jérémy Jammes, "Divination and Politics in Southern Vietnam: Roots of Caodaism," *Social Compass* 57:3 (2010), 363.

50. "Substance of Discussions of State-Joint Chiefs of Staff Meeting at the Pentagon Building, July 17, 1953, 11 a.m.," *FRUS,* 1952–1954, Indochina (vol. 13), 683.

51. For prior expressions of concern about Nguyen Van Tam's Francophilia, see "The Ambassador at Saigon (Heath) to the Department of State, " 25 January 1953, *FRUS,* 1952–1954, Indochina (vol. 13); Ellen J. Hammer, *The Struggle for Indochina* (Stanford: Stanford University Press, 1966), 281–286.

52. "Annee 1953—Affaire Caodaiste—Exposé Chronologique Succinct," especially pages 32 and 40, Caodistes Divers (1954–1955), SHAT, H10 3761.

53. "Activités Politiques du Ho Phap Pham Cong Tac," Le Directeur des Services Français de Sécurité en Indochine, 21 November 1953, CAOM, HCI, SPCE 15.

54. "The Ambassador in France (Dillon) to the Department of State," 3 July 1953. *FRUS,* 1952–1954, Indochina (Part 1), 634–635.

55. Cited in James Cable, *The Geneva Conference of 1954 on Indochina* (London: St. Martin's Press, 1986), 20.

56. Irving, *The First Indochina War,* 108.

57. "The Charge in France (Achilles) to the Department of State," 6 July 1953, *FRUS,* 1952–1954, Indochina, 635–637.

58. Statement made to *Le Monde,* 9 June 1953, cited in Henri Grimal, *Decolonization: The British, French, Dutch and Belgian Empires 1919–1963* (London: Routledge and Kegan Paul, 1965), 249.

59. "The Ambassador at Saigon (Heath) to the Department of State," 1 August 1953, *FRUS,* 1952–1954, Indochina.

60. See David W. P. Elliott, *The Vietnamese War: Revolution and Social Change in the Mekong Delta, 1930–1975,* vol. 1 (London: M. E. Sharpe, 2003), 115–162.

61. "Réunion Preparatoire du Congrès Nationale," 12 September 1953, CAOM, HCI, SPCE 15; "Bulletin des Renseignements: Conference de Presse du Comité d'Organisation du Congrès Nationale," 8 October 1953, CAOM, HCI, SPCE 27; see Buttinger, *Vietnam: A Dragon Embattled,* 815. Buttinger gives Ngo Dinh Nhu sole credit for leadership of the Movement for National Union and Peace.

62. "Viet-Nam Dan-Chu Xa-Hoi Dang, De That Chu-Nien Tuyen-Ngon," 21 September 1953, SHAT H10 4180.

63. "Réunion Inaugurale du Congrès Nationale—Meetings Populaires a Hanoi et Saigon le Dimanche 6 Septembre 1953," CAOM, HCI, SPCE 26; Buttinger, *Vietnam: A Dragon Embattled,* 785.

64. "The Ambassador at Saigon (Heath) to the Department of State," 11 September 1953. *FRUS,* 1952–1954, Indochina.

65. "Ambassador at Saigon (Heath) to the Department of State," 16 October 1953. *FRUS,* 1952–1954, Indochina.

66. "Texte d'une motion signée par vingt-deux congressistes et remise au Prince Buu Loc avant son depart pour Paris le dimanche 18 Octobre 1953," CAOM, HCI, SPCE 27; see also Hammer, *The Struggle for Indochina,* 305.

67. Bao Dai's position summarized in "The Ambassador in France (Dillon) to the Department of State," 17 October 1953, *FRUS,* 1952–1954, Indochina, 833–834.

68. Ibid.

69. "The Ambassador at Saigon (Heath) to the Department of State," 18 October 1953, *FRUS,* 1952–1954, Indochina, 834–835.

70. "The Ambassador in France (Dillon) to the Department of State," 20 October 1953, *FRUS,* 1952–1954, Indochina, 837–838.

71. Mark Bradley, *Imagining Vietnam and America: The Making of Postcolonial Vietnam, 1919–1950* (Chapel Hill: University of North Carolina Press, 2000); Seth Jacobs, *America's Miracle Man in Vietnam: Ngo Dinh Diem, Religion, Race, and U.S. Intervention in Southeast Asia, 1950–1957* (Durham: Duke University Press, 2004).

72. "The Ambassador at Saigon (Heath) to the Department of State," 18 October 1953, *FRUS,* 1952–1954, Indochina, 834–836.

73. "The Ambassador at Saigon (Heath) to the Department of State," 17 October 1953, *FRUS,* 1952–1954, Indochina, 828–830.

74. "The Ambassador at Saigon (Heath) to the Department of State," 18 January 1954, *FRUS,* 1952–1954, Indochina, 977–981.

75. "Bulletin des Renseignments: Activités de la Secte Caodaiste de Tay Ninh," 13 January 1954, CAOM, HCI, SPCE 15.

76. "Position de Caodiastes vis-à-vis le Gouvernment Buu Loc," 4 February 1954, SHAT, H10 3761.

77. "Bulletin des Renseignments Mensuels—Mois de Janvier 1954," 9, SHAT, H10 3761.

78. "Bulletin des Renseignments Mensuels—Mois de Janvier 1954," 6 and 10, SHAT, H10 3761.

79. "Discours Prononcé par le General Nguyen Thanh Phuong, Commandent en Chef des Forces Armées Caodistes a l'occasion du 7eme Anniversaire de la Lutte Anti-Communiste (11 Fevrier 1954)," SHAT, H10 3761.

Chapter 3

1. The "sink or swim" phrase used in the title of this chapter was coined by journalist Homer Bigart and was often used to describe Washington's policy of support for Ngo Dinh Diem. Cited in David Halberstam, *The Best and the Brightest* (New York, 1969), 191. Also "Memorandum for the Executive Officer, Operations Coordinating Board," 2 March 1954, White House Office, National Security Council Staff: Papers, 1948–1961, Box 37, OCB 091. Indo-China (File #1) (1) (November 1953–July 1954), DDEL.

2. "Sino-Soviet Direction and Nature of the Indochina Conflict," nd. White House Office, National Security Council Staff: Papers, 1948–1961, Box 37, OCB 091.Indo-China (File #1) (1) (November 1953–July 1954), DDEL.

3. "The Ambassador at Saigon (Heath) to the Department of State," 18 October 1953, *FRUS,* 1952–1954, Indochina, 834–836; Collins to Dulles, "Report on Vietnam for the National Security Council," 20 January 1955, White House Office, National Security Council Staff: Papers, 1948–1961, Disaster File, box 26, Vietnam (1), DDEL.

4. Ellen J. Hammer, *A Death in November: America in Vietnam, 1963* (New York: E. P. Dutton, 1987), 60.

5. William I. Hitchcock, *France Restored: Cold War Diplomacy and the Quest for Leadership in Europe, 1944–1954* (Chapel Hill: University of North Carolina Press, 1998), 188.

6. Kathryn C. Statler, *Replacing France: The Origins of American Intervention in Vietnam* (Lexington: University Press of Kentucky, 2007), 72.

7. Hitchcock, *France Restored*, 186; Laurent Cesari, "The Declining Value of Indochina: France and the Economics of Empire, 1950–1955," in Mark Atwood Lawrence and Fredrik Logevall, eds., *The First Vietnam War: Colonial Conflict and Cold War Crisis* (Cambridge: Harvard University Press, 2007), 191.

8. The issue of joint intervention in Indochina greatly strained the Anglo-American relationship. See Geoffrey Warner, "Britain and the Crisis over Dien Bien Phu, April 1954: The Failure of United Action," in Kaplan et al., *Dien Bien Phu and the Crisis of Franco-American Relations, 1954–1955* (Wilmington, DE: Scholarly Resources, 1990), 55–77; John Prados, *The Sky Would Fall: Operation Vulture: The US Bombing Mission in Indochina, 1954* (New York: The Dial Press, 1983); George C. Herring and Richard H. Immerman, "Eisenhower, Dulles, and Dienbienphu: 'The Day We Didn't Go to War' Revisited," *Journal of American History* 71 (1984): 343–363.

9. See Herring and Immerman, "Eisenhower, Dulles, and Dienbienphu," 343–363; Richard H. Immerman, "Between the Unattainable and the Unacceptable: Eisenhower and Dien Bien Phu," in Richard A. Melanson and David Mayers, eds., *Reevaluating Eisenhower: American Foreign Policy in the 1950s* (Urbana: University of Illinois Press, 1987), 120–154; Chester J. Pach Jr. and Elmo Richardson, *The Presidency of Dwight D. Eisenhower*, rev. ed. (Lawrence: University Press of Kansas, 1991), esp. 93–98.

10. Statler, *Replacing France*, 94. For one of the earliest thorough studies on the Geneva Conference, see Robert F. Randle, *Geneva 1954: The Settlement of the Indochinese War* (Princeton: Princeton University Press, 1969). For a reexamination of America's role in the conference, in light of recent revisionist scholarship on Eisenhower's diplomacy, see Richard H. Immerman, "The United States and the Geneva Conference of 1954: A New Look," *Diplomatic History* 14 (1990), 43–66. See also, James Cable, *The Geneva Conference of 1954 on Indochina* (London: St. Martin's Press, 1986); Philippe Devillers and Jean Lacouture, *End of a War: Indochina, 1954* (New York: Praeger, 1969), 121–313; and Gary Hess, "Redefining the American Position in Southeast Asia: The United States and the Geneva and Manila Conferences," in Kaplan et al., *Dien Bien Phu*.

11. "Année 1953—Affaire Caodaiste—exposé chronologique succinct," 5, SHAT, H10 3761; "Declaration Commune des Cao-Dai, Hoa-Hao, et Dai-Viet Remise a la Presse le 8-3-1954," SHAT, H10 3761.

12. "The Ambassador at Saigon (Heath) to the Department of State," 16 March 1954, *FRUS*, 1952–1954, Indochina, 1122–1124.

13. Ibid.

14. "The Ambassador at Saigon (Heath) to the Department of State," 24 March 1954, *FRUS*, 1952–1954, Indochina, 1155–1156.

15. "The Ambassador at Saigon (Heath) to the Department of State," 31 March 1954, *FRUS*, 1952–1954, Indochina, 1191–1192.

16. "Les Principaux Groupements Politiques et les sects Confessionelles de Tendances Nationalistes au Vietnam," July 1953, CAOM, HCI, SPCE 29.

17. "Dulles to Walter Beddel Smith, 12 May 1954, U.S. Congress, House, Committee on Armed Services," in *United States—Vietnam Relations, 1945–1967: A Study Prepared by the Department of Defense* (Washington: U.S. Government Printing Office, 1971), book 9:457–59. Cited in George C. Herring, "'A Good Stout Effort': John Foster Dulles and the Indochina Crisis, 1954–1955," in Richard Immerman, ed., *John Foster Dulles and the Diplomacy of the Cold War* (Princeton: Princeton University Press, 1992), 220.

18. "Année 1953—Affaire Caodaiste—exposé chronologique succinct," 13, SHAT, H10 3761.

19. Later in his administration he changed his rhetoric slightly to identify communism, disunion, and underdevelopment as the "three common enemies." See Republic of Vietnam, *Eight Years of the Ngo Dinh Diem Administration, 1954–1962* (Saigon: Republic of Vietnam, 1962), 236 and 263.

20. "Commissariat General de France en Indochine, Rapport Mensuel, Mois de Mai 1954," CAOM, HCI 5/30.

21. "Kien Nghi cua cac Dang-Phai va Nhan Si," *Saigon Moi*, 10 May 1954.

22. Ralph Smith, *Viet-Nam and the West* (London: Heinemann Educational Books, 1968), 151; Pierre Grosser, "La France et L'Indochine (1954–9156): Une 'Carte de Visite' en 'Peu de Chagrin,' Doctoral Thesis, Institut d'Etudes Politiques de Paris, Troisieme cycle d'histoire, September 2002, 1169.

23. "Traduction a Monsieur Nguyen-Ai-Quoc ou Ho-Chi-Minh," 1 May, 1954, SHAT, H10 3761.

24. "Chong Chia Xe V.N. o Nam Viet," *Saigon Moi*, 8 May 1954.

25. "La Voix Libre des Nationalistes Vietnamiennes Authentiques, l'Heure Historique," 28 May 1954, SHAT, H10 3761.

26. "Nos Impressions sur la Lettre de S.S. Le Pape Caodiste a M. Nguyen Ai Quoc (Le President Ho Chi Minh)," 6 May 1954, SHAT, H10 3761; "La Voix du Front de la Resistance Nationale, Personne ne Peut Aller Contre le Courant de l'Histoire," 13 May 1954, SHAT, H10 3761.

27. "Nuoc Viet Nam Thong Nhut Mot Giai tu Nam-Quan den Ca-Mau," *Saigon Moi*, 6 May 1954.

28. "Dan Chung Khap Noi Chong Cuoc Am Muu Chia Xe Nuoc V.N.," *Saigon Moi*, 22 May 1955.

29. "United States—Vietnam Relations, 1945–1967: Study Prepared by the Department of Defense" (Washington: U.S. Government Printing Office, 1971), B-7.

30. For documents indicative of Mendès-France's views and Washington's perception of him, see "The Ambassador in France (Dillon) to the Department of State," 17 June 1953, *FRUS*, 1952–1954, Indochina (vol. 13), 610–612; Irwin Wall, "Pierre Mendès-France vu par les Americains Accueil et et reactions des milieux gouvernementaux et des medias," in Rene Girault, ed., *Pierre Mendès-France et le role de la France dans le Monde* (Grenoble: Presses Universitaires de Grenoble, 1991), 229–248.

31. Pierre Mendès-France, "La Declaration d'Investiture," 17 June 1954, in *Pierre Mendès-France: Ouvres Completes III: Gouverner c'est Choisir, 1954–1955* (Paris: l'Institut Pierre Mendès-France, 1986), 50–69.

32. See George Herring, *America's Longest War: The United States and Vietnam, 1950–1975,* 4th ed. (New York: McGraw Hill, 2002), 43.

33. For more on the Soviet–Viet Minh relationship during the Geneva Conference, see Ilya V. Gaiduk, *Confronting Vietnam: Soviet Policy toward the Indochina Conflict, 1954–1963* (Washington, DC: Woodrow Wilson Center Press, 2003); For an analysis of Sino-Vietnamese diplomatic relations during the conference see Qiang Zhai, *China and the Vietnam Wars, 1950–1975* (Chapel Hill: University of North Carolina Press, 2000), 43–64.

34. "United States—Vietnam Relations, 1945–1967," D-13.

35. See Robert D. Schulzinger, *A Time For War: The United States in Vietnam, 1941–1975* (New York: Oxford University Press, 1991), 77.

36. The extent to which the United States influenced Bao Dai's decision to appoint Ngo Dinh Diem remains hotly debated. Many scholars agree that Bao Dai made the decision on

recognizing that Ngo Dinh Diem would be the most likely to channel American aid. See David L. Anderson, *Trapped by Success: The Eisenhower Administration and Vietnam, 1953–61* (New York: Columbia University Press, 1991), 53. See also See Philip E. Catton, *Diem's Final Failure: Prelude to America's War in Vietnam* (Lawrence: University Press of Kansas, 2002), 6–7; Denis Warner, *The Last Confucian* (New York: Macmillan, 1963), 65–66; Dennis J. Duncanson, *Government and Revolution in Vietnam* (New York: Oxford University Press, 1968), 210. According to rumors rampant in Saigon at the time, Bao Dai made his decision with the expectation that Ngo Dinh Diem's assumption of power would bring immediate direct American aid. See "Telegram from US Embassy Saigon to Department of State," 5 July 1954, NARA, RG 59, 751G.00/7-554. Seth Jacob goes further to claim, "Diem would never have been named premier had he not been Washington's candidate." Jacobs, *America's Miracle Man in Vietnam: Ngo Dinh Diem, Religion, Race, and U.S. Intervention in Southeast Asia, 1950–1957* (Durham, NC: Duke University Press, 2004), 52–56. Edward Miller occupies the opposite end of the spectrum, arguing that the United States had little effect on Bao Dai's decision; that Ngo Dinh Diem and Ngo Dinh Nhu's political activities within Vietnam backed the chief of state into a corner and left him with little choice but to place Ngo Dinh Diem in power. Miller, "Vision, Power, and Agency: The Ascent of Ngo Dinh Diem, 1945–1954," *Journal of Southeast Asian Studies* 3:35 (October 2004), 454–456. Miller and Jacobs continued this debate in an h-diplo roundtable: *America's Miracle Man in Vietnam* Roundtable Review, 12 June 2007, www.h-net.org/~diplo/roundtables/PDF/AmericasMiracleMan-Roundtable.pdf. For Bao Dai's own recollections, see Bao Dai, *Dragon d'Annam* (Paris: Plon, 1980), 329.

37. Thomas L. Alhern Jr., *CIA and the House of Ngo: Covert Action in South Vietnam, 1954–63*, Center for the Study of Intelligence 21, National Security Archive Electronic Briefing Book No. 283.

38. Alhern, *CIA and the House of Ngo*, 16–17 and 24.

39. Miller, "Vision, Power, and Agency," 447–452.

40. See Joseph G. Morgan, *The Vietnam Lobby: The American Friends of Vietnam, 1955–1975* (Chapel Hill: The University of North Carolina Press, 1997), 1–15. Among Ngo Dinh Diem's supporters in the United States were Michigan State University professor Wesley Fishel, Senator Mike Mansfield, Supreme Court justice William O. Douglass, and Cardinal Francis Spellman. See also Gregory Allen Olson, *Mansfield and Vietnam: A Study in Rhetorical Adaptation* (East Lansing: Michigan State University Press, 1995), 30; William Duiker, *U.S. Containment Policy and the Conflict in Indochina* (Stanford: Stanford University Press, 1994); Bao Dai, *Le Dragon D'Annam*, 328–332.

41. "Current Situation in Indochina," Memorandum by Ambassador Donald Heath to the Secretary of State, 28 April 1953, *FRUS, 1952–1954*, Indochina (vol. 13), 521–527.

42. "Telegram from US Embassy Saigon to Department of State," 27 May 1954, NARA, RG 59, 751G.00/5-2754; "Telegram from US Embassy Saigon to Department of State," 23 July 1954, NARA, RG 59, 751G.00/7-2354.

43. "The Ambassador at Saigon (Heath) to the Department of State," 17 October 1953, *FRUS, 1952–1954*, Indochina, 828–830.

44. "Telegram from US Embassy Saigon to Department of State," 8 June 1954, NARA, RG 59, 751G.00/6-854.

45. Cited in Jacobs, *America's Miracle Man*, 52.

46. "Telegram from US Embassy Saigon to Department of State," 28 July 1954, NARA, RG 59, 751G.00/7-2854.

47. "Telegram from US Embassy Paris to Department of State," 26 May 1954, NARA, RG 59, 751G.00/5-2654.

48. "Ngo Dinh Diem, Statement of 18 June 1954 (Paris)," in "Major Policy Speeches by President Ngo Dinh Diem" (Saigon, 1956), 5–6.

49. See Jeffrey Race, *War Comes to Long An: Revolutionary Conflict in A Vietnamese Province* (Los Angeles: University of California Press, 1972). According to Race, "In July 1954 . . . the end of violence was welcomed by all, but the 'return to normal' was not. A significant part of the population was either indifferent or strongly embittered toward the new government, both as sponsor of the returning landlords and village councils, and as the successor to the French" (11).

50. "Note au Sujet du President Tran Van Huu—Bruits Concernanant la Formation d'un Nouveau Gouvernement—Départ pour la France de M. Vuong Quang Nhuong, Ngo Dinh Diem," 27 July 1953, CAOM, HCI, SPCE 361; "Activités Politiques at Gouvernmentales Vietnamiennes," Haute Commisariat de France en Indochine, Direction des Services de Sécurité, 8 August 1953, CAOM, HCI 267/768.

51. "Telegram from US Embassy Hanoi to Secretary of State," 5 June 1954, NARA, RG 59, 751G.00/6-554.

52. "Telegram from US Embassy Saigon to Secretary of State," 7 July 1954, NARA, RG 59, 751G.00/7-554.

53. Cited in Jacobs, *America's Miracle Man,* 57.

54. See Kathryn Statler, "The Diem Experiment: Franco-American Conflict over South Vietnam, July 1954–May 1955," *Journal of American-East Asian Relations* 6:2–3 (summer–fall 1997), 145–173.

55. "Telegram from US Embassy Saigon to Secretary of State," 13 June 1954, NARA, RG 59, 751G.00/6-1354.

56. Statler, *Replacing France*, 118.

57. "Telegram from US Embassy Saigon to Secretary of State," 18 June 1954, NARA, RG 59, 751G.00/6-1854.

58. "The Ambassador in France (Dillon) to the Department of State, 24 may 1954, *FRUS, 1952–1954,* Indochina (vol. 13), 1608–1609.

59. Anthony Trawick Bouscaren, *The Last of the Mandarins: Diem of Vietnam* (Pittsburgh: Duquesne University Press, 1965), 3. Even Ngo Dinh Diem's most sympathetic biographer has written that "at the beginning, few thought Diem would last nine months, much less nine years."

60. "Rapport de le Commissariat General de France en Indochine, Semaine de 30 Juin de 6 Julliet 1954," CAOM, HCI 38/153; for more on the political and military problems Ngo Dinh Diem confronted as he came to power, see Duncanson, *Government and Revolution in Vietnam,* 204–210.

61. George C. Herring, Gary R. Hess, and Richard H. Immerman, "Passage of Empire: The United States, France, and South Vietnam, 1954–1955," in Kaplan et al., *Dien Bien Phu,* 171.

62. Jean LaCouture and Philippe Devillers, *La Fin d'une Guerre: Indochine 1954* (Paris: Editions du Seuil, 1960), 299.

63. Alfred W. McCoy, *The Politics of Heroin in Southeast Asia* (New York: Harper and Row, 1972), 94; Frances R. Hill, "Millenarian Machines in South Vietnam," *Comparative Studies in Society and History* 13:3 (July 1971), 341–342; Bernard Fall, "The Political-Religious Sects of Viet-Nam," *Pacific Affairs* 28 (September 1955), 250.

64. Joann L. Schrock et al., *Minority Groups in the Republic of Vietnam* (Washington, DC: Cultural Information Analysis Center, Ethnographic Study Series, 1966), 809; Duong Van Mai Elliott, *The Sacred Willow: Four Generations in the Life of a Vietnamese Family* (New York: Oxford University Press, 1999), 251–252.

65. Hill, "Millenarian Machines in South Vietnam," 342.

66. Schrock et al., *Minority Groups in the Republic of Vietnam*, 1031.

67. Savani, "Notes sur le Phat Giao Hoa Hao," Mimeographed, no publisher, no date, 62.

68. Savani, "Notes sur le Caodaisme," Mimeographed, no publisher, no date, 148; Nguyen Thanh Xuan, "Tim Hieu Cac Cuoc Van Dong Thong Nhat Dao Cao Dai Truoc Nam 1975," *Nghien Cuu Lich Su* (2003), 48–56.

69. For a hagiographic but informative account of Trinh Minh The's political and military activities, see Sergei Blagov, *Honest Mistakes: The Life and Death of Trinh Minh The (1922–1955): South Vietnam's Alternative Leader* (Huntington, NY: Nova Science Publishers, 2001), 29–30; Savani, "Notes sur le Caodaisme," 141.

70. Grosser, "La France et L'Indochine," 1169.

71. "Telegram de le Secretariat d'Etat aux Relations avec les Etats Associes sur le Gouvernement de Ngo Dinh Diem," 11 August 1954, CAOM, HCI 107/341.

72. "Note du Conseiller Diplomatique du Gouvernement, Mission aupres de Sa Majesté Bao Dai (6 Septembre 1954, Cannes), document 158, *Documents Diplomatiques Français, 1954 (21 Juillet–31 Decembre)* (Hereafter *DDF*), 320–326.

73. "Telegram from US Embassy Saigon to Secretary of State," 16 July 1954, NARA, RG 59, 751G.00/7-1654.

74. Grosser, "La France et L'Indochine," 1171.

75. Bishop Le Huu Tu was one of the most notable Catholic leaders in league with Nguyen Van Hinh and the politico-religious organizations at this time.

76. Edward Geary Lansdale, *In the Midst of Wars: An American's Mission to Southeast Asia* (New York: Harper and Row, 1972), 126–364; Cecil B. Currey, *Edward Lansdale: The Unquiet American* (Boston: Houghton Mifflin, 1988), 134–187.

77. Lansdale, *In the Midst of Wars*, 172. Lansdale claimed that Le Huu Tu "didn't have a prayer of being able to lead the Vietnamese nationalists" (171).

78. Quoted in Alhern, *CIA and the House of Ngo*, 19.

79. Hammer, *A Death in November*, 65.

80. "General Ely's views on the political situation in Vietnam, Telegram from Mr. Bonsal to Mr. Robertson," 16 August 1954, NARA, RG 59, 751.00G/8-1654.

81. Pierre Melandri, "The Repercussions of the Geneva Conference: South Vietnam under a New Protector," in Kaplan et al., *Dien Bien Phu*, 197–210.

82. Grosser, "La France et L'Indochine," 1178–1179.

83. "Telegram from US Embassy Saigon to Department of State," 13 August 1954, NARA, RG 59, 751G.00/8-1354.

84. Raphael-Leygues arrived in Saigon on April 10 on a mission intended to broaden support for the Southern government and to provide Mendès-France with an objective picture of the political situation.

85. Telegram from US Embassy Saigon to Department of State," 26 August 1954, NARA, RG 59, 751G.00/8-2654.

86. Ibid.

87. For Smith's thoughts, see "Telegram from Walter Bedell Smith to US Embassy Paris and US Embassy Saigon," 28 August 1954, NARA, RG 59, 751G.00/8-2754.

88. "Telegram from US Embassy Saigon to Department of State," 27 August 1954, NARA, RG 59, 751G.00/8-2754.

89. "Telegram from US Embassy Saigon to Secretary of State," 28 August 1954, NARA, RG 59, 751G.00/8-2854.

90. "Telegram from US Embassy Saigon to Secretary of State," 1 September 1954, NARA, RG 59, 751G.00/9-154.

91. "Plus que jamais dans la conjuncture actuelle prenons conscience de notre devoir," 4 September 1954, SHAT, H10 3761; "La révolution exterminatrice et la révolution liberatrice," 4 September 1954, SHAT, H10 3761.

92. "Telegram from US Embassy Saigon to Secretary of State," 8 September 1954, NARA, RG 59, 751G.00/9-854.

93. "Telegram from US Embassy Saigon to Secretary of State," 14 September 1954, NARA, RG 59, 751G.00/9-1454. Emphasis original.

94. "Telegram from US Embassy Saigon to Secretary of State," 17 September 1954, NARA, RG 59, 751G.00/9-1754.

95. "Telegram from US Embassy Saigon to Secretary of State," 19 September 1954, NARA, RG 59, 751G.00/9-1954.

96. Grosser, "La France et L'Indochine," 1186–1189.

97. "Telegram from US Embassy Saigon to Secretary of State," 24 September 1954, NARA, RG 59, 751G.00/9-2454.

98. Ibid.; "Telegram from US Embassy Saigon to Secretary of State," 25 September 1954, NARA, RG 59, 751G.00/9-2554.

99. Grosser, "La France et L'Indochine," 1190.

100. Ibid., 1195–1199.

101. Cited in Olson, *Mansfield in Vietnam*, 40.

102. Ibid., 39–40; see also, Robert Mann, *A Grand Delusion: America's Descent into Vietnam* (New York: Basic Books, 2001), 183.

103. Anderson, *Trapped by Success*, 84.

104. M. Henri Bonnet, Ambassadeur de France a Washington, a Mendès-France, Ministre des Affaires Étrangeres, 27 October, document 297, *DDF, 1954 (21 Juillet-31 Decembre)*, 616–617.

105. "Telegram from US Embassy Saigon to Secretary of State," 9 September 1954, NARA, RG 59, 751G.00/9-954.

106. "Telegram from US Embassy Saigon to Secretary of State," 15 September 1954, NARA, RG 59, 751G.00/9-1554; "Telegram from US Embassy Saigon to Secretary of State," 17 September 1954, NARA, RG 59, 751G.00/9-1754.

107. Currey, *Edward Lansdale*, 167; Hammer, *A Death in November*, 70.

108. "Emission de poste de radiodiffusion du Saint Siege de Tay Ninh," 23 December 1954, SHAT, H10 3761.

109. "Telegram de le Secretariat d'État aux Relations avec les États Associés," 14 September 1954, CAOM, HCI 107/371.

110. "Notes sur le Gouvernement de Ngo Dinh Diem," 116 December 1954, CAOM, HCI 37/149.

Chapter 4

1. Chapter originally published as Jessica M. Chapman, "The Sect Crisis of 1955 and the American Commitment to Ngo Dinh Diem," *Journal of Vietnamese Studies* 5:1 (winter 2010), 37–85. © 2010 by the Regents of the University of California.

2. David L. Anderson, *Trapped by Success: The Eisenhower Administration and Vietnam, 1953–61* (New York: Columbia University Press, 1991); Kai Bird, *The Color of Truth: McGeorge Bundy and William Bundy: Brothers in Arms* (New York: Simon and Schuster, 1998), 177; Stanley Karnow,

Vietnam: A History (New York: Penguin Books, 1983); and Marilyn B. Young, *The Vietnam Wars: 1945–1990* (New York: HarperCollins, 1991), 48–49. Several journalistic accounts and memoirs recount the day-to-day happenings of the sect crisis in some detail. See Joseph Buttinger, *Vietnam: A Dragon Embattled,* vol. 2 (London: Pall Mall Press, 1967); Bernard Fall, *Vietnam Witness, 1953–1966* (New York: Praeger, 1966); Ellen J. Hammer, *The Struggle for Indochina, 1940–1955* (Stanford: Stanford University Press, 1966); J. Lawton Collins, *Lightning Joe: An Autobiography* (Baton Rouge: Louisiana State University Press, 1979); Edward Geary Lansdale, *In the Midst of Wars: An American's Mission to Southeast Asia* (New York: Harper and Row, 1972).

3. Kathryn C. Statler, *Replacing France: The Origins of American Intervention in Vietnam* (Lexington: University Press of Kentucky, 2007), 125; for an analysis of the differing goals and perspectives of the French and the Americans in Vietnam after the Geneva agreements, see Kathryn Statler, "The Diem Experiment: Franco-American Conflict over South Vietnam, July 1954—May 1955," *Journal of American—East Asian Relations* 6:2–3 (summer—fall 1997), 145–173. Statler writes, "Although France and the United States had agreed to a policy of *action commune* (Joint action) in South Vietnam, their disagreement on goals and the means to achieve these goals led to conflict instead of cooperation between the two Western powers. . . . Nowhere was this battle for control more evident than in the debate over the viability of the Diem government" (145).

4. For more on the French side of the crisis, see Pierre Grosser, "La France et L'Indochine (1954–1956): Une 'Carte de Visite' en 'Peu de Chagrin,'" Doctoral Thesis, Institut d'Études Politiques de Paris, Troisieme cycle d'histoire, September 2002, 1498–1635; Statler, *Replacing France,* 117–153.

5. For recent research on Americans' attitudes toward Vietnamese people in the 1950s, in terms of race and religion, see Mark Bradley, *Imagining Vietnam and America: The Making of Postcolonial Vietnam, 1919–1950* (Chapel Hill: University of North Carolina Press, 2000); and Seth Jacobs, *America's Miracle Man in Vietnam: Ngo Dinh Diem, Religion, Race, and U.S. Intervention in Southeast Asia, 1950–1957* (Durham: Duke University Press, 2004). For firsthand evidence of U.S. officials referring to politico-religious leaders in terms such as "childlike," "naïve," and "irrational," see "The Ambassador at Saigon (Heath) to the Department of State," 17 October 1953, *FRUS, 1952–1954,* Indochina, 828–830; "Telegram from Dulles to Collins," 4 April 1955, National Archives II [NARA], Record Group [RG] 59, C0008, Reel 2, 751G.00/4-455; "Telegram from US Embassy Saigon to Secretary of State," 23 March 1955, NARA, RG 59, C0008, Reel 2, 751G.00/3-2355.

6. "Struggle Weird in Vietnam," *New York Times,* 29 April 1955.

7. Notable exceptions to this include Hoa Hao general Ba Cut and Binh Xuyen chief Bay Vien, who never welcomed Ngo Dinh Diem's leadership.

8. "Bulletin de renseignements. Le President Ngo Dinh Diem: Critique, par les milieux Vietnamiens, de son action et de la composition de son gouvernement," 8 July 1954. Centre des Archives d'Outre Mer [CAOM], Haut Commisariat de l'Indochine [HCI], Sérvice de Protection du Corps Expeditionnaire [SPCE] 8.

9. "Telegram from US Embassy Saigon to Secretary of State," 6 April 1955, NARA, RG 59, C0008, Reel 2, 751G.00/4-655; "Commissariat General de France en Indochine: Rapport Menuel, Mois de Janvier 1955," CAOM, HCI 5/30; Jayne Susan Werner, *Peasant Politics and Religious Sectarianism: Peasant and Priest in the Cao Dai in Viet Nam* (New Haven: Yale University Southeast Asian Studies, 1981); *Lich Su Khang Chien Chong My Cuu Nuoc 1954–1975: Tap II, Chuyen Chien Luoc* (Hanoi, 1996); Edward Garvey Miller, "Grand Designs: Vision, Power, and Nation Building in America's Alliance with Ngo Dinh Diem," Ph.D. diss., Harvard University, 2004, 162.

10. See George McTurnan Kahin and John W. Lewis, *The United States in Vietnam* (New York: Alfred A. Knopf, 1976), 70.

11. Donald Lancaster, *The Emancipation of French Indochina* (London: Oxford University Press, 1961), 379–380.

12. To U.S. officials, the term *loyal opposition* comprised all noncommunist nationalist politicians.

13. This refers to Ngo Dinh Nhu's *can lao nhan vi cach mang dang* (Personalist Labor Revolutionary Party).

14. Bernard Fall, *The Two Vietnams: A Political and Military Analysis,* 2nd rev. ed. (New York: Frederick A. Praeger, 1967), 241–242; Anthony Bouscaren, *The Last of the Mandarins: Diem of Vietnam* (Pittsburgh: Duquesne University Press, 1965), 14. According to the pro–Ngo Dinh Diem, anticommunist Anthony Bouscaren, Ngo Dinh Diem had a long history of anti-French sentiment, inherited from his father at an early age. Fall describes his participation in the anti-French National Extremist Movement in the late 1940s.

15. "Phuc Trinh Tong Quat Thang Hai Duong Lach 1955,"VNA2, PTTDICH, Folder 05.

16. J. Lawton Collins to the Secretary of State, "Report on Vietnam for the National Security Council," January 20, 1955, Box: Collins, J. Lawton Papers, 1896–1975, #25, Folder: Monthly Papers, January 1955(3), DDEL.

17. See Lansdale, *In the Midst of Wars,* 251; Cecil B. Currey, *Edward Lansdale: The Unquiet American* (Boston: Houghton Mifflin, 1988), 173. For details on Ngo Dinh Diem's plans for troop integrations and discharge subsidies for politico-religious soldiers, see "Telegram from the Special Representative in Saigon (Collins) to the Department of State," 15 March 1955, *FRUS,* Vietnam, 1955–1957, 125. For specifics on the amounts of these payments, see "Telegram from the Charge in Vietnam (Kidder) to the Department of State," 8 February 1955, *FRUS,* Vietnam, 1955–1957, 79–80; Miller, "Grand Designs," 162–163. Targeted politico-religious leaders include Cao Dai generals Trinh Minh The and Nguyen Thanh Phuong and Hoa Hao General Nguyen Giac Ngo.

18. "Commissariat General de France en Indochine, Bulletin des Renseignements," 19 January 1955, CAOM, HCI, SPCE 54.

19. See Anderson, *Trapped by Success,* 99.

20. Frances R. Hill, "Millenarian Machines in South Vietnam," *Comparative Studies in Society and History* 13:3 (July 1971), 333–334.

21. See Statler, *Replacing France,* 132.

22. See Nguyen Dinh Le, et al, "Cuoc Xung Dot Vu Trang Giua cac Giao Phai o Mien Nam voi Chinh Quyen, Ngo Dinh Diem (1955–1956)," *Nghien Cuu Lich Su* 6:1 (2001), 21.

23. "Telegram from US Embassy Saigon to Secretary of State," 8 March 1955, NARA, RG 59, C0008, Reel 2, 751G.00/3-855.

24. "Telegram from US Embassy Saigon to Secretary of State," 8 March 1955, NARA, RG 59, C0008, Reel 2, 751G.00/3-855. U.S. embassy representatives authenticated Nguyen Thanh Phuong and Trinh Minh The's signatures; "Telegram from the Special Representative in Saigon (Collins) to the Department of State," 10 March 1955, *FRUS,* Vietnam, 1955–1957, 119. Ngo Dinh Diem claimed that Nguyen Thanh Phuong and Trinh Minh The never had any intention of joining the coalition, but that they attended the front meeting merely to spy on its activities and report back to him.

25. "Vietnamese Ambassador's Comments on Events in Viet-Nam," 18 March 1955, NARA, RG 59, C0008, Reel 2, 751G.00/3-1855.

26. "Telegram from US Embassy Saigon to Secretary of State," 10 March 1955, NARA, RG 59, C0008, Reel 2, 751G.00/3-1055; "Vietnamese Ambassador's Comments on Events in Viet-Nam," 18 March 1955, NARA, RG 59, C0008, Reel 2, 751G.00/3-1855.

27. "CIA Current Intelligence Bulletin," 6 March 1955, CREST, CIA RDP79T00975A 001900270001-1.

28. "Hoat Dong va Am Muu cua Phap Chong Lai Chanh Phu Cong Hoa Viet Nam," 1 June 1956, Vietnamese National Archives II [VNARA], PTTDICH 4313.

29. For more on Bay Vien's relationship with French intelligence agents, see Alfred W. McCoy, *The Politics of Heroin in Southeast Asia* (New York: Harper and Row, 1973). For the broader thrust of French policy toward Vietnam at the time, see Statler, *Replacing France*, 117–153.

30. See Lansdale, *In the Midst of Wars*, 251; and Currey, *Edward Lansdale: The Unquiet American*, 173. For details on Ngo Dinh Diem's plans for troop integrations and discharge subsidies for politico-religious soldiers, see "Telegram from the Special Representative in Saigon (Collins) to the Department of State," 15 March 1955, *FRUS, Vietnam, 1955–1957*, 125.

31. For specifics on the amounts of these payments, see "Telegram from the Charge in Vietnam (Kidder) to the Department of State," 8 February 1955, *FRUS, Vietnam, 1955–1957*, 79–80; Miller, "Grand Designs," 162–163.

32. "CIA Current Intelligence Bulletin," 18 March 1955, CREST, CIA RDP79T00975A 001900180001-1.

33. "Tuong Lanh Hoa-Hao Nguyen Thanh Day ve Hop Tac voi Chinh Phu," *Thoi Luan*, 13 March 1955; "23 Binh Si Xung Phong Binh Xuyen o Quan Khu Da Lat ve Hop Tac Chanh Phu Quoc Gia," *Thoi Luan*, 7 April 1955.

34. "Telegram from US Embassy Saigon to Secretary of State" containing full text of 21 March declaration of United Front of Nationalist Forces and 21 March motion by politico-religious organizations transmitted to Ngo Dinh Diem, 22 March 1955, NARA, RG 59, C0008, Reel 2, 751G.00/3-2255; see also "Premiers Reactions Gouvernementales a l'Ultimatum du 'Front Unifé de Toutes les Forces Nationalistes'," Le Directeur de Service du Protection de la Représentation Civile du Francaise et du Corps Expeditionaire en Indochine, 23 March 1955, CAOM, HCI, SPCE 24.

35. Even the text of this declaration was prevented from appearing in the press due to censorship, lending great credence to this indictment.

36. "Telegram from Department of State to US Embassy Saigon and US Embassy Paris," 21 March 1955, NARA, RG 59, C0008, Reel 2, 751G.00/3-1955.

37. "Telegram from US Embassy Saigon to Secretary of State," 26 March 1955, NARA, RG 59, C0008, Reel 2, 751G.00/3-2655.

38. "Telegram from US Embassy Saigon to Secretary of State," 23 March 1955, NARA, RG 59, C0008, Reel 2, 751G.00/3-2355.

39. Miller, "Grand Designs," 163–170; Sergei Blagov, *Honest Mistakes: The Life and Death of Trinh Minh The (1922–1955): South Vietnam's Alternative Leader* (Huntington, NY: Nova Science Publishers, 2001), 113–114.

40. "Telegram from US Embassy Saigon to Secretary of State," 22 March 1955, NARA, RG 59, C0008, Reel 2, 751G.00/3-2255.

41. "CIA Current Intelligence Bulletin," 24 March 1955, CREST, CIA-RDP97T00975A 001900080001-2.

42. "Telegram from US Embassy Saigon to Secretary of State," 23 March 1955, NARA, RG 59, C0008, Reel 2, 751G.00/3-2355.

43. "Telegram from US Embassy Saigon to Secretary of State," 23 March 1955, NARA, RG 59, C0008, Reel 2, 751G.00/3-2355.

44. Buttinger, *Vietnam: A Dragon Embattled*, 705; see also Joan L. Schrock, William Stockton, Jr., Elaine M. Murphy, Marilou Fromme, *Minority Groups in the Republic of Vietnam* (Washington, DC: Cultural Information Analysis Center, Ethnographic Study Series, 1966). According to this

report, the "system of alternating support and opposition as a means of extracting favors was indicative of the opportunism characteristic of French, Cao Dai relations" (839).

45. See John T. McAlister Jr. and Paul Mus, *The Vietnamese and Their Revolution* (New York: Harper and Row, 1970), 114–123. Mus points to a traditional tendency amongst Vietnamese to adopt wait-and-see "attentiste" attitudes toward political conflicts in order to avoid allying with the losing side. In this case, though, the politico-religious organizations strove to influence the political outcome without committing irrevocably to any one side.

46. "Telegram from Department of State to US Embassy Saigon and US Embassy Paris," 28 March 1955, NARA, RG 59, C0008, Reel 2, 751G.00/3-2855; "Telegram from Department of State to US Embassy Saigon and US Embassy Paris," 25 March 1955, NARA, RG 59, C0008, Reel 2, 751G.00/3-2555; "Telegram from the Director of the Office of Philippine and Southeast Asian Affairs (Young) to the Department of State," 23 March 1955, *FRUS, Vietnam, 1955–1957*, 144.

47. "Telegram from US Embassy Saigon to Secretary of State," 24 March 1955, NARA, RG 59, C0008, Reel 2, 751G.00/3-2455; "CIA Current Intelligence Bulletin," 25 March 1955, CREST, CIA-RDP79T00975A001900090001-1.

48. "Telegram from US Embassy Saigon to Secretary of State," 25 March 1955, NARA, RG 59, C0008, Reel 2, 751G.00/3-2555; "CIA Current Intelligence Bulletin," 18 March 1955, CREST, CIA-RDP79T00975A001900180001-1.

49. Grosser, "La France et L'Indochine," 1522.

50. "Telegram from US Embassy Saigon to Secretary of State," 26 March 1955, NARA, RG 59, C0008, Reel 2, 751G.00/3-2655; "Memorandum from the Chief of the National Security Division of the Training Relations and Instruction Mission (Lansdale) to the Special Representative in Vietnam (Collins)," 27 March 1955, *FRUS, Vietnam, 1955–1957*, 148–149.

51. Buttinger, *Vietnam: A Dragon Embattled*, 869; Blagov, *Honest Mistakes*, 115; Grosser, "La France et L'Indochine," 1523; Dong Tan, *Tim Hieu Dao Cao Dai hay Giay Dap 231 Cau Phong Van cua Gioi tri Thuc Dai Hoc Quoc Te ve Dao Cao Dai* (Saigon: Cao Hien, 1974), 26 and 139.

52. "Letter from Ngo Dinh Diem to Tran Van Soai and the United Front of Nationalist Forces," 27 March 1955, VNARA, PTTDICH, Folder 4320.

53. "Telegram from US Embassy Saigon to Secretary of State," 27 March 1955, NARA, RG 59, C0008, Reel 2, 751G.00/3-2755.

54. "Telegram from US Embassy Saigon to Secretary of State," 23 March 1955, NARA, RG 59, C0008, Reel 2, 751G.00/3-2355.

55. "Telegram from US Embassy Saigon to Secretary of State," 29 March 1955, NARA, RG 59, C0008, Reel 2, 751G.00/3-2955.

56. "J. Lawton Collins to the Secretary of State," March 29, 1955, Box: Collins, J. Lawton Papers, 1896–1975, #25, Folder: Monthly Papers, March 1955, DDEL.

57. "Background—South Vietnam Status of Defense Minister Minh," NSC Briefing, 31 March 1955, CREST, CIA-RDP79R00890A000500030062-1.

58. "Telegram from the Special Representative in Saigon (Collins) to the Department of State," 30 March 1955, *FRUS*, 159–163.

59. For Ngo Dinh Diem's official statement on the clash, depicting the Binh Xuyen as the aggressors, see "Cuon Phim No Sung tai Sai Gon nhung Chi Tiet Quan Trong," *Thoi Luan*, 3 April 1955. This article includes a message from Ngo Dinh Diem blaming the 30 March violence on Bay Vien's troops.

60. "Memorandum for the Director of Central Intelligence from the Board of National Estimates: 'The Crisis in Saigon'," 4 April 1955, CREST, CIA-RDP79R009004A00020002 0005-2.

61. See Statler, "The Diem Experiment," 145.

62. "Hoat Dong va Am Muu cua Phap Chong Lai Chanh Phu Cong Hoa Viet Nam," 1 June 1956, VNA2, PTTDICH 4313.

63. "J. Lawton Collins to the Secretary of State," March 31, 1955, Box: Collins, J. Lawton Papers, 1896–1975, #25, Folder: Monthly Papers, March 1955, DDEL.

64. "Telegram from the Secretary of State to the Embassy in France," 3 April 1955, *FRUS, Vietnam, 1955–1957,* 193–194; "M. Laforest, Secrétaire d'État aux États Associés, au General Ely, Commissaire General de France en Indochine," 31 March 1955, *Documents Diplomatiques Français, 1955, Tome I* (hereafter DDF), document 161 (Paris, 1987), 373–374; "Le General Ely, Commissaire General de France en Indochine, a M. Laforest, Secrétaire d'État Aux États Associés," 31 March 1955, *DDF, 1955, Tome I,* document 162, 364–377.

65. "Telegram from Secretary of State to US Embassy Saigon," 31 March 1955, NARA, RG 59, C0008, Reel 2, 751G.00/3-3155.

66. Grosser, "La France et L'Indochine," 1527.

67. Arthur J. Dommen, *The Indochinese Experience of the French and the Americans: Nationalism and Communism in Cambodia, Laos, and Vietnam* (Bloomington: Indiana University Press, 2001), 285.

68. "Telegram from US Embassy Saigon to Secretary of State," 30 March 1955, NARA, RG 59, C0008, Reel 2 751G.00/3-3055.

69. "Telegram from the Special Representative in Vietnam (Collins) to the Department of State," 31 March 1955, *FRUS,* Vietnam, 1955–1957, 171–174.

70. "Telegram from US Embassy Saigon to Secretary of State," 30 March 1955, NARA, RG 59, C0008, Reel 2 751G.00/3-3055.

71. "Telegram from US Embassy Saigon to Secretary of State," 31 March 1955, NARA, RG 59, C0008, Reel 2, 751G.00/3-3155.

72. "Memorandum from W. Park Armstrong, Jr. to Secretary of State Regarding Cao Dai Rally to Diem," 31 March 1955, NARA, RG 59, C0008, Reel 2, 751G.00/3-3155.

73. "Memorandum for the Director of Central Intelligence from the Board of National Estimates: 'The Crisis in Saigon'," 4 April 1955, CREST, CIA-RDP79R009004A000200020005-2.

74. "Telegram from Secretary of State to US Embassy Saigon and US Embassy Paris," 1 April 1955, NARA, RG 59, C0008, Reel 2, 751G.00/4-155.

75. "Memorandum for the Director of Central Intelligence from the Board of National Estimates: 'The Crisis in Saigon'," 4 April 1955, CREST, CIA-RDP79R009004A000200020005-2.

76. Grosser, "La France et L'Indochine," 1532.

77. "Y Chung Toi," *Thoi Luan,* 31 March 1955.

78. "Trung Tuong Nguyen Thanh Phuong Tuyen Bo ve Lap Truong Quan Doi Cao Dai Truoc Thoi Cuoc," *Thoi Luan,* 10 April 1955.

79. "CIA Current Intelligence Bulletin," 2 April 1955, CREST, CIA-RDP79T00975A 001900020001-8.

80. "Telegram from US Embassy Saigon to Secretary of State," 5 April 1955, NARA, RG 59, C0008, Reel 2, 751G.00/4-655. For more on U.S.-French fears of a sect–Viet Minh alliance, see "Memorandum of Conversation between the Special Representative in Vietnam (Collins) and the French Commissioner General in Vietnam (Ely), Saigon," 29 March 1955, *FRUS, Vietnam, 1955–1957,* 155. On Ely's frustration with Ngo Dinh Diem and with Washington's position on the developing crisis, see "Le General Ely, Commissaire General de France en Indochine, a M. Laforest, Secrétaire d'État aux États Associés," 6 April 1955, *DDF, 1955, Tome I,* document 178, 410–414; Grosser, "La France et L'Indochine," 1530.

81. Buttinger, *Vietnam: A Dragon Embattled,* 875.

82. Grosser, "La France et L'Indochine," 1564.

83. "Telegram from US Embassy Saigon to Secretary of State," 7 April 1955, NARA. RG 59, C0008, Reel 2, 751G.00/4-755.

84. Ibid.

85. Ibid.

86. "Telegram from US Embassy Saigon to Secretary of State," 5 April 1955, NARA, RG 59, C0008, Reel 2, 751G.00/4-555.

87. See George McT. Kahin, *Intervention: How America Became Involved in Vietnam* (New York: Alfred A. Knopf, 1986), 82–82; Collins, *Lightning Joe,* 406.

88. "Telegram from Secretary of State to US Embassy Saigon," 9 April 1955, NARA, RG 59, C0008, Reel 2, 751G.00/4-955.

89. French officials were keenly aware that Dulles feared that Ngo Dinh Diem's ouster might be perceived as a victory for the Binh Xuyen and the French over the United States. See Grosser, *La France et l'Indochine,* 1568.

90. Department of State Memorandum of Conversation between Mike Mansfield and Kenneth T. Young, Jr., "Situation in Free Vietnam," 8 April 1955, NARA, RG 59, C0008, Reel 2, 751G.00/4-855; Joseph G. Morgan, *The Vietnam Lobby: The American Friends of Vietnam, 1955–1975* (Chapel Hill: University of North Carolina Press, 1997).

91. "Telegram from Secretary of State to US Embassy Saigon," 11 April 1955, NARA, RG 59, C0008, Reel 2, 751G.00/4-1155.

92. Grosser, *La France et l'Indochine,* 1569.

93. "Telegram from Secretary of State to US Embassy Saigon and US Embassy Paris," 12 April 1955, NARA, RG 59, C0008, Reel 2, 751G.00/4-1255.

94. "Telegram from US Embassy Paris to Secretary of State," 13 April 1955, NARA, RG 59, C0008, Reel 2, 751G.00/4-1355; US Government Office Memorandum, "General Collins' Proposed Press Conference re. Diem," 13 April 1955, NARA, RG 59, C0008, Reel 2, 751G.00/4-1355.

95. Statler, "The Diem Experiment," 168.

96. "Telegram from US Embassy Paris to Secretary of State," 16 April 1955, NARA, RG 59, C0008, Reel 3, 751G.00/4-1655; see also "M. Couve de Murville, Ambassadeur de France a Washington, a M. Pinay, Ministère des Affaires Étrangères," 18 April 1955, *DDF, 1955, Tome I,* document 210, 466–471.

97. "Telegram from US Embassy Saigon to Secretary of State," 19 April 1955, NARA, RG 59, C0008, Reel 3, 751G.00/4-1955; Grosser, "La France et L'Indochine," 1573.

98. "Telegram from US Embassy Saigon to Secretary of State," 17 April 1955, NARA, RG 59, C0008, Reel 3, 751G.00/4-1755.

99. Tran Van Van, a southern politician who resented the dominance of northerners in Ngo Dinh Diem's government, would later sign the Caravelle Manifesto.

100. "Telegram from US Embassy Saigon to Secretary of State," 18 April 1955, NARA, RG 59, C0008, Reel 3, 751G.00/4-1855.

101. "Telegram from US Embassy Saigon to Secretary of State," 19 April 1955, NARA, RG 59, C0008, Reel 3, 751G.00/4-1955.

102. "Telegram from US Embassy Saigon to Secretary of State," includes text of note from Diem to Collins, 19 April 1955, NARA, RG 59, C0008, Reel 3, 751G.00/4-1955.

103. "Telegram from US Embassy Saigon to Secretary of State," 20 April 1955, NARA, RG 59, C0008, Reel 3, 751G.00/4-2055.

104. "Telegram from US Embassy Paris to Secretary of State," 21 April 1955, NARA, RG 59, C0008, Reel 3, 751G.00/4-2155; "Memorandum of Conversation between Nguyen De, William M. Gibson, and David Bane," 21 April 1955, NARA, RG 59, C0008,

Reel 3, 751G.00/4-2155; "M. Laforest. Secrétaire d'État aux États Associés, au General Ely, Commissaire General de France en Indochine," 25 April 1955, document 221, *DDF, 1955 (Tome I)*, 505–506.

105. "Memorandum of Conversation between Nguyen De, William M. Gibson, and David Bane," 21 April 1955, NARA, RG 59, C0008, Reel 3, 751G.00/4-2155.

106. Memorandum from the Assistant Secretary of State to the Secretary of State, "Report on Vietnamese Political Situation," 23 April 1955, NARA, RG 59, C0008, Reel 3, 751G.00/4-2355; on France's position see "M. Laforest, Secrétaire d'État aux États Associés, au General Ely, Commissaire General de France en Indochina," 25 April 1955, *DDF, 1955, Tome I*, document 221, 505–506.

107. "Telegram from US Embassy Paris to Secretary of State," 25 April 1955, NARA, RG 59, C0008, Reel 3, 7511G.00/4-2555.

108. Memorandum from William J. Sebald to Secretary of State, "Viet-Nam Situation," 27 April 1955, NARA, RG 59, C0008, Reel 3, 751G.00/4-2755; "Telegram from US Embassy Saigon to Secretary of State," 26 April 1955, NARA, RG 59, C0008, Reel 3, 751G.00/4-2655; Buttinger, *Vietnam: A Dragon Embattled,* 879.

109. "Telegram from US Embassy Saigon to Secretary of State," 27 April 195, NARA, RG 59, C0008, Reel 3, 751G.00/4-2755.

110. Ibid.

111. "Memorandum from the Deputy Assistant Secretary of State for Far Eastern Affairs (Sebald) to the Secretary of State," 27 April 1955, *FRUS, Vietnam, 1955–1957,* 291–292.

112. "Telegram from US Embassy Saigon to Secretary of State," 27 April 1955, NARA, RG 59, C0008, Reel 3, 751G.00/4-2755.

113. "John Foster Dulles to J. Lawton Collins to the Secretary of State," April 20, 1955, Box: Collins, J. Lawton Papers, 1896–1975, #25, Folder: Monthly Papers, March 1955, DDEL. For more on Dulles's attitudes towards Ngo Dinh Diem and Vietnam during the crisis, see Ronald W. Pruessen, "John Foster Dulles and the Road Not Taken: Vietnam, April 1955," in Christopher Goscha and Karine Laplante, eds, *L'Échec de la paix en Indochine, 1954–1962* (Paris: Les Indes Savantes, 2010), 199–217.

114. "Telegram from Secretary of State to US Embassy Saigon and US Embassy Paris," 27 April 1955, NARA, RG 59, C0008, Reel 3, 751G.00/4-2755.

115. "John Foster Dulles to U.S. Embassy Paris and U.S. Embassy Saigon," April 28, 1955, Box: Collins, J. Lawton Papers, 1896–1975, #25, Folder: Monthly Papers, April 1955, DDEL.

116. "Telegram from Secretary of State to US Embassy Saigon and US Embassy Paris," 28 April 1955, NARA, RG 59, C0008, Reel 3, 751G.00/4-2855.

117. Denis Warner, *The Last Confucian* (New York: Macmillan, 1963), 84–85; see also Duong Van Mai Elliott, *The Sacred Willow: Four Generations in the Life of a Vietnamese Family* (New York: Oxford University Press, 1999), 253–256. Elliot claims that no one knew the exact figure for civilian casualties, but that the estimate of five hundred killed and a thousand wounded was probably low.

118. "Telegram from US Embassy Saigon to Secretary of State," 28 April 1955, NARA, RG 59, C0008, Reel 3, 751G.00/4-2855; "Le General Ely, Commissaire general de France en Indochine, a M. Laforest, Secretaire d'Etat aux Etats Associes," 29 April 1955, document 235, *DDF, 1955, Tome I,* 536–540.

119. Buttinger, *Vietnam: A Dragon Embattled,* 879; Lancaster, *Emancipation of French Indochina,* 389.

120. "Memorandum from the Director of the Office of Philippine and Southeast Asian Affairs (Young) to the Assistant Secretary of State for Far Eastern Affairs (Robertson)," 30 April 1955, *FRUS,* Vietnam, 1955–1957, 337–338.

121. "Telegram from the Secretary of State to the Embassy in Vietnam," 1 May 1955, *FRUS, Vietnam, 1955–1957*, 344.

122. Quoted in Marilyn B. Young, *The Vietnam Wars, 1945–1990* (New York: Harper Collins, 1991), 49.

123. "Message from His Majesty Bao Dai to President Ngo Dinh Diem," Telegram from US Embassy Saigon to Secretary of State, 29 April 1955, NARA, RG 59, C0008, Reel 3, 751G.00/4-2955.

124. "Telegram from US Embassy Saigon to Secretary of State," 29 April 1955, NARA, RG 59, C0008, Reel 3, 751G.00/4-2955; Telegram from US Embassy Saigon to Secretary of State, 30 April 1955, NARA, RG 59, C0008, Reel 3, 751G.00/4-3055.

125. See Buttinger, *Vietnam: A Dragon Embattled*, 880–884; Scigliano, "Political Parties in South Vietnam under the Republic," *Pacific Affairs* 33:4 (December 1960), 339.

126. "Briefing on Conditions in Vietnam." US Department of State Memorandum of Conversation, 2 May 1955, NARA, RG 59, C0008, Reel 3, 751G.00/4-3055. Kenneth Young noted that the orientation, composition, and purposes of the Revolutionary Committee were not fully known at this time, but that it appeared to be a creation of the Cao Dai and had potential to undermine Ngo Dinh Diem's government.

127. "Telegram from US Embassy Saigon to Secretary of State," 1 May 1955, NARA, RG 59, C0008, Reel 3, 751G.00/5-155.

128. "Telegram from US Embassy Saigon to Secretary of State," 30 April 1955, NARA, RG 59, C0008, Reel 3, 751G.00/4-3055.

129. See Jacobs, *America's Miracle Man*.

130. See Catton, *Diem's Final Failure: Prelude to America's War in Vietnam* (Lawrence: University Press of Kansas, 2002), 1–24.

131. Ngo Dinh Diem started the "Denounce the Communists" (*to cong*) campaign in 1955 following a three-hundred-day waiting period imposed by the Geneva agreements and increased its force in January 1956 by issuing Ordinance 6, which removed most restrictions on combating political opponents. See Frances FitzGerald, *Fire in the Lake: The Vietnamese and the Americans in Vietnam* (New York: Vintage Books, 1972), 131–135.

132. See Jessica M. Chapman, "Staging Democracy: South Vietnam's 1955 Referendum to Depose Bao Dai," *Diplomatic History* 30:4 (September 2006), 671–703.

Chapter 5

1. For examples of exuberant responses from Eisenhower's administration and the American press to Ngo Dinh Diem's victory over the politico-religious organizations, see Seth Jacobs, *America's Miracle Man in Vietnam: Ngo Dinh Diem, Religion, Race, and U.S. Intervention in Southeast Asia, 1945–1954* (Durham, NC: Duke University Press, 2004), 220–223.

2. "Dulles to Collins," 5 May 1955, J. Lawton Collins Papers, box 26, Monthly Papers, May 1955 (1), DDEL.

3. Republic of Vietnam, Presidency of the Republic of Vietnam Press Office (hereafter PRVNPO), "President Ngo Dinh Diem on Asia (Extracts from Speeches by President Ngo Dinh Diem)" (Saigon: October 1957), 14.

4. "President Ngo Dinh Diem," 13.

5. For a statement of Ngo Dinh Diem's revolutionary principles, see Pham Thanh Nghi, *Dao Duc Cach Mang Cua Chi Si Ngo Dinh Diem* (Saigon: Press Office, Presidency of the Republic of Vietnam, 1956).

6. David W. P. Elliott, *The Vietnamese War: Revolution and Social Change in the Mekong Delta, 1930–1975*, vol. 1 (Armonk, NY: M. E. Sharpe, 2003); Ngo Dinh Diem, "Statement of June 18, 1954," in "President Ngo Dinh Diem on Democracy (Addresses Relative to the Constitution)" (Saigon: Presidency of the Republic of Vietnam Press Office, 1957), 5.

7. See Elliott, *The Vietnamese War*, 181. Elliot notes, "At bottom, the government's fear of communism was a politically motivated cover for their fear of revolutionary socioeconomic programs rather than real concern of the revolutionaries' foreign connections."

8. Philip Catton, *Diem's Final Failure: Prelude to America's War in Vietnam* (Lawrence: University Press of Kansas: 2002), 28; William Egan Colby, *Lost Victory: A Firsthand Account of America's Sixteen Year Involvement in Vietnam* (New York: Contemporary Books, 1990), 110.

9. *Major Policy Speeches by President Ngo Dinh Diem* (Saigon: Presidency of the Republic of Vietnam Press Office, 1956), 34.

10. "Achievements of the Campaign of Denunciation of Communist Subversive Activities (First Phase)" (Republic of Vietnam: The People's Committee for the C.D.C.S.A., May 1956), 51.

11. Ibid., 67.

12. Robert Scigliano, *South Vietnam: Nation under Stress* (Boston: Houghton Mifflin, 1963), 167.

13. Ronald H. Spector, *Advice and Support: The Early Years of the U.S. Army in Vietnam, 1941–1960* (New York: The Free Press, 1985), 252–253. Edward Lansdale shared Ngo Dinh Diem's view that his sectarian enemies needed to be defeated or incorporated into his political platform. See Jonathan Nashel, *Edward Lansdale's Cold War* (Boston: University of Massachusetts Press, 2005), 144.

14. "Achievements of the Campaign of Denunciation of Communist Subversive Activities," 35.

15. Ibid. Ngo Dinh Diem's motto was, "Abolish Feudalism, Fight Colonialism and Annihilate Communism." According to Tran Chanh Thanh, Chairman of People's Central Directive Committee for the Campaign of Denunciation of Communist Subversive Activities, "Communism was the most important among these three enemies; Colonialism and Feudalism were but disintegrated forces before the progress of humanity and there was no longer room for them in this world. To carry out the President's policy, to triumph over our adversary, we have found a wonderful formula: to denounce communist subversion. The campaign, aimed at annihilating Communism, necessarily destroys its allies: Colonialism and Feudalism" (15); See also Frances FitzGerald, *Fire in the Lake: The Vietnamese and the Americans in Vietnam* (New York: Vintage Books, 1972), 131.

16. Edward Garvey Miller, "Grand Designs: Vision, Power and Nation Building in America's Alliance with Ngo Dinh Diem, 1954–1960," Ph.D. diss., Harvard University, 2004, 218.

17. John C. Donnell, "Politics in South Vietnam: Doctrines of Authority in Conflict," Ph.D. diss., University of California, Berkeley, 1964, 101–105.

18. Bernard B. Fall, *The Two Vietnams: A Political and Military Analysis* (Boulder, CO: Westview Press, 1984), 247; Emmanuel Mounier, *A Personalist Manifesto*, translated by the Monks of St. John's Abbey (New York: Longmans, Green, 1938); John Hellman, *Emmanuel Mounier and the New Catholic Left, 1930–1950* (Toronto: University of Toronto Press, 1981), 5–6 and 53–74; Eugene Weber, *The Hollow Years: France in the 1930s* (New York: W. W. Norton, 1994), 201–202; Jean-Louis Loubet del Bayle, *Les non-conformistes des années 30: un tentative de renouvellement de la pensée politique Française* (Paris: Editions de Seuil, 1969).

19. Matthew B. Masur, "Hearts and Minds: Cultural Nation Building in South Vietnam," Ph.D. diss., Ohio State University, 2004, 18.

20. See Catton, *Diem's Final Failure*, 14, 45; Masur, "Hearts and Minds," 24–27; John C. Donnel, "Personalism in Vietnam," in *Problems of Freedom: South Vietnam since Independence*, ed. Wesley R. Fishel (Glencoe, IL: The Free Press, 1961).

21. For some examples of Ngo Dinh Diem's references to human dignity and reciprocal social responsibility, see Ngo Dinh Diem, "Democratic Development in Vietnam," in Paul K. T. Sih, ed., *Democracy in East Asia* (Taiwan: China Culture Publishing Foundation, 1957), 86; PRVNPO, "President Ngo Dinh Diem on Democracy (Address Relative to the Constitution)" (Saigon, February 1958); PRVNPO, "The Emergence of Free Viet-Nam: Major addresses delivered by President Ngo-Dinh-Diem during his official visit to the United States of America, May 8–18, 1957" (Saigon, 1957), 26; "President Ngo Dinh Diem," 7.

22. Loubet del Bayle, *Les non-conformistes des années 30*, 226.

23. Mounier, *Personalist Manifesto*, 247.

24. In Mounier's view, however, the power of these elites would be limited to running national institutions like the military and the postal service, while local political initiative would fall to a range of councils and cooperative groups that would serve as intermediaries between the government and the people. In his own words, "The power of the state, even in its political function, is limited from below not only by the authority of the spiritual person, but also by the spontaneous powers and customs of all the natural societies which compose the nation." See Mounier, *Personalist Manifesto*, 234; Hellman, *Mounier and the New Catholic Left*, 141–148.

25. Catton, *Diem's Final Failure*, 49–50.

26. Dipesh Chakrabarty, "The Legacies of Bandung: Decolonization and the Politics of Culture," in Christopher J. Lee, ed., *Making a World After Empire: The Bandung Moment and its Political Afterlives* (Athens: Ohio University Press), 53–54.

27. See William Safran, "Citizenship and Nationality in Democratic Systems: Approaching to Defining and Acquiring Membership in the International Community," *International Political Science Review* 18:3 (July 1997), 313. For more on the concept of citizenship, see Thomas Janoski, *Citizenship and Civil Society: A Framework of Rights and Obligations in Liberal, Traditional, and Social Democratic Regimes* (New York: Cambridge University Press, 1998); Charles Tilly, "A Primer on Citizenship," *Theory and Society* 26 (1997): 599–602; Kerry J. Kennedy, ed., *Citizenship Education and the Modern State* (Washington, DC: Flamer Press, 1997); Will Kymlicka and Wayne Norman, "Return of the Citizen: A Survey of Recent Work on Citizenship Theory," *Ethics* 104 (January 1994): 257–289. In this state-of-the-field review article, the authors point out the difficulties of creating an overarching theory of citizenship, "because there are two different concepts which are sometimes conflated in these discussions: citizenship as legal status, that is, full membership in a particular political community; and citizenship-as-desirable-activity, where the extent and quality of one's citizenship is a function of one's participation in that community" (353).

28. Quoted in Anthony Bouscaren, *Last of the Mandarins: Diem of Vietnam* (Pittsburgh: Duquesne University Press, 1965), 86; and FitzGerald, *Fire in the Lake*, 120. Ngo Dinh Diem's emphasis on virtue, and his abhorrence of vice, was a recurring theme of his administration. He later accused Bao Dai of the same sort of moral degeneracy displayed by Bay Vien. And in late-1955, he launched an "Anti–Four Vices Campaign" intended to eradicate prostitution, gambling, opium smoking, and alcoholism. See John C. Donnel, "Personalism in Vietnam," in Wesley R. Fishel, ed., *Problems of Freedom: South Vietnam since Independence* (Glencoe, IL: The Free Press, 1961), 33.

29. Trinh Minh The participated in the United Front of Nationalist Forces until rallying his Cao Dai Lien Minh troops to the government at some point in early April.

30. "Hanh-dong khieu-khich cua Quan-Doi Phat-Giao Hoa-Hao," April 25, 1955, Vietnamese National Archives II (VNA2), Phu Tong Thong De Nhat Vietnam Cong Haa (PTTDeNhat), File no. 4320.

31. *Time,* June 20, 1955, 34; see also Joseph Buttinger, *Vietnam: A Dragon Embattled,* vol. 2 (London: Pall Mall Press, 1967), 886.

32. Donald Lancaster, *The Emancipation of French Indochina* (London: Oxford University Press, 1961), 395. According to this account, Bao Dai sent Nguyen Van Hinh to Saigon on April 29 with orders to contact the Cochinchinese politico-religious organizations. Upon learning of the Binh Xuyen defeat he diverted his plane to Phnom Penh, but he eventually made his way into southwest Vietnam in mid-May to liaise with the Hoa Hao generals.

33. Bernard Fall, *Vietnam Witness, 1953–1956* (New York: Praeger, 1966), 159.

34. CIA Current Intelligence Bulletin, 4 June 1955, United States National Archives and Records Administration (NARA), CREST, CIA-RDP79T00975A002000500001-3; "National Security Council Agenda for the Meeting to be held in the Conference Room of the White House, Thursday, June 9, 1955," June 6, 1955, NARA, CREST, CIA-RDP80R01443R000400040002-3.

35. "NSC Briefing," June 8, 1955, NARA, CREST, CIA-RDP80R01443R000400040002-3.

36. "Thieu-Tuong Nguyen-Giac-Ngo Len An Nam Lua [Tran Van Soai] va Ba Cut," *Thoi Dai,* June 10, 1955.

37. "Tr-V-Soai yeu cau tam Ngung Ban De Dieu-Dinh Tro Ve Hop-Tac Voi Chanh Phu Q.G.?" *Thoi Dai,* June 16, 1955; Fall, *Vietnam Witness,* 159, According to Bernard Fall, this overture took place on May 29.

38. Buttinger, *A Dragon Embattled,* 889.

39. For accounts of Nguyen Thanh Phuong's activities see Buttinger, *A Dragon Embattled,* 886; Lancaster, *Emancipation of French Indochina,* 397; Joann L. Schrock et al., *Minority Groups in the Republic of Vietnam* (Washington, DC: Cultural Information Analysis Center, Ethnographic Study Series, 1966), 844.

40. "Bo Tong Tham-muu Quan-Doi Quoc Gia Viet-Nam Thong Cao," *Thoi Dai,* November 23, 1955.

41. "Telegram from US Embassy Saigon to Department of State," February 20, 1956, NARA, Record Group (RG) 59, C0008, Reel 7, 751G.00/2-2056.

42. "Phuc Trinh Cua Thieu Tuong Duong Van Minh Tu Linh Chien Dich Nguyen Hue v/v bat Le Quang Vinh tuc Ba Cut," April 27, 1956, PTTDeNhat, Folder no. 4322, VNA2.

43. "Achievements of the Campaign of Denunciation of Communist Subversive Activities," 73–75.

44. For more information on Tran Chanh Thanh and the activities undertaken by the Ministry of Information and Youth, see "Record of Government Achievement, July 1955–July 1956," (Saigon, 1956), 67–83. The National Revolutionary Movement, a propaganda and political front for the government, was founded in 1954 by Tran Chanh Tranh and two of Ngo Dinh Diem's brothers, Ngo Dinh Nhu, Ngo Dinh Can. It established cells in every level of national and provincial administration as a means of influencing politics and silencing opposition to the government throughout the countryside. It provided the canopy for the National Revolutionary Civil Servants' League, the Republican Youth Movement, and the Women's Solidarity Movement, all of which served to organize, track, and propagandize to employees and loyalists of the administration. The latter two comprised paramilitary units for the government's defense.

45. Scigliano, *South Vietnam,* 75; and Pho Ba Hai, *Vietnamese Public Management in Transition: South Vietnam Public Administration, 1955–1975* (Lanham, MD: University Press of America, 1990), 364.

46. See Catton, *Diem's Final Failure,* 14; Denis Warner, *The Last Confucian* (New York: Macmillian, 1963), 14; Buttinger, *A Dragon Embattled,* 977; Fall, *The Two Vietnams,* 272; Donnell, "Politics in South Vietnam," 240–243 and 290–291; and FitzGerald, *Fire in the Lake,* 129.

47. Scigliano, *South Vietnam,* 167; Masur, "Hearts and Minds," 40–41.

48. Masur, "Hearts and Minds," 20–24; Scigliano, *South Vietnam,* 167; "Achievements of the Campaign of Denunciation of Communist Subversive Activities." According to this document produced by the South Vietnamese government, "With the third wave, the press began to play an active part in the Campaign of Denunciation of Communist Subversive Activities" (74).

49. François Guillemot, "Révolution Nationale et Lutte pour L'Indépendance au Viêt-Nam: L'Échec de la Troisieme Voie, 1938–1955," Thèse de doctorat, École Practiques Des Hautes Études, Paris, 2003, 637–643; Bernard Fall, "South Viet-Nam's Internal Problems," *Pacific Affairs* 31:3 (September 1958), 254.

50. Phuc Thien, *Ngo Dinh Diem of Viet-Nam* (Saigon: Saigon: Press Office, Presidency of the Republic of Vietnam, 1957), 12.

51. For a thorough review of the circumstances and theories surrounding Trinh Minh The's death see Sergei Blagov, *Honest Mistakes: The Life and Death of Trinh Minh The, South Vietnam's Alternative Leader* (New York: Nov Science Press, 2001), 173–194. He concludes that "Diem and Nhu were mixed up in The's demise" as a means of preventing him from seizing power in South Vietnam (193).

52. Lancaster, *Emancipation of French Indochina,* 394.

53. See Buttinger, *A Dragon Embattled,* 882–885; "CIA Current Intelligence Bulletin," May 1, 1955, NARA, CREST, CIA-RDP79T00975A002000200001-6.

54. Buttinger, *A Dragon Embattled,* 884.

55. Robert Shaplen, *The Lost Revolution: The Story of Twenty Years of Neglected Opportunities in Vietnam and of America's Failure to Foster Democracy There* (New York: Harper and Row, 1955), 125–126; U.S. Department of State, *Foreign Relations of the United States, Vietnam, 1955–1957* (FRUS), "Telegram from Special Representative in Vietnam (Collins) to the Department of State, 4 May 1955," 357; see also Mark Moyar, *Triumph Forsaken: The Vietnam War, 1954–1965* (New York: Cambridge University Press, 2006), 34.

56. For the South Vietnamese government's official account of Trinh Minh The's death see "Thieu Tuong Trinh Minh The," *Thoi Dai,* 5 May 1955; see translation of "The Anti-French Campaign Is Expanding in Saigon," from *Le Journal d'Extreme-Orient,* May 3, 1955, NARA, RG 59, C0008, Reel 3, 751G.00/5-355.

57. "Telegram from US Embassy Saigon to Secretary of State," May 5, 1955, NARA, RG 59, C0008, Reel 3, 751G.00/5-455.

58. Patricia Pelley, *Postcolonial Vietnam: New Histories of the National Past* (Durham, NC: Duke University Press, 2002); 43–45; see also Masur, "Hearts and Minds," 36–40; Tuong Vu, "Vietnamese Political Studies and Debates on Vietnamese Nationalism," *Journal of Vietnamese Studies* 2:2 (2006), 175–230.

59. For examples of such themes among Vietnam's reformers of the 1920s see Mark Philip Bradley, *Imagining Vietnam and America: The Making of Postcolonial Vietnam, 1919–1950* (Chapel Hill: The University of North Carolina Press, 2000), 10–25.

60. Pelley, *Postcolonial Vietnam,* 142–143.

61. See Ellen J. Hammer, *The Struggle for Indochina, 1940–1955* (Stanford: Stanford University Press, 1955), 284–285; Buttinger, *A Dragon Embattled,* 784.

62. See, for example, see Pham Thanh Nghi, *Dao Duc Cach Mang Cua Chi Si Ngo Dinh Diem,* 21.

63. "Telegram from US Embassy Saigon to Secretary of State," May 5, 1955, NARA, RG 59, C0008, Reel 3, 751G.00/5-455.

64. Nguyen Thenh Danh, "Tieng Noi cua *Thoi Dai*: Phai Hoc Tap Guong Chien Dau Cua Thieu Tuong Trinh Minh The," *Thoi Dai*, May 5, 1955.

65. Ibid.

66. "Tieu-Su Cua Thieu Tuong Trinh Minh The," *Thoi Dai*, May 5, 2005.

67. "Thieu Tuong Trinh Minh The," *Thoi Dai*, May 5, 2005; for more on Trinh Minh The's rallying see Cecil B. Currey, *Edward Lansdale: The Unquiet American* (Boston: Houghton Mifflin, 1988), 169; Edward Geary Lansdale, *In the Midst of Wars: An American's Mission to Southeast Asia* (New York: Harper and Row, 1972), 184–199.

68. For more on Ngo Dinh Diem's use of American-funded bribes to secure the allegiance of Trinh Minh The and other Hoa Hao and Cao Dai generals see David L. Anderson, *Trapped by Success: The Eisenhower Administration and Vietnam, 1953–61* (New York: Columbia University Press, 1991), 85; Warner, *The Last Confucian,* 82; Lansdale, *In the Midst of Wars,* 251; Currey, *Unquiet American,* 173; Miller, "Grand Designs," 163.

69. Lansdale, *In the Midst of Wars,* 184; "Telegram from US Embassy Saigon to Secretary of State," 4 May 1955, NARA, RG59, C0008, Reel 3, 751G.00/5-455.

70. "Décrete de sa Majesté Bao Dai, Chef de l'État: Les Obseques Nationales Seront Organisées pour le General Trinh Minh The, Tombe au Champ d'Honneur," May 4, 1955, PTTDeNhat, File no. 1257, VNA2.

71. "Le Quoc Tang Cua Trung Tuong Trinh Minh The da cu hanh truoc su hien dien cua Thu-Tuong," *Thoi Luan*, May 8, 1955; "Tat ca nghieng minh truoc linh cuu vi anh hung dan toc da hy sinh cho To quoc Trung Tuong Trinh Minh The," *Thoi Dai*, May 6, 1955.

72. "Thieu Tuong Trinh Minh The da tu tran trong truong hop nao," *Thoi Luan*, 8 May 2005; "Sac Lenh So 153" [Order number 153], May 13, 1955, PTTDeNhat, File no. 1257, VNA2; "Decrete de sa Majeste Bao Dai, Chef de l'Etat," PTTDeNhat, File no. 1257, VNA2. Ngo Dinh Diem officially promoted The Trinh Minh The from his title of Brigade General to the posthumous title of Division general on May 4, 1955. He issued the decree formalizing The Trinh Minh The's Medal of Honor on May 13, 1955.

73. "Tat ca nghieng minh truoc linh cuu vi anh hung dan toc da hy sinh cho To quoc Trung Tuong Trinh Minh The," *Thoi Dai,* May 6, 1955.

74. Blagov, *Honest Mistakes,* 180. Blagov cites Nhi Lang, who claimed to be present to witness these events; see also Warner, *The Last Confucian,* 84.

75. Lansdale, *In the Midst of Wars,* 309–310.

76. "Phien nhom dai hoi cua hoi dong Do-thanh da duoc nhung ket qua gi? Anh Hung Dan Toc Trinh Minh The se duoc nhan dan V.N. dat ten nguoi vao 1 dai lo trong do thenh S.C.," *Thoi Dai,* July 13, 1955.

77. Vu Ngu Chieu, "The Other Side of the 1945 August Revolution: The Empire of Viet-Nam (March-August 1945)," *Journal of Asian Studies* 45:2 (February 1986), 309.

78. Wynn Wilcox, "Allegories of the U.S.-Vietnam War: Nguyen Anh, Nguyen Hue, and the 'Unification Debates,'" *Crossroads: An Interdisciplinary Journal of Southeast Asian Studies* 17:1 (2003), 129–160.

79. "Tin Tuc Lien Quan Den V.N. Qua Dai Phat Thanh Viet Cong," May 3, 1956, DICH, File no. 4177, VNA2.

80. "Tom tat phuc-trinh cua nha tong giam doc C.S.C.A. ve thang 11 nam 1955," PTTDeNhat, File no. 4018, VNA2.

81. "Return of the Cao Dai Troops to the Maquis," Telegram from US Embassy Saigon to Department of State, January 23, 1956, NARA, RG 59, C0008, Reel 6, 751G.00/1-2356.

82. Ibid.

83. "CIA Current Intelligence Bulletin," May 5, 1955, NARA, CREST, CIA-RDP79T00975A002000230001-3.

84. "Tu 1 tuong cuop vo danh, Bay Vien da nhay vao truong chanh tri do the luc Bao Dai? hay la: chuoi ngay tan cua ten V.G. Bay Vien," May 17, 1955, *Thoi Dai;* "Hoat dong va am muu cua phap chong lai chanh phu cong hoa Vietnam," June 1, 1956, PTTDeNhat, File no. 4313, VNA2.

85. "Nhung Trang Tinh-Su Ly-Ky cua ten luu manh: Bay Vien," *Thoi Dai*, May 18, 1955.

86. Ibid.

87. Ibid., and May 20, 1955.

88. "Nhung Trang Tinh-Su Ly-Ky cua ten luu manh: Bay Vien," *Thoi Dai*, May 18, 1955.

89. For more on the Bình Xuyen's key role in Vietnam's opium network, see Alfred W. McCoy, *The Politics of Heroin in Southeast Asia* (New York: Harper and Row, 1972).

90. "Tai Toa Thuong tham, Buon thuoc phien lau voi Bay Vien," *Thoi Luan*, October 26, 1955.

91. "Bay Vien hien thoi o dau?" *Thoi Luan,* November 24, 1955.

92. "Cuoc Song Hien Thoi cua Bao Dai va Bay Vien o Phap Nhu The Nao?" *Thoi Luan,* December 28, 1955.

93. Schrock et al., *Minority Groups,* 1021–1048.

94. "La Capture de Ba Cut Marque la Fin de Toute Opposition Armee Contre le Gouvernment du President Ngo-Dinh-Diem," *Vietnam Presse*, April 18, 1956, PTTDeNhat, File no. 4322, VNA2.

95. "Capture of Hoa Hao Rebel Leader Ba Cut," Telegram from US Embassy Saigon to Department of State, May 23, 1956, NARA, RG 59, C0008, Reel 7, 751G.00/5-2356.

96. Ibid.

97. Lansdale, *In the Midst of Wars,* 322.

98. "L'Ex-Chef Rebelle Ba Cut Comparait Aujourd'Hui Devant la Cour Martiale a Can-Tho," *Vietnam Presse*, PTTDeNhat, File no. 4322, VNA2.

99. To which government they were referring is not entirely clear, as the State of Vietnam was not formed until 1949. The SVN was preceded by the Provisional Central Government of Vietnam (1948–49), which replaced the colonial administration of Cochin China.

100. "Phieu tin tuc hoat dong quoc gia Hoa Hao Le Quang Vinh tuc Ba Cut: Lien ket voi Viet Cong hoat dong pha roi chanh quyen quoc gia," November 7, 1955, PTTDeNhat, File no. 4321, VNA2; "Phieu tin tuc hoat dong quoc gia Hoa Hao Le Quang Vinh tuc Ba Cut: Dua Quan Doi Hoa Hao gia nhap vao mat tran to quoc cua Viet Minh," November 16, 1955, PTTDeNhat, File no. 4321, VNA2; "Phieu tin tuc hoat dong quoc gia Hoa Hao Le Quang Vinh tuc Ba Cut: Moi bat hoa giua Quan Doi Ba Cut va Viet Cong," November 18, 1955, PTTDeNhat, File no. 4321, VNA2.

101. "Le General Mai Huu Xuan a Requis Contre Ba Cut La Peine Capitale," *Vietnam Presse,* July 4, 1956, PTTDeNhat, File no. 4322, VNA2.

102. "Kien nghi cua dan chung cac gioi thon Mythoi (sic) kinh dang Cu Ngo-Tong-Thong," no date, PTTDeNhat, File no. 4322, VNA2; "Kien nghi kinh goi Ngo-Tong-Thong kinh nho ong dai bieu chanh phu tai Nam Viet ong Tinh Truong Long Xuyen chuyen de," May 1, 1956, PTTDeNhat, File no. 4322, VNA2; "Ban kien nghi kinh de len cu Tong-Thong nuoc Cong Hoa Vietnam de to thai do doi voi Le-Quang Vinh tuc Ba Cut," May 17, 1956, PTTDeNhat, File no. 4322, VNA2; "Sau khi bi bat Ba Cut se phai lanh mot hinh phat gat gao: tu hinh?" *Le Song,* April 17, 1956.

103. "Capture of Hoa Hao Rebel Leader Ba Cut," Telegram from US Embassy Saigon to Department of State, May 23, 1956, NARA, RG 59, C0008, Reel 7, 751G.00/5-2356.

104. "L'Ex Leutenant-Colonel Le-Quang-Vinh Dit Ba Cut est Condamné a la Peine de Mort avec Military Degradation Militaire et Confiscation de ses Biens," *Vietnam Presse*, July 5, 1956, PTTDeNhat, File no. 4322, VNA2; "Execution of Ba Cut," Telegram from US Embassy Saigon to Department of State, July 16, 1956, NARA, RG 59, C0008, Reel 7, 751G.00/7-1656.

105. "Sac Lenh cua Tong Thong Viet Nam Cong Hoa," July 4, 1956, PTTDeNhat, File no. 4322, VNA2; "Bien Ban Buoi Nhom cua Hoi Dong An Xa," July 6, 1956, PTTDeNhat, File no. 4322, VNA2.

106. Two of Ba Cut's lawyers, Vuong Quang Nhuong and Le Ngoc Chan, were famous in South Vietnam. Le Ngoc Chan was a former Quoc Dan Dang activist and served as defense minister in Ngo Dinh Diem's first cabinet, and Vuong Quang Nhuong was head of the Lawyers' Association and worked as justice minister under Tran Van Huu. For more on the trial, see Nguyen Long Thanh Nam (translated by Sergei Blagov), *Hoa Hao Buddhism in the Course of Vietnam's History* (New York: Nova Science Publisher, 2003), 122–126.

107. "Viet Nam Dan Chu Xa Hoi Dang Bach Thu," June 15, 1956, PTTDeNhat, File no. 4322, VNA2.

108. "Execution of Ba Cut," Telegram from US Embassy Saigon to Department of State, July 16, 1956, NARA, RG 59, C0008, Reel 7, 751G.00/7-1656.

109. "L'Ex-Chef Rebelle Le-Quang-Vinh Dit Ba-Cut est Executé ce Matin a Cantho," *Vietnam Presse*, July 13, 1956, PTTDeNhat, File no. 4322, VNA2; "Posthumous Retrial for Vietnam Sect Leader," *New York Times*, March 7, 1965.

110. "Execution of Ba Cut," Telegram from US Embassy Saigon to Department of State, July 16, 1956, NARA, RG59, C0008, Reel 7, 751G.00/7-1656.

111. "CIA Geographic Intelligence Review," January 1957, NARA, CREST, CIA-RDP79-01005A000300020002-9.

Chapter 6

1. Chapter originally published as Jessica M. Chapman, "Staging Democracy: South Vietnam's 1955 Referendum to Depose Bao Dai," *Diplomatic History* 30:4 (September 2006), 671–703. © 2006 by the Society for Historians of American Foreign Relations (SHAFR).

2. Existing scholarship on the referendum is U.S.-centric. The most thorough accounts of the event have been written by journalists and firsthand observers. See Joseph Buttinger, *Vietnam: A Dragon Embattled*, vol. 2, *Vietnam at War* (London: Pall Mall Press, 1967), 889–893; Chester L. Cooper, *The Lost Crusade: America in Vietnam* (New York: Dodd, Mead, 1970), 148–152; Robert Scigliano, *South Vietnam: Nation under Stress* (Boston: Houghton Mifflin, 1964), 23–24; Howard R. Penniman, *Elections in South Vietnam* (Washington, DC: American Enterprise Institute for Public Policy Research, 1972), 20–21; Denis Warner, *The Last Confucian* (New York: Macmillan, 1963), 86; Bernard B. Fall, *The Two Viet-Nams: A Political and Military Analysis*, 2nd rev. ed. (New York: Praeger, 1963), 256–259; Donald Lancaster, *The Emancipation of French Indochina* (New York: Oxford University Press, 1961), 398–399; Robert Shaplen, *The Lost Revolution: The Story of Twenty Years of Neglected Opportunities in Vietnam and of America's Failure to Foster Democracy There* (New York: Harper and Row, 1965), 129–130; Anthony Trawick Bouscaren, *The Last of the Mandarins; Diem of Vietnam* (Pittsburgh: Duquesne University Press, 1965), 56–57. For more recent scholarly accounts, which also dismiss the referendum as an undemocratic exercise, see David L. Anderson, *Trapped by Success: the Eisenhower Administration and Vietnam, 1953–1961* (New York: Columbia University Press, 1991), 127–128; Seth Jacobs, *America's Miracle Man in Vietnam: Ngo Dinh Diem,*

Religion, Race, and U.S. Intervention in Southeast Asia (Durham, NC: Duke University Press, 2004), 224–225. See also Edward Garvey Miller, "Grand Designs: Vision, Power, and Nation Building in America's Alliance with Ngo Dinh Diem, 1954–1960," Ph.D. diss., Harvard University, 2004. Miller has situated the referendum within the context of Vietnamese politics and noted that Ngo Dinh Diem did subscribe to a particular illiberal set of democratic ideals. Yet, he concludes, "By structuring the plebiscite as a choice for or against a deeply unpopular absentee king, and by linking that choice to the almost universally popular concept of republicanism, Diem cast the question in such a way that an overwhelmingly favorable response was assured" (208).

3. Since modernization theory as an explanation for political and social change emerged in the 1950s, scholars have problematized the concept of tradition versus modernity. Whereas the architects of the theory saw modernization as a progressive, systematic, revolutionary process by which traditional forms would be replaced, revisionists have attacked the reductionistic equation of tradition with backwardness and modernity with economic progress and social virtue. Moreover, they have pointed out that modernity does not simply replace tradition, but combines with it to produce new political and social practices and institutions. For a thorough review of this literature see Samuel P. Huntington, "To Change to Change: Modernization, Development, and Politics," *Comparative Politics* 3:2 (April 1971), 283–322; for more recent assessments see Ronald Inglehart and Wayne E. Baker, "Modernization, Cultural Change, and the Persistence of Traditional Values," *American Sociological Review* 65:1 (February 2000), 19–51; David C. Engerman, Nils Gilman, Mark H. Haefele, Michael E. Latham, eds., *Staging Growth: Modernization, Development, and the Global Cold War* (Boston: University of Massachusetts Press, 2003); see also Partha Chatterjee, *The Politics of the Governed: Reflections on Popular Politics in Most of the World* (New York: Columbia University Press, 2004), 6–8. Partha Chatterjee refers to the coexistence of the traditional and the modern as "dense and heterogeneous time." In the case of South Vietnam at this time, the terms *inherited* and *borrowed* could be used to replace *traditional* and *modern* in order to avoid the impression of value judgments. I have chosen to use the terms *modern* and *traditional* because they appeared prevalently in the twentieth-century Vietnamese anticolonial vocabulary, and are thus the terms that Vietnamese politicians would have used to understand their nation's ongoing process of social and political change.

4. Struggles over modernization versus the return to traditional values and practices marked the Vietnamese anticolonial movement throughout the twentieth century. One of the most relevant examples for this study is the debate between traditionalist Phan Boi Chau and modernizer Phan Chau Trinh over the relative merits of monarchy versus democracy. See William J. Duiker, "Phan Boi Chau: Asian Revolutionary in a Changing World," *Journal of Asian Studies* 31:1 (November 1971), 77–88. Duiker demonstrates that even Phan Boi Chau, the more conservative of these two anticolonial leaders, was torn between his longing for a return to traditional forms and his understanding of the need to modernize to ensure national survival and independence in a changing world.

5. Tony Smith, *America's Mission: The United States and the Worldwide Struggle for Democracy in the Twentieth Century* (Princeton: Princeton University Press, 1994), 4. Smith identifies the greatest ambition of U.S. foreign policy since the Spanish-American war as follows: "to promote democracy abroad as a way of enhancing the national security."

6. Kathryn Statler, "The Diem Experiment and Franco-American Conflict over South Vietnam, July 1954–May 1955," *Journal of American-East Asian Relations* 6:2–3 (summer–fall 1997): 145–173; Daniel P. O'C. Greene, "John Foster Dulles and the End of Franco American Entente in Indochina," *Diplomatic History* 16:4 (fall 1992): 551–571. Both Statler and Greene have demonstrated that the United States largely succeeded in eliminating the remnants of French influence in Saigon through a series of talks in mid-May 1955. Nonetheless, the French

government retained an interest in influencing the political future of its former colony and especially in preventing violence and injustice toward French citizens still living in Vietnam. Indeed, it was not until after the referendum and Ngo Dinh Diem's proclamation of the Republic of Vietnam on October 26 that Ngo Dinh Diem moved to demand the immediate withdraw of the French Expeditionary Corps from South Vietnam.

7. See Miller, "Grand Designs," 194.

8. Buttinger, *A Dragon Embattled*, 880–884; Robert G. Scigliano, "Political Parties in South Vietnam Under the Republic," *Pacific Affairs* (September 1960), 328–329; US Department of State Memorandum of Conversation, "Briefing on Conditions in Vietnam," 2 May 1955, National Archives and Records Administration (hereafter NARA), Record Group 59 (hereafter RG), C0008, Reel 3, 751G.00/4-3055. Cao Dai generals Trinh Minh The and Nguyen Thanh Phuong played leading roles in the Revolutionary Council, as did Hoa Hao general Nguyen Giac Ngo.

9. Robert R. Nathan, "The Consequences of Partition," in Wesley R. Fishel, ed., *Problems of Freedom: South Vietnam since Independence* (Glencoe, IL: The Free Press, 1961), 16.

10. Miller, "Grand Designs," 197.

11. Fall, *The Two Viet-Nams*, 257; Buttinger, *a Dragon Embattled*, 884.

12. "Ban Tuyen Cao cua Phu Ton Nhon Luc 15 Gio Ngay 15-6-1955,"Vietnamese National Archives #2 (hereafter VNA2), Phu Tong Thong De Nhat Cong Hoa (hereafter PTTDICH), Folder 18091.

13. "Telegram from US Embassy Saigon to Secretary of State," 27 June 1955, NARA, RG59, C0008, Reel 4, 751G.00/6-2755.

14. "Telegram from Secretary of State to US Embassy Saigon and US Embassy Paris," 29 June 1955, NARA, RG59, C0008, Reel 4, 751G.00/6-2955.

15. "Telegram from US Embassy Saigon to Secretary of State," 7 October 1955, NARA, RG59, C0008, Reel 5, 751G.00/10-755; Telegram from US Embassy Saigon to Department of State, "The Government's Case Against Bao Dai," 18 October 1955, NARA, RG59, C0008, Reel 5, 751G.00/10-1855.

16. See Lancaster, *The Emancipation of French Indochina*, 398.

17. "Telegram from US Embassy Paris to Secretary of State," 14 October 1955, NARA, RG59, C0008, Reel 5, 751G.00/10-1355; "Bao Dai Condemns Diem Referendum," *New York Times*, 14 October 1955; "Diem and Bao Dai," *New York Times*, 15 October 1955.

18. See "Telegram from US Embassy Paris to Secretary of State" (contains text of message addressed by Bao Dai to the Vietnamese people), 19 October 1955, NARA, RG59, C0008, Reel 5, 751G.00/10-1955. Bao Dai did deliver a message to the Vietnamese people, but there is no evidence that it was broadcast widely, if at all, within the borders of South Vietnam.

19. "La Révocation de Ngo Dinh Diem Par Bao Dai—Extrait du Bulletin des Écoutes du Haut Commissariat de la Republique Française au Vietnam No. 2849 du 20 Octobre 1955," VNA2, PTTDICH, Folder 18092; "Bao Dai 'Removes' Vietnam Premier," *New York Times*, 19 October 1955; "Telegram from US Embassy Paris to Secretary of State" (containing text of Bao Dai's letter), 18 October 1955, NARA, RG59, C0008, Reel 5, 751G.00/10-1855.

20. "Telegram from US Embassy Paris to Secretary of State," 20 October 1955, NARA, RG59, C0008, Reel 5, 751G.00/10-2055.

21. *Lua Song*, 27 October 1955; "Ket Qua Cuoc Trung Cau Dan Y Ngay 23 Thang 10 Nam 1955," 26 October 1955, VNA2, PTTDICH, Folder 639. Official election returns show 5,721,735 of 5,828,907 ballots cast in favor of removing Bao Dai from office and charging Ngo Dinh Diem with the responsibility to establish a republican government.

22. "Ban Tuyen Cao Cua Quoc Truong Viet Nam," 26 October 1955, VNA2, PTTDICH, Folder 18097.

23. Philip Catton, *Diem's Final Failure: Prelude to America's War in Vietnam* (Lawrence: University Press of Kansas, 2002), 37; Edward Miller, "Vision, Power and Agency: The Ascent of Ngo Dinh Diem, 1945–1954," *Journal of Southeast Asian Studies* 35:3 (October 2004), 433.

24. Republic of Vietnam, "President Ngo Dinh Diem," Saigon: Presidency of the Republic of Vietnam Press Office, 1957, 13.

25. The real significance of the "mandate of heaven" within Vietnam has been much debated. For basic explanations of the concept and its application to leadership and succession, see Lee H. Yearley, "Toward a Typology of Religious Thought: A Chinese Example," *Journal of Religion* 55:4 (October 1975), 428; Robert Petit, *La Monarchie Annamite* (Paris: Les Editions Domat-Montchrestien, 1931), especially 37–47. For works that emphasize the centrality of the mandate to Vietnamese life and politics, see Stephen B. Young, "The Mandate and Politics in Vietnam," in John C. Donnell and Charles A. Joiner, ed. *Electoral Politics in South Vietnam* (Lexington, MA: Lexington Books, 1974), 13–34; John T. McAlister Jr. and Paul Mus, *The Vietnamese and Their Revolution* (New York: Harper and Row, 1970), 67–69 and 114; D. Howard Smith, "The Significance of Confucius for Religion," *History of Religions* 2:2 (winter 1963), 248; Frances FitzGerald, *Fire in the Lake: The Vietnamese and the Americans in Vietnam* (New York: Vintage Books, 1972); Peter R. Moody, Jr., *Political Opposition in Post-Confucian Society* (New York: Praeger, 1988). According to Moody, "No country in the Confucian cultural area has shown great tolerance for competitive politics" (1).

26. Shawn Frederick McHale, *Print and Power: Confucianism, Communism, and Buddhism in the Making of Modern Vietnam* (Honolulu: University of Hawaii Press, 2004), 76. See also Gerald Cannon Hickey, *Village in Vietnam* (New Haven: Yale University Press, 1964), xv; K. W. Taylor, "Vietnamese Confucian Narratives," in Benjamin Elman, John B. Duncan, Herman Ooms, eds., *Rethinking Confucianism* (Los Angeles: UCLA Asia Pacific Monograph Series, 2002), 337.

27. R. B. Smith, "The Development of Opposition to French Rule in Southern Vietnam, 1880–1940," *Past and Present* 54 (February 1972), 95.

28. See also Nguyen The Anh, "From Indra to Maitreya: Buddhist Influence in Vietnamese Political Thought," *Journal of Southeast Asian Studies* 33:2 (June 2002), 225–241.

29. These latter ideas clearly were borrowed from Europe and the United States by Vietnamese reformers throughout the twentieth century in a self-conscious process of civilization. See Mark Bradley, *Imagining Vietnam and America: The Making of Postcolonial Vietnam, 1919–1950* (Chapel Hill: University of North Carolina Press, 2000); Bradley, "Becoming *Van Minh*: Civilizational Discourse and Visions of the Self in Twentieth-Century Vietnam," *Journal of World History* 15:1 (2004), 65–83.

30. Quoted in Thomas L. Alhern Jr., *CIA and the House of Ngo: Covert Action in South Vietnam, 1954–63*, Center for the Study of Intelligence, 21 (National Security Archive Electronic Briefing Book No. 283), 73.

31. Emmanuel Mounier, *A Personalist Manifesto*, trans. Monks of St. John's Abbey (New York: Longmans, Green, 1938), 247–248.

32. Cao Van Luan, one of Ngo Dinh Diem's former cabinet members, claims that the Ngos' brand of Personalism was insufficiently grounded in traditional Vietnamese political thought, and that it therefore undermined the prime minister's claims of populist leadership. See Cao Van Luan, *Ben Giong Lich Su, 1940–1965* (Glendale: Co So Xuat Ban Dai Nam, 1986), 282–287.

33. Fall, *The Two Viet-Nams*, 237. Fall writes, "It was perhaps out of faithfulness to the *mystique* of the monarchy as such that that Diem decided in 1955 to oust its unworthy representative, Bao-Dai"; See Ngo Dinh Diem, "Democratic Development in Vietnam," in Paul K. T. Sih, ed., *Democracy in East Asia* (Taiwan: China Culture Publishing Foundation, 1957). In this article, penned by Ngo Dinh Diem prior to his assumption of the premiership in South Vietnam, the

following were identified as a principles universally accepted by the Vietnamese people: "The Mandate of Heaven held by the Sovereign was revocable if he proved himself to be unworthy thereof; The voice of the people was the voice of Heaven."

34. "Telegram from US Embassy Saigon to Secretary of State," 21 October 1955, NARA, RG59, C0008, Reel 5, 751G.00/10-2155.

35. "Mot Tai Lieu Dac Biet Chua Bao Nao Noi Toi: Cuoc Doi cua Bao Dai," *Thoi Dai,* 4 August 1955. For evidence suggesting that Diem's government made every effort to circulate the newspapers cited here as widely as possible throughout the countryside, see "Record of Governmental Achievements, July 1955—July 1956" (Saigon, 1956). According to this RVN publication, "Substantial efforts have been put out by information services on various scales, in an accelerated rhythm in a move to enable all our compatriots—even those in the remotest hamlets,—to be aware of current topics inland and abroad. Newspapers, magazines, booklets, etc. . . . of all kinds were sent to them" (15).

36. For a brief description of Khai Dinh's apparently unremarkable and often criticized reign, see Oscar Chapuis, *The Last Emperors of Vietnam: From Tu Duc to Bao Dai* (Westport, CT: Greenwood Press, 2000), 27; and Bruce McFarland Lockhart, *The End of the Vietnamese Monarchy* (New Haven: Yale University Press, 1993).

37. "Cuoc Doi Tinh Ai Ly Ky cua Bao Dai: Bao Dai la Con Mot . . . Thang Mu An Luong cua Tu Cung Thai Hau," *Thoi Dai,* 5 August 1955.

38. Anticolonialism and anti-French sentiments were, of course, nothing new to Vietnam by this time. Up until Ngo Dinh Diem's appointment, however, leaders of the State of Vietnam had been relative Francophiles. For discussion of earlier anticolonial movements see Peter Zinoman, *The Colonial Bastille: A History of Imprisonment in Vietnam, 1862–1940* (Berkeley: University of California Press, 2001); Mus and McAlister, *The Vietnamese and their Revolution*; David G. Marr, *Vietnamese Tradition on Trial, 1920–1945* (Berkeley: University of California Press, 1981); Hue-Tam Ho-Tai, *Radicalism and the Origins of the Vietnamese Revolution* (Boston: Harvard University Press, 1992); William J. Duiker, *The Rise of Nationalism in Vietnam, 1900–1941* (Ithaca: Cornell University Press, 1976). For discussion of Ngo Dinh Diem's anti-French background see Warner, *The Last Confucian*; Miller, "Vision, Power and Agency," 433–458.

39. "Cuoc Doi Tinh Ai Ly Ky cua Bao Dai: Tu Cung Thai Hau So Con Lau Ay Vo Dam de Con Tay Lai," *Thoi Dai,* 8 August 1955.

40. "Cuoc Doi Tinh Ai Ly Ky cua Bao Dai: Bao Dai Lay Vo voi Cai Ten Tay," *Thoi Dai,* 9 August 1955.

41. *Thoi Dai,* 9 August 1955.

42. "Cuoc Doi Tinh Ai Ly Ky cua Bao Dai: Co Marie Jeanne Henriette la Con Nao ma Quyen Ru Noi Bao Dai," *Thoi Dai,* 11 August 1955.

43. "Cai An Tinh Ai Lich Su cua Bao Dai: Vua Co The Lay Vo Ngoai Quoc co Nhieu Vo, Nhieu Con Khong?" *Thoi Dai,* 27 August 1955.

44. "Cuoc Doi Tinh Ai Cua Bao Dai: Mot Cuoc Chay Dua Chinh Tri Bang . . . Ai Tinh Giua Nam Phuong Henriette va Co Gai Hop Dem Evelyn Riva," *Thoi Dai,* 16 August 1955.

45. "Truat Phe Bao Dai la Y Nguyen cua Nhan Dan," *Thoi Dai,* 21 October 1955.

46. "Tuyen Cao cua Uy Ban Nhan Dan Trung Cau Dan Y Goi Dong Bao Toan Quoc," *Tieng Chuong,* 8 October 1955; see also "Bao Dai Con Mua Roi Den Bao Gio," *Lua Song,* 30 September 1955; "Bao Dai: Tru Danh Bu Ninh Dang Dao Ho Chon Minh Trong Am Muu Tay Sai Cho Viet Cong," *Lua Song,* 10 Oct 1955; "Bao Dai va Viet Cong," *Dan Chu,* 26 September 1955; "La Collusion de Bao Dai avec les Communistes et les Colonialistes," *Vietnam Presse,* 11 October 1955, VNA2, PTTDICH, Folder 18092. These are just a few examples of the barrage of articles in the South Vietnamese press in the month prior to the referendum that identified Bao

Dai as a puppet emperor and accused him of colluding with the communists and the French to sell Vietnam to outside forces.

47. "Chung Quanh Vu Bao Dai Bi Mat Lien Lac Voi Viet Cong Tron Trach Nhiem," *Lua Song*, 30 September 1955.

48. For several examples of these formulaic petitions, see VNA2, PTTDICH, Folder 18091.

49. Nguyen Van Hinh was the son of former State of Vietnam prime minister Nguyen Van Tam, and there was some speculation that he sought to overthrow Ngo Dinh Diem to make room for his father's return to power in South Vietnam.

50. For more on the roots of Bao Dai's relationship with the sects, see Jayne Susan Werner, *Peasant Politics and Religious Sectarianism: Peasant and Priest in the Cao Dai in Viet Nam* (New Haven: Yale University Press, 1981), 53; See also Archimedes A. Patti, *Why Vietnam? Prelude to America's Albatross* (Berkeley: University of California Press, 1980), 445.

51. "Biet Xu Dung La Phieu Nghia la Biet Bao Ve Quyen Loi Cho Chinh Minh," *Lua Song*, 20 October 1955.

52. Lancaster, *The Emancipation of French Indochina*, 382–397.

53. "Chung Quang Vu Bao Dai Bi Mot Lien Lac Voi Viet Cong," *Saigon Moi*, 30 September 1955; "Bu Nhin Bao Dai Lien Lac voi Doc Tai V.C. de Du Dinh No Le Hoa Nhan Dan Viet Nam Mot Lan Nua," *Lua Song*, 1 October 1955; "Bao Dai va Viet Cong," *Dan Chu*, 26 September 1955; Petitions to depose Bao Dai, VNA2, PTTDICH, Folder 18091.

54. Chatterjee, *The Politics of the Governed*, 27.

55. Miller, "Grand Designs," 204–210. In his dissertation, Miller uses Vietnamese sources to provide a more nuanced interpretation of Ngo Dinh Diem's goals surrounding the referendum. He notes that Ngo Dinh Diem intended the referendum to be "an initial exercise in democracy which would pave the way for the early establishment of a directly elected National-Assembly." He does not, however, delve into the details of Ngo Dinh Diem's efforts to disseminate his notions of democracy within Vietnam.

56. "Tuyen Bo Cua Ong Tong Tuong Noi Vu Phat Ngon Nhan Chinh Phu ve Trung Cau Dan Y," VNA2, PTTDICH, Folder 18094.

57. Ibid.

58. "Translation of the Governmental Declaration October 19, 1955," VNA2, PTTDICH, Folder 18094.

59. "Loi Tuyen Bo Truyen Thanh Cua Thu Tuong Chanh Phu," 22 October 1955, VNA2, PTTDICH, Folder 639.

60. "Tai Lieu Hoc Tap Ve Cuoc Trung Cau Dan Y Ngay 23-10-1955," VNA2, PTTDICH, Folder 639.

61. "Muc Dich va Y Nghia Truat Phe Bao Dai," VNA2, PTTDICH, Folder 639. This educational pamphlet explains Ngo Dinh Diem's reasons for deposing Bao Dai at the current time and the potential benefits of doing so.

62. "Quan Niem Doc Tai va Quan Niem Dan Chu," *Thoi Luan*, 20 August 1955.

63. See Carlyle A. Thayer, *War by Other Means: National Liberation and Revolution in Viet-Nam 1954–1960* (Sydney: Allen and Unwin, 1989), especially 26–45.

64. "Cuoc Dau Phieu Dan Chu Nhat tu Xua Toi Nay o Viet Nam," *Lua Song*, 15 October 1955.

65. For a discussion of the international response to this, see Ilya V. Gaiduk, *Confronting Vietnam: Soviet Policy toward the Indochina Conflict, 1954–1963* (Washington, DC: Woodrow Wilson Center Press, 2003), especially 69–83.

66. "Telegram from the Ambassador to Vietnam (Reinhardt) to the Department of State, June 29, 1955," *FRUS*, 1955–1957, vol. 1 (Washington, D.C., 1985), 470; "Telegram from US

Embassy Saigon to Secretary of State," 29 June 1955, NARA, RG59, C0008, Reel 4, 751G.00/6-2955. Ambassador Reinhardt reported to Secretary Dulles that Vu Van Mau informed him in strictest confidence that Ngo Dinh Diem's cabinet was considering holding a referendum to depose Bao Dai at this time.

67. See Gaiduk, *Confronting Vietnam,* 69. This announcement was a response to Pham Van Dong's June statement that the DRV was willing to hold a consultative conference on elections. By taking this step, Ngo Dinh Diem defied American advice to pursue consultations with the DRV in hopes the communists would balk at numerous provisions for free elections and thus assume the blame for breaching the Geneva agreement.

68. "Loi Tuyen Bo Truyen Thanh cua Ngo Thu Tuong Ngay 16-7-55," *Thoi Dai,* 18 October 1955; Nguyen Van Minh, *Lich Su Khang Chien Chong My Cuu Nuoc, 1955–1975* (Tap II) (Hanoi: Nha Xuat Ban Chinh Tri Quoc Gia, 1996), 63; Patti, *Why Vietnam,* 447.

69. *Ngon Luan,* 8 August 1955.

70. See Fall, *The Two Viet-nams,* 270.

71. "Lam The Nao Mot Cuoc Tong Tuyen Cu Tu Do o Viet Nam," *Thoi Luan,* 15 August 1955.

72. "Tuyen Bo Cua Ong Tong Tuong Noi Vu Phat Ngon Nhan Chinh Phu ve Trung Cau Dan Y," VNA2, PTTDICH, Folder 18094.

73. "Telegram from US Embassy Saigon to Secretary of State," 27 September 1955, NARA, RG59, C0008, Reel 5, 751G.00/9-2755.

74. "Vietnamese National Assembly and other Political Reforms," Memo from Kenneth T. Young to Mr. Robertson and Mr. Sebald, 5 October 1955, NARA, RG59, C0008, Reel 5, 751G.00/10-555.

75. "Telegram from US Embassy Saigon to Secretary of State," 29 September 1955, NARA, RG59, C0008, Reel 5, 751G.00/9-2955.

76. "Telegram from US Embassy Saigon to Secretary of State," 17 October 1955, NARA, RG59, C0008, Reel 5, 751G.00/10-1755.

77. "Telegram from Secretary of State to US Embassy Paris, US Embassy London, and US Embassy Saigon," 20 October 1955, NARA, RG59, C0008, Reel 5, 751G.00/10-2055.

78. "Diem Makes Plea on Today's Vote," *New York Times,* 23 October 1955.

79. "Nhung Dieu Quan Trong ve Viec Trung Cau Dan Y Ngay 23–10 Toi Day," *Tieng Chuong,* 12 October 1955; see also "Organization du Referendum," 10 October 1955, VNA2, PTTDICH, Folder 18093.

80. Ballot for 23-10-1955 referendum to depose Bao Dai, VNA2, PTTDICH, Folder 18093; "Background of Plebiscite," *New York Times,* 23 October 1955; "Les Électeurs du Sud-Vietnam Vont Choisir sur Photographie Entre le Bon Ngo Dinh Diem el le Vilain Bao-Dai," *Libération,* 11 October 1955; "Mr. Diem's Lucky Color," *The Economist,* 29 October 1955.

81. Edward Geary Lansdale, *In the Midst of Wars: an American's Mission to Southeast Asia* (New York: Harper and Row, 1972), 333–334.

82. "A Review of Election Processes in South Vietnam," Directorate of Intelligence, 9 March 1966, NARA, CREST, CIA-RDP79T00826A000400010040-7.

83. Ibid.

84. "Telegram from US Embassy Saigon to Secretary of State," 25 October 1955, NARA, RG59, C0008, Reel 5, 751G.00/10-2555.

85. "Phieu Tin Tuc Hoat Dong Quoc Gia Hoa Hao Tran Van Soai," 4 November 1955, VNA2, PTTDICH, Folder 4320.

86. "New Leader in Asia," *Missourian,* 25 October 1955, VNA2, PTTDICH, Folder 18096; "South Vietnam and the Saar," *Desert News,* 25 October 1955, VNA2, PTTDICH, Folder 18096;

"Diem Gives South Vietnam Rallying Point and a Chance," Milwaukee, Wisconsin *Journal*, 26 October 1955, VNA2, PTTDICH, Folder 18096. This folder includes clippings from several American and French newspapers regarding the Vietnamese referendum.

87. "Vietnam Sticks with Diem," Dayton, Ohio *News*, 25 October 1955, VNA2, PTTDICH, Folder 18096.

88. Henry R. Lieberman, "Diem Moves to Strengthen an Independent Vietnam," *New York Times*, 30 October 1955.

89. "South Viet-Nam Voters Repudiate Ex-Emperor," *Los Angeles Times*, 24 October 1955.

90. "Diem Sees Delay on Unity Upheld," *New York Times*, 26 October 1955.

91. Lieberman, "Diem Moves to Strengthen an Independent Vietnam."

92. "Retired by Request: Bao Dai Joins the Exes," New Orleans, Louisiana *Item*, 26 October 1955, VNA2, PTTDICH, Folder 18096; "The Boot for Bao Dai," Snyder, Texas *News*, 26 October 1955, VNA2, PTTDICH, Folder 18096.

93. Assorted articles from the Luce Press Clipping Bureau, VNA2, PTTDICH, Folder 18096.

94. "US Embassy Saigon to Secretary of State," 20 October 1955, NARA, RG59, C0008, Reel 5, 751G.00/10-1955.

95. "La Signification Politique du Referendum du 23 Octobre au Sud-Vietnam," *La Tribune des Nations*, 21 October 1955, VNA2, PTTDICH, Folder 18096.

96. "Les Électeurs Choisissent Entre Diem et Bao Dai," *France-Soir*, 24 October 1955, VNA2, Folder 18096.

97. "Le Vietnam de M. Diem se Prononce Demain Pour ou Contre Bao Dai," *Combat*, 22 October 1955, VNA2, PTTDICH, Folder 18096; "Le Cirque Diem Organisé le Referendum Anti-Bao Dai," *Le Populaire*, 22 October 1955, VNA2, PTTDICH, Folder 18096.

98. "Vietnam: Succés de Diem Assure, Mais 50% d'Abstentions," *L'Express*, 24 October 1955, VNA2, PTTDICH, Folder 18096; "Sud-Vietnam: 50% d'Abstentions au 'Referendum Diem,'" *l'Humanite*, 24 October 1955, VNA2, PTTDICH, Folder 18096.

99. Nathan, "The Consequences of Partition," 13–14. Some historians, on the contrary, have argued against the political relevance and sincerity of Diem's critics. Nathan claims that, as a consequence of America's replacement of France as the predominant foreign influence on Vietnamese political affairs, there was "a burst of democratic and pseudo-democratic ideas and propaganda across the political spectrum. Pious democratic credos were uttered by men who had till then been considered power-hungry political scoundrels." Such uses of democratic rhetoric by Cao Dai and Hoa Hao generals and their allies were, according to Nathan, insignificant because none of these men ended up rising to power.

100. Cao Van Luan, *Ben Giong Lich Su*, 282–287.

101. Nguyen Van Minh, *Lich Su Khang Chien*, 73; see also Gabriel Kolko, *Anatomy of a War: Vietnam, the United States, and the Modern Historical Experience* (New York: Pantheon Books, 1985), 89. Kolko estimates that twelve thousand were killed from 1955 to 1957 in South Vietnam; Frances FitzGerald, *Fire in the Lake*. FitzGerald claims that by the end of 1956, RVN prison camps primarily intended for communist subversives housed approximately twenty thousand prisoners, including the leaders of the sects and nonstate political parties, as well as uncooperative members of the press and trade unions (112).

102. Vietnamese nationalists in France and the United States did raise some objections to Ngo Dinh Diem's handling of the elections, but they did not gain hearing in South Vietnam.

103. "Communication du General Hoa Hao Tran Van Soai au sujet des élections," 22 October 1955, VNA2, PTTDICH, Folder 4312.

104. "Ngo Dinh Diem Dang Lam Gi???," 3 October 1955, VNA2, PTTDICH, Folder 4321; see also "Chung Toi Phan Doi Ngo Thu Thuong," 3 October 1955, VNA2, PTTDICH, Folder

4321. A GVN document in this same file regarding the activities of Ba Cut's forces identifies the source of these documents as Ba Cut's Hoa Hao.

105. "Letter from the Commander of the Army of the Vietnamese Socialist Party to the various branches of the Army," 14 October 1955, VNA2, PTTDICH, Folder 4321.

106. See Fall, *The Two Viet-nams*, 258.

Chapter 7

1. See Seth Jacobs, *America's Miracle Man in Vietnam: Ngo Dinh Diem, Religion, Race, and U.S. Intervention in Southeast Asia, 1950–1957* (Durham, NC: Duke University Press, 2004), 221–222.

2. John Prados, *Vietnam: The History of an Unwinnable War, 1945–1975* (Lawrence: University Press of Kansas, 2009), 58.

3. Philip Catton, *Diem's Final Failure: Prelude to America's War in Vietnam* (Lawrence: University Press of Kansas, 2002), 2.

4. "Proclamation of the Republic," 26 October 1955, in Republic of Vietnam, *Major Policy Speeches by President Ngo Dinh Diem* (Saigon: Presidency of the Republic of Vietnam Press Office, 1956), 23–24.

5. Cited in Robert G. Scigliano, "The Electoral Process in South Vietnam: Politics in an Underdeveloped State," *Midwest Journal of Political Science* 4:2 (May 1960), 142.

6. J. A. C. Grant, "The Viet Nam Constitution of 1956," *American Political Science Review* 52 (June 1958): 437–462.

7. "Tong Tuyen Cu Quoc Hoi o Viet-Nam Tu Do," *Saigon Moi*, 19 January 1956.

8. See David L. Anderson, *Trapped by Success: The Eisenhower Administration and Vietnam, 1953–61* (New York: Columbia University Press, 1991), 131. Anderson claims that Diem's campaign practices were practically identical to those used by the Viet Minh in selecting the DRV's first constituent assembly in 1946.

9. "Telegram from US Embassy Saigon to Secretary of State," 6 December 1955, NARA, RG 59, 751G.00/12-655.

10. "Telegram from US Embassy Saigon to Secretary of State," 30 November 1955, NARA, RG 59, 751G.00/11-3055.

11. "Telegram from US Embassy Saigon to Secretary of State," 17 December 1955, NARA, RG 59, 751G.00/12-1755; "Telegram from US Embassy Saigon to Secretary of State," 10 January 1956, NARA, RG 59, 751G.00/1-1056; "Telegram from US Embassy Saigon to Secretary of State," 23 January 1956, NARA, RG 59, 751G.00/1-2356.

12. "Telegram from US Embassy Saigon to Secretary of State," 11 January 1956, NARA, RG 59, 751G.00/1-1156; "Telegram from US Embassy Saigon to Secretary of State," 13 January 1956, NARA, RG 59, 751G.00/1-1356.

13. "Telegram from US Embassy Saigon to Secretary of State," 17 December 1955, NARA, RG 59, 751G.00/12-1755; "Telegram from US Embassy Saigon to Secretary of State," 20 January 1956, NARA, RG 59, 751G.00/1-2056; "Telegram from Young to Kattenburg," 23 January 1956, NARA, RG 59, 751G.00/1-2056.

14. "Telegram from US Embassy Saigon to Secretary of State," 20 January 1956, NARA, RG 59, 751G.00/1-2056.

15. Cited in Scigliano, "The Electoral Process in South Vietnam," 143.

16. "A Review of Election Processes in South Vietnam," 10 March 1966, NARA, CIA-RDP79T00826A000400010040-7.

17. "South Vietnam: A Political History, 1954–1970," Keesling's Research Report (New York: Scribner, 1970), 18; "Tin Tuc Lien Quan Den V.N. Qua Dai Phat Thanh Viet Cong," Vietnamese National Archives #2 (hereafter VNA2), PTTDICH, Folder 4112.

18. "Tin Tuc Lien Quan Den V.N. Qua Dai Phat Thanh Viet Cong va Ngoai Quoc, 28/2/1956," VNA2, PTTDICH, Folder 4112.

19. "A Review of Election Processes in South Vietnam," 10 March 1966, NARA, CIA-RDP79T00826A000400010040-7.

20. *Saigon Moi*, 2 January 1956; *Saigon Moi*, 3 January 1956; *Saigon Moi*, 4 January 1956; *Saigon Moi*, 10 January 1956; *Saigon Moi*, 16 January 1956.

21. Scigliano, "The Electoral Process in South Vietnam," 151.

22. "Tin Tuc Lien Quan Den Viet Nam Qua Dai Phat Thanh Viet Cong, 4/3/1956," VNA2, PTTDICH, Folder 4112. This news roundup, produced by the RVN Security agency, served to inform Diem's regime of Viet Minh propaganda content. It does not specify who wrote the original article, nor does it indicate where it was first published.

23. "Report of the Office of the Secretary of Defense Vietnam Task Force," January 15, 1969, Part IV.A.5 Evolution of the War. Origins of the Insurgency, 19.

24. Nguyen Tuyet Mai, "Electioneering: Vietnamese Style," *Asian Survey* 2:9 (November, 1962) 11–18. Madame Nhu was the wife of Ngo Dinh Nhu who would become infamous in South Vietnam for her political insensitivity.

25. "A Review of Election Processes in South Vietnam," 10 March 1966, NARA, CIA-RDP79T00826A000400010040-7, Catton, *Diem's Final Failure*, 13.

26. "A Review of Election Processes in South Vietnam," 10 March 1966, NARA, CIA-RDP79T00826A000400010040-7.

27. "Editorial Note," *FRUS, Vietnam, 1955–1957*, 649.

28. Anderson, *Trapped by Success*, 130.

29. Scigliano, "The Electoral Process in South Vietnam," 153.

30. Grant, "The Vietnam Constitution of 1956," 444. Eisenhower's administration dispatched Grant to South Vietnam in summer 1956 to comment on the assembly's draft constitution, but Ngo Dinh Diem ignored the bulk of his advice.

31. Bernard B. Fall, *The Two Viet-Nams: A Political and Military Analysis*, 2nd rev. ed. (New York: Praeger, 1967), 259–275.

32. Quoted in Grant, "The Vietnam Constitution of 1956," 457.

33. Marilyn Young, *The Vietnam Wars, 1945–1990* (New York: Harper Collins, 1991), 60–71.

34. Stanley Karnow, *Vietnam: A History* (New York: Viking Press, 1983), 227; Catton, *Diem's Final Failure*, 64.

35. Mark Bradley, *Vietnam at War* (New York: Oxford University Press. 2009), 85.

36. Anderson, *Trapped by Success*, 164.

37. U.S. Operations Mission to Vietnam, *Saigon Daily News Round-Up*, May 14, 1956, 3, cited in Robert Scigliano, *South Vietnam: Nation under Stress* (Westport, CT: Greenwood Press, 1963), 168.

38. Carlyle A. Thayer, *War by Other Means: National Liberation and Revolution in Vietnam 1954–1960* (Sydney: Allen and Unwin, 1989), 81.

39. "Report of the Office of the Secretary of Defense Vietnam Task Force," January 15, 1969, Part IV.A.5 Evolution of the War. Origins of the Insurgency, 21.

40. Frances FitzGerald, *Fire in the Lake: The Vietnamese and the Americans in Vietnam* (New York: Vintage Books, 1972), 112.

41. FitzGerald, *Fire in the Lake*, 112; see also Gabriel Kolko, *Anatomy of War: Vietnam, the United States, and the Modern Historical Experience* (New York: New Press, 1985); Thayer, *War by Other Means*, 82.

42. Peter Zinoman, *The Colonial Bastille: A History of Imprisonment in Vietnam, 1862–1940* (Berkeley: University of California Press, 2001).

43. Young, *The Vietnam War,* 64.

44. Robert D. Schulzinger, *A Time for War: The United States and Vietnam, 1941–1975* (New York: Oxford University Press, 1997), 93.

45. Young, *The Vietnam War,* 63.

46. "Report of the Office of the Secretary of Defense Vietnam Task Force," January 15, 1969, Part IV.A.5 Evolution of the War. Origins of the Insurgency, 21.

47. George McT. Kahin, *Intervention: How America Became Involved in Vietnam* (New York: Alfred A. Knopf, 1986), 108.

48. Thayer, *War by Other Means,* 131.

49. Young, *The Vietnam War,* 63; See Thayer, *War by Other Means,* 136–138; see also Kolko, *Anatomy of War.* Kolko argues that "the Cao Dai and Hoa Hao sects, which had always been something of a polyglot, offered Party military personnel the best cover for their work" (101).

50. "Daniel V. Anderson to Department of State," November 2, 1956, NARA, RG 59, 751G.00/11-1256.

51. "Dillon to Secretary of State," December 19, 1956, NARA, RG 59, 751G.00/12-1956.

52. "Dulles to U.S. Embassy Paris and U.S. Embassy Saigon," NARA, RG 59, 751G.00/12-2156.

53. Robertson to Eric Kocher, "Letter forwarded by Senator Long attacking Government of Viet-Nam," February 13, 1957, NARA, F.W. 751G.00/2-875.

54. Daniel V. Anderson to Department of State, "Recent anti-government activity in the Cao Dai," March 14, 1957, NARA, 751G.00/3-1457.

55. Daniel V. Anderson to Department of State, "Conditions in Five Southern Provinces of Vietnam, March 1957," April 13, 1957, NARA, 751G.00/4-1357.

56. Daniel V. Anderson to Department of State, "Summary of Internal Security Situation in Viet Nam, June 1957," July 18, 1957, NARA, 751G.00/7-1857

57. "NSC Briefing, South Vietnam," 30 September 1958, CREST, CIA-RDP79R00890A 001000050030-8.

58. Lam Quang Thi, *The Twenty-five Year Century: A South Vietnamese General Remembers the Indochina War to the Fall of Saigon* (Chicago: Ivan Dee, 1995), 60–70.

59. Truong Nhu Tang, *A Viet Cong Memoir: An Inside Account of the Vietnam War and Its Aftermath* (New York: Vintage Books, 1985), 68.

60. Ta Xuan Linh, "How Armed Struggle Began in South Vietnam," *Vietnam Courier* 22 (March 1974), 20–23. This article is an abridged translation of Viet Hong, "Vai net ve dau tranh vo trang va luong vo trang o Nam Bo truoc cuoc dong khoi 1959–1960," *Nghien Cuu Lich Su* 155 (March and April 1974), 39–55.

61. Douglas Eugene Pike, *Viet Cong: The Organization and Techniques of the National Liberation Front of South Vietnam* (Cambridge: MIT Press, 1966), 68–69; see also Arthur J. Dommen, The *Indochinese Experience of the French and the Americans: Nationalism and Communism in Cambodia, Laos, and Vietnam* (Bloomington: Indiana University Press, 2001), 423; David W. P. Elliott, *The Vietnamese War: Revolution and Social Change in the Mekong Delta, 1930–1975* (New York: M. E. Sharpe, 2003), 147; Neil L. Jameson, *Understanding Vietnam* (Berkeley: The University of California Press, 1995), 238.

62. Pike, *Viet Cong,* 83.

63. Pierre Asselin, "Hanoi between the Two Geneva Accords: The Evolution of Vietnamese Revolutionary Strategy, 1959–1962" in Christopher Goscha and Karine Laplante, eds., *L'Échec*

de la Paix en Indochine (The Failure of Peace in Indochina) (1954–1962) (Paris: Les Indes Savantes, 2010), 17–38.

64. Thayer, *War by Other Means*, 116.

65. "Report of the Office of the Secretary of Defense Vietnam Task Force," January 15, 1969, Part IV.A.5 Evolution of the War. Origins of the Insurgency, 21.

66. Jeffrey Race, *War Comes to Long An: Revolutionary Conflict in a Vietnamese Province* (Berkeley: University of California Press, 1972), 99.

67. Asselin, "Hanoi Between the Two Geneva Accords," 19.

68. Ibid., 23.

69. Ibid., 20.

70. Ibid., 21; Karnow, *Vietnam: A History*, 238–239.

71. "Report of the Office of the Secretary of Defense Vietnam Task Force," January 15, 1969, Part IV.A.5 Evolution of the War. Origins of the Insurgency, 19–20.

72. Ibid.

73. Philip Taylor, *Goddess on the Rise: Pilgrimage and Popular Religion in Vietnam* (Honolulu: University of Hawai'i Press, 2004), 39–40.

74. Janet Hoskins, "Cao Dai Exile and Redemption: A New Vietnamese Religion's Struggle for Identity," in Pierrette Hondagneu-Sotelo, ed., *Religion and Social Justice for Immigrants* (Piscataway, NJ: Rutgers University Press, 2007), 200.

75. Philip Taylor, "Apocalypse Now? Hoa Hao Buddhism Emerging from the Shadows of War," *The Australian Journal of Anthropology* 12:3 (2001), 351; Janet Hoskins, "Diaspora as Religious Doctrine: An 'Apostle of Vietnamese Nationalism' Comes to California," *Journal of Vietnamese Studies* 6:1 (winter 2011), 43–86;

76. For connections between the transnational Hoa Hao organization and some success in pressing for greater government recognition within Vietnam, see Jérémy Jammes, "Réflexions sur l'institutionnalisation du bouddhisme Hoa Hao: Remise en perspective historique de la reconnaissance de 1999," *Social Compass* 53:7 (2010), 372–385.

77. Taylor, *Goddess on the Rise*, 44.

78. Carlyle A. Thayer, "Vietnam and the Challenge of Political Civil Society," *Contemporary Southeast Asia* 31:1 (April 2009), 1–27.

79. Ibid., 23.

80. See Philip Taylor, *Modernity and Re-enchantment in Post-revolutionary Vietnam* (Lanham, MD: Lexington Books, 2007).

Conclusion

1. Christopher J. Lee, "Between a Moment and an Era: The Origins and Afterlives of Bandung," in Christopher J. Lee, ed., *Making a World After Empire: The Bandung Moment and Its Political Afterlives* (Athens: Ohio University Press, 2010), 8.

2. See Tuong Vu, "To be Patriotic Is to Build Socialism," in Tuong Vu and Wasana Wongsurawat, eds., *Dynamics of the Cold War in Asia: Ideology, Identity, and Culture* (New York: Palgrave Macmillan, 2009), 33–52.

3. Matthew Connelly, "Taking Off the Cold War Lens: Visions of North-South Conflict During the Algerian War for Independence," *American Historical Review* 1905:3 (June 2000), 739–769.

4. David Schmitz, *Thank God They're on Our Side: The United States and Right-Wing Dictatorships, 1921–1965* (Chapel Hill: University of North Carolina Press, 1999).

5. Quoted in Connelly, "Taking off the Cold War Lens," 754.

6. Robert J. McMahon, "The Illusion of Vulnerability: American Reassessments of the Soviet Threat, 1955–1956," *International History Review* 18:3 (August 1996), 591–619.

7. Rodric Braithwaite, *Afgantsy: The Russians in Afghanistan, 1979–1989* (Oxford: Oxford University Press, 2011), 8.

8. See Odd Arne Westad, *The Global Cold War: Third World Interventions and the Making of Our Times* (New York: Cambridge University Press, 2007); Artemy M. Kalinovsky, *A Long Goodbye: The Soviet Withdrawal from Afghanistan* (Cambridge: Harvard University Press, 2011).

9. Philip Taylor, "Modernity and Re-Enchantment in Post-revolutionary Vietnam," in Philip Taylor, ed., *Modernity and Re-Enchantment: Religion in Post-Revolutionary Vietnam* (New York: Rowman and Littlefield, 2007), 1–56.

Bibliography

Archives and Libraries

France

Centre des Archives d'Outre Mer, Aix-en-Provence (CAOM)
Haut Commissariat de l'Indochine (HCI)
Service Historique de l'Armée de Terre, Château de Vincennes, Paris
(SHAT)
Service de Protection du Corps Expeditionnaire (SPCE)

United States

CREST, Central Intelligence Agency Database
Dwight D. Eisenhower Presidential Library, Abilene, KS (DDEL)
Hoover Institution Library and Archives, Stanford University, Palo Alto,
CA
Douglas Pike Collection
RG 59, US State Department Central Files
RG 273, Records of the National Security Council

Texas Tech Vietnam Virtual Archive (TTVA)
United States National Archives II, College Park, MD (NARA)

Vietnam

General Sciences Library (Thu Vien Khoa Hoc Tong Hoc), Ho Chi Minh
    City
Pho Tong Thong De Nhat Cong Hoa (PTTDeNhat)
Phu Thu Thuong (PTTDICH)
Vietnamese National Archives II (Trung Tam Luu Tru Quoc Gia Viet Nam),
    HCMC (VNA2)

Newspapers

Dan Chu
Los Angeles Times
Lua Song
Le Monde
New York Times
Nghien Cuu Lich Su
Saigon Moi
Thoi Dai
Thoi Luan
Tieng Chuong
Time

Government Publications

Alhern, Thomas Jr. *CIA and the House of Ngo: Covert Action in South Vietnam, 1954–63
    (U)*. Center for the Study of Intelligence, 21. National Security Archive Electronic
    Briefing Book No. 283.
Ministère des Affaires Étrangeres Français. *Documents Diplomatiques Français, 1954*.
    Tome I (21 Juillet–31 Decembre). Paris: Imprimerie Nationale, 1987.
——. *Documents Diplomatiques Français, 1955*. Tome I (1 Janvier–30 Juin). Paris:
    Imprimerie Nationale, 1987.
——. *Documents Diplomatiques Français, 1955*. Tome II (1 Juiller–31 Decembre). Paris:
    Imprimerie Nationale, 1987.
Pierre Mendès-France: Ouvres Completes III: Gouverner c'est Choisir, 1954–1955. Paris:
    l'Institut Pierre Mendès-France, 1986.

Republic of Vietnam. "Achievements of the Campaign of Denunciation of Communist Subversive Activities (First Phase)." Saigon: The People's Committee for the CDCSA, May 1956.

———. *Major Policy Speeches by President Ngo Dinh Diem.* Saigon: Presidency of the Republic of Vietnam Press Office, 1956.

———. "Record of Government Achievement, July 1955–July 1956." Saigon: Presidency of the Republic of Vietnam Press Office, 1956.

———. "President Ngo Dinh Diem." Saigon: Presidency of the Republic of Vietnam Press Office, 1957.

———. "President Ngo Dinh Diem on Democracy (Addresses Relative to the Constitution)." Saigon: Presidency of the Republic of Vietnam Press Office, 1957.

———. "Seven Years of the Ngo Dinh Diem Administration, 1954–1961." Saigon: Information Print Office, 1961.

———. *Eight Years of the Ngo Dinh Diem Administration, 1954–1962.* Saigon: Republic of Vietnam, 1962.

U.S. Department of Defense. "Report of the Office of the Secretary of Defense Vietnam Task Force," January 19, 1969.

U.S. Department of State. *Foreign Relations of the United States, 1952–1954.* Vol. 13. *Indochina (Part 1).* Washington, DC: Government Printing Office, 1982. [Hereafter *FRUS*].

———. *FRUS, 1952–1954.* Vol. 13. *Indochina (Part 2).* Washington, DC: Government Printing Office, 1982.

———. *FRUS, 1952–1954.* Vol. 16. *The Geneva Conference.* Washington, DC: Government Printing Office, 1981.

———. *FRUS, 1955–1957.* Vol. 1. *Vietnam.* Washington, DC: Government Printing Office, 1985.

Secondary Sources and Published Memoirs

Adas, Michael. *Prophets of Rebellion: Millenarian Protest Movements against the European Colonial Order.* Chapel Hill: University of North Carolina Press, 1979.

Anderson, Benedict. *Imagined Communities: Reflections on the Origin and Spread of Nationalism.* New York: Verso Press, 1983.

Anderson, David L. *Trapped By Success: The Eisenhower Administration and Vietnam, 1953–61.* New York: Columbia University Press, 1991.

Anderson, David L., and John Ernst, eds. *The War that Never Ends: New Perspectives on the Vietnam War.* Lexington: University Press of Kentucky, 2007.

Appleby, Joyce. "Modernization Theory and the Formation of Modern Social Science Theories in England and America." *Comparative Studies in Society and History* (April 1978): 259–285.

Asselin, Pierre. "Choosing Peace: Hanoi and the Geneva Agreement on Vietnam, 1954–1955." *Journal of Cold War Studies* 9:2 (spring 2007): 95–126.

Bao Dai. *Le Dragon D'Annam*. Paris: Plon, 1980.

Bator, Victor. *Vietnam: A Diplomatic Tragedy, The Origins of United States Involvement.* New York: Oceana, 1965.

Bergerud, Eric M. *The Dynamics of Defeat: The Vietnam War in Hau Nghia Province.* Boulder, CO: Westview Press, 1991.

Betz, Christiaan J. "Vietnam: Social Transformation from Confucianism to Communism." Ph.D. diss., California Institute of Asian Studies, 1977.

Bhabha, Homi K. *Nation and Narration*. New York: Routledge, 1980.

Biggs, David. *Quagmire: Nation Building and Nature in the Mekong Delta.* Seattle: University of Washington Press, 2010.

The Biography and Teachings of Prophet Huynh Phu So. Santa Fe Springs, CA: Hoa Hao Buddhist Church, 1983.

Bird, Kai. *The Color of Truth: McGeorge Bundy and William Bundy, Brothers in Arms.* New York: Simon and Schuster, 1998.

Blagov, Sergei. *Honest Mistakes: The Life and Death of Trinh Minh The (1922–1955): South Vietnam's Alternative Leader.* Huntington, NY: Nova Science Publishers, 2001.

Bouscaren, Anthony Trawick. *The Last of the Mandarins: Diem of Vietnam.* Pittsburgh: Duquesne University Press, 1965.

Bradley, Mark. *Imagining Vietnam and America: The Making of Postcolonial Vietnam, 1919–1950.* Chapel Hill: University of North Carolina Press, 2000.

——. "Becoming *Van Minh*: Civilizational Discourse and Visions of the Self in Twentieth-Century Vietnam." *Journal of World History* 15:1 (2004): 65–83.

——. *Vietnam at War.* New York: Oxford University Press. 2009.

Bradley, Mark, and Robert K. Brigham. "Vietnamese Archives and Scholarship on the Cold War Period: Two Reports." Cold War International History Project Working Paper #7. Washington, DC: September 1993.

Brigham, Robert K. *Guerrilla Diplomacy: The NLF's Foreign Relations and the Viet Nam War.* Ithaca: Cornell University Press, 1999.

——. *ARVN: Life and Death in the South Vietnamese Army.* Lawrence: University Press of Kansas, 2006.

Brocheux, Pierre. *The Mekong Delta: Ecology, Economy, and Revolution, 1860–1960.* Madison: University of Wisconsin-Madison Center for Southeast Asian Studies, 1995.

Brocheux, Pierre, and Daniel Hémery. *Indochina: An Ambiguous Colonization, 1858–1954.* Berkeley: University of California Press, 2009.

Brown, Weldon A. *Prelude to Disaster: The American Role in Vietnam, 1940–1963.* Port Washington, NY: Kennikat Press, 1975.

Buttinger, Joseph. *Vietnam: A Dragon Embattled.* Vol. 2. London: Pall Mall Press, 1967.

Buzzanco, Robert. "Fear and (Self) Loathing in Lubbock: How I Learned to Quit Worrying and Love Vietnam and Iraq," *Counterpunch* 16/17 (April 2005), http://counterpunch.org/buzzanco04162005.html.

Cable, James. *The Geneva Conference of 1954 on Indochina.* London: St. Martin's Press, 1968.

Cao Van Luan. *Ben Giong Lich Su, 1940–1965.* Glendale, CA: Co So Xuat Ban Dai Nam, 1986.

Carter, James M. *Inventing Vietnam: The United States and State Building, 1954–1968.* New York: Cambridge University Press, 2008.

Catton, Philip. *Diem's Final Failure: Prelude to America's War in Vietnam.* Lawrence: University Press of Kansas, 2002.

Cesari, Laurent. *L'Indochine en guerres, 1945–1993.* Paris: Éditions Belin, 1995.

Chapman, Herrick. "Modernity and National Identity in Postwar France." *French Historical Studies* 22:2 (spring 1999): 291–314.

Chapman, Jessica M. "Staging Democracy: South Vietnam's 1955 Referendum to Depose Bao Dai." *Diplomatic History* 30:4 (September 2006): 671–703.

——. "The Sect Crisis of 1955 and the American Commitment to Ngo Dinh Diem." *Journal of Vietnamese Studies* 5:1 (winter 2010): 37–85.

Chapuis, Oscar. *A History of Vietnam from Hong Bang to Tu Duc.* Westport, CT: Greenwood Press, 1995.

——. *The Last Emperors of Vietnam: From Tu Duc to Bao Dai.* Westport, CT: Greenwood Press, 2000.

Chatterjee, Partha. *Nationalist Thought and the Colonial World: A Derivative Discourse.* Minneapolis: University of Minnesota Press, 1986.

——. *The Nation and Its Fragments: Colonial and Postcolonial Histories.* Princeton: Princeton University Press, 1993.

——. *The Politics of the Governed: Reflections on Popular Politics in Most of the World.* New York: Columbia University Press, 2004.

Chesneaux, Jean. *Tradition et Revolution au Vietnam.* Paris: Editions Anthropos, 1971.

Cohen, Paul A. *History in Three Keys: The Boxers as Event, Experience, and Myth.* New York: Columbia University Press, 1997.

Colby, William Egan. *Lost Victory: A Firsthand Account of America's Sixteen Year Involvement in Vietnam.* New York: Contemporary Books, 1990.

Collins, J. Lawton. *Lightning Joe: An Autobiography.* Baton Rouge: Louisiana State University Press, 1979.

Cooper, Chester L. *The Lost Crusade: America in Vietnam.* New York: Dodd, Mead, 1970.

Currey, Cecil B. *Edward Lansdale: The Unquiet American.* Boston: Houghton Mifflin, 1988.

Dalloz, Jacques. *The War in Indochina, 1945–1954.* Dublin: Barnes and Noble, 1990.

Daum, Andreas W., Lloyd C. Gardner, and Wilfried Mausbach, eds. *America, the Vietnam War, and the World.* New York: Cambridge University Press, 2003.

DeCarmoy, Guy. *Les Politiques Étrangeres de la France.* Paris: La Table Ronde, 1967.

Despeuch, Jacques. *Le Traffic de Piastres.* Paris: Deux-Rives, 1953.

Devillers, Philippe. *Histoire du Vietnam du 1940 au 1952.* Paris: Editions du Seuil, 1952.

Devillers, Philippe, and Jean Lacouture. *End of a War: Indochina, 1954.* New York: Praeger, 1969.

Dommen, Arthur J. *The Indochinese Experience of the French and the Americans: Nationalism and Communism in Cambodia, Laos, and Vietnam.* Bloomington: Indiana University Press, 2001.

Dong Tan. *Tim Hieu Dao Cao Dai Hay Giay Dap 231 Cau Phong Van Cua Gioi Thi Thuc Dai Hoc Quoc Te ve Dao Cao Dai.* Saigon: Cao Hien, 1974.

Donnell, John C., and Charles A. Joiner. *Electoral Politics in South Vietnam.* Lexington, MA: Lexington Books, 1974.

Douglass, William O. *North from Malaya: An Adventure on Five Fronts.* Garden City, NY: Doubleday, 1953.

Draper, Theodore. *Abuse of Power.* New York: Viking Press, 1967.

Duara, Prasenjit. *Rescuing History from the Nation: Questioning Narratives of Modern China.* Chicago: University of Chicago Press, 1995.

Duiker, William J. "Phan Boi Chau: Asian Revolutionary in a Changing World." *Journal of Asian Studies* 31:1 (November 1971): 77–88.

——. *The Rise of Nationalism in Vietnam, 1900–1941.* Ithaca: Cornell University Press, 1976.

——. *The Communist Road to Power in Vietnam.* Boulder, CO: Westview Press, 1981.

——. *U.S. Containment Policy and the Conflict in Indochina.* Stanford, CA: Stanford University Press, 1994.

Duncanson, Dennis J. *Government and Revolution in Vietnam.* New York: Oxford University Press, 1968.

Duong Kinh Quoc. *Chinh Quyen Thuoc Dia O Viet Nam Truoc Cach Mang Thang Tam Nam 1945.* Hanoi: Nha Xuat Ban Khoa Hoc Xa Hoi, 1988.

Dutton, George Edson. "The Tay Son Uprising: Society and Rebellion in Late Eighteenth-Century Viet Nam, 1771–1802." Ph.D. diss., University of Washington, 2001.

Eisenstadt, S. N. "Studies of Modernization and Sociological Theory." *History and Theory: Studies in the Philosophy of History* 13:3 (October 1974): 225–252.

Eldridge, Philip J. *The Politics of Human Rights in Southeast Asia.* New York: Routledge Press, 2002.

Elkind, Jessica Breiteneicher. "The First Casualties: American Nation Building Programs in South Vietnam, 1955–1965." Ph.D. diss., University of California, Los Angeles, 2005.

Elliott, David W. P. *The Vietnamese War: Revolution and Social Change in the Mekong Delta, 1930–1975.* New York: M. E. Sharpe, 2003.

Elliott, Duong Van Mai. *The Sacred Willow: Four Generations in the Life of a Vietnamese Family.* New York: Oxford University Press, 1999.

Elman, Benjamin A., John B. Duncan, and Herman Ooms, eds. *Rethinking Confucianism: Past and Present in China, Japan, Korea, and Vietnam.* Los Angeles: UCLA Asia Pacific Monograph Series, 2002.

Engerman, David C., Nils Gilman, Mark Haefele, and Michael Latham, eds. *Staging Growth: Modernization, Development, and the Global Cold War.* Boston: University of Massachusetts Press, 2003.

Ernst, John. *Forging a Fateful Alliance: Michigan State University and the Vietnam War.* East Lansing: Michigan State University Press, 1998.

Fall, Bernard. "The Political-Religious Sects of Viet-Nam." *Pacific Affairs* 28 (September 1955): 235–253.

——. "South Viet-Nam's Internal Problems." *Pacific Affairs* 31:3 (September 1958): 241–260.

——. *Vietnam Witness, 1953–1966.* New York: Praeger, 1966.

——. *The Two Viet-Nams: A Political and Military Analysis.* 2nd rev. ed. New York: Praeger, 1967.

——. *Street without Joy: The French Debacle in Indochina.* London: Greenhill, 2005.

Farley, Miriam S. "Vietnam Kaleidoscope." *Far Eastern Survey* 24:5 (May 1955): 77–78.

Fishel, Wesley, ed. *Problems of Freedom: South Vietnam since Independence.* Glenco, IL: Free Press, 1961.

——. "Political Realities in Vietnam." *Asian Survey* 1:2 (April 1961): 15–23.

——. *Vietnam: Anatomy of a Conflict.* Itasca, IL: F. E. Peacock, 1968.

FitzGerald, Frances. *Fire in the Lake: The Vietnamese and the Americans in Vietnam.* New York: Vintage Books, 1972.

Gaddis, John Lewis. *Strategies of Containment: A Critical Appraisal of Postwar American National Security Policy.* New York: Oxford University Press, 1982.

——. *We Now Know: Rethinking Cold War History.* New York: Oxford University Press, 1997.

Gaiduk, Ilya V. *The Soviet Union and the Vietnam War.* Chapel Hill: University of North Carolina Press, 2000.

——. *Confronting Vietnam: Soviet Policy toward the Indochina Conflict, 1954–1963.* Washington, DC: Woodrow Wilson Center Press, 2003.

Gardner, Lloyd C. *Approaching Vietnam: From World War II through Dien Bien Phu.* New York: W. W. Norton, 1988.

Geary, Patrick J. *The Myth of Nations: The Medieval Origins of Europe.* Princeton: Princeton University Press, 2002.

Gellner, Ernest. *Nations and Nationalism.* Ithaca, New York: Cornell University Press, 1983.

Gibbons, William Conrad. *The U.S. Government and the Vietnam War: Executive and Legislative Roles and Relationships (Part I: 1945–1960).* Princeton: Princeton University Press, 1986.

Gildea, Robert. *France since 1945.* Oxford: Oxford University Press, 2002.

Giles, Frank. *The Locust Years: The Story of the Fourth French Republic, 1946–1958.* New York: Carroll and Graf, 1991.

Girault, Rene, ed. *Mendès-France et le role de la France dans le Monde.* Grenoble: Presses Universitaires de Grenoble, 1991.

Gittinger, J. Price. "Progress in South Vietnam's Agrarian Reform (I)." *Far Eastern Survey* 29:1 (January 1960): 1–5.

Gobron, Gabriel. *History and Philosophy of Caodaism.* Saigon: Le Van Tan Printing House, 1950.

Goscha, Christopher E. *Thailand and the Southeast Asian Networks of the Vietnamese Revolution, 1885–1954.* Surrey, UK: Curzon Press, 1999.

——. "La guerre par d'Autres Moyens: Réflexions sur la Guerre du Viet Minh dans le Sud-Vietnam de 1945 à 1951." *Guerres Mondiales et Conflits Contemporains* 206 (April–June 2002): 29–57.

Goscha, Christopher E., and Karine Laplante, eds. *L'Échec de la paix en Indochine (The Failure of Peace in Indichina), 1954–1962.* Paris: Les Indes Savantes, 2010.

Goscha, Christopher E., and Christian Ostermann, eds. *Connecting Histories: Decolonization and the Cold War in Southeast Asia, 1945–1962.* Washington, DC: Woodrow Wilson Center Press, 2009.

Goscha, Christopher E., and Benoît de Tréglodé, eds. *Naissance d'un État-Parti: Le Vietnam depuis 1945.* Paris: Les Indes Savantes, 2004.

Grant, J. A. C. "The Viet Nam Constitution of 1956." *American Political Science Review* 52:2 (1958): 437–462.

Gravel, Mike. *The Pentagon Papers: The Defense Department History of United States Decision Making on Vietnam*, Vol. 1. Boston: Beacon Press, 1971.

Greene, Daniel P. O'C. "John Foster Dulles and the End of Franco-American Entente in Indochina." *Diplomatic History* 16:4 (fall 1992): 551–571.

Greene, Graham. *The Quiet American.* New York: Penguin Books, 1955.

Grimal, Henri. *Decolonization: The British, French, Dutch, and Belgian Empires, 1919–1963.* London: Routledge and Kegan Paul, 1965.

Grosser, Alfred. *The Western Alliance: European-American Relations since 1945.* New York: Vintage Books, 1980.

Grosser, Pierre. "La France et l'Indochine (1954–1956): Une 'Carte de Visite' en 'Peu de Chagrin.'" Thèse de doctorat, Institute d'Études Politiques de Paris, Troisieme cycle d'histoire, September 2002.

Gruening, Ernest, and Herbert Wilton Beaser. *Vietnam Folly.* Washington, DC: National Press, 1968.

Guillemot, François. "Révolution Nationale et Lutte pour L'Indépendance au Viêt-Nam: L'Échec de la Troisieme Voie, 1938–1955." Thèse de doctorat, École Practiques Des Hautes Études, Paris, 2003.

——. "Autopsy of a Massacre: On a Political Purge in the Early Days of the Indochina War (Nam Bo 1947)." *European Journal of East Asian Studies* 9:2 (2010): 225–265.

Halberstam, David. *The Best and the Brightest.* New York: Random House, 1972.

Hammer, Ellen J. "The Bao Dai Experiment." *Pacific Affairs* 32:1 (March 1950): 46–58.

——. "Progress Report on Southern Vietnam." *Pacific Affairs* (September 1957): 221–235.

——. *The Struggle for Indochina, 1940–1955.* Stanford, CA: Stanford University Press, 1966.

——. *A Death in November: America in Vietnam, 1963.* New York: E. P. Dutton, 1987.

Harrison, Michael M. *The Reluctant Ally: France and Atlantic Security.* Baltimore: Johns Hopkins University Press, 1981.

Hassler, Alfred. *Saigon, U.S.A.* New York: Richard W. Baron, 1970.

Hellman, John. *Emmanuel Mounier and the New Catholic Left, 1930–1950.* Toronto: University of Toronto Press, 1981.

Herring, George C. "'Peoples Quite Apart': Americans, South Vietnamese, and the War in Vietnam." *Diplomatic History* 14:1 (January 1990): 1–23.

——. *America's Longest War: The United States and Vietnam, 1950–1975.* 4th ed. New York: McGraw Hill, 2002.

Herring, George C., and Richard H. Immerman. "Eisenhower, Dulles, and Dienbienphu: 'The Day We Didn't Go to War' Revisited." *Journal of American History* 71 (1984): 343–363.

Hess, Gary R. "The First American Commitment to Indochina: The Acceptance of the 'Bao Dai Solution,' in 1950." *Diplomatic History* 2:4 (fall 1978): 331–350.

Hickey, Gerald Cannon. *Village in Vietnam.* New Haven: Yale University Press, 1964.

Hill, Frances R. "Millenarian Machines in South Vietnam." *Comparative Studies in Society and History* 13:3 (July 1971): 325–350.

Hitchcock, William I. *France Restored: Cold War Diplomacy and the Quest for Leadership in Europe, 1944–1954.* Chapel Hill: University of North Carolina Press, 1998.

Hixon, Walter L. *The Roots of the Vietnam Wars.* New York: Garland, 2000.

Hoang Van Dao, *Viet-Nam Quoc-Dan Dang.* Hanoi: n.p., 1970.

Hobsbawm, E. J. *Nations and Nationalism since 1780: Programme, Myth, Reality.* New York: Cambridge University Press, 1992.

Hoopes, Townsend. "God and John Foster Dulles." *Foreign Policy* 13 (winter 1973–74), 154–177.

Hoskins, Janet. "Cao Dai Exile and Redemption: A New Vietnamese Religion's Struggle for Identity." In Pierrette Hondagneu-Sotelo, ed., *Religion and Social Justice for Immigrants.* Piscataway, NJ: Rutgers University Press, 2007.

——. "Diaspora as Religious Doctrine: An 'Apostle of Vietnamese Nationalism' Comes to California." *Journal of Vietnamese Studies* 6:1 (winter 2011): 43–86.

Hue-Tam Ho-Tai. *Millenarianism and Peasant Politics in Vietnam.* Cambridge, MA: Harvard University Press, 1983.

——. *Radicalism and the Origins of the Vietnamese Revolution.* Cambridge, MA: Harvard University Press, 1992.

——. *Passion, Betrayal, and Revolution in Colonial Saigon: The Memoirs of Bao Luong.* Berkeley: University of California Press, 2010.

Hunt, Michael. *Ideology and U.S. Foreign Policy.* New Haven: Yale University Press, 1987.

Huntington, Samuel P. "To Change to Change: Modernization, Development, and Politics." *Comparative Politics* 3:2 (April 1971): 283–322.

Huynh Kim Khanh. *Vietnamese Communism, 1925–1945.* Ithaca: Cornell University Press, 1982.

Immerman, Richard H., ed. *John Foster Dulles and the Diplomacy of the Cold War.* Princeton: Princeton University Press, 1990.

——. "The United States and the Geneva Conference of 1954: A New Look." *Diplomatic History* 14 (1990): 43–66.

Inglehart, Ronald, and Wayne E. Baker. "Modernization, Cultural Change, and the Persistence of Traditional Values." *American Sociological Review* 65:1 (February 2000): 19–51.

Irving, R. E. M. *The First Indochina War: French and American Policy, 1945–54.* London: Croom Helm, 1975.

Jacobs, Seth. *America's Miracle Man in Vietnam: Ngo Dinh Diem, Religion, Race, and U.S. Intervention in Southeast Asia, 1950–1957.* Durham, NC: Duke University Press, 2004.

Jamieson, Neil L. *Understanding Vietnam*. Berkeley: University of California Press, 1993.

Jammes, Jérémy. "Divination and Politics in Southern Vietnam: Roots of Caodaism." *Social Compass* 57:3 (2010): 357–371.

———. "Réflexions sue l'institutionnalisation du bouddhisme Hoa Hao. Remise en perspective historique de la reconnaissance de 1999." *Social Compass* 53:7 (2010): 372–285.

Janoski, Thomas. *Citizenship and Civil Society: A Framework of Rights and Obligations in Liberal, Traditional, and Social Democratic Regimes*. New York: Cambridge University Press, 1998.

Jumper, Roy. "Mandarin Bureaucracy and Politics in South Vietnam." *Pacific Affairs* 30:1 (March 1957): 47–58.

———. "Problems of Public Administration in South Vietnam." *Far Eastern Survey* 26:12 (December 1957): 183–190.

Kahin, George McT. *Intervention: How America Became Involved in Vietnam*. New York: Alfred A. Knopf, 1986.

Kahin, George McT., and John W. Lewis. *The United States in Vietnam*. New York: Dial Press, 1967.

Kahn, Joel S. "Peasant Ideologies in the Third World." *Annual Review of Anthropology* 14 (1985): 49–75.

Kaplan, Lawrence S., Denise Artaud, and Mark P. Rubin. *Dien Bien Phu and the Crisis of Franco-American Relations, 1954–1955*. Wilmington, DE: Scholarly Resources, 1990.

Karnow, Stanley. *Vietnam: A History*. New York: Viking Press, 1983.

Kattenburg, Paul M. *The Vietnam Trauma in American Foreign Policy, 1945–75*. New Brunswick, NJ: Transaction Books, 1980.

Kelley, Liam. "Vietnam as 'Domain of Manifest Civility' (Van Hien chi Bang)." *Journal of Southeast Asian Studies* 34:1 (February 2003): 63–76.

Kennedy, Kerry J., ed. *Citizenship Education and the Modern State*. Washington, DC: Flamer Press, 1997.

Knudson, Albert C. *The Philosophy of Personalism: A Study in the Metaphysics of Religion*. New York: Abingdon Press, 1927.

Kolko, Gabriel. *Anatomy of a War: Vietnam, the United States, and the Modern Historical Experience*. New York: Pantheon Books, 1985.

Kuisel, Richard F. "Coca-Cola and the Cold War: The French Face Americanization, 1948–1953." *French Historical Studies* 17:1 (spring 1991): 96–116.

———. *Seducing the French: The Dilemma of Americanization*. Berkeley: University of California Press, 1993.

Kuzmarov, Jeremy. "Modernizing Repression: Police Training, Political Violence, and Nation-Building in the 'American Century.'" *Diplomatic History* 33:2 (April 2009): 191–221.

Kymlicka, Will, and Wayne Norman. "Return of the Citizen: A Survey of Recent Work on Citizenship Theory." *Ethics* 104 (January 1994): 257–289.

LaCouture, Jean. *Vietnam: Between Two Truces*. New York: Vintage Books, 1966.

Lam Quang Thi. *The Twenty-five Year Century: A South Vietnamese General Remembers the Indochina War to the Fall of Saigon*. Chicago: Ivan Dee, 1995.

Lancaster, Donald. *The Emancipation of French Indochina*. London: Oxford University Press, 1961.

Lansdale, Edward Geary. *In the Midst of Wars: An American's Mission to Southeast Asia*. New York: Harper and Row, 1972.

Latham, Michael. *Modernization as Ideology: American Social Science and "Nation Building" in the Kennedy Era*. Chapel Hill: University of North Carolina Press, 2000.

Laurent, Arthur. *La Banque de l'Indochine et la Piastre*. Paris: Deux-Rives, 1954.

Lawrence, Mark Atwood. *Assuming the Burden: Europe and the American Commitment to War in Vietnam*. Los Angeles: University of California Press, 2005.

Lawrence, Mark Atwood, and Fredrik Logevall, eds. *The First Vietnam War: Colonial Conflict and Cold War Crisis*. Cambridge, MA: Harvard University Press, 2007.

Li Tana. *Nguyen Cochinchina: Southern Vietnam in the Seventeenth and Eighteenth Centuries*. Ithaca, Cornell University Press, 1998.

Lieberman, Victor. *Strange Parallels: Southeast Asia in Global Context, c. 800–1830*. Vol. 1. *Integration on the Mainland*. Cambridge: Cambridge University Press, 2003.

Lind, Michael. *Vietnam, The Necessary War: A Reinterpretation of America's Most Disastrous Military Conflict*. New York: Free Press, 1999.

Lindholm, Richard W., ed. *Vietnam: The First Five Years*. East Lansing: Michigan State University Press, 1959.

Logevall, Fredrik. *Choosing War: The Lost Chance for Peace and the Escalation of War in Vietnam*. Berkeley: University of California Press, 1999.

——. "Bringing in the 'Other Side': New Scholarship on the Vietnam Wars." *Journal of Cold War Studies* 3 (fall 2001): 77–93.

Loubet del Bayle, Jean-Louis. *Les non-conformistes des années 30: un tentative de renouvellement de la pensée politique Française*. Paris: Editions de Seuil, 1969.

Mann, Robert. *A Grand Delusion: America's Descent into Vietnam*. New York: Basic Books, 2001.

Marlay, Ross, and Clark Neher. *Patriots and Tyrants: Ten Asian Leaders*. New York: Rowan and Littlefield, 1999.

Marr, David. *Vietnamese Anticolonialism, 1885–1925*. Berkeley: University of California Press, 1971.

——. *Vietnamese Tradition on Trial, 1920–1945*. Berkeley: University of California Press, 1981.

——. *1945: The Quest for Power*. Berkeley: University of California Press, 1997.

——. "Concepts of Statecraft in Vietnam," *PROSEA* Reach Paper No. 33 (June 2000).

Masur, Matthew B. "Hearts and Minds: Cultural Nation Building in South Vietnam, 1954–1963." Ph.D. diss., Ohio State University, 2004.

——. "Exhibiting Signs of Resistance: South Vietnam's Struggle for Legitimacy, 1954–1960." *Diplomatic History* 33:2 (April 2009): 293–313.

Masur, Matthew B., and Edward Miller. "Saigon Revisited: Researching South Vietnam's Republican Era (1954–1975) at Archives and Libraries in Ho Chi Minh City." Washington, DC: Cold War International History Project, 2006.

McAlister, John T. Jr., and Paul Mus. *The Vietnamese and Their Revolution.* New York: Harper and Row, 1970.

McCoy, Alfred W. *The Politics of Heroin in Southeast Asia.* New York: Harper and Row, 1972.

McFarland Lockhart, Bruce. *The End of the Vietnamese Monarchy.* New Haven: Yale University Press, 1993.

McHale, Shawn Frederick. *Print and Power: Confucianism, Communism, and Buddhism in the Making of Modern Vietnam.* Honolulu: University of Hawaii Press, 2004.

——. "Understanding the Fanatic Mind? The Viet Minh and Race Hatred in the First Indochina War (1945–1954)." *Journal of Vietnamese Studies* 4:3 (fall 2009): 98–138.

McMahon, Robert J. *The Limits of Empire: The United States and Southeast Asia since World War II.* New York: Columbia University Press, 1999.

McNamara, Robert S., and Brian VanDeMark. *In Retrospect: The Tragedy and Lessons of Vietnam.* New York: Vintage Books, 1996.

Melanson Richard A., and David Mayers, eds. *Reevaluating Eisenhower: American Foreign Policy in the 1950s.* Urbana: University of Illinois Press, 1987.

Mendès-France, Pierre. *Pierre Mendès-France: Ouvres Completes III: Gouverner c'est Choisir, 1954–1955.* Paris: l'Institut Pierre Mendès-France, 1986.

Miller, Edward Garvey. "Grand Designs: Vision, Power, and Nation Building in America's Alliance with Ngo Dinh Diem." Ph.D. diss, Harvard University, 2004.

——. "Vision, Power, and Agency: The Ascent of Ngo Dinh Diem, 1945–1954." *Journal of Southeast Asian Studies* 3:35 (October 2004): 433–458.

——. "War Stories: The Taylor-Buzzanco-Debate and How We Think about the Vietnam War." *Journal of Vietnamese Studies* 1:1–2 (2006): 453–484.

Miller, Edward Garvey, and Tuong Vu. "The Vietnam War as a Vietnamese War: Agency and Society in the Study of the Second Indochina War." *Journal of Vietnamese Studies* 4:3 (fall 2009): 1–16.

Moody, Peter R. Jr. *Political Opposition in Post-Confucian Society.* New York: Praeger, 1988.

Morgan, Joseph G. *The Vietnam Lobby: The American Friends of Vietnam, 1955–1975.* Chapel Hill: University of North Carolina Press, 1997.

Mounier, Emmanuel. *A Personalist Manifesto.* Translated by the Monks of St. John's Abbey. New York: Longmans, Green, 1938.

Moyar, Mark. *Triumph Forsaken: The Vietnam War, 1954–1965.* New York: Cambridge University Press, 2006.

Murray, Henry A., ed. *Myth and Mythmaking.* Boston: Beacon Press, 1960.

Nashel, Jonathan. *Edward Lansdale's Cold War.* Boston: University of Massachusetts Press, 2005.

Navarre, Henri. *Agonie de l'Indochine.* Paris: Plon, 1957.

Nghiem Dang. *Vietnam: Politics and Public Administration.* Honolulu: East-West Center Press, 1966.

Ngo Dinh Diem. "Democratic Development in Vietnam." In Paul K. T. Sih, ed., *Democracy in East Asia.* Taipei: China Culture Publishing Foundation, 1957.

Nguyen Duc Dieu. *Nho Giao tai Viet Nam.* Ha Noi, Nha Xuat Ban Khoa Hoc Xa Hoi, 1994.

Nguyen Hung. *Nguoi Binh Xuyen.* T.P Ho Chi Minh: Nha Xuat Ban Cong An Nhan Dan, 1988.

Nguyen Long Thanh Nam. *Hoa Hao Buddhism in the Course of Vietnam's History.* New York: Nova Science, 2003.

Nguyen Thanh Xuan. "Tim Hieu Cao Cuoc Van Dong Thong Nhat Dao Cao Dai Truoc Nam 1975." *Nguyen Cuu Lich Su* (2003): 48–56.

Nguyen The Anh. "From Indra to Maitreya: Buddhist Influence in Vietnamese Political Thought." *Journal of Southeast Asian Studies* 33:2 (June 2002): 225–241.

Nguyen Tuyet Mai. "Electioneering: Vietnamese Style." *Asian Survey* 2:9 (November 1962): 11–18.

Nguyen Van Minh. *Lich Su Khang Chien Chong My Cuu Nuoc 1954–1975: Tap II, Chuyen Chien Luoc.* Hanoi: Nha Xuat Ban Chinh Tri Quoc Gia, 1996.

Nguyet Dam, and Than Phong. *Chin Nam Mau Lua Duoi Che Do Gia Dinh Tri Ngo Dinh Diem.* Hanoi: Tac Gia Xuat Ban, 1964.

Oliver, Victor L. *Caodai Spiritism: A Study of Religion in Vietnamese Society.* Leiden, Netherlands: E. J. Brill, 1976.

Olson, Gregory Allen. *Mansfield and Vietnam: A Study in Rhetorical Adaptation.* East Lansing: Michigan State University Press, 1995.

Pach, Chester J. Jr., and Elmo Richardson. *The Presidency of Dwight D. Eisenhower.* Rev. ed. Lawrence: University Press of Kansas, 1991.

Patti, Archimedes A. *Why Vietnam? Prelude to America's Albatross.* Berkeley: University of California Press, 1980.

Pelley, Patricia. *Postcolonial Vietnam: New Histories of the National Past.* Durham, NC: Duke University Press, 2002.

Penniman, Howard R. *Elections in South Vietnam.* Washington, DC: American Enterprise Institute for Public Policy Research, 1972.

Petit, Robert. *La Monarchie Annamite.* Paris: Les éditions Domat-Montchrestien, 1931.

Pham Thanh Nghi. *Dao Duc Cach Mang Cua Chi Si Ngo Dinh Diem.* Saigon: Press Office, Presidency of the Republic of Vietnam, 1956.

Phan Thu Lang. *Bao Dai: Vi Vua Trieu Nguyen Cuoi Cung.* Ha Noi: Nha Xuat Ban Cong An Nhan Dan, 1999.

Phillips, Rufus. *Why Vietnam Matters.* Annapolis: Naval Institute Press, 2008.

Pho Ba Hai. *Vietnamese Public Management in Transition: South Vietnam Public Administration, 1955–1975.* Lanham, MD: University Press of America, 1990.

Phuc Thien. *President Ngo Dinh Diem's Political Philosophy.* Saigon: Review Horizons, 1956.

——. *Ngo Dinh Diem of Viet-Nam.* Saigon: Press Office, Presidency of the Republic of Vietnam, 1957.

Pike, Douglas Eugene. *Viet Cong: The Organization and Techniques of the National Liberation Front of South Vietnam.* Cambridge: MIT Press, 1966.

Popkin, Samuel L. *The Rational Peasant: The Political Economy of Rural Society in Vietnam.* Berkeley: University of California Press, 1979.

Porter, Gareth. *Perils of Dominance: Imbalance of Power and the Road to War in Vietnam.* Berkeley: University of California Press, 1995.

Prados, John. *The Sky Would Fall: Operation Vulture: The U.S. Bombing Mission in Indochina, 1954.* New York: Dial Press, 1983.

——. *Vietnam: The History of an Unwinnable War, 1945–1975.* Lawrence: University Press of Kansas, 2009.

Pye, Lucian W. "Political Modernization: Gaps between Theory and Reality." *Annals of the Academy of Political and Social Science* 442 (March 1979): 28–39.

Qiang Zhai. *China and the Vietnam Wars, 1950–1975.* Chapel Hill: University of North Carolina Press, 2000.

Race, Jeffrey. *War Comes to Long An: Revolutionary Conflict in a Vietnamese Province.* Los Angeles: University of California Press, 1972.

Randle, Robert F. *Geneva 1954: The Settlement of the Indochinese War.* Princeton: Princeton University Press, 1969.

Razi, G. Hossein. "Legitimacy, Religion, and Nationalism in the Middle East." *American Political Science Review* 84:1 (March 1990): 69–91.

Reynolds, Andrew. *The Architecture of Democracy: Constitutional Design, Conflict Management, and Democracy.* New York: Oxford University Press, 2002.

Rostow, Walt Whitman. *The Stages of Economic Growth: A Non-Communist Manifesto.* London: Cambridge University Press, 1960.

Rotter, Andrew J. "The Triangular Route to Vietnam: The United States, Great Britain, and Southeast Asia." *International History Review* 6:3 (August 1984): 404–423.

——. *The Path to Vietnam: Origins of the American Commitment to Southeast Asia.* Ithaca: Cornell University Press, 1987.

Roy, Jules. *The Battle of Dienbienphu.* New York: Harper and Row, 1963.

Safran, William. "Citizenship and Nationality in Democratic Systems: Approach to Defining and Acquiring Membership in the International Community." *International Political Science Review* 18:3 (July 1997): 313–335.

SarDesai, D. R. *Vietnam: Trials and Tribulations of a Nation.* Long Beach, CA: Long Beach Publications, 1988.

——. *The Struggle for National Identity.* Boulder, CO: Westview Press, 1992.

Savani, A. M. "Notes Sur le Caodaisme." Mimeographed, no publisher, no date.

——. "Notes Sur le Binh Xuyen." Mimeographed, no publisher, no date.

——. "Notes Sur le Phat Giao Hoa Hao." Mimeographed, no publisher, no date.

Scheer, Robert. *How the United States Got Involved in Vietnam: A Report to the Center for the Study of Democratic Institutions.* Santa Barbara, CA: Center for the Study of Democratic Institutions, 1965.

Schmitz, David F. *Thank God They're on Our Side: The United States and Right-Wing Dictatorships, 1921–1965.* Chapel Hill: University of North Carolina Press, 1999.

Schrock, Joann L., William Stockton, Jr., Elaine M. Murphy, and Marilou Fromme, eds. *Minority Groups in the Republic of Vietnam.* Washington, DC: Cultural Information Analysis Center, Ethnographic Study Series, 1966.

Schulzinger, Robert D. *A Time for War: The United States and Vietnam, 1941–1975.* New York: Oxford University Press, 1997.

Scigliano, Robert. "Political Parties in South Vietnam under the Republic." *Pacific Affairs* 33:4 (December 1960): 327–346.

———. "The Electoral Process in South Vietnam: Politics in an Underdeveloped State." *Midwest Journal of Political Science* 4:2 (May 1960): 138–161.

———. *South Vietnam: Nation under Stress.* Boston: Houghton Mifflin, 1963.

Scigliano, Robert, and Guy Fox. *Technical Assistance in Vietnam: The Michigan State University Experience.* New York: Praeger, 1965.

Shaplen, Robert. *The Lost Revolution: The Story of Twenty Years of Neglected Opportunities in Vietnam and of America's Failure to Foster Democracy There.* New York: Harper and Row, 1955.

Shastri, Amita, and A. Jeyaratnam Wilson, eds. *The Post-Colonial States of South Asia: Democracy, Development, and Identity.* New York: Palgrave Press, 2001.

Sih, Paul K. T., ed. *Democracy in East Asia.* Taiwan: China Culture Publishing Foundation, 1957.

Silverman, Jerry M. "Local Government and National Integration in South Vietnam." *Pacific Affairs* 47:3 (1974): 305–325.

Smith, Anthony D. *The Ethnic Origins of Nations.* New York: Basil Blackwell, 1986.

Smith, D. Howard. "The Significance of Confucius for Religion." *History of Religions* 2:2 (winter 1963): 242–255.

Smith, Ralph B. *Viet-Nam and the West.* London: Heinemann Educational Books, 1968.

———. "An Introduction to Caodaism I. Origins and Early History." *Bulletin of the School of Oriental and African Studies* 33: 2 (1970): 335–349.

———. "An Introduction to Caodaism II: Beliefs and Organization." *Bulletin of the School of Oriental and African Studies* 33:3 (1970): 573–589.

———. "The Development of Opposition to French Rule in Southern Vietnam, 1880–1940." *Past and Present* 54 (February 1972): 94–129.

———. "The Japanese Period in Indochina and the Coup of 9 March 1945." *Journal of Southeast Asian Studies* 9:2 (September 1978): 268–301.

Smith, Tony. *America's Mission: The United States and the Worldwide Struggle for Democracy in the Twentieth Century.* Princeton: Princeton University Press, 1994.

"South Vietnam: A Political History, 1954–1970." Keesling's Research Report. New York: Scribner, 1971.

Spector, Ronald H. *The United States Army in Vietnam: Advice and Support, the Early Years, 1941–1960.* Washington, DC: U.S. Army Center for Military History, 1983.

Statler, Kathryn Claire. "The Diem Experiment: Franco-American Conflict Over South Vietnam, July 1954–May 1955." *Journal of American-East Asian Relations* 6 (summer–fall 1997): 145–173.

———. "From the French to the Americans: Intra-Alliance Politics, Cold War Concerns, and Cultural Conflict in Vietnam, 1950–1960." Ph.D. diss., University of California, Santa Barbara, 1999.

———. *Replacing France: The Origins of American Intervention in Vietnam.* Lexington: University Press of Kentucky, 2007.

Summers, Harry G. *On Strategy: A Critical Analysis of the Vietnam.* Novato, CA: Presidio Press, 1982.

Taylor, Keith Weller. *The Birth of Vietnam*. Berkeley: University of California Press, 1983.

———. "How I Began to Teach about the Vietnam War." *Michigan Quarterly Review* 43:4 (fall 2004): 637–647.

———. "Robert Buzzanco's 'Fear and (Self) Loathing in Lubbock.'" *Journal of Vietnamese Studies* 1:1–2 (2006): 463–452.

Taylor, Philip. "Apocalypse Now? Hoa Hao Buddhism Emerging from the Shadows of War." *Australian Journal of Anthropology* 12:3 (December 2001): 339–354.

———. *Goddess on the Rise: Pilgrimage and Popular Religion in Vietnam*. Honolulu: University of Hawai'i Press, 2004.

———. *Modernity and Re-enchantment in Post-revolutionary Vietnam*. Lanham, MD: Lexington Books, 2007.

Tertrais, Hugues. *La Piastre et le Fusil: Le Coûte de la Guerre d'Indochine, 1945–1954*. Paris: Ministére de l'Économie des Finances et de l'Industrie, 2002.

Thayer, Carlyle A. *War by Other Means: National Liberation and Revolution in Vietnam 1954–1960*. Sydney: Allen and Unwin, 1989.

———. "Vietnam and the Challenge of Political Civil Society." *Contemporary Southeast Asia* 31:1 (April 2009): 1–27.

Thomas, Martin, Bob More, and L. J. Butler, eds. *Crises of Empire: Decolonization and Europe's Imperial States, 1918–1975*. London: Hodder Education, 2008.

Tilly, Charles. "A Primer on Citizenship." *Theory and Society* 26 (1997): 599–602.

Tonnesson, Stein, and Hans Antlov. *Asian Forms of the Nation*. New York: Curzon Press, 1996.

Tran Quang Vinh. *Hoi Ky Tran Quang Vinh va lich Su Quan Doi Cao Dai*. Vietnam: no publisher, 1997.

Tran Van-My. "Japan and Vietnam's Caodiasts: A Wartime Relationship (1939–1945)." *Journal of Southeast Asian Studies* 27:1 (March 1996): 179–193.

Trinh Van Thao, *Vietnam du Confucianisme au Communisme: Un Essai Itineraire Intellectuel*. Paris: Editions L'Harmattan, 1990.

Trullinger, James Walker Jr. *Village at War: An Account of Revolution in Vietnam*. New York: Longman, 1980.

Truong Nhu Tang. *A Viet Cong Memoir: An Inside Account of the Vietnam War and Its Aftermath*. New York: Vintage Books, 1986.

Tuong Vu. "Vietnamese Political Studies and Debates on Vietnamese Nationalism." *Journal of Vietnamese Studies* 2:2 (2006): 175–230.

———. "'It's Time for the Indochinese Revolution to Show Its True Colors': The Radical Turn of Vietnamese Politics in 1948." *Journal of Southeast Asian Studies* 40:3 (October 2009): 519–542.

Viet Nam Quoc Dan Dang (VNQDD): Tai Ban Ky II. Hanoi: Viet Dan Hoang Van Dao.

Vu Ngu Chieu. "The Other Side of the 1945 Vietnamese Revolution: The Empire of Viet-Nam (March-August 1945)." *Journal of Asian Studies* 45:2 (February 1986): 293–328.

Wall, Irwin. *The United States and the Making of Postwar France, 1945–1954*. New York: Cambridge University Press, 1991.

Warner, Denis. *The Last Confucian*. New York: Macmillan, 1963.

Weber, Eugene. *The Hollow Years: France in the 1930s.* New York: W. W. Norton, 1994.

Werner, Jayne Susan. *Peasant Politics and Religious Sectarianism: Peasant and Priest in the Cao Dai in Vietnam.* New Haven: Yale University Southeast Asian Studies, 1981.

Williams, William Appleman. *The Tragedy of American Diplomacy.* New York: W. W. Norton, 1959.

Windrow, Martin. *The Last Valley: Dien Bien Phu and the French Defeat in Vietnam.* Cambridge, MA: Da Capo Press, 2004.

Winters, Francis X. *The Year of the Hare: America in Vietnam, January 25, 1963–February 15, 1964.* Athens: University of Georgia Press, 1997.

Woodside, Alexander. *Vietnam and the Chinese Model: A Comparative Study of the Nguyen and Ch'ing Civil Government in the First Half of the Nineteenth Century.* Cambridge, MA: Harvard University Press, 1971.

Wook, Choi Byung. *Southern Vietnam under the Reign of Minh Mang (1820–1841): Central Policies and Local Response.* Ithaca: Cornell University Press, 2004.

Wurfel, David. "Agrarian Reform in the Republic of Vietnam." *Far Eastern Survey* 26:6 (June 1957): 81–92.

Yearley, Lee H. "Toward a Typology of Religious Thought: A Chinese Example." *Journal of Religion* 55:4 (October 1975): 426–443.

Young, Marilyn. *The Vietnam Wars, 1945–1990.* New York: Harper Collins, 1991.

Zhai, Qiang. *China and the Vietnam Wars, 1950–1975.* Chapel Hill: University of North Carolina Press, 2000.

Zinoman, Peter. *The Colonial Bastille: A History of Imprisonment in Vietnam, 1862–1940.* Berkeley: University of California Press, 2001.

Index

CPSIA information can be obtained
at www.ICGtesting.com
Printed in the USA
LVHW02s1956230118
563563LV00008B/59/P